The Unified Operations of The Human Soul

The Unified Operations of The Human Soul

Jonathan Edwards's Theological
Anthropology and Apologetic

Jeffrey C. Waddington

RESOURCE *Publications* · Eugene, Oregon

THE UNIFIED OPERATIONS OF THE HUMAN SOUL
Jonathan Edwards's Theological Anthropology and Apologetic

Copyright © 2015 Jeffrey C. Waddington. All rights reserved. Except for brief quotations in critical publications or reviews, no part of this book may be reproduced in any manner without prior written permission from the publisher. Write: Permissions. Wipf and Stock Publishers, 199 W. 8th Ave., Suite 3, Eugene, OR 97401.

Resource Publications
An Imprint of Wipf and Stock Publishers
199 W. 8th Ave., Suite 3
Eugene, OR 97401

www.wipfandstock.com

ISBN 13: 978-1-62564-860-0

Manufactured in the U.S.A.   07/02/2015

It is my distinct privilege to dedicate this study:

*to my father Charles LeRoy Waddington and
my mother Carole Lynn Morris Waddington.*

On 9 September 2010 my mother entered glory where she has joined the chorus singing "Worthy is the Lamb" (Rev. 5:1–14).

I also desire to dedicate this study to three special women in my life:

*my wife Ruth Eileen Wiebe Waddington,
my daughter Suzannah Emily Ruth Waddington, and
my daughter Carolynne Muriel Eileen Waddington*

who have given me joy and supported me in this long pilgrimage.

Contents

Acknowledgements | ix
Abbreviations | xi

1 Introduction | 1
   Prolegomena | 1
   Outline of Chapter | 3
   A Brief Survey of Edwards Scholarship | 4
   History and Current State of the Edwards Scholarship | 16
   Survey of Edwards-as-Apologist Scholarship | 21
   Contribution of the this Study | 30
   Classical Apologetics: A Brief Description | 32
   Methodological Considerations | 36
   Conclusion | 38

2 Man as The Imago Dei | 39
   Introduction | 39
   The Historical Setting for Jonathan Edwards' Discussion of Man Created in the Image of God | 41
   Jonathan Edwards and the Donum Superadditum | 49
   Augustine's Understanding of Adam's Nature | 60
   Thomas Aquinas, the Image of God, and the Doctrine of the Donum Superadditum | 72
   John Calvin on the Image of God | 75
   Francis Turretin on the Image of God | 77
   A Return to a Consideration of Gerstner | 89
   Conclusion | 92

3 Man's Knowledge of God | 95
   Introduction | 95
   John Gerstner on Natural Theology and Jonathan Edwards | 97
   Jonathan Edwards, Deism, Natural Revelation,
   and Natural Theology | 102
   Jonathan Edwards on Man's Knowledge of God | 114
   A Brief Historical Survey on Man's Knowledge of God | 131
   Edwards and Man's Knowledge of God and His Apologetic | 143

4 The Relation of Intellect and Will: A Unity | 148
   Introduction | 148
   Gerstner on "Indirect" Total Depravity | 150
   Edwards on the Intellect and Will in the Great Awakening | 154
   Alvin Plantinga's Consideration of Edwards on the
   Intellect and Will | 168
   Edwards on the Unified Operations of the Human Soul
   and His Apologetics | 182
   Conclusion | 185

5 Edwards' Apologetic and Anthropology & Summation of The Whole | 187
   Introduction | 187
   Outline | 188
   Two Perspectives on Jonathan Edwards and Apologetics | 189
   Elements of Edwards' Apologetic and Their Context | 191
   Preliminary Conclusions | 214
   Recapitulation of the Whole Study | 216
   Final Conclusions | 223

Bibliography | 229

Acknowledgements

I WOULD LIKE TO thank William Edgar for his encouragement and keen eye. Thanks also are due to Jeffrey K. Jue and Paul Kjoss Helseth. This manuscript would be much less useful without their input. I also want to thank Kenneth P. Minkema of the Jonathan Edwards Center at Yale University for making available to me a then unpublished Edwards lecture transcript.

I would be remiss if I did not thank my colleagues at the *Reformed Forum:* Camden Bucey, James Cassidy, Nick Batzig, Craig Biehl, and David Filson. We have been a band of brothers that I look forward to ministering with for many years to come. I would also like to thank the fathers and brothers of the Presbyteries of New Jersey and of Philadelphia of the Orthodox Presbyterian Church. I would especially thank the congregations I have had the privilege to serve as a licentiate, minister, and pulpit supply, particularly Calvary Church of Amwell in Ringoes, NJ and Knox Orthodox Presbyterian Church of Lansdowne, PA. I also need to thank my Westminster Theological Seminary bookstore family with whom I spent four wonderful years, especially Lane Tipton and Brian Belh. Grateful thanks are also due to the gracious kindnesses of Drs. Vern and Diane Poythress. I would not have made it this far without their gentle prodding and powerful prayers.

I would also like to salute those whom I have already noted in the dedication. I want to pay honor to my father Charles L. Waddington of Asbury Park, NJ. Unfortunately for me, my mother Carole Lynn Morris Waddington, went home to be with the Lord on 9 September 2010 and was not able to see the completion of this study. Even as she joyfully contemplated her home-going she encouraged me to carry this project onto completion. Words cannot convey how much I owe to my dear wife Ruth Eileen Wiebe Waddington. She is a Proverbs 31 woman and I am greatly blessed. Ruth and I are blessed together with two beautiful daughters who make their parents proud: Suzannah Emily Ruth Waddington and Carolynne Muriel Eileen Waddington.

Finally I desire with my whole heart to present this study as an offering of praise to the God of my salvation: Father, Son, and Holy Spirit.

Abbreviations

WJE/1   *The Works of Jonathan Edwards/Vol. 1: Freedom of the Will*. Edited by Paul Ramsey. New Haven: Yale University Press, 1957.

WJE/2   *The Works of Jonathan Edwards/Vol. 2: Religious Affections*. Edited by John E. Smith. New Haven: Yale University Press, 1959.

WJE/3   *The Works of Jonathan Edwards/Vol. 3: Original Sin*. Edited by Clyde A. Holbrook. New Haven: Yale University Press, 1970.

WJE/4   *The Works of Jonathan Edwards/Vol. 4: The Great Awakening*. Edited by C. C. Goen. New Haven: Yale University Press, 1972.

WJE/5   *The Works of Jonathan Edwards/Vol. 5: Apocalyptic Writings*. Edited by Stephen J. Stein. New Haven: Yale University Press, 1977.

WJE/6   *The Works of Jonathan Edwards/Vol. 6: Scientific and Philosophical Writings*. Edited by Wallace E. Anderson. New Haven: Yale University Press, 1980.

WJE/7   *The Works of Jonathan Edwards/Vol. 7: The Life of David Brainard*. Edited by Norman Pettit. New Haven: Yale University Press, 1985.

WJE/8   *The Works of Jonathan Edwards/Vol. 8: Ethical Writings*. Edited by Paul Ramsey. New Haven: Yale University Press, 1989.

WJE/9   *The Works of Jonathan Edwards/Vol. 9: A History of the Work of Redemption*. Edited by John F. Wilson. New Haven: Yale University Press, 1989.

WJE/10	*The Works of Jonathan Edwards/Vol. 10: Sermons and Discourses, 1720–1723.* Edited by Wilson H. Kimnach. New Haven: Yale University Press, 1992.
WJE/11	*The Works of Jonathan Edwards/Vol. 11: Typological Writings.* Edited by Wallace E. Anderson, Mason I. Lowance, Jr. with David Watters. New Haven: Yale University Press, 1993.
WJE/12	*The Works of Jonathan Edwards/Vol. 12: Ecclesiastical Writings.* Edited by David D. Hall. New Haven: Yale University Press, 1994.
WJE/13	*The Works of Jonathan Edwards/Vol. 13: The "Miscellanies," a-500.* Edited by Thomas A. Schafer. New Haven: Yale University Press, 1994.
WJE/14	*The Works of Jonathan Edwards/Vol. 14: Sermons and Discourses, 1723–1729.* Edited by Kenneth P. Minkema. New Haven: Yale University Press, 1997.
WJE/15	*The Works of Jonathan Edwards/Vol. 15: Notes on Scripture.* Edited by Stephen J. Stein. New Haven: Yale University Press, 1998.
WJE/16	*The Works of Jonathan Edwards/Vol. 16: Letters and Personal Writings.* Edited by George S. Claghorn. New Haven: Yale University Press, 1998.
WJE/17	*The Works of Jonathan Edwards/Vol. 17: Sermons and Discourses, 1730–1733.* Edited by Mark Valeri. New Haven: Yale University Press, 1999.
WJE/18	*The Works of Jonathan Edwards/Vol. 18: The "Miscellanies," 501–832.* Edited by Ava Chamberlain. New Haven: Yale University Press, 2000.
WJE/19	*The Works of Jonathan Edwards/Vol. 19: Sermons and Discourses, 1734–1738.* Edited by M. X. Lesser. New Haven: Yale University Press, 2001.
WJE/20	*The Works of Jonathan Edwards/Vol. 20: The "Miscellanies," 833–1152.* Edited by Amy Plantinga-Pauw. New Haven: Yale University Press, 2002.

WJE/21	*The Works of Jonathan Edwards/Vol. 21: Writings on the Trinity, Grace, and Faith.* Edited by Sang H. Lee. New Haven: Yale University Press, 2003.
WJE/22	*The Works of Jonathan Edwards/Vol. 22: Sermons and Discourses, 1739–1742.* Edited by Harry S. Stout, Nathan O. Hatch, and Kenneth P. Farley. New Haven: Yale University Press, 2003.
WJE/23	*The Works of Jonathan Edwards/Vol. 23: The "Miscellanies," 1153–1360.* Edited by Douglas A. Sweeney. New Haven: Yale University Press, 2004.
WJE/24	*The Works of Jonathan Edwards/Vol. 24 A & B: The "Blank Bible."* Edited by Stephen J. Stein. New Haven: Yale University Press, 2006.
WJE/25	*The Works of Jonathan Edwards/Vol. 25: Sermons and Discourses, 1743–1758.* Edited by Wilson H. Kimnach. New Haven: Yale University Press, 2006.
WJE/26	*The Works of Jonathan Edwards/Vol. 26: The Reading Catalog.* Edited by Peter J. Thuesen. New Haven: Yale University Press, 2008.
WJEB	*The Works of Jonathan Edwards.* 2 vols. Edited by Edward Hickman. Edinburgh: Banner of Truth, 1974.
WJEO	*The Works of Jonathan Edwards Online.* Edited by Harry S. Stout, Kenneth P. Minkema, and Adriaan C. Neele, 2012. Sponsored by the Jonathan Edwards Center at Yale University at http://edwards.yale.edu/archive/ (Accessed 5 October 2012).

1

Introduction

Prolegomena

THIS STUDY IS CONCERNED with Jonathan Edwards's theological anthropology and its relationship to his apologetic practice.[1] It will seek to ascertain *what sort of* theological anthropology Edwards held and *how that was related* to his apologetic practice. It has been suggested by one well-known Reformed theologian that Edwards was a "classical" apologist.[2] It is the contention of this study that Jonathan Edwards was an eclectic, ad hoc apologist[3] who (evincing no self-conscious commitment to any particu-

---

1. The matter is stated this way because Edwards was not a Christian apologist *simpliciter*, but rather a pastor-theologian who engaged in the occasional apologetic endeavor. However, his apologetical interests developed during the course of his ministerial career, especially with the rise of Deism. For more on this see Gerald. R. McDermott, *Jonathan Edwards Confronts the Gods: Christian Theology, Enlightenment Religion, and Non-Christian Faiths* (New York: Oxford University Press, 2000).

2. See John Gerstner, *The Rational Biblical Theology of Jonathan Edwards* 3 vols. (Powhatan/Orlando: Berea/Ligonier, 1991–93).

3. Edwards' apologetic eclecticism reflects the age in which he lived and the education he received in the home of his parents Timothy and Esther Edwards and at what later became known as Yale University. Three sources are especially helpful in determining the breadth of Edwards' liberal arts and ministerial training. These are William Sparks Morris' *The Young Jonathan Edwards: A Reconstruction* The Jonathan Edwards Classic Studies Series (Eugene, OR: Wipf and Stock, 2005), Norman Fiering's *Jonathan Edwards' Moral Thought in its British Context* (Chapel Hill, NC: University of North Carolina Press, 1981) and its companion volume, *Moral Philosophy at Seventeenth-Century Harvard: A Discipline in Transition* (Chapel Hill, NC: University of North Carolina Press, 1981). It should be noted that the eclectic nature of Edwards' training does not necessarily militate against its generally Reformed character.

lar apologetic method) drew upon various and sundry philosophical and theological sources as he sought to defend a generally orthodox Calvinistic Christianity and to critique unbelief.[4] For instance, Stephen Nichols has recently noted that

> The best tool for understanding Edwards may be found in his own analogy of providence . . . Pressing the analogy, we find there were diverse influences from different areas. This is indeed literally true; Edwards was influenced by current thought on the Continent and by that in England and New England. It is also true metaphorically; Edwards was influenced from different areas of learning-from logic to geography, from mathematics to natural science, and from rhetoric to divinity. And he managed to bring them together. This may account for the diversity of interpretations.[5]

At the heart of the argument for this contention is an examination of Edwards's view of the *unified operations of the human soul*.[6] One key to ascer-

---

4. Edwards predates the conscious awareness of different apologetic schools. See Avery Dulles, *A History of Apologetics* (Philadelphia: Westminster Press, 1971), who notes that it was with the rise of the Enlightenment and the influence of German philosopher Immanuel Kant that Christians became self-conscious of their epistemological assumptions and how those more or less related to their theologies, 158-247. Gerstner makes the same point in his *Rational Biblical Theology*, "If Edwards' great contemporary Kant was the great divide in Christian thought on which side was Jonathan Edwards?...Edwards was undoubtedly an intellectual defender of traditional theism. It is also true that he defended it in his own unique manner," 1:55.

5. Stephen J. Nichols, *An Absolute Sort of Certainty: The Holy Spirit and the Apologetics of Jonathan Edwards* (Phillipsburg, NJ: Presbyterian & Reformed Publishing, 2003), 15. The analogy that Nichols is referring to is explicated in Edwards' series of sermons that have come to be known as "A History of the Work of Redemption" where he compares the providences of God to meandering streams and rivers that seem to be unrelated and going in different directions but which ultimately empty into the same ocean. See Jonathan Edwards, *The Works of Jonathan Edwards: Vol. 9/A History of the Work of Redemption* Edited by John F. Wilson (New Haven, CT: Yale University Press, 1989), 520.

6. See the interesting research by Paul Kjoss Helseth of Northwestern College. Helseth has written extensively on the place of reason in Reformed theology, especially as exemplified in the works of Old Princetonians such as Archibald Alexander, Charles Hodge, B. B. Warfield, and J. Gresham Machen. See "B. B. Warfield's Apologetical Appeal to 'Right Reason': Evidence of a 'Rather Bald Rationalism'?," *SBET* 16 (Autumn 1998): 156-77; "'Right Reason' and the Princeton Mind: The Moral Context," *JPH* 77/1 (Spring 1999): 13-28; "The Apologetical Tradition of the OPC: A Reconsideration," *WTJ* 60/1 (Spring 1998): 109-29; "B. B. Warfield on the Apologetic Nature of Christian Scholarship: An Analysis of His Solution to the Problem of the Relationship Between Christianity and Culture," *WTJ* 61/1 (Spring 2000): 89-111; "'Re-imagining' the Princeton Mind: Postconservative Evangelicalism, Old Princeton, and the Rise of

taining how to classify an apologetic method is to examine the apologist's view of the nature of man as created, fallen, and redeemed. This, the following study will attempt to do. The upshot of this study is that Edwards's theological anthropology would not appear to support a *self-conscious* classical approach to apologetics. It will be the burden of this dissertation to demonstrate this.[7]

Outline of Chapter

This chapter will unfold in the following manner. First, a brief survey of Edwards scholarship since the Second World War (and a special focus on the scholarship of Edwards's anthropology and the more recent Edwards-as-apologist scholarship) will help to set the context in which this study will proceed. Second, with this background having been filled in, a discussion of the contribution of this study to Edwards research will follow. Third, a focused description of "classical" apologetics will be offered. Fourth and finally, the methodology of this study will be delineated, including a discussion of the fact that Edwards did not write a treatise on apologetics as such so that an evaluation of his apologetic practice will involve an analysis of various texts from his voluminous corpus (sermons, polemical treatises, semi-private notebooks of a biblical, theological, and philosophical nature) as well as synthesis wherein all the disparate data are correlated in order to obtain a unified view of Edwards's anthropology and apologetic. It will also be stressed that this study is an examination of Edwards's theology in terms of its *conceptuality* and not in terms of its *historical setting* per se.[8]

Neo-Fundamentalism," *JETS* 45/3 (Spring 2002): 427–50; "Christ-Centered, Bible-Based, and Second-Rate? 'Right Reason' as the Aesthetic Foundation of Christian Education," *WTJ* 69/2 (Fall 2007): 383–401. Helseth's work is mentioned here (and will be interacted with later in this study) because he and the author of this study have come to similar conclusions about Edwards' view of reason. In other words, Edwards and the Old Princeton theologians have been seen as "bald rationalists," and Helseth's research questions that assessment.

7. It should be noted that this study is not intended to be a repudiation *en toto* of John Gerstner's scholarship on Jonathan Edwards. Rather, it is a refinement or nuance of that body of research. While this author differs with Dr. Gerstner in his own apologetic commitment (he is a presuppositionalist whereas Gerstner was committed to the classical school), he recognizes the massive amount of erudition in Gerstner's work on Edwards and stands shoulder to shoulder *with* him as over against the preponderance of scholarship done on Edwards over the years. The disagreements of this writer with Gerstner will become obvious in the pages to follow, but it needs to be stressed, especially in this postmodern age, that Gerstner gets more right than wrong, with regard to Jonathan Edwards. That fact needs to be remembered throughout this study.

8. Having said this, it is understood that no theologian can be abstracted from his

A Brief Survey of Edwards Scholarship

The story of Edwards scholarship has been told well and often.[9] The account given here will be selective, beginning with the renaissance of Edwardsian academic research around the time of the second world war and will provide an extended focus on the studies of Edwards's anthropology and the Edwards-as-apologist scholarship.[10] The survey here will follow a basically chronological approach with an emphasis on secondary studies that deal with Edwards's life, philosophy, theology and biblical studies within two broad streams, the academic and the ecclesiastical.

Secondary literature on Jonathan Edwards was relatively pervasive throughout the early to middle 19th century and then interest seemed to have fallen off with the rise of classical Liberalism and the concomitant disapproval of Edwards's brand of Calvinistic theology.[11] At this time about the

---

place and time. This is simply a recognition that historical theology has different methods and concerns. At the same time it needs to be said that this study will be informed by historical theological studies.

9. The most comprehensive telling of the story of Edwards scholarship is found in M. X. Lesser's *Reading Jonathan Edwards: An Annotated Bibliography in Three Parts: 1729–2005* (Grand Rapids: Eerdmans, 2007). Kenneth Minkema, executive editor of the Yale edition of *The Works of Jonathan Edwards*, notes in a recent article that there are now more than four thousand secondary sources on Edwards. See his "Jonathan Edwards in the Twentieth Century," *JETS* 47 (December 2003): 659–87.

10. Given the number of times this story has been told it will not surprise the reader to know that it is nearly impossible to come up with some new way of organizing the history. One can do a simple chronological account. One can also divide the history into academic and ecclesiastical as was recently done in the magazine *Christian History* in a special issue devoted to Edwards, *Jonathan Edwards: The Warm-Hearted Genius Behind the Great Awakening* (Carol Stream: Christian History, 2002). Or one can categorize the materials on Edwards into different disciplines as Minkema has done in the previously cited *JETS* article.

11. While pre-Miller scholarship will not be discussed in any detail it should not be assumed that there is no interesting material to be considered. The contrary is true. Just to give the reader some idea of the interesting discussions that are out there, consider nineteenth century discussion of Edwards. Mark Noll, in his "The Contested Legacy of Jonathan Edwards in Antebellum Calvinism: Theological Conflict and the Evolution of Thought in America," *Canadian Review of American Studies* 19 (Summer 1988): 149–64, for instance, has shown the intensity of the debate between Old Princeton and Andover over who was the true heir of the Edwardsean heritage. And there was the question of whether Edwards was an orthodox trinitarian that arose from the musings of Oliver Wendell Holmes over the nature of certain unpublished writings (at the time) of Edwards on the topic. And the nature of Edwards' philosophical idealism provided fodder for nineteenth century discussion as well. And Edwards' treatment of the freedom of the will has always been a perennial favorite. Another debate circling around Edwards was what role, if any, his thought had to play in the rise of New School Presbyterianism.

only people interested in Edwards were hide-bound religious conservatives and Edwards family members.[12] But between the first and second world wars interest in Jonathan Edwards was rekindled. Amazingly it was not a theologian, Reformed or otherwise, that brought new attention to Edwards. In fact, the renaissance of Edwards research arose with the interest in Puritans more generally which was kindled in the thought of an atheist Harvard University American literature professor, Perry Miller.[13]

Miller became an expert in Puritan thought and in Edwards in particular.[14] For our purposes, the bomb that fell on the playground of religious scholarship was Miller's 1949 biography on Edwards in the *American Men of Letters* Series.[15] It was Miller's view that Edwards was a man ahead of his times and a prodigy in the backwater colonial wilderness.[16] Miller went so far as to say that Edwards was a man ahead of his time to such an extent that Miller's own generation was just then beginning to catch up with him.[17] What was it that made Edwards such a wonder? It was his reading of John Locke and his embrace of Lockean empiricism.[18] Unfortunately for Miller,

---

12. See *Jonathan Edwards: The Two Hundreth Anniversary of His Birth. Union Meeting of the Berkshire North and South Conferences. Stockbridge, Mass. October Fifth, 1903* (Stockbridge, MA: Berkshire Conferences, 1903).

13. Recent scholarship has been done on Miller himself, including focus on his atheism, alcoholism, and propaganda/intelligence work done for the US government during World War II. See Randall Fuller, "Errand into the Wilderness: Perry Miller as American Scholar," *American Literary History* 18/1 (2006): 102–28.

14. One should consult Miller's *The New England Mind: The Seventeenth Century* (Cambridge, MA: Belknap/Harvard, 1939); *The New England Mind: From Colony to Province* (Cambridge, MA: Belknap/Harvard, 1953); *Errand into the Wilderness* (Cambridge, MA: Belknap, 1956); *The Great Awakening: Documents Illustrating the Crisis and Its Consequences* (Co-edited by Alan Heimert. Indianapolis, IN: Bobbs-Merrill Company, 1967); and *The Puritans: A Sourcebook of Their Writings* (Co-edited with Thomas H. Johnson. Mineola, NY: Dover, 2001). It is an ongoing debated question as to whether Edwards was a Puritan in the true sense of that term. An adequate answer to that question is beyond the purview of this study. It is sufficient for our purposes to note that Edwards stood within the tradition of New England Puritanism and drank from the fountain of Puritan spirituality and evinced in his own life and thought the traits of Puritan thinking. For some discussion of this issue, see www.reformedforum.org/ctc106/.

15. Perry Miller, *Jonathan Edwards* American Men of Letters Series (Westport, CT: Greenwood Press, 1949).

16. Recent scholarship suggests that Miller's view of Edwards as the lone prodigy in the American colonial wilderness may have been influenced by his propagandistic view of American exceptionalism. See Fuller, "Errand."

17. Miller, *Jonathan Edwards*, xiii.

18. *Ibid*, 46 and especially 52. Miller calls Edwards' reading of Locke's *Essay* the "central and decisive event in his intellectual life."

his portrayal of Edwards reads more like fiction than fact. Two areas stand out for comment. Firstly, Miller's reading is selective and secondly it appears to us to be theologically problematic. Miller is selective in that he reads Edwards as a philosopher or scientist in abstraction from his rather obvious Christian theological convictions. Miller finds it hard to believe Edwards would actually believe what he professed to believe. Edwards's sermons and treatises become a kind of cryptic code to hide his problematic views from the uninitiated.[19] Additionally, Miller offers a questionable interpretation of Edwards's theology. Miller echoes what has subsequently come to be called the "Calvin verses the Calvinists" historiographical debate.[20]

Miller argues that Edwards was a throwback to Calvin in the midst of a problematic covenant theological milieu.[21] Calvin stressed an arbitrary God who predestines the elect for inconceivable reasons. Additionally, Miller construed covenant theology as an Arminianizing of Calvinism in which men were able to bind God to his promises. Covenant theology made God manageable. God was humanized in this scheme according to Miller's way of thinking. Edwards stands out as the lone exception in a sea of covenantalism. The problem with this is, of course, that it is debatable on both counts. While covenant is not an architectonic principle in the theology of Calvin, it does play a significant role nonetheless.[22] And covenant theology is not an Arminianizing of Calvinism.[23] More importantly, Edwards was a covenant theologian of the first order.[24] All one has to do is read widely across the full

---

19. Miller, *Jonathan Edwards*, 50–51.

20. See Richard A. Muller, *Christ and the Decree: Christology and Predestination in Reformed Theology from Calvin to Perkins* 3rd Ed. (Grand Rapids, MI: Baker, 2009); *The Unaccommodated Calvin: Studies in the Foundation of a Theological Tradition* (New York: Oxford University Press, 2000); *After Calvin: The Development of a Theological Tradition* (New York: Oxford University Press, 2003); *Post-Reformation Reformed Dogmatics: The Rise and Development of Reformed Orthodoxy, ca. 1520 to ca. 1725* 4 vols. (Grand Rapids, MI: Baker, 2003).

21. Miller, *Jonathan Edwards*, 76 and *Errand into the Wilderness*, 48–98.

22. See Peter Lillback, *The Binding of God: Calvin's Role in the Development of Covenant Theology* Texts & Studies in the Reformation & Post-Reformation Thought (Grand Rapids, MI: Baker, 2001).

23. See Carl W. Bogue's *Jonathan Edwards and the Covenant of Grace* Jonathan Edwards Classic Studies Series (Eugene, OR: Wipf and Stock, 2008), 165ff.

24. How Miller could have read Edwards as he did is a huge question. More recent scholarship has demonstrated serious problems with Miller's treatment of Edwards. See Gerstner's *Rational Biblical Theology* 2:78–141, Bogue's *Jonathan Edwards and the Covenant of Grace*, and, with mixed results, Conrad Cherry, *The Theology of Jonathan Edwards: A Reappraisal* (Bloomington and Indianapolis, IN: Indiana University Press, 1990). More recently, Harry S. Stout in *The New England Soul* (New York: Oxford University Press, 1986) has also demonstrated that Edwards was squarely planted within

extent of his voluminous corpus. It would appear that Miller's attempt to read Edwards as a modern Lockean (and Newtonian) who wrote in cryptograms misled him here. Perry Miller is a scholar to whom almost every student of Edwards must pay homage and then quickly move on. Scholars recognize the debt they owe Miller for reopening the Edwardsean scholarly enterprise, especially as he served as the first editor of the Yale edition of *The Works of Jonathan Edwards*.[25] It is true that, humanly speaking, Edwards studies owes its Phoenix like rebirth to Miller. But if it is hoped that his misunderstanding of Edwards has been completely transcended, it would be a vain hope. Miller began a school of Edwards scholarship that still has its adherents to this day. And this is a school of interpretation that succeeds in misreading Edwards because it bifurcates him. Typically Edwards gets read through the lens of one viewpoint. Edwards is either a scientist, philosopher, theologian, or biblical exegete. But rarely is he all of that and more. It will be seen that this selective reading of Edwards is a perennial plague.[26]

Of course interest in Edwards has never really died out completely. As already noted, Edwardsean literature can be usefully divided into two major camps, the academic and ecclesiastical. While this distinction can rightly be made, it should not be understood to be a hard and fast distinction as there are scholars in the church as well as in the secular academy. Interest in Edwards in the church was *primarily* limited to the evangelical wing and in the academy the study of Edwards has branched out into the several disciplines of theology, philosophy, history, literature, and now gender studies and sociology.[27] If there is a *tendenz* in the ecclesiastical literature it would move in the direction of ignoring Edwards's philosophical and scientific interests in favor of his theological and pastoral concerns with the stress usually falling on his defense of and articulation of the aims of the Great Awakening.[28] The

---

the covenant theological school of New England Puritanism, maintaining one major hallmark of covenant theology, the national covenant.

25. Begun in 1957, the Yale letter press edition of Edwards' *Works* completed publication in 2008 with the 26th and final volume which was devoted to Edwards' reading catalogs. See Jonathan Edwards, *The Works of Jonathan Edwards: Vol. 26/Reading Catalogs* Peter J. Thuesen, ed. (New Haven, CT: Yale University Press, 2008).

26. One does not have to agree with the specific details of Miller's thesis to be an adherent of his approach to Edwards. John Smith, a subsequent editor of the Yale edition of Edwards' *Works*, would be one example of a scholar in the Miller vein, as would be Alan Heimert. More recently, Gerald McDermott evidences the same tendency to read Edwards selectively. Of course one needs to distinguish between treating selective aspects of Edwards' thought and treating his thought in an overly selective manner.

27. See Minkema, "Edwards in the Twentieth Century."

28. Iain Murray's *Jonathan Edwards: A New Biography* (Edinburgh, UK: Banner of Truth, 1987) is an example of this. See Nichols, *Absolute Sort of Certainty*, 7, 9, and 15.

Banner of Truth Trust out of the United Kingdom has kept the Edwardsean spirit alive in the republication of the two-volume Hickman edition of Edwards's *Works* and various affordable editions of his writings.[29] And one of the founding members of the Banner of Truth Trust, Iain Murray in 1987 produced a *New Biography* which still remains useful and is clearly appreciative of Edwards. However, some, such as George Marsden, think it lacks an appropriately critical assessment of its subject.[30] Other ecclesiastical Edwards volumes would include those produced by Soli Deo Gloria Publishers and new series by Presbyterian and Reformed Publishing and Christian Focus in which the language of Edwards's writings is modernized.[31]

On the academic side, the most significant publication has been the Yale University Press critical edition of *The Works of Jonathan Edwards* which now has 26 volumes with its recent completion in 2008.[32] These volumes each have significant introductory essays that elucidate the various

---

29. Jonathan Edwards, *The Works of Jonathan Edwards* 2 vols. Edward Hickman, ed. (Carlisle, PA: Banner of Truth, 1974).

30. For instance, see Marsden's comments explaining why he was offering another study of the life of Edwards, "Part of the answer is that, despite the vast specialized literature about Edwards, there is no recent full critical biography. The last was Ola Winslow's Pulitzer Prize-winning *Jonathan Edwards, 1703–1758*, published in 1940. Perry Miller's influential, brilliant, and often misleading *Jonathan Edwards* (1949) was a sketch of Edwards' intellectual life. Patricia Tracy's *Jonathan Edwards: Pastor* (1980) dealt only with his years in Northampton. Iain Murray's *Jonathan Edwards: A New Biography* (1987) provides a well-documented updating of biographies in the honorable but uncritical tradition of Edwards' earlier admirers," *Jonathan Edwards*, xvii.

31. For instance, see the Presbteryian & Reformed Publishing series edited by T. M. Moore, "Jonathan Edwards for Today's Reader." To date three titles have appeared in this series, *Growing in God's Spirit*, *Praying Together for True Revival*, and *Pursuing Holiness in the Lord*. Banner of Truth has produced paperback and less-expensive hardback editions of material found in its two-volume Hickman edition of Edwards' *Works* such as *Religious Affections*, *Charity and Its Fruits*, and *A History of the Work of Redemption*. Similarly Soli Deo Gloria, now an imprint of Reformation Heritage Books, offers beautifully produced and less expensive editions of Edwards' material such as *Freedom of the Will* and *Justification by Faith*. Publishers such as Christian Focus/Mentor offers similar items that keep Edwards in the hands of readers not inclined to want to read the critical edition of Edwards' *Works* published by Yale University Press.

32. Volume 26 of the *Works*, which is Edwards' reading catalog, came out in the fall of 2008 and brought the print edition of the Edwards corpus to completion. Begun in 1957, it has taken almost 48 years and three general editors (Perry Miller, John Smith, and Harry Stout) to publish these volumes. Even with the reaching of this milestone, not all of the Edwards materials will be available in print. However, the Jonathan Edwards Center at Yale University now has an online searchable database of Edwards' *Works* and the goal is to put everything Edwards penned on the website over the next several years. As of the spring of 2007 there were 25,000 pages of material (mostly the Miscellanies and sermons) and the plan was to add another 35,000 pages of text online annually until all the material is available.

issues related to subject matter contained in the respective volumes. Perhaps the most significant volumes of this set are those which demonstrate Edwards's commitment to Scripture and contain his theological ruminations. In 2006 Edwards's "Blank Bible" was finally published in two huge volumes and these will undoubtedly help to restore the Bible to its place at the center of Edwards's thought.[33]

The academic publishing arm of the Edwards renaissance can be helpfully categorized into the theological, philosophical, and historical studies. It is fair to say that the philosophical has predominated. On the philosophical side there are several landmark studies of Edwards's thought. One of the more significant contributions would have to be Roland Delattre's 1968 volume *Beauty and Sensibility in the Thought of Jonathan Edwards: An Essay in Aesthetics and Theological Ethics* in which the centrality of beauty and proportionality were highlighted as foundational elements in Edwards's thought.[34] This seminal study was then followed by the ground-breaking work of Norman Fiering, *The Moral Thought of Jonathan Edwards in Its British Context*. Fiering argues for an Edwards who is not the lone intellectual prodigy in a howling wilderness, who falls under the spell of John Locke (contra Miller). Rather, he presents an Edwards who is a member of the republic of letters intimately familiar with the philosophical discussions of his day and more in line with continental theocentric metaphysicians like Nicholas Malebranche.[35] More recently this aspect of Edwards studies has been dominated by the fruitful insights of Sang Hyun Lee and *The Philosophical Theology of Jonathan Edwards*. Lee argues for an Edwards who eschewed Aristotelian metaphysics with its distinction between substance and accidents and adopted a dispositional ontology in which God replicates his *ad intra* glory *ad extra* in creation so that God himself increases.[36] Many

33. Jonathan Edwards, *The Works of Jonathan Edwards: Vols. 24A & B/The "Blank Bible"* Edited by Stephen J. Stein. (New Haven: Yale University Press, 2006).

34. Roland Delattre, *Beauty and Sensibility in the Thought of Jonathan Edwards: An Essay in Aesthetics and Theological Ethics* Jonathan Edwards Classic Studies Series (Eugene, OR: Wipf and Stock, 2007). Aesthetics is a significant element in Edwards' thought. Wherever one finds the use of words like "fitness" or "appropriateness" one is sure to find the concern for aesthetics not far below the surface. For Edwards, God and his creation are beautiful and exhibit proportionality. This suggests that Edwards operated with what is called an *analogia entis* or chain of being. For more on this, see Thomas Schafer, *The Concept of Being in the Thought of Jonathan Edwards* (Ph.D. diss., Duke University, 1951).

35. Fiering, *Jonathan Edwards' Moral Thought*.

36. Sang Hyun Lee, *The Philosophical Theology of Jonathan Edwards* (Princeton, NJ: Princeton University Press, 2000). See Stephen R. Holmes' critical assessment of Lee's proposal in "Does Jonathan Edwards Use a Dispositional Ontology?: A Response to Sang Hyun Lee" in *Jonathan Edwards, Philosophical Theologian*. Paul Helm and Oliver

studies that we will note in the theological section gain their initial impetus from the work of Lee.

While the philosophical focus predominated early on in the renaissance of Edwards studies, various theologians were also interested in Edwards. Neo-Orthodox theologians such as Joseph Haratounian offered a theological assessment of the decline of theology in New England from after the time of Edwards in his *Piety Vs Moralism*.[37] After many years of the neglect of Edwards's theology Conrad Cherry returned to the centrality of faith in the theology of Edwards in his *The Theology of Jonathan Edwards: A Reappraisal*. Cherry reminded the academic community that Edwards was first and foremost a Calvinistic theologian and this was a bracing turn of events.[38] Another significant contribution to understanding Edwards's theological mind is C. Samuel Storms's *Tragedy in Eden*. In this volume Storms recounts Edwards's defense of the doctrine of original sin against his nemesis John Taylor. Storms discusses Edwards's unique exposition of the imputation of Adam's sin to his posterity in terms of divinely constituted identity.[39] At the end of the day, however, Edwards ended up in an unenviable position by suggesting that Adam fell because he was in some sense ontologically defective and that, in effect, only the God-man Jesus Christ

---

Crisp, eds. (Burlington, VT: Ashgate, 2003), 99–114. More recently, Oliver Crisp has offered his own criticisms of Lee, especially with regard to Edwards' occasionalism and continuous creationism, in his article, "Jonathan Edwards' Ontology: a critique of Sang Lee's dispositional account of Edwardsian metaphysics," *Religious Studies* 46 (2010): 1–20.

37. Joseph Haratounian, *Piety Versus Moralism: The Passing of New England Theology from Edwards to Taylor* Studies in Religion and Culture: American Religion Series, no. 4 (New York: Henry Holt & Co., 1932).

38. Conrad Cherry, *The Theology of Jonathan Edwards: A Reappraisal* Stephen J. Stein, intro. (Bloomington and Indianapolis, IN: Indiana University Press, 1990).

39. C. Samuel Storms, *Tragedy in Eden: Original Sin in the Theology of Jonathan Edwards* (Lanham, MD: University Press of America, 1986). There is scholarly dispute over the specific nature of Edwards' formulation of the imputation of Adam's sin. See the treatments of the issue in Charles Hodge's *Systematic Theology* (Grand Rapids, MI: Eerdmans, 1971), 2:217–21; B. B. Warfield in his "Edwards and the New England Theology," *The Works of Benjamin B. Warfield: Studies in Theology* (Grand Rapids, MI: Baker, 2000), 513–38; John Murray's *The Imputation of Adam's Sin* (Phillipsburg, NJ: Presbyterian and Reformed Publishing, 1959), 52–64; Oliver Crisp's *Jonathan Edwards and the Metaphysics of Sin* (Burlington, VT: Ashgate, 2005), 25–45, 96–119; and Storms' helpful discussion in *Tragedy in Eden*, 214–92. While Edwards' discussion of imputation looks like a combination of both the realist and federalist positions, it is in fact a unique exposition of federalism built upon Edwards' understanding of divinely constituted identity. Just as God constitutes individual personal identity over time (perduration), he also constitutes racial identity between Adam and his posterity. Whether this is a fit and proper exposition of the imputation of Adam's sin is a matter for debate and will be touched upon later in this study.

could have passed the primeval probation.[40] More recently, the rediscovery of Edwards's Trinitarianism has garnered attention. While this was a contentious topic in the late nineteenth century, and has been a continuing interest as connected with Edwards's concern with the religious affections and the general contours of his theology as a whole, it had not regained focused attention until Amy Plantinga Pauw had published her *The Supreme Harmony of All* in which she argued for the centrality of the doctrine of the Trinity for Edwards and for the idea that Edwards held two incompatible models of the Trinity, the psychological model traced through the Western church back to Augustine and the social model attributed to the Eastern church, especially to the Cappadocian Fathers.[41] Since the publication of Pauw's dissertation studies of various aspects of Edwards's Trinitarianism have become a veritable cottage industry.[42]

40. We will revisit this discussion below.

41. Amy Plantinga Pauw, *The Supreme Harmony of All: The Trinitarian Theology of Jonathan Edwards* (Grand Rapids, MI: Eerdmans, 2002). This is a reworking of her doctoral work, *The 'Supreme Harmony of All': Jonathan Edwards and the Trinity* (Ph.D. diss. Yale University, 1990). Steven Studebaker has offered trenchant criticisms of Pauw's thesis in his dissertation, *Jonathan Edwards' Augustinian Social Trinitarianism: A Criticism of and an Alternative to Recent Interpretations* (Milwaukee, WI: Marquette University, 2003). In the 19th century a debate arose about the orthodoxy of Edwards' Trinitarian views. This revolved around missing treatises of Edwards that have since come to light and been published. When these writings came to light, it was seen that Edwards' ruminations on the Trinity, while somewhat abstract, continued in the venerable tradition of Augustine and Anselm. See Egbert C. Smyth, "Introduction," *Observations Concerning the Scripture Oeconomy of the Trinity and Covenant of Redemption* (New York: Charles Scribner's Sons, 1880); Edwards Amasa Park, "Remarks of Jonathan Edwards on the Trinity," *Bibliotheca Sacra* 38 (January 1881): 147-87, (April 1881): 333-369; George P. Fisher, *An Unpublished Essay of Edwards on the Trinity* (New York: Charles Scribner's Sons, 1903); Richard D. Pierce, "A Suppressed Edwards Manuscript on the Trinity," *Crane Review* 1 (Winter 1959): 66-80; and Paul Helm, "Introduction," *Treatise on Grace and Other Posthumously Published Writings* (Cambridge and London: James Clarke & Co., 1971). A review of Lesser's *Reading Jonathan Edwards* will reveal that concern for Edwards' Trinitarian theology was ongoing throughout the 20th century, but usually as it related to some other aspect of Edwards' theology. However, prior to Pauw, there were two significant, though typically neglected dissertations on Edwards' Trinitarianism, namely: Herbert Warren Richardson's *The Glory of God in the Theology of Jonathan Edwards (A Study in the Doctrine of the Trinity)* (Ph.D. diss., Harvard University, 1962) and Krister Sairsingh's *Jonathan Edwards and the Idea of Divine Glory: His Foundational Trinitarianism and Its Ecclesial Import* (Ph.D. diss., Harvard University, 1986).

42. See for instance, Stephen R. Holmes, *God of Grace & God of Glory: An Account of the Theology of Jonathan Edwards* (Grand Rapids, MI: Eerdmans, 2000); William Danaher, *The Trinitarian Ethics of Jonathan Edwards* (Louisville, KY: Westminster John Knox Press, 2004); Michael A. G. Haykin, *Jonathan Edwards: The Holy Spirit in Revival: The Lasting Influence of the Holy Spirit in the Heart of Man* (Darlington, UK: Emmaus/Evangelical Press, 2005); and Robert N. Caldwell, *Communion in the Spirit: The Holy*

Anri Morimoto painted an Edwards overly sympathetic to Roman Catholic theology in his *Jonathan Edwards and the Catholic Vision of Salvation*. Edwards, we are told, understood that salvation is obtained by a holy disposition which might or might not evidence itself so that it is seen that Edwards embraced the idea of anonymous Christianity before it had been formulated by the Catholic theologian Karl Rahner. The difference between the Christian and the non-Christian was not the possession of salvation but the knowledge of that possession and the triggering of the evidence of faith as the anonymous believer came into contact with the church and the proclamation of the gospel.[43] Avihu Zakai's *Jonathan Edwards' Philosophy of History* introduced readers to Edwards's concern for the manifestation of God's redemptive activity in history through a successive undulating series of revivals. Edwards cut against the grain of Enlightenment trends that reduced history to human agency by stressing that history was the arena of God's redemptive activity and spread of his own glory.[44]

A concern for the place of Jonathan Edwards in history is evident in the various volumes that have come about as the result of symposiums such as *Jonathan Edwards and the American Experience*, *Benjamin Franklin, Jonathan Edwards and the Representation of American Culture*, *Jonathan Edwards' Writings* and *Edwards in Our Time*. These volumes also reflect the general scholarly interest in philosophical and theological issues.[45] Edwards

---

Spirit as the Bond of Union in the Theology of Jonathan Edwards Studies in Evangelical History and Thought (Eugene, OR: Wipf & Stock/Paternoster, 2006).

43. Anri Morimoto, *Jonathan Edwards and the Catholic Vision of Salvation* (University Park, PA: Pennsylvania State University Press, 1995), see especially 160-61. The argument of this book has been summarized in his article "Salvation as Fulfillment of Being: The Soteriology of Jonathan Edwards and Its Implications for Missions." *The Princeton Seminary Bulletin* 20 (1999): 13–23. That Edwards held that an individual actually had to trust in Christ for salvation (infants and mentally disabled excepted) has been ably demonstrated by John J. Bombaro, "Dispositional Peculiarity, History, and Edwards' Evangelistic Appeal to Self-Love," *WTJ* 66 (Spring 2004): 121–57 and Jeffrey C. Waddington, "Must We Believe? Jonathan Edwards and Conscious Faith in Christ," *Confessional Presbyterian Journal* 6 (Fall 2010): 11- 21.

44. Avihu Zakai, *Jonathan Edwards' Philosophy of History: The Reenchantment of the World in the Age of the Enlightenment* (Princeton, NJ: Princeton University Press, 2003).

45. Nathan O. Hatch and Harry S. Stout, eds. *Jonathan Edwards and the American Experience* (New York: Oxford University Press, 1988); Barbara B. Oberg and Harry S. Stout, eds. *Benjamin Franklin, Jonathan Edwards and the Representation of American Culture* (New York: Oxford University Press, 1993); Stephen J. Stein, ed. *Jonathan Edwards' Writings: Text, Context, Interpretation* (Bloomington, IN: Indiana University Press, 1996); and Sang H. Lee and Allen C. Guelzo, eds. *Edwards in Our Time* (Grand Rapids, MI: Eerdmans, 1999). These volumes also provide ample evidence of the failure of the scholarly community to reach any consensus on how to interpret the significance of Edwards.

has also figured prominently in Mark Noll's *America's God* in which Edwards serves as the standard for American religion that steadily declined with the merger of evangelical religion, republicanism, and common sense realism.[46] In E. Brooks Hollifield's *Theology in America* is found a more than competent chapter length consideration of Edwards and his theology.[47] Hollifield notes that it is an irony of history that the theologian of harmony and proportion split his church and birthed a theological movement that divided the Reformed community in America.[48] More recently *Jonathan Edwards at Home and Abroad* has provided us with a look at the significance of Edwards in the United States and around the world.[49]

The three hundredth anniversary of Edwards's birth in 2003 saw not only a multitude of conferences and symposiums, but also another spate of articles and books. Probably the most significant publishing event of the time was George Marsden's *Jonathan Edwards: A Life* which endeavored to make Edwards understandable to the 21st century in terms of the 18th century. Marsden succeeded in presenting a complex, historically believable and unified picture of Edwards that quickly garnered high praise and achieved classic status. It is not too much to say that Marsden has written the standard biography of Edwards for many years to come.[50] Four ecclesiastical and academic volumes deserve mention as they offer a salient testimony to the continuing influence of Edwards. *The Legacy of Jonathan Edwards for American Evangelicalism* and *The God-Enchanted Vision of All Things* provide us with appreciative yet critical assessments of Edwards's continuing value in the church.[51] The first volume stems from the Reformed

---

46. Mark Noll, *America's God: From Jonathan Edwards to Abraham Lincoln* (New York: Oxford University Press, 2002).

47. E. Brooks Hollifield, *Theology in America: Christian Thought from the Age of the Puritan to the Civil War* (New Haven, CT: Yale University Press, 2003).

48. Hollifield, *Theology in America*, 126. In what sense Edwards can be held responsible for the various theological perspectives present in the so called "New England theology" or "New Divinity," is a disputed question beyond the purview of this study. Hollifield, however, does devote a chapter to the question, 127–56.

49. David W. Kling and Douglas A. Sweeney, eds., *Jonathan Edwards at Home and Abroad: Historical Memories, Cultural Movements, Global Horizons* (Columbia, SC: University of South Carolina Press, 2003).

50. George Marsden, *Jonathan Edwards: A Life* (New Haven, CT: Yale University Press, 2003). Recently Marsden produced a much more condensed life with an emphasis on a comparison between Edwards and Benjamin Franklin in his *A Short Life of Jonathan Edwards* (Grand Rapids, MI: Eerdmans, 2008).

51. D. G. Hart, Sean Michael Lucas, and Stephen J. Nichols, eds. *The Legacy of Jonathan Edwards: American Religion and the American Tradition* (Grand Rapids, MI: Baker, 2003) and John Piper and Justin Tayler, eds. *The God-Enchanted Vision of All Things* (Wheaton, IL: Crossway, 2003).

Bible Conference at Westminster Presbyterian Church in Lancaster, PA in October 2001 and the second volume arose out of a similar conference connected with the ministry of John Piper and Bethlehem Baptist Church in Minneapolis, MN. These two volumes demonstrate that it is possible to appreciate and even identify with the kind of Christianity practiced by Edwards and still maintain a critical distance. Students of Edwards will also greatly benefit from two new guides to Edwards's thought, *The Princeton Companion to Jonathan Edwards* edited by Sang Hyun Lee and *The Cambridge Companion to Jonathan Edwards* edited by Stephen Stein. Both of these volumes are encyclopedic and offer helpful introductions to various aspects of Edwards's life and thought.[52] These last two volumes are targeted to academic audiences and tend to be less interested in Edwards as a spiritual mentor and more interested in Edwards as a factum of history. Each of these four books gives evidence of the multivalent if not conflicting nature of Edwards studies.

The most recent contributions to the ongoing Edwardsean scholarly discussion involve both appreciative and critical assessments of his life and work. Three new biographies have graced bookshelves. Philip Gura offers a brief portrait of Edwards with his *Jonathan Edwards: America's Evangelical*. Gura argues that Edwards's contribution to American religion focuses on his writings about personal religious experience and that his influence was most pronounced in nineteenth century thinkers such as Harriet Beecher Stowe and the Transcendentalists.[53] George Marsden revisited the Northampton pastor with his *A Short Life of Jonathan Edwards* where he does not merely condense his masterful full scale 2003 biography, but also provides an intriguing comparison/contrast between Edwards and his contemporary Benjamin Franklin.[54] The latest life of Edwards is Douglas Sweeney's *Jonathan Edwards and the Ministry of the Word* in which the author writes for a specifically Christian audience in setting out Edwards's appreciation of and reliance upon God's Word.[55]

---

52. Sang Hyun Lee, ed. *The Princeton Companion to Jonathan Edwards* (Princeton, NJ: Princeton University Press, 2005) and H Stephen J. Stein, ed. *The Cambridge Companion to Jonathan Edwards* (Cambridge: Cambridge University Press, 2007). However, it should be noted that only a few of the chapters in each volume evidence interest in and agreement with the Reformed Christian heritage which Edwards embraced and propagated.

53. Phillip F. Gura, *Jonathan Edwards: America's Evangelical* (New York: Hill and Wang, 2005).

54. See note 50 above.

55. Douglas A. Sweeney, *Jonathan Edwards and the Ministry of the Word: A Model for Faith and Thought* (Downers Grove, IL: Inter Varsity Press, 2009).

Another development in recent years is the team publishing effort of the Jonathan Edwards Center at Yale University and Wipf and Stock publishers called *The Jonathan Edwards Classic Studies Series*. This series to date includes twelve previously out-of-print titles which have figured significantly in the last century of Edwards studies and is to be welcomed by a new generation of Edwards scholars.[56] Doctoral dissertations also continue to be produced. Three that relate to contemporary theological debate revolve around the nature of justification. Brandon Withrow's study, *"Full of Wondrous and Glorious Things"* concentrated on the Anglo-American exegetical context in which Edwards wrestled with the doctrine of justification.[57] Michael McClenahan's study, *Jonathan Edwards and His Doctrine of Justification in the Period Up to The First Great Awakening* is an exemplary study in the historical and theological setting of Edwards's justification discourse and ably applies the Muller historiographical method to Edwards studies.[58] It will be a standard treatment of its subject for years to come. Craig Biehl's Westminster Theological Seminary dissertation has been recently published as *The Infinite Merit of Christ* and has the benefit of concentrating on an exposition of what Edwards himself has said on God's unchanging rule of righteousness, justification, and the imputation of Christ's active and passive obedience by faith.[59]

---

56. This series includes the following titles: William Sparkes Morris, *The Young Jonathan Edwards: A Reconstruction*; Patricia Tracey, *Jonathan Edwards, Pastor*; Norman Fiering, *Jonathan Edwards' Moral Thought and its British Context*; Roland A. Delattre, *Beauty and Sensibility in the Thought of Jonathan Edwards: An Essay in Aesthetics and Theological Ethics*; Alan Heimert, *Religion and the American Mind*; Joseph A. Conforti, *Samuel Hopkins and the New Divinity Movement*; Allen C. Guelzo, *Edwards on the Will: A Century of American Theological Debate*; Alexander V. G. Allen, *Jonathan Edwards: The First Critical Biography, 1889*; Carl W. Bogue, *Jonathan Edwards and the Covenant of Grace*; Harvey G. Townsend, ed., *The Philosophy of Jonathan Edwards: From His Private Notebook*; Harold P. Simonson, *Jonathan Edwards: Theologian of the Heart*; and finally, Joseph Haratounian, *Piety Vs Moralism: The Passing of the New England Theology from Edwards to Taylor*.

57. Brandon Withrow, *"Full of Wondrous and Glorious Things": The Exegetical Mind of Jonathan Edwards in its Anglo-American Cultural Context* (Ph.D. Diss., Westminster Theological Seminary, 2007).

58. Michael McClenahan, *Jonathan Edwards' Doctrine of Justification in the Period up to the First Great Awakening* (D. Phil. Diss. Oxford: Oxford University, 2006). This would be the method adopted by historical theologian Richard A. Muller and his disciples and exemplified in such masterful works as noted in note 22 above. Muller has co authored a volume with James Bradley where he spells out his approach to historiographical issues, *Church History: An Introduction to Research, Reference Works, and Methods* (Grand Rapids, MI: Eerdmans, 1995).

59. Craig Biehl, *The Infinite Merit of Christ: The Glory of Christ's Obedience in the Theology of Jonathan Edwards* (Jackson, MS: Reformed Academic Press, 2009).

Jonathan Edwards has come in for some criticism within the ecclesiastical domain in the last few years while not being the main subject of focus in the following three items. For instance, Michael Horton has suggested in his book *Covenant and Salvation* that because of his philosophical idealism, Edwards was guilty of compromising the doctrine of justification and held to some form of theosis or divinization.[60] John V. Fesko has made similar criticisms in his recent *Doctrine of Justification* as has R. Scott Clark in his *Recovering the Reformed Confession*. Clark additionally criticizes Edwards for his concern with true religious affections and considers that concern a "quest for illegitimate religious experience."[61]

The history of Edwardsean scholarship is filled with twists and turns. It is filled with careful scholarship as well as doubtful expositions of Edwards's thought. This section has included a brief consideration of some of the more significant secondary studies of Edwards's life and thought. The reader has hopefully gained a sense of the varying readings of Edwards. A similar variety is reflected in the focused examination of the Edwards-as-apologist scholarship.

History and Current State of the Scholarship about Edwards's Anthropology and Apologetics

The story of the renaissance of academic interest in Jonathan Edwards has already been touched upon here. Edwards studies have focused on a variety of aspects of his life and thought. One aspect of Edwards's theology that has received a modicum of attention is his understanding of anthropology or the doctrine of man. Since the present study is an attempt to bring Edwards's anthropology and apologetics together, a brief description and assessment

---

60. Michael S. Horton, *Covenant and Salvation: Union with Christ* (Louisville, KY: Westminster John Knox Press, 2007), 288–89. Horton enlists the support of Charles Hodge of old Princeton in his criticisms of Edwards. However, upon closer inspection, Hodge was critical of Edwards' continuous creationism but thought his doctrine of justification was thoroughly sound. See Hodge, *Systematic Theology*, 3:116–18, 148.

61. John V. Fesko, *The Doctrine of Justification: Understanding the Classic Reformed Doctrine* (Phillipsburg, NJ: Presbyterian and Reformed Publishing, 2008), 34–39 and R. Scott Clark, *Recovering the Reformed Confession: Our Theology, Piety, and Practice* (Phillipsburg, NJ: Presbyterian and Reformed Publishing, 2008). Clark devotes the third chapter of this book to a look at "QIRE" or the quest for illegitimate religious experience. The whole chapter is a criticism of Edwards' general approach to the Christian faith and life from a modern day advocate of the old life and old side position. Space and different focus does not allow an in-depth response to Clark and his colleagues at Westminster Seminary California. Horton, Fesko, and Clark all appear to rely upon problematic secondary sources and admit they are not students of Edwards.

Studies of Edwards's Anthropology

Das Kelly Barnett

Das Kelly Barnett's study of Edwards's anthropology is the first of its kind in the twentieth century.[62] The author provides a thorough discussion of Edwards's doctrine of man as made in the image of God and finding the essence of that imaging relationship in the natural and moral aspects of each. Just as God has natural and moral attributes, so too does man have a natural and a moral image.[63] Barnett also gives in-depth discussion to the nature of the soul in Edwards and his understanding of the unified operations of the human soul, with its two powers of understanding and will.[64] Understandably there is concern with how man was created, how he was affected by the fall, and what is involved in his restoration. This is all set within the context of God's emanating his *ad intra* Trinitarian glory *ad extra* so that it is re-manated back to him by his sentient creatures in both knowing and loving him. Barnett shows that for Edwards, the essence of true religion is renewed affections and these affections result in an empirically verifiable piety.[65]

However, for Barnett, Edwards's empirically verifiable piety had the misfortune of being expressed in terms of a moribund Calvinism. "Jonathan Edwards, failing to find new channels for expressing his theocentric anthropology, gave to the metaphysical, logical, antiquated Calvinistic form he employed a vitality seldom known."[66] There is a sense, for Barnett, that Edwards's concern is with the abiding and universal experience of piety and that the Calvinist theology in terms in which it is expressed is incidental or of no real concern to Edwards. This comes across as the now familiar, if not worn out, distinction raised by Friedrich Schleiermacher between what is universal in human experience and the ever-changing doctrine formulated to explain the experience, an explanation needing revision with each new circumstance. For Barnett, Edwards's concern for vital piety was the kernel and his reliance on Calvinistic theological categories was the husk.

---

62. Das Kelly Barnett, *The Doctrine of Man in the Theology of Jonathan Edwards* (Th.D. diss., Southern Baptist Theological Seminary, 1943).

63. Barnett, *Doctrine of Man*, 132.

64. Barnett, *Doctrine of Man*, 157–58.

65. Barnett, *Doctrine of Man*, 107–08.

66. Barnett, *Doctrine of Man*, 209. Similar sentiments can also be found at 107–08.

Arthur Bamford Crabtree

Arthur Bamford Crabtree presents the reader with a relatively brief but significant study of Edwards's anthropology.[67] Crabtree offers a detailed discussion of Edwards's understanding of Adam as created, fallen and restored, with the emphasis falling upon the fall. The author covers familiar ground here as well, dealing with such issues as the relation of revelation and reason, the nature of Edwards's Calvinism, and the nature of sin. It is Crabtree's analysis of Edwards's exposition of Adam's fall that is most significant for the purposes of this study.

Crabtree believes that Edwards's distinction between the natural and moral image in Adam is tantamount to the *adiutorium* or *donum superadditum*.[68] Edwards's essential error, according to the author, is that he thought Adam was created righteous rather than neutral. Adam was, said Edwards, under a "rule of right action."[69] Crabtree is correct that Edwards will find it challenging to account for the fall if Adam was created upright. The Reformed tradition as a whole has affirmed that Adam and Eve were created in a state of positive righteousness, yet were mutable. Crabtree also thinks the discussion of the retention and loss of the *imago Dei* within the Reformed tradition is "somewhat cloudy." And this applies equally to Edwards in particular.[70] Edwards's discussion of the natural and moral image in man mirrors the broad and narrow senses of image.

In the end, Crabtree offers informed discussions of Edwards's view of revelation and reason, his unique exposition of the imputation of Adam's sin to his posterity, the noetic effects of sin, and the nature of redemption. However, as an Arminian, Crabtree criticizes Edwards as an example of a Calvinist theologian who sacrifices the integrity of human nature on the altar of divine sovereignty.[71] Much of his criticism of Edwards is in fact a generic criticism of the Reformed faith as a whole. It should be said that Crabtree has the merit of addressing most if not all of the issues germane to Edwards's anthropology and so he is a source one must turn to, to understand Edwards on the subject.

---

67. Arthur Bamford Crabtree, *Jonathan Edwards' View of Man: A Study in Eighteenth Century Calvinism* (Wallington, Surrey: The Religious Education Press, LTD, 1948). By brief, it is noted that this dissertation comes in at just under seventy pages.

68. Crabtree, *View of Man*, 17–18, 23–26. The adiutorium goes back at least as far as Augustine. More about this below.

69. Crabtree, *View of Man*, 22.

70. Crabtree, *View of Man*, 24.

71. Crabtree, *View of Man*, 57.

George Arthur Tattrie

George Arthur Tattrie provides a study of Edwards's understanding of man's place within the whole created order in his McGill University dissertation of 1973.[72] Simply put, the author believes that Edwards has insight to offer in the contemporary ecological controversy. The world was created to reflect God's glory back to him and this is achieved principally through the human creation. God sustains his creation by continually creating it anew every moment and fighting off the chaos that threatens to destroy it.[73] One of the distinguishing characteristics, for Tattrie, of Edwards's cosmology, is his view of God permeating his creation. While not to be identified, God and his creation are not totally separate either. Edwards the theocentric idealist is also, then, a sort of panentheist.[74] In contrast to the traditional view of transcendence, "Edwards holds that the Creator and creation exist in personal relationship. The creation is not that which is set "over against" the Creator but that which participates in him. Apart from this relationship the created order has no reality. Its participation in the Creator is the source of its value, integrity, and life."[75]

Since God permeates the whole of his creation, Tattrie holds that Edwards held to a sacramental view of the universe. The author realizes that this sort of language is not present in Edwards but that it fairly well explains his perspective. Not surprisingly, Tattrie understands revelation to be omnipresent in creation along with the Creator. This is one reason why Edwards rejected the Deistic notion of the sufficiency of natural religion. Man was never created to think autonomously.[76] If man is to act rightly toward God then he requires knowledge and this only comes through revelation.[77] Revelation enables man to fulfill his *raison d'être* and that is to serve as the crowning touch of the creation of the universe. Tattrie concludes his study by assessing whether Edwards is an *internalist* (man is simply one species among many within creation) or an *externalist* (man is completely separate from the creation) and concludes that Edwards sees that man shares some characteristics of both views.

---

72   George Arthur Tattrie, *Jonathan Edwards' Understanding of the Natural World and Man's Relationship to It* (Ph.D. diss., McGill University, 1973).
73. Tattrie, *Natural World*, 79.
74. Tattrie, *Natural World*, 81.
75. Tattrie, *Natural World*, 92.
76. Tattrie, *Natural World*, 98.
77. Tattrie, *Natural World*, 226–27.

The Unified Operations of the Human Soul
David Leroy Weddle

In the same year that saw Tattrie produce his study on Edwards's view of the natural world and man's relationship to it, David Leroy Weddle presented a comparative study of the views of conversion in the theologies of Jonathan Edwards and Charles Grandison Finney.[78] The center of this study on contrasts is the role of divine sovereignty and human responsibility in conversion. Edwards, as a Calvinist, was a monergist and Finney a synergist. For Edwards conversion was the result of divine activity, for Finney, it was a non-miraculous and non-supernatural decision made by man to obey God. For Edwards, salvation truly appropriated could not be lost, for Finney it could be gained and lost frequently.

The differences between the views of Edwards and Finney on conversion relate to the nature of the fall and the role of the Holy Spirit in regeneration. For Finney,[79] the fall affected Adam and Eve only[80] and regeneration involved only moral suasion. Contrarily, for Edwards, who admitted that as a teen he was horrified by divine sovereignty, Adam's sin was imputed to his posterity by means of divinely constituted identity and regeneration involved the direct work of the Holy Spirit producing a new principle of life in the believer, what he called the "new sense."[81] The new sense did not impart new doctrine or information, but by it the Holy Spirit enabled the regenerate to love the truth which before they hated with vehemence.[82] In the end, conversion for Edwards was a work of God implanting a relish for the beauty of divine things whereas for Finney conversion was simply the persuasion of the sinner that it was in his best interest to trust in Christ, a trust he was fully capable of exhibiting without supernatural change. Weddle notes that for Edwards, conversion or experience of the new sense is a "form of 'aesthetic' appreciation."[83]

> Specifically, it is the perception of divine beauty in the image of Christ. The "vision" of Christ's excellency informs the "principle"

---

78. David Leroy Weddle, *The New Man: A Study in the Significance of Conversion for the Theological Definition of Self in Jonathan Edwards and Charles G. Finney* (Ph.D. diss., Harvard University, 1973).

79. It should be noted that while Edwards was not familiar with the specifics of Finney's theology due to historical location, Finney was quite familiar with the theology of Edwards and rejected it.

80. Adam's posterity sins by following the example of those in their immediate environment.

81. Weddle, *New Man*, 224–26.

82. Weddle, *New Man*, 139, 325–30.

83. Weddle, *New Man*, 330.

of one's moral responses, expressed by Edwards as the indwelling of the Holy Spirit. The illumination of grace creates within the believer a "new power of mind" which orders perception and governs volition.[84]

The foregoing studies of Jonathan Edwards's doctrine of man indicate both his defense of traditional Calvinistic doctrine, and at the same time the often unique ways he does it. Edwards's theocentric idealism impinges upon his understanding of man. Man is created to receive the glorious communications of the Triune God and to refund them back to God. But because of the fall, redemption is now required so that man can fulfill his purpose. It has also been shown that Edwards's defense of the doctrine of the imputation of Adam's sin was unfolded in its own unique way building on Edwards's own notion of divinely constituted identity. Man is born in sin and is not capable of regenerating himself. The Holy Spirit must infuse a new principle of action by which he is then able to sense the beauty of God and the things of God. Regenerate man, then, is the only man who is able to refund the glory due to God. And this glory is most evident in the person and work of Jesus Christ. It is the perception and appreciation of the glory that is found in Christ and his work of redemption that comprises the "new sense."

The survey of Edwardsean anthropological scholarship reveals a range of theological perspectives. This is typical of the guild as a whole. While each of these studies noted Edwards's apologetic defense of Calvinism, none of them made any explicit connection between Edwards's anthropology and his apologetic practice. Below, this study turns to what is a recent attempt to overcome the perspectival fragmentation evident in Edwards studies noted earlier.

Survey of Edwards-as-Apologist Scholarship

One route to a more holistic and integrated picture of Jonathan Edwards has been to look at him through the lens of his apologetic work. This approach holds much promise.[85] But until recently it remained a road less travelled. For many years the only significant work on Edwards as an apologist was the work of John Gerstner. He has been joined by five others who provide further insight into the place of apologetics in the theological thought of Edwards. While apologetics provides a new entrée into Edwards's widely variant thought, it is somewhat surprising that it forms a miniscule trickle

---

84. Weddle, *New Man*, 330.

85. Michael McClymond and Stephen J. Nichols see apologetics as an especially fruitful unifying theme in Edwards. See below.

in the Niagara Falls of Edwards scholarship. The fact that the apologetics angle is relatively recent and small actually assists in the attempt to ascertain some coherence in Edwards's thought.

John Gerstner

Any discussion of the history of Jonathan Edwards-as-apologist scholarship would have to begin with John Gerstner. Gerstner's lifelong passion was the study of Jonathan Edwards in all his various facets.[86] One central element of his understanding of Edwards was Edwards's role as a Christian apologist. There are three principle sources from which we can gain familiarity with how Gerstner views Edwards as apologist. The first is his four-part series "An Outline of the Apologetics of Jonathan Edwards."[87] In this series Gerstner builds off comments Edwards makes in his *Freedom of the Will*[88] to argue that Edwards was a classical apologist. The second source is a book that Gerstner co-authored with R. C. Sproul and Arthur Lindsley, *Classical Apologetics*.[89] Here Edwards is not the center of attention but he serves as an occasional example of the classical method. This volume is especially revealing about what Gerstner understands the classical apologetic method to involve. The third source is Gerstner's magnum opus, the three-volume

---

86. See the following: John Gerstner, "An Outline of the Apologetics of Jonathan Edwards." *Bibliotheca Sacra* 133 (1976): 3–10, 99–107, 195–201, 291–98; and Jonathan Gerstner. "Edwardsean Preparation for Salvation." *WTJ* 42 (Fall 1979): 5–71; *John Gerstner: The Early Writings* (Morgan: Soli Deo Gloria, 1997); "Jonathan Edwards." *Eternity* 39 (Jan 1998): 36–37; "Jonathan Edwards and the Bible." *Tenth* 9 (1979): 1–90; "Jonathan Edwards: Insights That Shaped History." *Fundamentalist Journal* 4 (April 1985): 43–44; "Jonathan Edwards on the Bible and Reason." Sound Recording. Philadelphia: Westminster Media, 1979; "Jonathan Edwards on Natural Theology." Sound Recording. 1975; *Jonathan Edwards: A Mini-Theology* (Wheaton, IL: Tyndale House Press, 1987); *Jonathan Edwards on Heaven and Hell* (Carlisle, PA: Banner of Truth, 1980); *Jonathan Edwards, Evangelist* (Morgan, PA: Soli Deo Gloria, 1995); *Rational Biblical Theology*; *Reasons for Faith* (New York: Harper & Brothers, 1960); *Steps to Salvation: The Evangelistic Message of Jonathan Edwards* (Philadelphia: Westminster Press, 1960); and *The Theology of Jonathan Edwards* Sound Recordings (Grand Rapids, MI: Institute of Theological Studies, 1986). Gerstner also co-authored an apologetics text with R. C. Sproul and Arthur Lindsley where Edwards is used as an exemplar: *Classical Apologetics: A Rational Defense of the Christian Faith and a Critique of Presuppositional Apologetics* (Grand Rapids, MI: Zondervan, 1984).

87. John Gerstner, "An Outline of the Apologetics of Jonathan Edwards."

88. Jonathan Edwards, *The Works of Jonathan Edwards/Vol. 1: Freedom of the Will*. Paul Ramsay, ed. (New Haven, CT: Yale University Press, 1957).

89. Sproul, Gerstner, Lindsley, *Classical Apologetics*.

Rational Biblical Theology of Jonathan Edwards.[90] Here Gerstner endeavors to provide a systematic and comprehensive exposition of Edwards's theology in the standard systematic theology loci format. However, the first 189 pages of volume one are devoted to a consideration of Edwards's place in the history of Christian theology more generally and apologetics specifically. As one might expect, Edwards is portrayed as the epitome of classical apologetic method.

So what is the picture we gather from these three sources? Edwards follows the traditional practice of classical apologetics with a view of the human soul that reflects a hierarchical faculty psychology and that sees natural theology as the foundation for special revelation. Edwards also agrees with classical apologetics that before we can discern whether God has spoken to the human race, we need to ascertain that there is a God who can communicate. This is done with the assistance of what have come to be called the "theistic proofs." Once it is determined that there is in fact such a God as can be philosophically established, attention turns to the Bible. The Bible is then evaluated as a historically veracious book and since it is so its witness to Jesus as divine can be accepted and Jesus gives his imprimatur that the Bible is divinely inspired.[91] Gerstner is convinced that these ostensive elements in Edwards add up to a classical apologetic methodology. This study will focus on the first element relating to the nature of man and his ability to receive a communication from God.

Additionally Gerstner believes that Edwards embraced the classical synthesis in which there is an attempt to build a Christian superstructure upon the foundation of secular philosophy. Gerstner goes so far as to say that ancient Greek philosophy is to the Gentiles what the Old Testament was to the Hebrews, a preparation for the gospel. This can be framed as a question about the relationship of theology to philosophy.[92] Gerstner notes

---

90. Gerstner, *Rational Biblical Theology of Jonathan Edwards*. See especially the first 189 pages of volume one.

91. Gerstner in his *Rational Biblical Theology*, offers a brief summary of the classical method of apologetics: "While the church rests on special revelation, special revelation rests on common revelation. A person is in the world before he enters the church. He must be persuaded that there is a God before he can entertain a special revelation from God. Theistic proofs naturally and logically precede Christian evidences. A person may believe that there is a God without believing in Christ. He cannot believe in Christ without believing in God (John 14:2). He must be persuaded that there is a God before he can be persuaded that Christ is the Son of God (Matt. 16:16). Attempts to short-cut the route to Christianity by eliminating the theistic argument seem logically absurd, intellectually futile," 1:22.

92. According to Steven Cowan in his introduction to *The Five Views of Apologetics* (Grand Rapids, MI: Zondervan, 2000), pp.7–20, this is really a form of the faith/reason relationship.

three approaches to this relation: There is the rejection of any interaction, arguably exemplified in Tertullian. Then there is Augustine's perspective in which philosophy serves as the handmaid of theology providing conceptual tools. Finally there is the view of Thomas Aquinas in which philosophy has its own legitimacy apart from its role as handmaiden to theology.[93] In fact, philosophy provides the foundation upon which theology is built. Where might Jonathan Edwards fall within this spectrum? Clearly, Gerstner sees Edwards as typifying the third approach.[94] That is, unassisted reason is able to ascertain limited knowledge about God but that salvation requires revelation. Thirdly, there is an utter confidence in human reason. Reason is able to operate, even subsequent to the fall, so that it can ascertain whether there is a God and whether the Bible is a revelation whatsoever.

Michael J. McClymond

Michael J. McClymond has written a critically acclaimed volume entitled *Encounters with God: An Approach to the Theology of Jonathan Edwards*.[95] McClymond argues that Edwards's theology can be fruitfully characterized as theocentric and that his writings cluster around spiritual perception and apologetics.[96] Unlike many in his context, Edwards was concerned with both subjective and objective elements of the Christian faith. In other words, for Edwards, the spiritual sense itself was an argument for God's existence. But he never abandoned rational argumentation either. Edwards was able to

---

93. Gerstner, *Rational Biblical Theology*, 1: 21–50. See also the discussion of the relationship of theology to philosophy in Bernard Ramm, *Varieties of Christian Apologetics* (Grand Rapids, MI: Baker, 1961), 17–18.

94. Gerstner, *Rational Biblical Theology*, "If my view of Edwards is correct-as remains to be seen-Edwards' place in the history of Christian theology is secure as one of orthodoxy's greatest champions of Christian philosophy no less than theology." Further Gerstner clearly identifies Edwards as an exemplar of classical apologetics, "Yet today, though the classical apologetics of Jonathan Edwards is not dead, it is surely under severe attack," 1:55–56.

95. Michael McClymond, *Encounters with God: An Approach to the Theology of Jonathan Edwards* (New York: Oxford University Press, 1998). Other items about Edwards that McClymond has authored are the following: "God the Measure: Toward a Theocentric Understanding of Jonathan Edwards' Metaphysics." *SJT* 47 (1994): 43–59; "Spiritual Perception in Jonathan Edwards." *JR* 77 (1997): 195–216. Most recently McClymond has co-authored with Gerald McDermott, *The Theology of Jonathan Edwards* (New York: Oxford University Press, 2012).

96. McClymond, *Encounters*, v. McClymond further compares these two concerns as two rivers that join together, "... one might say that spiritual perception is the Blue Nile and apologetics the White Nile of Edwards' thought, two major tributaries of one river," vi.

maintain an orthodox theology while also taking Enlightenment thought captive to the gospel. McClymond unpacks Edwards's apologetic as having two aspects, implicit and explicit. The explicit was his rational argumentation and implicit was his holistic view of the universe with God at the center. The benefit of McClymond's work is that he shows sensitivity to all these elements in Edwards's thought. In conclusion, McClymond attempts to situate and show resonances between Edwards on the one hand and Paley and Schleiermacher on the other hand.

Gerald R. McDermott

Gerald R. McDermott has offered a ground-breaking and thought provoking thesis in his recent study of "a strange, new Edwards." Capitalizing on the greater availability of Edwards's "Miscellanies," McDermott presents us with a closet religious inclusivist in *Jonathan Edwards Confronts the Gods*.[97] Arguing that Edwards's main opponents were the Deists, McDermott notes that Edwards attempted to answer the Deist twin arguments of there being no necessity for special revelation as natural revelation was sufficient and the so-called "scandal of particularity." That is, the only religion there is, is the religion of morality based upon revelation given in nature and as such available to all men. The scandal of particularity was the problem of why special revelation would be limited to such as a small percentage of the world population which belief in the Bible as God's Word suggested. Old Testament Israel and New Testament Christianity comprise a miniscule portion of the world's people and so the God of the Bible would seem to be a miserable tyrant.

---

97. Gerald R. McDermott, *Jonathan Edwards Confronts the Gods*. Other materials of related interest include *Can Evangelicals Learn from World Religions? Jesus, Revelation, and Religious Traditions* (Downer's Grove, IL: Inter Varsity Press, 2000); "Jonathan Edwards and the Salvation of Non-Christians." *PE* 10 (2001): 208–27; "Jonathan Edwards, Deism, and the Mystery of Revelation." *JPH* 77 (1999): 211–24; *One Holy and Happy Society: The Public Theology of Jonathan Edwards* (University Park, PA: Pennsylvania State University Press, 1992); "Response to Gilbert: 'The Nations Will Worship: Jonathan Edwards and the Salvation of the Heathen.'" *TJ* 23 (2002): 77–80; *Seeing God: Jonathan Edwards and Spiritual Discernment* (Vancouver, BC: Regent University Press, 2000); *God's Rivals: Why Has God Allowed Different Religions? Insights from the Bible and the Early Church* (Downers Grove, IL: Inter Varsity Press, 2007); *Understanding Jonathan Edwards: An Introduction to America's Theologian* (New York: Oxford University Press, 2009); "Jonathan Edwards and the American Indians: the Devil Sucks Their Blood," *NEQ* 72/4 (1999): 539–58; "What Jonathan Edwards Can Teach Us About Politics," *CT* 38/8 (18 July 1994): 32; "Jonathan Edwards on Justification-More Protestant Or Catholic?," *PE* 17/1 (Winter 2008): 92–111.

McDermott goes on to show that Edwards answered the Deist argument with a three pronged attack. First, he argued for the presence of revelation in all parts of the world. Contrary to the Deist supposition, all men everywhere had access to divine revelation. Here Edwards drew upon the tradition of *prisca theologia* or primitive theology which held that God had given special revelation of himself to such persons as Noah that was then passed down through myriad generations but which also got twisted and obscured, not to say perverted, in the multiple retellings. Second, Edwards countered Deism with his unusual typology. As was typical of Christian theologians, Edwards held that certain persons, events, and institutions in the Old Testament pointed forward to fulfillment in the New Testament, especially in the person and work of Jesus Christ. However, Edwards held that typology was actually built into the universe by God so that various physical aspects of the world pointed to greater, more significant spiritual realities. These were not merely read off creation by over active imaginations, but were part of the divinely intended warp and woof of creation. Third, McDermott argues that Edwards entertained the possibility of salvation for the non-Christian inasmuch as he held that all that was needed for one to be saved was the possession of a holy disposition which may or may not be manifested in overt faith in Christ.[98]

Robert Brown

Robert Brown has advanced scholarly discussion of Edwards's specific apologetic aimed at a defense of the Scriptures in the face of the criticisms of Deism. He has written a short article on the subject and a prize-winning book, *Jonathan Edwards and the Bible*.[99] In his book he argues for a shift in apologetic strategy over time as Edwards was confronted by the detailed criticisms leveled at the Bible. As Edwards addressed questions raised about such things as the Mosaic authorship of the Pentateuch he edged away from his traditional Reformed apologetic with its emphasis on the necessity of a new sense to a more evidential approach. Due to the fact that Edwards had to defend the foundational text of the church, and can no longer assume its

---

98. McDermott is building upon the work of Sang Lee, *The Philosophical Theology of Jonathan Edwards* (Princeton, NJ: Princeton University Press, 2000) and Anri Morimoto's *Jonathan Edwards and the Catholic Vision of Salvation* (University Park, PA: Pennsylvania State University Press, 1995).

99. Robert E. Brown, *Jonathan Edwards and the Bible* (Bloomington & Indianapolis, IN: Indiana University Press, 2002). Brown has also authored "Edwards, Locke, and the Bible," *JR* 79/3 (July 1999): 361–84.

veracity and divine nature, he spends much more time delving into historical issues.

Brown sees a shift in Edwards's apologetic strategy in that he had to adapt to the contemporary challenges brought against the Christian faith and the Bible. Edwards argued for the derivation of so-called natural religion from historical religion so that what seems to be "rational" is in many ways determined by socialization. That is, one thinks that natural religion is rational because he has been brought up in a Christian land. Whereas the Deists argued for the primacy of an autonomous natural religion which was then polluted through priestcraft into such specific historical religions as Christianity, Edwards argued that biblical religion was original and that so-called natural religions were a corrupted descendent of Christianity.

At the end of the day, Brown does not argue that Edwards rejected the traditional Reformed emphasis on the necessity of the new birth in order properly to understand the Bible and the world, but that he added the more Enlightenment oriented *more historico*[100] method which demanded that he demonstrate the historical veracity of the Christian faith and the Bible on Enlightenment terms. For Brown, Edwards is almost completely a child of his time.

Stephen Nichols

Stephen Nichols has amply demonstrated his familiarity with the life and thought of Jonathan Edwards. He has authored, edited, or contributed to several scholarly discussions of Edwards.[101] Our concern is with the revision of his PhD dissertation known as *An Absolute Sort of Certainty*.[102] Nichols attempts to connect Edwards the theologian with Edwards the philosopher and this is best done, so he argues, through looking at Edwards the apologist.

---

100. Brown believes that Edwards accepted some of the presuppositions of his age. One of these would be the view that true knowledge must conform to the standard of geometry, a view called the *more geometrico*. In other words, for something to be considered a science or knowledge, it must approximate the mathematical rigor of geometry.

101. These include *Jonathan Edwards: A Guided Tour of His Life and Thought* (Phillipsburg, NJ: Presbyterian & Reformed Publishing, 2001); an annotated edition of *Jonathan Edwards' Resolutions and Advice to Young Converts* (Phillipsburg, NJ: Presbyterian & Reformed Publishing, 2001); *The Legacy of Jonathan Edwards*; and *Heaven on Earth: Capturing Jonathan Edwards' Vision of Living in Between* (Wheaton, IL: Crossway, 2006).

102. Stephen J. Nichols, *An Absolute Sort of Certainty: The Holy Spirit and the Apologetics of Jonathan Edwards* (Phillipsburg, NJ: Presbyterian and Reformed Publishing, 2003). This is a reworking of his 2000 Westminster Theological Seminary dissertation.

Doing this pulls together what may appear at first glance to be rather disparate elements into a cohesive, systematic whole. Nichols helpfully looks at Edwards's views on revelation, inspiration, illumination, regeneration and assurance (as well as Edwards's views on knowledge, perception, and testimony) and he shows what roles these play in his apologetic, producing what Edwards referred to as "an absolute sort of certainty." In other words, Nichols examines and brings together Edwards's theology and epistemology.[103]

Nichols argues that for Edwards, the Holy Spirit is the one who makes apologetics possible and effective. It takes the Holy Spirit's transformation of sinful man for man to see God and the world as it really is. The "new sense" is at the heart of this transformation. With this stress on the new sense, Edwards notes the difference between speculative or notional knowledge and spiritual knowledge. One can have speculative knowledge without spiritual knowledge but one cannot have spiritual knowledge without the speculative. The Holy Spirit, in other words, works through means. Specifically, the Holy Spirit, who inspired the writing of Scripture, is the one who illuminates it. One cannot understand Scripture aright without the renewing work of the Spirit, often referred to as the *testimonium internum Spiritu Sancti* or internal witness of the Holy Spirit. Scripture evidences that it is divinely inspired, but sinful man rejects this self-evidence and so needs to have his mind clarified. And so reason is not sufficient in itself to prove the truth of Christianity. God does use human reason in the process of coming to faith, but reason is not the *source* of belief. Sanctified reason can *see* that Scripture is divine and sweet. But it must be sanctified. Finally, Nichols provides evidence of Edwards's apologetic in his use of the medium of the sermon. Here Edwards drives home his apologetic message (argumentation with various forms of unbelief) which the Holy Spirit enables sinful men to truly appreciate through the new sense.

Josh Moody

Josh Moody approaches Edwards's apologetic method indirectly by means of his appropriation and correction of Enlightenment motifs and themes. In his insightful study of Edwards, *Jonathan Edwards and the Enlightenment*, Moody shows that the key to understanding Edwards's theology and his

---

103. This present study clearly builds upon Nichols' *An Absolute Sort of Certainty*. However Nichols' study is concerned to show how Edwards' apologetic provides integration for his theology as a whole and is irenic. This study seeks to address the particular argument of John Gerstner that Edwards was a classical apologist. Nichols' work does not address the specific concerns dealt with here, although we believe that this study coheres with and builds upon Nichols' fine research.

apologetic is his concern with "knowing the presence of God."[104] The author builds his study around four themes: true salvation, true experience, true reality, and true light. Edwards, says Moody, was a child of his times with his concern for certainty and use of the metaphor of light. Light, a common analogy in vogue at the time, features prominently in Edwards's voluminous writings. What we see from this study is that Edwards embodied the view of Augustine that the Christian was to "plunder the Egyptians," taking all that was worthwhile from a pagan source, but purifying it in the process. Moody notes that Edwards felt free to do this because he remained within the Reformed, Puritan tradition. According to Moody this meant at least two things. First, Edwards reflected the New England respect for science and philosophy and second, Edwards was free to rework the Enlightenment to conform it to his own biblical worldview.[105]

Brief Mentions

This discussion of the scholarship that deals with Edwards the apologist needs to mention two articles that have appeared in recent apologetics encyclopedias and a recent journal article. Norman Geisler includes a lengthy chapter on Edwards in his apologetics encyclopedia[106] and Robert Caldwell has written a concise but helpful treatment of Edwards the apologist in the *IVP Dictionary of Apologetics*.[107] Geisler's discussion, while of considerable length, is clearly dependent upon and derivative of the work of John Gerstner and offers no new assessment. Caldwell, on the other hand, draws together the insights from the latest research into Edwards's apologetic. Caldwell notes that Edwards left us no apologetic treatise, but that apologetics suffuses his corpus of literature. The author continues with four observations about Edwards's apologetic. First, Edwards was concerned to defend Scripture and in this task he looks like the traditional evidentialist. Second, when Edwards lauded reason (which he did), he was always speaking of *sanctified*

---

104. This is actually the subtitle of Moody's book. Josh Moody, *Jonathan Edwards and the Enlightenment: Knowing the Presence of God* (Lanham, MD: University Press of America, 2005). Additionally, Moody has authored *The God-Centered Life: Insights from Jonathan Edwards for Today* (Leicester, UK: Inter Varsity Press, 2006) and edited *Jonathan Edwards and Justification* (Wheaton, IL: Crossway, 2012).

105. Moody, *Jonathan Edwards and the Enlightenment*, 2.

106. Norman L. Geisler, *The Baker Encyclopedia of Christian Apologetics* (Grand Rapids, MI: Baker, 1998), 209–12.

107. W. C. Campbell-Jack and Gavin McGrath, eds. C. Stephen Evans, Cons. Ed. *The New IVP Dictionary of Apologetics* (Downers Grove, IL: IVP, 2006), Robert Caldwell, 228–29.

reason. Third, Edwards adopted the use of the *prisca theologia* to combat the "scandal of particularity" and fourth, Edwards stressed the direct spiritual perception of God necessary to salvation.[108] Finally, Joseph Woodall has recently published an article on Edwards and apologetics, "Jonathan Edwards, Beauty, and Apologetics" in which he argues that Edwards was concerned that the Christian life be an aesthetically beautiful life that would be winsome and therefore apologetically attractive.[109]

Contribution of This Study

While recent interest in Edwards's apologetic has surfaced afresh, most of these studies have contented themselves with discussions of Edwards's historical and theological milieu or with the role of the Holy Spirit in regeneration of the unbeliever and how that relates to the apologetic encounter. These are all important advances of our understanding of Edwards's theology and practice. However, none of these studies specifically focus upon the relationship of Edwards's theology of man and his apologetic practice or consider how these relate to the architectonic systematic structures of his thought.[110] John Gerstner comes close to doing this. However, Gerstner could be understood to be overly systematic in his presentation. It has been said that Gerstner has forced a foreign grid onto the Edwards corpus or has flattened the complexity of his thought.[111] This criticism needs to be

---

108. One can detect the influences of Michael McClymond, Gerald McDermott, Robert Brown, and Stephen Nichols in this dictionary article.

109. Joseph D. Woodall, "Jonathan Edwards, Beauty, and Apologetics," *Criswell Theological Review* 5/1 (Fall 2007): 81–95. This article is drawn from Woodall's Ph.D. dissertation, "Aesthetic Christian Apologetics" conferred by Southwestern Baptist Seminary in 2005.

110. Back in 2003 when this writer participated in a PhD seminar on the theology of Jonathan Edwards with Sang Hyun Lee at Princeton Theological Seminary, Lee was asked where the major lacunae lay in the field of Edwards studies and he unhesitatingly answered that two areas which were wide open for further scholarship were examinations of Edwards' biblicism and particular theological or doctrinal formulations. This study aims to partially fill that void.

111. This has been said to me by various scholars who would otherwise be sympathetic with Gerstner's own theological commitment. In other words, Gerstner makes Edwards too neatly conformed to the Reformed confessional tradition. It is worth considering whether Gerstner himself was influenced by Enlightenment thinking (even the so-called "moderate" Enlightenment thinking of Scottish Common Sense Realism). Interestingly enough, Gerstner, who is known for his scholarship on Edwards, actually did his dissertation on James McCosh, president of Princeton College, a student and advocate of Scottish Common Sense Realism. But that is outside the purview of our study.

taken seriously, but it is not the assumption of this project that Gerstner is problematic simply for being systematic.[112] The approach taken here, while not a historical theological study as such, will endeavor to be sensitive to historical context and the possibility of both theological maturation and retrogression. This study will endeavor to allow Edwards to be himself, to speak for himself, and to depart from the Reformed confessional consensus as he so desires.[113] Edwards, like his fellow New England ministers, held firmly to his independence of thought, even though he is quite properly categorized as a Calvinist.[114]

There is evidence, however, that Gerstner misreads Edwards at the point of his treatment of Edwards and faculty psychology.[115] So it would seem that a fresh examination of Edwards's Reformed theological anthropology is in order with a view to gaining a correct understanding of his perspective on the relations of the various capacities of the human soul as created, fallen, and restored and how this connects with his apologetics as ascertained from his actual practice. This writer does not see this study as a repudiation of the mammoth scholarly efforts of John Gerstner in general nor of all the particulars of his work on Edwards. What is being attempted here is a correction of certain aspects. Admittedly corrections here will have

112. Harry S. Stout is illustrative of this critical anti-systematic mindset. In his address turned paper on Edwards' tri-world vision of reality in *The Legacy of Jonathan Edwards*, 27–46, he discusses Edwards' desire to take his series of sermons now known as the "history of the work of redemption" and turn them into a theology done in a totally new form. This new form, perhaps an adumbration of the later Reformed biblical theological movement, Stout avers, would replace the standard systematic theological method of writers like Thomas Aquinas. Stout seems to simply equate Thomas with systematic theology when in fact Thomas is an exemplar of a *particular kind* of systematic theology, embodying the Medieval scholastic method as Francis Turretin would illustrate the high water mark of post reformation Reformed orthodox scholasticism. So criticisms of Gerstner on this count may reflect an anti-systematic bias or they reflect an aspect of truth even if overwrought.

113. Edwards' treatment of the imputation of Adam's sin comes to mind as an example of an apparent departure from the confessional tradition. Edwards, in his discussion of the fall and the transmission of sin to Adam's progeny in his treatise *Original Sin* (*The Works of Jonathan Edwards, Vol. 3: Original Sin*. Clyde A. Holbrook, ed. New Haven, CT: Yale University Press, 1970) does not stick with a purely federal conception of Adam's relation to the rest of the human race. There has been some debate over exactly what Edwards was doing in his discussion, and this will be examined more closely below, but most scholars understand that Edwards was not following the well-worn paths of the federal theology exemplified in the Westminster Confession of Faith. See the discussions of B. B. Warfield, John Murray and Oliver Crisp on this perennial issue noted in footnote 36 above.

114. See Edwards' comments in his *Freedom of the Will*.

115. K. Scott Oliphint has drawn attention to this problem in his "Jonathan Edwards: Reformed Apologist." *WTJ* 57/1 (Spring 1995): 165–186.

systemic effects throughout the Gerstner project. The upshot of all this is that there are aspects of Edwards apologetic which *do* fit a classical model and aspects that *do not*. This examination will reveal at least one area where reconsideration is called for.

Classical Apologetics: A Brief Description

It would seem to be necessary briefly to discuss just what classical apologetics is in order to ascertain whether Edwards's theological anthropology and apologetic practice reflect a classical perspective. So what is classical apologetics? It might be best to first determine what apologetics itself is. Apologetics is the defense of the Christian faith.[116] There is a negative and a positive aspect to this. Negatively, apologetics is the discipline of answering charges brought against and accusations made about the Christian faith. Positively, apologetics involves a commendation of the faith. And to these two standard divisions we would add a third element: the polemical. There is a legitimate place for the criticism of unbelief and less consistent forms of Christianity. So we see that there are three essential elements to Christian apologetics as the defense of the faith.

Christian apologetics began in the New Testament and since that time has developed in different ways. Different ways of doing apologetics have developed, often closely related to the theological perspective of specific apologists.[117] Additionally, these different ways can be variously classified as well.[118] It must be granted that these apologists were not all self-conscious members of a particular apologetic school but that we find it helpful to use these classifications for our own benefit. Bernard Ramm in his *Varieties of Christian Apologetics* divides the various approaches into three families: systems that stress the encounter of faith, systems that stress the use of natural

---

116. The locus classicus for apologetics is 1st Peter 3:15 where we find the word ἀπολογίαν from which we get the English word apologetics. We are told to always be ready to give the reason for the hope that is in us.

117. See Ramm, *Varieties*, for an example of the different apologetic systems that have arisen in defense of the faith. For primary texts from significant apologists over the last two thousand years, see William Edgar and K. Scott Oliphint, eds., *Christian Apologetics: Past & Present* (Wheaton, IL: Crossway, 2009–10), 2 vols.

118. In addition to Ramm, one can find different classifications in Steven Cowan, *Five Views on Apologetics* (Grand Rapids, MI: Zondervan, 2000); Kenneth Boa and Robert Bowman, *Faith Has Its Reasons* (Colorado Springs, CO: NavPress, 2001); and for a more historically oriented discussion, see Dulles, *A History of Apologetics*. Lengthier discussions can be found in Geisler, *Baker Encyclopedia of Christian Apologetics* and Campbell-Jack, McGrath, and Evans, *New Dictionary of Christian Apologetics*.

theology, and systems that stress the authority of revelation.[119] Kenneth Boa and Robert Bowman classify apologetics schools in the following manner: classical apologetics with a stress on proof, evidentialism with a stress on objective facts, Reformed apologetics with a concern for divine revelation and refutation of unbelief, and fideism with its emphasis on the uniqueness of the experience of faith.[120] Steve Cowan in his *Five Views on Apologetics* offers a similar classification of apologetic strategies, although with a concern for contemporary practice rather than historical or theoretical description. He sets forth five major schools: classical apologetics, evidentialism, cumulative case, presuppositionalism, and Reformed epistemology.[121]

Each of these treatments of the various schools of apologetic methodology discuss in some depth the issues that divide the methods. Ramm is particularly helpful in this regard. He points out that various apologetic strategies have arisen due to how different apologists have answered the following questions: What is the relationship between Christianity and philosophy? Is there any usefulness to the so-called "theistic proofs"? Does an apologist have to work with a specific theory of truth? How does an apologist understand the noetic effects of sin? What is the nature of revelation? Does the Christian faith offer certainty and if so, what kind? Is there common ground between the believer and unbeliever? What is the nature of faith? What usefulness do Christian evidences possess? And what is the relationship of faith and reason?[122]

We shall now consider the classical apologetic method in more detail. As has been frequently pointed out, this school of apologetics is referred to as "classical" because it is understood to be the way apologetics was done by the early apologists and has been followed by the mainstream of apologetics. It is also called "classical" because it reflects a commitment to the "classical synthesis" between Christian theology and philosophy. It is argued by some that philosophy was to the Greeks what the Old Testament was to the Hebrews.[123] However, the relationship of philosophy to theology is more complex than that would seem to suggest. Bernard Ramm notes that there have been at least three approaches to this relationship. There is the utter rejection of philosophy which we find voiced in the question of Tertullian,

---

119. Ramm, *Varieties*, 11–27.

120. Boa and Bowman, *Faith Has Its Reasons*, 55–60.

121. Cowan, *Five Views*, 11–27.

122. Ramm, *Varieties*, 17–27. Cowan, *Five Views*, 11–27, suggests that these questions all revolve around the relationship of faith to reason.

123. Ramm, *Varieties*, 12 and 17, notes this and Gerstner, *Rational Biblical Theology*, 1:25–26, hails it as obviously true.

"what does Jerusalem have to do with Athens?"[124] At the opposite end of the spectrum was the view that philosophy had a right to exist independently of theology. Thomas Aquinas is an illustration of this view.[125] In the middle was the position espoused by Augustine that philosophy was ancillary to theology, that is, it served as a handmaiden.

Not surprisingly, classical apologetics is understood to embrace the view adopted by Thomas Aquinas.[126] Thomas held that there was a philosophy that could be taken up in theology but could stand on its own as well. All of this is background to the roles that philosophy and theology play. Philosophy was to lay the foundation upon which theology would rear its superstructure. And this can be seen in classical apologetics. This apologetic method can be described as a two step procedure.[127] That is, one must first demonstrate that there is a divine being and only after that can one examine the Bible. The logic of this apologetic approach is that before one can ascertain whether the Bible is a communication from God, one must demonstrate that there is such a God as can communicate. The demonstration of the existence of this God must draw from philosophy since the purported revelation in the Bible is what is in question.

Another way to look at this is this: the Bible is filled with miraculous events and the apologist must be able to demonstrate from some other source than the Bible that there is a God to be able to communicate. If the God of the Bible does exist, it would not be surprising that he had communicated with

---

124. It has been pointed out that one must not read Tertullian naively. He was a trained lawyer and was therefore adept at rhetoric. Rhetoric called for a speaker or writer to admit his amateur status. So, ironically, a sure sign of philosophical training was for someone to call into question philosophy. Tertullian evinces signs of a Stoic influence as well.

125. Ramm, *Varieties*, 18.

126. See Ramm's discussion of Thomas, *Varieties*, 88–105. Thomas argues that natural reason (unassisted by divine revelation or the Holy Spirit) is able to function competently within the natural sphere. Natural reason is not so much tainted as it is limited. Therefore for reason to know certain theological truths beneficial for salvation, it then depends on divine revelation. Whether Thomas ought to be classified as a "classical" apologist is an open question. Like Anselm, Thomas offers his theistic arguments in the context of Christian meditation, not apologetic encounter, strictly speaking. See Thomas' comments on apologetic methodology in his *Summa Contra Gentiles* (5 vols. Anton C. Pegis, trans. Notre Dame: Notre Dame University Press, 1975), 9.1–5.

127. What Cornelius Van Til called the "blockhouse method" which seeks to defend the Christian faith seriatum. See his *Defense of the Faith* 4th ed. (Phillipsburg, NJ: Presbyterian & Reformed Publishing, 2008), 136–43. By two-step method, it is meant that classical apologetics seeks to argue for God's existence first before consideration of the nature of Scripture as a divine communication or of Jesus Christ as the Son of God. Another way to say this is that classical apologetics argues for generic theism as a foundation for the specific Christian form of theism.

his creatures. So before one examines the Bible to determine whether it is a species of revelation one must demonstrate that a revelation capable God exists in the first place. This first step, in which a demonstration of the existence of a God is attempted, is conducted with the assistance of philosophy. This philosophy is said to serve an analogous role for the Gentile which the Old Testament played for the Jews. It is a preparation for the gospel. Typically, the existence of God is demonstrated through the use of "theistic proofs" such as those formulated by Anselm and Thomas Aquinas. Anselm of Canterbury developed the ontological argument[128] and Thomas formulated the famous "five ways" which include an argument from contingency to necessity, from motion to rest, from cause to effect, from gradations of being, and from teleological purpose in the universe. The point is these are interpreted by many as attempts by these apologists to argue for the existence of God without reference to Holy Scripture. This view of Thomas, for instance, is assisted by his comments in the *Summa Contra Gentiles*[129] to the effect that the Christian missionary can reason from the New Testament with the heretic, from the Old Testament with a Jew, and since the Bible is not accepted by the Muslim, the Christian missionary must argue from reason.[130]

Additionally, the philosophical proof of God's existence often proceeds with a consideration of logical laws. The law of non-contradiction, the law of identity, and the law of the excluded middle are often drawn upon in this type of apologetic method. Similarly, a classical apologist may argue from the law of cause and effect or he or she may use the principle of sufficient reason (known as *PSR*). That is, an event must have a sufficient explanation

---

128. This is the name given to Anselm's argument by Immanuel Kant. It was not used by the archbishop of Canterbury himself.

129. Thomas Aquinas, *Summa contra Gentiles*, was ostensibly written as a missionary manual for Christians working with Muslims.

130. Aquinas, *Summa contra Gentiles*, 2.3. Thomas says, "To proceed against individual errors, however, is a difficult business, and this for two reasons. In the first place, it is difficult because the sacrilegious remarks of individual men who have erred are not so well known to us that we may use what they say as the basis of proceeding to a refutation of their errors. This is, indeed, the method that the ancient Doctors of the Church used in the refutation of the errors of the Gentiles. For they could know the positions taken by the Gentiles since they themselves had been Gentiles, or at least had lived among the Gentiles and had been instructed in their teaching. In the second place, it is difficult because some of them, such as the Mohammedans and the pagans, do not agree with us in accepting the authority of any Scripture, by which they may be convinced of their error. Thus, against the Jews we are able to argue by means of the Old Testament, while against heretics we are able to argue by means of the New Testament. But the Mohammedans and the pagans accept neither the one nor the other. We must, therefore, have recourse to the natural reason, to which all men are forced to give their assent. However, it is true, in divine matters the natural reason has its failings."

of its cause. These kinds of apologetic arguments usually end in the demonstration of the existence of some sort of divine being, although the specific kind of deity is unspecified. With the demonstration of the existence of God brought to the satisfactory conclusion of the apologist, the next step is to examine the Bible to see if it evidences itself to be a revelation from God.

The typical classical apologetic examination of the Bible proceeds in the following manner: the apologist moves from an assessment of historical veracity or adequacy, through the recognition that Jesus claimed to be the Son of God, performed miracles, and claimed the Old Testament was of divine provenance, as was the forthcoming New Testament. The conclusion reached is that given the historical veracity of the New Testament, Jesus's claims and the reports of his miraculous escapades are more likely than not (i.e., more probabilistic) to be taken as true. This is especially to be understood of the ultimate miracle, the resurrection.

The two step classical apologetic method can take various forms and can draw upon various types of philosophy. Some classical apologists argue the first step probabilistically while others argue with the goal of epistemological certainty. The second step can only be probable as it argues *a posteriori* or after the fact or from historical events. Now that the classical apologetic method has been explained, we will be a in a better position to examine the evidence in the case of Edwards. Before we get to that, however, the methodology of this study must be delineated and a summary of the remaining chapters must be given.

Methodological Considerations

It has already been noted that Jonathan Edwards did not write a systematic treatise on apologetics. In other words, there is no evidence that he understood himself to embody, represent, or stand within, a given apologetic school. If Avery Dulles is correct, this may simply be a reflection of Edwards's historical location.[131] That is, Edwards's predates substantial apologetic methodological self-consciousness. That there are various schools or methods of understanding apologetic theory and praxis may be a matter of modern self-awareness. Dulles attributes such self-consciousness to our own post-Kantian historical context.[132]

---

131. Avery Dulles, *A History of Apologetics*. As noted earlier, Gerstner also sees Kant as providing a watershed for apologetic self-awareness.

132. Dulles, *History of Apologetics*, 158–247. This fact will also have to be considered when Edwards' view of human reason is taken into consideration. Is Edwards a bald rationalist? This will be addressed below.

This study's task will involve both analysis and synthesis. The first step in the examination of the relation of Edwards's theological anthropology to his apologetic is to survey the field. Edwards's discourses on the freedom of the will and original sin are prime examples of polemical documents. His treatise on the religious affections, while having a polemical tinge, is more accurately classified as an expository essay. These sources will have to be examined and sifted for specific evidence of views about the nature of man as created in the image of God, or as fallen into sin, or about his view of apologetics and what, if any, view he may have expressed about the relation that exists between anthropology and apologetics.

Edwards's semi-private notebooks are well known since they have been published in the Yale University Press edition of his works. Edwards constantly read and thought with quill in hand. These notebooks are referred to here as "semi-private" for a reason. There has been ongoing scholarly discussion on how to interpret these notebooks. Are they purely private journals for Edwards's own benefit?[133] Or did he pen them with the intention that they be available to the greater public? The various notebooks actually fall somewhere in between. Not everything in the notebooks came to public notice in Edwards's lifetime. However, two facts mitigate seeing them as merely private journals. The first is that he often allowed friends and family to read them. We have evidence that he allowed his ministerial interns (Hopkins and Bellamy come to mind) to read them. Also we know for a fact that large swaths of material were taken from his notebooks and used in his sermons and treatises. These notebooks involve the "Miscellanies," the "Notes on the Mind," the "Notes on Scripture," the "Apocalyptic Writings," "Controversies" notebooks, and the "Blank Bible."

The sermons round out the genres examined in this study. These include individual sermons on Scripture passages germane to the topic under investigation and sermon series such as "Charity and its Fruits," and the "History of the Work of Redemption." In addition to careful analysis of appropriate texts, this project will quite obviously require a pulling together of insights from these various documents. So then there is the inevitable synthetic element. Not only will this occur across genres but also across topics

---

133. Perry Miller suggested that the Miscellanies were written as hidden notebooks in which Edwards could express his *true* thoughts on various theological topics. See his *Jonathan Edwards*, 50–51. In other words, the notebooks were private and Edwards could express himself freely whereas in his sermons and public treatises he had to measure and trim his words. Something similar is evident in the recent scholarship of Gerald McDermott, especially in his *Jonathan Edwards Confronts the Gods* where a "strange, new Edwards" arises from a fresh reading of the notebooks.

or loci. Edwards nowhere ties his anthropology to his apologetic method in any obvious way.

It should also be noted that this is an apologetics study and not a church history or historical theology project as such. While Robert Brown has called attention to development within Edwards's apologetic practice in the face of Deist attacks on Christianity and the Bible, development will not be our focus in this study. On the other hand, it has been said that Gerstner's Edwards scholarship shows an annoying lack of historical awareness. Gerstner is driven by systematic theological concerns. This study will be conducted with eyes open to the possibility of development, but that will not be the subject of research. Truth be told, Edwards was a systematic thinker. But given the voluminous literary output of this man, it would not be impossible for him to have matured in his thinking, to have made improvements, to have even changed his mind at points. But one of the consistent comments of scholars across the ages and theological spectrum is that Edwards was amazingly consistent with himself. Additionally, where Edwards's historical context helps to shed light on his thinking, it will prove beneficial.[134]

Lastly, in order to gain clarity in our understanding of Jonathan Edwards's theological anthropology and its relationship to his apologetic, it will do well to compare and contrast his thinking with examples from the history of Christian theology. Such comparisons and contrasts should highlight and isolate commonalities and disparities. An examination of these thinkers should help us to get a grasp of Edwards's position.

Conclusion

In the end it will be shown that Edwards's apologetic practice *does not wholly conform* to the classical model. However, Jonathan Edwards was a man of his time and he does exhibit some tendencies of a traditional apologetic method. But he lacks a stated commitment to a specific school of apologetics. He did, though, defend the faith against attacks and he also criticized many non-Christian perspectives. At the end of the day, Edwards's view of the unified operations of the human soul does not seem to square with the hierarchical faculty psychology foundational to and operative within a classical approach to apologetics.

---

134. See Michael J. McClymond and Gerald R. McDermott, *The Theology of Jonathan Edwards* (New York: Oxford University Press, 2012), who devote a whole chapter to development in Edwards' thought, 77–88.

2

Man as the Imago Dei

Introduction

THIS CHAPTER WILL SEEK to examine Jonathan Edwards's view of man as created in the image of God. One may well wonder what this has to do with his apologetic. The fact of the matter is that Christian theology, and apologetics as a sub-discipline of theology, is, or ought to be, systematic.[1] That is, whether self-conscious about this fact or not, Christian theologians and apologists have entertained views about the nature of man that impinge on their apologetic *praxis*.[2] For instance, is the essential problem with the human race *ontological finitude* or *ethical rebellion*? Throughout history philosophers have wrestled with the finite nature of man's being and consider it to be the major problem with which we have to do. However a biblical perspective would suggest that finitude is not a problem but a fact of our created status. The human predicament is not that we are limited because we are creatures, but that we are in ethical rebellion against our Creator. One could even say that the basis for the ethical rebellion was a failure to accept our human finitude. Apologetics is caught up in this matter. Does the apologist cater to the assumption that the major problem with the human race is finitude or limitation? Or does he or she face the problem as sin or ethical

---

1. For a valuable discussion of this that postdates Edwards, see Benjamin B. Warfield's discussion of the systematic propensity of the human mind as created by God as the basis for systematic theology in "The Rights of Systematic Theology," in *The Selected Shorter Writings of Benjamin B. Warfield* John Meeter, ed. (Phillipsburg, NJ: Presbyterian & Reformed Publishing, 1973), 2: 219–279.

2. See the discussion of the theological issues that impinge upon apologetics in Bernard Ramm, *Varieties of Christian Apologetics* (Grand Rapids, MI: Baker, 1961), 17–27.

rebellion? An apologist's view of the essential problem with the human race will determine methods and strategies.[3]

To illustrate the point, consider the problem of knowledge. Human knowledge is limited. Are humans therefore ignorant of God and who he is? Or, if they have knowledge of God, how do they come by it? Does man possess knowledge of God simply by virtue of his being created in God's image or does he acquire knowledge of God through consideration of proofs and arguments alone? Is man's mind a *tabula rasa* or is it created with both the capacity to know God and actually possesses such knowledge? One's answer to these questions will color how one does apologetics. In the first case, the apologist knows that the man or woman he addresses was created by God in his own image and possesses both the capacity to know God and actually does have an awareness of God because such knowledge is implanted by God himself (Rom. 1:18f). This knowledge is denied and repressed, but it is present nonetheless. Because this natural knowledge of God is present, though repressed, there is something to which the apologist can appeal in an apologetic encounter. In the second case, the apologist faces a person who knows nothing about God and so has to build a case from the ground up. The Christian apologist will then appeal to standards that hold whether or not the Christian God exists. To put it another way, the apologist who starts with the belief that man's mind is a blank slate will use theistic proofs or arguments in a pre-dogmatic way so as to build a foundation upon which to rear a specifically Christian defense.[4] The reality of man's being made in the image of God and what that means involves more than consideration of man's natural knowledge of God, but this has been offered as an illustration.

We have already had occasion to note in the previous chapter, that apologetic self-consciousness is most likely a product of a post-Kantian historical context and that Edwards predates this phenomenon.[5] However, this does not mean that there is no systematic coherence or integration between Edwards's view of man as made in God's image and his apologetic practice. It only means that he himself may not have been aware of it.

---

3. It is also the case that apologetics is not done in a subjective vacuum. That is, the apologist himself has a specific theology that colors his approach. An Arminian is likely to offer one kind of defense and a Calvinist another, and a Roman Catholic a third alternative. Edwards' apologetic efforts typically defended Reformed theological distinctives.

4. More will be said about this in the next chapter.

5. Avery Dulles, *A History of Apologetics* (Philadelphia: Westminster Press, 1971), 158–247, has made the suggestion that it was the Kantian revolution that brought in its wake Christian apologetic self-awareness, especially regarding epistemological issues.

Whether or not there is such a systematic integration between Edwards's theological anthropology and his apologetics remains to be demonstrated later in this study. For now it is sufficient to examine Edwards's understanding of man as created in the *imago Dei*. As it turns out, Jonathan Edwards has plenty to say about this, and in some significant depth. There are several significant sources for understanding what Edwards held about man as created in the image of God, including (but not limited to) the sermon "East of Eden" on Genesis 3:24, several *Miscellanies* entries dealing with Adam and the nature of man, and his treatises on *Freedom of the Will* and *Original Sin*.[6]

Finally this chapter will wrestle with whether Edwards held to some form of the so-called *donum superadditum* and why that matters. To help the reader place Edwards within the stream of Christian thinking on this subject, a comparison of Edwards with Augustine, Thomas Aquinas, John Calvin, and Francis Turretin will be made. The reader should come away with a better grasp of Jonathan Edwards's theology of man as made in the image of God. Some comment will be made about how this discussion relates to apologetics, although a fuller discussion will be reserved for later in the study.

The Historical Setting for Jonathan Edwards's Discussion of Man Created in the Image of God

Over the next several pages, this study will seek to examine the context in which Edwards's fullest formulations of the *imago Dei* occur. It will be seen that Edwards speaks at length about the image, especially in terms of man

---

6. The sermon "East of Eden" on Genesis 3:24 can be found in *The Works of Jonathan Edwards/Vol. 17: Sermons and Discourses, 1730-1733* (Mark Valeri, ed. New Haven, CT: Yale University Press, 1999), 331-348, the *Miscellanies* entrees can be found in *The Works of Jonathan Edwards/Vol. 13: The "Miscellanies" a-500* (Thomas A. Schafer, ed. New Haven, CT: Yale University Press, 1994), *The Works of Jonathan Edwards/Vol. 18: The "Miscellanies" 501-832* (Ava Chamberlain, ed. New Haven, CT: Yale University Press, 2000), *The Works of Jonathan Edwards/Vol. 20: The "Miscellanies" 833-1152* (Amy Plantinga Pauw, ed. New Haven, CT: Yale University Press, 2002), and *The Works of Jonathan Edwards/Vol. 23: The "Miscellanies" 1153-1360* (Douglas A. Sweeney, ed. New Haven, CT: Yale University Press, 2004), *Freedom of the Will* is located in *The Works of Jonathan Edwards/Vol. 1: Freedom of the Will* (Paul Ramsey, ed. New Haven, CT: Yale University Press, 1957 & 1985) and *Original Sin* comprises *The Works of Jonathan Edwards/Vol. 3: Original Sin* (Clyde A. Holbrook, ed. New Haven, CT: Yale University Press, 1970). Hereafter references to volumes in *The Works of Jonathan Edwards* series will be given in full for the first reference and then in the following abbreviated format: *WJE* followed by the backslash and volume number, comma and appropriate page numbers as in this example involving the *Original Sin* volume: *WJE*/3, 223-234.

as possessing both a natural and moral image and it will be seen that in this regard man reflects the Triune God who possesses both natural and moral attributes. Man can be said to be an analogue of God.

> As there are two kinds of attributes in God, according to our way of conceiving of him, his moral attributes, which are summed up in his holiness, and his natural attributes, of strength, knowledge, etc. that constitute the greatness of God; so there is a two-fold image of God in man, his moral and spiritual image, which is his holiness . . . and God's natural image, consisting in men's reason and understanding, his natural ability, and dominion over the creatures, which is the image of God's natural attributes.[7]

Jonathan Edwards did not wrestle with the nature of man as created in the image of God in a vacuum. Rather, he looked into the whole matter in the context of defending an orthodox, Calvinistic understanding of the fall and its effects. Edwards's most complete discussion is found in his treatise on *Original Sin*, although related discussion is also found in his famous *Freedom of the Will*. Edwards's nemesis was the British Presbyterian John Taylor. Taylor, whose works were apparently gaining a hearing in the New England of Edwards's day, argued for some highly heterodox views about the fall and the inheritance of a sinful nature by Adam's progeny.[8]

Taylor's book, *The Plain Scripture-Doctrine of Original Sin* argued for several unusual theses.[9] Two of Taylor's theses are a concern for this study: (1) Adam and Eve were created in a neutral position and (2) death is not a punishment for sin but God's method of restricting the ravages of sin. Rejecting the Reformed position that Adam and Eve were created in a condition of knowledge, righteousness, and holiness, Taylor argued that Adam and Eve were created in a neutral state. That is, the first couple was created in a state of moral equilibrium. They were neither good nor evil. To be good or evil requires the exercise of moral choice and Adam and Eve could not have been created with knowledge, righteousness, and holiness as these characteristics would require choices to have been made and moral fiber to have developed.

---

7. Jonathan Edwards, *The Works of Jonathan Edwards/Vol. 2: Religious Affections* (John E. Smith, ed. New Haven, CT: Yale University Press, 1959 & 1987), 256.

8. See the fascinating and enlightening discussion about Taylor's influence in New England in Clyde Holbrook's editorial introduction in Edwards, *WJE/3*, 2–27.

9. John Taylor, *The Plain Scripture-Doctrine of Original Sin, Proposed to Free and Candid Examination* (London: 1738). Further treatment of John Taylor and his theological position can be found in C. Samuel Storms, *Tragedy in Eden: The Doctrine of Sin in Jonathan Edwards* (Lanham, MD: University Press of America, 1985), 31–78.

It is, I think, Demonstration, that we cannot, as moral agents, observe what is right and true, or be righteous and holy, without our own free and explicit Choice. And in consequence, *Adam* could not be originally created in Righteousness and true Holiness, because he must choose to be righteous before he could be righteous, and therefore he must exist, he must *be created*, yea, he must exercise Thought and Reflection, before he *was righteous*.[10]

Taylor also rejected the traditional Reformed understanding of death as a judicial punishment imposed by God upon creation because of the disobedience of the first parents. Rather, Taylor argued, death is God's loving limitation placed upon the human race. Sin would be much more serious if God had not introduced death to curb sin's ramifications.[11]

Man as Natural and Moral Image

The Christian tradition has debated the particulars of the *imago Dei* and Jonathan Edwards himself participated in that ongoing exegetical and theological discussion. Not surprisingly, he has brought his own unique insights to bear on the discussion.[12] While the broader Christian tradition has historically distinguished between a broader and narrower image, Edwards rather spoke of a *natural* and *moral* image in man.[13] This kind of distinction is typical of Edwards and we will see similar bifurcations in his understanding of the nature of God and human epistemology.[14]

While Edwards did not use the terminology, it would not be inaccurate to substitute the terms *metaphysical* for natural and *ethical* for moral so as to see that Edwards understood the image of God in man in terms

---

10. Taylor, *Plain Scripture-Doctrine*, 182. See also the *Supplement* which contains a fairly lengthy refutation of original righteousness, 148–157.

11. Taylor, *Plain Scripture-Doctrine*, 65–72. Taylor argues that death is beneficial in that it disciplines humanity, dissuading from vanity, and it is a "striking demonstration" of the heinous nature of sin in the eyes of God.

12. A thorough consideration of the nature of the image of God can be found in G. C. Berkouwer's *Man: The Image of God* in his Studies in Dogmatics series (Dirk W. Jellema, trans. Grand Rapids, MI: Eerdmans, 1962). For a helpful examination of the history of the theological discussion about the image of God, see also Anthony A. Hoekema's *Created in God's Image* (Grand Rapids, MI: Eerdmans, 1986), 33–65.

13. Edwards, *WJE/2*, 256.

14. Edwards himself makes this connection in his sermon on the necessity of knowledge, "The Importance and Advantage of a Thorough Knowledge of Divine Truth," in *The Works of Jonathan Edwards/Vol. 22: Sermons and Discourses, 1739-1742* (Harry S. Stout, ed. New Haven, CT: Yale University Press, 2003), 83–104, especially 87.

of both a metaphysical and an ethical image.[15] In other words, the natural image could be said to create the possibility of the moral image. It would be fair to say that without the metaphysical or natural image, there could be no ethical or moral image. This raises the question as to whether Edwards understood the ethical image as an optional extra added to the metaphysical or natural image. This question will be dealt with below when the question of whether Edwards held to a doctrine of the *donum superadditum* is examined. Is it possible for the natural image to exist apart from the moral or the moral from the natural? Before we wrestle with these fascinating and significant questions, a look at what Edwards understood each facet of the *imago Dei* to involve will be in order.

The Natural Image

As already suggested by the use of the substitute term *metaphysical* image, the natural image may be said to provide the preconditions for the moral image. According to Jonathan Edwards, the natural image is comprised of man's intellectual, volitional, linguistic, and relational capacities. It is helpful to remember that, among other things, what distinguishes man from beast is the possession of the *imago Dei*. The natural image would thus include man's ability to reason. Man is a thinking creature who does not merely act on instinct, as do others of God's creation. Man can reason according to logical principles. He can follow chains of reasoning and argue points of view. It is doubtful that man as we know him would be man without this rational capacity.

Man also has volition.[16] That is, Edwards affirmed what the mainstream of the Christian tradition has affirmed. Prior to the fall, Adam and Eve had free will and after the fall they no longer had such free will. Is Edwards suggesting that prior to the fall, Adam and Eve had *libertarian* free

---

15. These distinctions are owed to the insights of K. Scott Oliphint in his "Jonathan Edwards: Reformed Apologist," in *WTJ* 57/1 (Spring 1995): 184.

16. John Gerstner notes in *The Rational Biblical Theology of Jonathan Edwards* (Powhatan, VA & Orlando, FL: Berea Publications & Ligonier Ministries, 1992), 2:308, 314, that Edwards was inconsistent in affirming both that Adam had libertarian freedom of will prior to his fall in the garden and that there is no such thing as libertarian free will or a will unmotivated by causes outside itself. That is, Gerstner understands Edwards to affirm *libertarian* free will in the garden pre-fall and to deny such libertarian free-will after the fall. The inconsistency, if there be such inconsistency, lies in the fact that Edwards argues in excruciating detail against the idea of a will abstracted or detached from the nature of the person who possesses that will. Not even God has that kind of will. If Adam was created in righteousness, holiness, and knowledge, by definition he cannot have been created with libertarian free will.

will or is he simply suggesting that prior to the fall, their wills were unencumbered by sin? Is it possible that prior to the fall, Adam and Eve's wills were motivated by a holy disposition so that, for a time at least, they only sought to do God's will?[17] Given Edwards's general concern for cause and effect relationships, it would seem that he would not posit an unconstrained or unmotivated will in the garden.

The natural image of God in man would also involve man's ability to communicate. For Edwards, the quintessence of being, human and divine, is *consent* to being. Consent would seem to require both relationality and linguistic capacity. How could one "relate" to another without the ability to communicate? So Edwards would understand these capacities to be prerequisites to man communing with man and more importantly, man communing with God.[18]

The question naturally arises, and will be addressed in greater detail below, can the natural (or metaphysical) image stand alone or does it require the moral (or ethical) image to function properly? Does the natural image function adequately without the moral image or does it necessarily malfunction? In other words, is the moral image integral to the image as a whole or is it an added extra?

The Moral Image

In addition to the natural image of God in man, there is also the moral image.[19] The moral image involves the possession of a holy disposition. Love to God and enjoyment of him would most certainly be included within the purview of the moral image. The desire to be holy as God is holy and the love of God and the things of God would be in view as well. Related to this would be one of Edwards's favorite ways of describing man's appropriate response to God: "beings consent to being" and the remanation of God's glorious emanation.[20]

---

17. This fact, of course, only makes the problematic nature of how a sinful disposition, fleeting or settled, could have arisen in Adam and Eve at all more obvious.

18. See Edwards' "Miscellanies" "tt" and "178" in *WJE/13*, 189–191 and 327 respectively.

19. Is it possible that Edwards' natural/moral distinction is similar to the broader/narrower distinction which is more typical in the Christian tradition? What is different about the two ways of understanding the *imago Dei*? Is the difference merely terminological? It would seem that Edwards would agree with Albert Wolters' distinction between the *structures* and *direction* of creation pre- and post-fall. See Wolters, *Creation Regained* (Grand Rapids, IL: Eerdmans, 1985).

20. Again, see Edwards' Miscellanies "tt" and "178" in *WJE/13*, 189–191 and 327.

Edwards would recognize that man was created to have fellowship with God and to worship him. He would agree wholeheartedly with the Westminster divines' answer to the first question of the shorter catechism. "What is the chief end of man?" "Man's chief end is to glorify God and to enjoy him forever."[21] Even in heaven the saints would continue to grow in their love and praise for God-their consent to being in general. In his final sermon in his series on 1 Corinthians 13, later to become known as "Charity and its Fruits," Edwards spoke of heaven as a "world of love."[22] In heaven the saints would get to exercise their moral image without earthly limitations. The saints would grow increasingly closer to God and to one another without losing individual identity. The exercise of the moral image is, of course, not limited to the new heavens and the new earth.

The saints on earth were to be visible. That is, Christians are called to make visible their moral image. Another way to approach this is to say that Christians are to experience true religious affections.[23] After all, what are the true religious affections other than the progressive restoration of the moral image of God in man? Edwards would have resonated with the apostle Paul when Paul referred to the life of sanctification as a "putting off of the old man" and a "putting on of the new man" in knowledge, righteousness, and true holiness (as he does in Ephesians 4:24 and Colossians 3:10). Paul was undoubtedly thinking of Adam's original state of integrity, what was lost in the fall and eventually regained in sanctification.

The Relation of the Natural and Moral Image of God

If, as has already been suggested, the natural image provides the preconditions for the moral image, what is the exact nature of the relationship of these two aspects of the *imago Dei*? Is the relationship analogous to what Edwards understands about *speculative* and *spiritual* knowledge?[24] While

---

For a fully developed articulation of emanation and remanation, see Edwards' "Concerning the End for Which God Created the World," in *The Works of Jonathan Edwards/Vol.8: Ethical Writings* (Paul Ramsey, ed. New Haven, CT: Yale University Press, 1989), 403–536.

21. Q & A 1 of the *Westminster Shorter Catechism*.

22. Edwards, "Charity and Its Fruits," *WJE/8*, 123–398. Sermon fifteen, "Heaven is a World of Love," can be found at 366–398.

23. Edwards, *WJE/2*, see especially the twelfth sign of true religious affections, namely Christian practice which Edwards explicates at 383–461.

24. Edwards, *WJE/22*, in his sermon on the necessity of the knowledge of divine truth notes, "That there are two kinds of knowledge of the things of divinity, viz. speculative and practical, or in other terms, natural and spiritual. The former remains only in

we will deal with the speculative/spiritual knowledge issue in more detail below, it is worth considering whether there is an analogy here. Perhaps an analogy lies here: just as it is possible for a person to have speculative knowledge of God without spiritual knowledge, and so an unregenerate man may serve as a superb theologian, so also would it be true to say that the natural image remains intact subsequent to the fall while the moral image is lost? In other words, does Edwards allow for not only the remainder of some form of the natural image (which most orthodox theologians would grant), but does he allow for a properly functioning natural image *sans* moral image?[25]

Man as Analogue of the Triune God

Jonathan Edwards stood within the grand Christian theological tradition which understands the *imago Dei* to constitute man a finite analogue of his God. To understand this relationship better it makes sense to first consider Edwards's discussion of the divine attributes. God, says Edwards, possesses *natural* and *moral* attributes. The natural attributes embrace God's omniscience, his omnipotence, and omnipresence. These are attributes that tend to focus on power. Edwards would say these are characteristics that, considered by themselves, would cause men to tremble and cower in fear, but not make them love and adore God. For Edwards, one of the glories of the incarnation of the Son of God and the gospel is that both the natural and moral attributes are revealed together.

---

the head. No other faculty but the understanding is concerned in it. It consists in having a natural or rational knowledge of the things of religion, or such a knowledge as is to be obtained by the natural exercise of our own faculties, without any special illumination of the Spirit of God. The latter rests not entirely in the head, or in the speculative ideas of things; but the heart is concerned in it: it principally consists in the sense of the heart. The mere intellect, without the heart, the will or inclination, is not the seat of it. And it may not only be called seeing, but feeling or tasting. Thus there is a difference between having a right speculative notion of the doctrines contained in the Word of God, and having a due sense of them in the heart. In the former consists speculative or natural knowledge of the things of divinity; in the latter consists the spiritual or practical knowledge of them," 87.

25. Anticipating further consideration of this question below, it should be noted here that Edwards does *not* hold that the natural image of God remains *fully intact* subsequent to the fall. For instance, in his sermon "East of Eden," commenting on the perfect state in which Adam was created and so possessed harmonious faculties, Edwards notes, "And his soul was in a very perfect state, the faculties of it in full strength, not broken, impaired, and weakened and ruined, as they are now . . . " and after the fall, "He lost the vigor and strength of his faculties. His understanding was clouded and broken, and the whole man in all its faculties was but the ruins of what it before was," Edwards, *WJE/17*, 333–334.

> For the better understanding of this matter, we may observe that God in the revelation that he has made of himself to the world by Jesus Christ, has taken care to give proportionable manifestation of two kinds of excellencies or perfections of his nature, viz. those that especially tend to possess us with awe and reverence, and to search and humble us, and those that tend to win and draw and encourage us. By the one he appears as an infinitely great, pure, holy, and heart-searching judge; by the other, as a gentle and gracious Father and a loving friend: by the one he is a pure, searching, and burning flame; by the other a sweet, refreshing light.[26]

On the other hand, the moral attributes are those characteristics that make God praiseworthy and loveable. These would include God's holiness, righteousness, and love. These make his natural attributes amiable and attractive. These are the attributes Edwards primarily had in mind when he discussed man's love to God as "being's consent to being."[27]

So we find that God has natural and moral attributes and man has a natural and moral image. How do these relate? At one point Edwards suggests that if you take man's nature and remove the effects of sin and finitude you end up with the mind of God.[28] By use of the *via negativa* and the *via eminentia* one can move from man to God.[29] These two familiar ways of speaking about God in human language have an honorable pedigree. Theologians who thrived during the Middle Ages, Reformation and Post-Reformation eras would be familiar with these methods. The *via negativa* involved taking human attributes and removing sinful effects and thereby ending with some legitimate way of thinking about God. The *via eminentia*, also called the "way of heightening" involved the removal of finite limitations and raising a particular characteristic to the "n"th degree. The combination of these two "ways" led Edwards to make the suggestion already noted.

Is it possible for God to exist without his moral attributes or his natural attributes? What we ask about God in this regard may be reflective of what we can ask about man and his natural and moral image. Or perhaps this is

---

26. Edwards, *WJE/4*, 463.

27. Edwards, *WJE/2*, 257.

28. Edwards makes the comment that "If we should suppose the faculties of a created spirit to be enlarged infinitely, there would be the Deity to all intents and purposes . . . ," Jonathan Edwards, *The Works of Jonathan Edwards/Vol. 6: Scientific and Philosophical Writings* (Wallace E. Anderson, ed. New Haven, CT: Yale University Press, 1980), 363. It should be noted that Anderson locates this comment in Misc. 150. An examination of the Yale edition of the Miscellanies reveals that this is Miscellanies 135.

29. See Richard A. Muller, *Dictionary of Latin and Greek Theological Terms: Drawn Principally from Protestant Scholastic Theology* (Grand Rapids, MI: Baker, 1985), 326.

where man and God differ. God cannot add or subtract from his attributes. God is simple. He *is* his attributes. Man, however, can gain and lose characteristics. Man is still man even after the fall. He changes from being holy and righteous man to sinful man, but man he is still.

This discussion brings us to a consideration of whether or not Jonathan Edwards held to what is known as the doctrine of the superadded gift or the *donum superadditum*.

Jonathan Edwards and the Donum Superadditum

John Gerstner has suggested that Edwards had his own form of the (Thomistic) doctrine of the *donum superadditum*.[30] C. Samuel Storms, while altogether too brief, suggests to the contrary, that despite appearances, Edwards did not hold to the doctrine of the *donum*.[31] The most useful way to explore this issue is to give as thorough an exposition of Edwards's view of Adam pre-and post-fall and as possible compare this with the best example of a thoroughgoing *donum* teaching in the theology of Thomas Aquinas.[32] This will allow us to compare and contrast the two views. To help provide some context, further exploration will be made of the doctrinal formulations of Augustine, John Calvin, and Francis Turretin.

Edwards on Adam

John Gerstner states that for Edwards, Adam was created "almost fallen."[33] What does Gerstner mean by this? After considering Gerstner's perspective on Edwards and Adam, a closer look and exposition of Edwards's view will follow. What Gerstner is suggesting is that for Edwards, God stacked the decks, as it were, against Adam. It was not possible for Adam to have passed

---

30. Gerstner, *Rational Biblical Theology*, 2:316–319.

31. Storms, *Tragedy in Eden*, 276n175. Storms notes that Edwards' distinction in his *Original Sin* treatise between Adam's natural and supernatural principles might lead some to conclude that Edwards held to the doctrine of the *donum superadditum*. Storms thinks such a view would be erroneous. Unfortunately nothing further is mentioned about this.

32. Thomas Aquinas, *The Summa Theologica* 5 vols. (Fathers of the English Dominican Province, trans. Allen: Christian Classics, 1948 & 1981), 1a.93.1–102.4 [1:469–502]. The Latin text is taken from the following website: http://www.corpusthomisticum.org/iopera.html. The print edition from which the text is drawn is the Leonine edition of the *Summa Theologica* (Rome: Ex Typographia Polyglotta S. C. de Propaganda Fide, 1888–89).

33. Gerstner, *Rational Biblical Theology*, 2:237.

the test to which he was put in the Garden of Eden. At the end of the day, only the Son of God could have sustained the probation to which Adam was put. And, as it turns out, it was the Son of God who ultimately did pass the probation.[34]

Adam as Created

Edwards's discussion is dense and must be carefully and closely read. As Edwards's theology of Adam is unpacked it will become clear why Gerstner thinks for Edwards Adam was created almost fallen. In order to prevent painting God as the author of sin Edwards ends up making him the Creator of a defective creature.[35] The sole question directing Edwards's discussion is this: how could a holy creature fall into sin? How could a creature come from the hands of God and deliberately rebel against his maker without there being some *definable* cause? It is questions like these that drive Edwards's discussion.

The situation is somewhat aggravated, for Edwards, standing in the mainstream of the Reformed tradition, affirmed that Adam was not merely created with moral neutrality[36] but was positively righteous and holy.

> In a moral agent, subject to moral obligations, it is the same thing, to be perfectly *innocent*, as to be perfectly *righteous*. It must be the same, because there can no more be any *medium* between sin and righteousness, or between being right and being wrong, in a moral sense, than there can be a medium between straight and crooked, in a natural sense . . . therefore he was immediately under a rule of right action: he was obliged as soon as he existed, to act right.[37]

---

34. Gerstner is no doubt correct when he notes that Edwards, like Augustine before him, and others would follow, painted himself into a corner by trying to understand how a creature created good fresh from the hands of the Creator, who is not only innocent, but holy and righteous, could fall into sin. What Gerstner means is that ultimately neither Augustine nor Edwards can explain how a holy creature could rebel against God. Their attempts to do so end up attributing the fall to a defective creation. See Gerstner's thoughtful comments, *Rational Biblical Theology*, 2:307, 319–321.

35. There is more here than *mutability*. Edwards seeks to exonerate God from the authorship of sin. But in doing so he goes beyond *finitude* and *changeability* to attribute the fall to both inattention on the part of Adam and a withdrawal of the Holy Spirit prior to the fall.

36. This is one of the disagreements Edwards has with John Taylor in *Original Sin*. For Taylor, Adam could not have been created with a good or holy nature as that would require *choice*. See Edwards, *WJE/2*, 223–236.

37. Edwards, *WJE/3*, 228.

Like John Calvin before him, Edwards would understand Adam's nature from what the New Testament says is restored in salvation (namely righteousness, holiness, and knowledge per Ephesians 4:24 and Colossians 3:10).[38] That is, what Adam lost in the fall is recovered in redemption and so since these virtues are restored Adam must have had them in the Garden prior to the fall. Edwards speaks of this in terms of Adam's possession of a holy *habit* or *disposition*.

There is an interesting debate occurring amongst Edwards scholars concerning the nature of Edwards's understanding of *habits* or *dispositions*. The two schools have been labeled the "Korean-American" school and the "British" school. The "Korean-American" school is exemplified in the scholarship of Sang Hyun Lee, professor of theology at Princeton Theological Seminary, who has published widely on Edwards's reconceptualization of the traditional Aristotelian nature-habits-act scheme. Lee argues that for Edwards, habits or dispositions are law-like entities which guarantee that when they converge or intersect that such and such an event will transpire or such and such a being will arise. Habits can exist in either a virtual or actual state, but each is just as real as the other. It is safe to say that Lee's thesis is the majority report among mainstream Edwards scholars. Such scholars as Anri Morimoto, Gerald McDermott, and Amy Plantinga-Pauw assume or further his thesis. More recently questions have arisen about the viability of the Lee thesis. One such response comes from British historical theologian Stephen R. Holmes who challenges the idea that Edwards reformulated the Aristotelian notion of habits and suggests that Edwards can be read more than adequately against the traditional background. Holmes also challenges the pantheistic and process-oriented conclusions Lee draws from his own thesis.[39] Holmes is basically correct that Edwards's treatment of habits or dispositions can be understood against the background of a traditional Christianized form of the Aristotelian understanding of human nature. Human nature is understood as comprised of three elements: sub-

---

38. Edwards, *WJE/3*, 367–371.

39. Lee's thesis, which has major ramifications for understanding Edwards, cannot be unpacked here due to limitations of space, can be found in his *The Philosophical Theology of Jonathan Edwards* (Princeton, NJ: Princeton University Press, 2000. 2nd ed.), his editor's introduction to *The Works of Jonathan Edwards/Vol. 21: Writings on Grace, Faith, and the Trinity* (New Haven, CT: Yale University Press, 2003), and in his edited volume *The Princeton Companion to Jonathan Edwards* (Princeton, NJ: Princeton University Press, 2005). Holmes articulates his concerns with Lee in his, "Does Edwards Use a Dispositional Ontology: A Response to Sang Hyun Lee" in the volume *Jonathan Edwards, Philosophical Theologian* (Paul Helm and Oliver Crisp, eds. Burlington, VT: Ashgate, 2003), 99–114. Scholars who follow this trail include Paul Helm, Michael McClenahan, and Craig Biehl.

stance (or nature), habits, and acts. In this schematic, habits stand between substance and acts. When Adam fell he still remained a man, although he mutated or changed from being a holy to a sinful creature. Man's substance remained intact but his habits and acts changed. In other words, Adam did not become another species of creature when he fell. God created Adam with a holy habit or disposition and it is this which was corrupted in the fall. Acts, as Edwards would affirm, proceed from habits. So the basis of a holy or righteous act is a holy disposition and conversely the basis of a sinful act is a sinful disposition.

As already noted, Adam is not only not created in moral ambivalence or equilibrium, but he possesses a positively holy disposition.[40] He is inclined toward love of God and holiness. In the Garden, Adam (and Eve) is disposed to love and obey God. So one can see how Edwards would have a harder time explaining how a holy creature such as Adam could possibly sin. Again, for Edwards, one must possess a given habit or disposition before one can act *from* that disposition. In other words, acts are the *results of* dispositions or, to put it another way, dispositions *tend towards* overt acts. However, it must also be noted that Adam and Eve were not immutable in the sense that the saints in heaven are. That is, at the very least, Adam and Eve were "mutable." To put it positively, the first couple was not yet confirmed in righteousness. Negatively, the potential was there for them to fall.[41] But still the question remains, how did a holy creature, with a holy disposition, fall into sin?

How does Edwards deal with this conundrum? Gerstner argues that Edwards does not so much explain as merely label. That is, Edwards thinks he has come up with a viable explanation for the fall, how a holy creature could fall into sin. Gerstner begs to differ.[42] Edwards may offer a taxonomy of terms, but at the end of the day, he provides no real explanation of the

---

40. Edwards, *WJE/17*, 333–334. Edwards notes, "And his soul was in a very perfect state, the faculties of it in full strength, not broken, impaired, and weakened and ruined, as they are now. The soul of man with regard to quickness and clearness of its faculties was then like the heavenly intelligences-as a flame of fire. The natural image of God that consists in reason and understanding was then complete. And man then had excellent endowments. His mind shone with the perfect spiritual image of God, being without any defect in its holiness and righteousness, or any spot or wrinkle to mar its spiritual beauty. God had put his own beauty upon it; it shone with the communication of his glory. And man enjoyed uninterrupted spiritual peace and joy that hence arose. His mind was full of spiritual light and peace as the atmosphere in a cool and calm day."

41. That is, Adam and Eve, even though created "good," indeed, "very good," were not in a state of confirmed righteousness. That state was the eschatological blessing implicitly promised to them had they passed the probation. See Edwards, *WJE/17*, 332.

42. Gerstner, *Rational Biblical Theology*, 2:303–322 The same problem is discussed at some length in Gerstner's taped series on the theology of Edwards.

fall.⁴³ Even if it is granted that Edwards is ultimately unsatisfactory, what does he say? This is what he says:

Adam was created with *sufficient* grace to stand up under the probation, however he did not possess *efficacious* grace.⁴⁴ Had Adam made use of the grace proffered, he could have passed the probation and entered into a state of confirmed righteousness from which he could not have fallen. But this is tantamount to saying that God set Adam up for a fall. In other words, God gave Adam sufficient grace to hold up under the test, but that Adam did not take full advantage of what he possessed. At the end of the day, only the Son of God could have passed the probation.⁴⁵

This, of course, is not all that could be said. Up to this point, Edwards has been trying to protect God from the charge that he is the author of sin. But in order to avoid that conclusion, the route Edwards has taken lands him in the sorry predicament of suggesting that God is a Creator of defective goods. In order to (rightly) preserve God's glory and honor in this affair, does Edwards end up making Adam into an ontologically defective creature?

> Adam, the first surety of mankind, failed in his work, because he was a mere creature, and so a mutable thing. Though he had so great a trust committed to him, as the care of the eternal welfare of all his posterity, yet, being not unchangeable, he failed, and transgressed God's holy covenant. He was led aside, and drawn away by the subtle temptation of the devil. He being a changeable being, his subtle adversary found means to turn him aside, and so he fell, and all his posterity fell with him.⁴⁶

Adam sins because he could not help it given his finite nature.⁴⁷ In fact, there are two problems here. One, finite Adam cannot help but fall because

---

43. As will be seen below, the same criticism may be offered of Francis Turretin in his *Institutes of Elenctic Theology* (George Musgrave Geiger, trans. James T. Dennison, ed. Phillipsburg, NJ: P&R Publishing, 1992).

44. That is, God provided grace which should have been enough to enable Adam to pass the probation in the Garden of Eden. It was therefore sufficient. However Adam failed to make effective use of this grace because God withheld the measure of grace which would have enabled Adam to stand the test. So it is not clear how we should understand this grace. It appears to be *neither* sufficient *nor* efficacious.

45. So says Gerstner, and rightly so, in *Rational Biblical Theology*, 2:307.

46. Jonathan Edwards, from a sermon on Hebrews 13:8, "Sermon XIV," *The Works of Jonathan Edwards*, 2 vols. (Edward Hickman, ed. Carlisle, PA: Banner of Truth, 1974), 2:951. Hereafter references to the Banner edition of Edwards' *Works* will be to *WJEB*.

47. Edwards in his *Freedom of the Will* treatise puts it this way, "It was meet, if sin did come into existence, and appear in the world, it should arise from the imperfection which properly belongs to a creature, as such, as should appear so to do, that it might

he has efficacious grace withheld from him. Two, God withholds the grace he knows would have prevented Adam from falling.

These are not the only problems. The problem of the possession of a holy disposition needs to be revisited. A habit or disposition (holy or otherwise) is a law-like tendency toward act. Before there can be holy acts there must first be a holy disposition to ground the holy acts. The same thing, of course, can be said for sinful acts. Before a sinful act can be performed, it must be grounded in a sinful disposition.[48] Edwards (rightly) argues that Adam and Eve were created upright. That is, they were not created in a merely neutral position, but they possessed a positively holy disposition. So where did the unholy disposition come from?

There is more still. Earlier in his treatise *Original Sin*, Edwards noted that a prevalent and universal effect argues for a prevalent and universal cause and such was the case with the problem of original sin in the human race. That is, with the human race subsequent to the fall, the *repetitive* nature of sinful acts yields a constant or sustained sinful disposition underlying them.

> A common and steady effect shews, that there is somewhere a preponderance, a prevailing exposedness or liableness in the state of things, to what steadily comes to pass. The natural dictate of reason shews, that where there is an effect, there is a cause, and a cause sufficient for the effect; because if it were not sufficient, it would not be effectual: and that therefore, where there is a stated prevalence in the cause; a steady effect argues a steady cause.[49]

This is all well and good when considering the condition of the human race after the fall of Adam. But how does this account for the one act of sin in the Garden of Eden? In other words, Adam and Eve did not fall as a result

---

appear not to be from God as the efficient or fountain. But this could not have been, if man had been made at first with sin in his heart; nor unless the abiding principle and habit of sin were first introduced by an evil act of the creature. If sin had not arose from the imperfection of the creature, it would not have been so visible, that it did not arise from God, as the positive cause, and real source of it," *WJE/1*, 413. This appears to be the perennial temptation of unchristian and sub-Christian thought, to confuse finitude with sinfulness. The Scriptures nowhere condemn humans for their finitude. Rather, there is ample Scriptural testimony to the heinousness of sin. Sin is the result of ethical rebellion, not the inevitable outcome of being finite creatures (i.e., not God).

48. Edwards, *WJE/3*, 389–408. Edwards discusses the dispositional foundation of acts in various and sundry locations throughout the *Original Sin* treatise.

49. Edwards, *WJE/3*, 121.

of already having a sinful nature. So where did the sinful disposition come from? Was there a sinful disposition underlying the sin that brought the fall?

Jonathan Edwards argues that there was not. Contrary to his logic, that holy acts require the prior possession of a holy disposition and that sinful acts would seem to require analogous possession of a sinful disposition, he argues that the first sin arose *not* from the possession of a sinful disposition but that the first sin was a *transient* act.[50] This looks suspiciously like an effect without a cause.[51] How did this happen? How did this transient act occur? Why did Adam fail to appropriate the efficacious grace or make use of the sufficient grace which was, so to speak, at arm's reach? Perhaps the first sin was not so much an effect without a cause as it was an effect of a non-perduring cause (i.e., transient). While the universal and prevalent nature of sin requires something like original sin, the first sin arose because the reason of Adam was distracted by a lesser desire.[52] That is, whereas Edwards argues in his treatise on original sin that the universality and prevalent nature of sin (as an effect) requires an equally universal and prevalent cause of the sin, with the fall there is no enduring sinful habit or disposition behind the first sin of our first parents. The cause of the effect (of the fall) in this instance is something temporary or passing. This discussion begs the question of what Edwards understood Adam's nature prior to the fall to be. It is in this context that a look at the question of the *donum superadditum* would seem appropriate.

Jonathan Edwards's Doctrine of the Donum Superadditum?

When Edwards discusses the metaphysical or ontological preconditions for the fall (i.e., the way things really were that provided the context for Adam's sin), he enters territory that may bring him within a hair's breadth of the traditional doctrine of the superadded gift.[53] First, Edwards states that Adam had a "higher" and "lower" nature. Nature here seems to serve as a synonym for faculty or capacity. The higher nature would surely include the intellect or understanding. The lower nature would include "animal" desires such

---

50. Edwards, *WJE*/3, 191–195.

51. This would be, of course, a problem for Edwards, because he relies quite strongly on the fact that every effect must have a cause.

52. Edwards, *WJE*/3, 381–382.

53. The doctrine of the *donum superadditum* is traditionally associated with Roman Catholic theology and especially with the theology of the "Angelic Doctor," Thomas Aquinas.

as the need to eat, have sex, and the need for sleep. Edwards notes that the higher nature is meant to rule over the lower nature.[54]

It turns out that for Edwards this additional something is none other than the Holy Spirit himself.[55] It is the presence of the Holy Spirit at work in Adam that accounts for his holy disposition. Indeed it more than accounts for it. The Holy Spirit may actually be the holy disposition itself.[56] It is the presence and activity of the Holy Spirit within the first couple that accounts for their love of God and obedience to him. It is the Holy Spirit in Adam that inclines him to consent to God's being. This leads to a question. If the Holy Spirit constitutes the holy disposition possessed by Adam, so that he could and did perform holy acts for a time, whence the arrival of even a *transient* sinful act? Edwards's argumentation makes sense for humans who come after the fall and therefore already possess a sinful disposition. But how does such a disposition arise within one who possesses a holy disposition, indeed, who is inhabited by the Holy Spirit himself?

Edwards's answer is that Adam succumbed to temptation by being distracted.[57] Adam was briefly forgetful of his duty to God. He was transiently overcome in a moment. Edwards goes so far as to imply that Adam fell because the Holy Spirit was withdrawn from him.[58] So these all seem

---

54. One significant difference between Edwards and the traditional articulation of the *donum* is that the inferior principles of human nature overtake the superior principles only after the fall and the withdrawal of the Holy Spirit and the loss of original righteousness whereas in the doctrine of the *donum* this is man's condition prior to and apart from consideration of the fall.

55. It is the presence of the Holy Spirit to account for Adam's righteousness and holiness, and not some inherent human disposition or habit that leads John Gerstner to hold that Edwards had a doctrine of the *donum superadditum*. See Gerstner, *Rational Biblical Theology*, 2:316–319. See also the subsequent note.

56. There is a question within Edwardsean studies about whether the holy disposition is a human disposition created by the Holy Spirit which is a *tertium quid* between the Holy Spirit and the human nature or whether the holy disposition simply *is* the Holy Spirit at work in the individual believer. This difference may be reflected in the medieval debate between Thomas Aquinas and Peter Abelard about created grace (*gratia creata*) and uncreated grace (*gratia increata*). See Anri Morimoto's discussion of this in his *Jonathan Edwards and the Catholic Vision of Salvation* (University Park, PA: Pennsylvania State University Press, 1995), 41–47, and Sang Lee's treatment of the same issue in his editor's introduction to *WJE/21*, 46–48.

57. That is, absent an evil disposition, Adam was distracted from his divine duties and because of his frailty as a creature, fell into sin. Edwards, *WJE/13*, 485.

58. Edwards argues in several places that God was not under any obligation to grant to Adam the presence of the Holy Spirit nor was he obligated to allow the continued presence of the Holy Spirit and this lies behind the sufficient and efficacious grace distinction. It seems as if the Holy Spirit was *withheld* prior to the fall, or that seems necessitated by Edwards' line of argument. See Gerstner, *Rational Biblical Theology*,

to amount to the same thing. (1) Adam had sufficient but not efficacious grace. (2) Adam was distracted from his duty to God. (3) Adam experienced a transient sinful desire and acted on it, and (4) the Holy Spirit was withdrawn and so Adam was left with his "natural" (?) self-love, which, in the absence of the Holy Spirit, was then inordinate.[59]

In response to these matters one needs to ask how these things are so? Why did Adam fail to avail himself of efficacious grace? Why was he distracted from his duty to God? Where did the transient sinful inclination come from? Why would the Holy Spirit be withdrawn before Adam's disobedience, and thus give rise to it, rather than the withdrawal being the result of the fall?

The moment of the fall is not the only consideration. What did Edwards think was the result of Adam's fall, in terms of his constituent nature? In other words, what are the noetic effects of sin or what are the effects on the progeny? Does Edwards think that man's whole nature is infected by sin? Does he privilege one faculty (the intellect or the will) over another?[60] It will come as no surprise to realize that Edwards has been read as an intellectualist,[61] a voluntarist,[62] some combination of the two,[63] others can't decide and some think it is simply beside the point.[64] At the end of the day, the question *is* significant and gets to the heart of Edwards's view of man and his nature. And it relates to his apologetics.

2:316–317.

59. Edwards, *WJE*/3, 381–382.

60. In asking these types of questions it needs to be kept in mind that there may be development and change in Edwards' thinking over time or he may have been inconsistent with himself. In other words, we may be dealing with an early, middle, and late Edwards.

61. Gerstner would be in this category.

62. Norman Fiering would be one scholar who interprets Jonathan Edwards as an Augustinian voluntarist. See his *Jonathan Edwards' Moral Thought and Its British Context* (Chapel Hill, NC: University of North Carolina Press, 1981), 261–271.

63. Steven Studebaker sees Edwards as a voluntarist with an intellectualist tinge. See his *Jonathan Edwards' Augustinian Social Trinitarianism: A Criticism of and an Alternative to Recent Interpretations* (Ph. D. Diss., Milwaukie, WI: Marquette University, 2003), 148–186.

64. Alvin Plantinga is one philosopher who has wrestled with the question of which comes first in regeneration, the intellect or the will. He himself cannot decide. See his *Warranted Christian Belief* (New York: Oxford University Press, 2000), 301. More will said about Plantinga and Edwards in a following chapter. Brandon Withrow suggests that the question itself is wrong headed. See his *"Full of Wondrous and Glorious Things": The Exegetical Mind of Jonathan Edwards in its Anglo-American Cultural Context* (Ph. D. Diss., Westminster Theological Seminary, 2007).

The concern with this question is with the noetic effects of sin, not the ordering the faculties in the human soul, which *will be* the subject of another chapter in this study. Here the concern is with whether Edwards denied in substance, if not in theory, total depravity or undermined his commitment to the doctrine through various formulations in his sermons, treatises, and his semi-private notebooks. Does Edwards privilege one faculty or somehow mitigate the effects of sin on one faculty (capacity of the soul) over another? What is not being asked here is whether the fall totally vitiated Adam's faculties. Such thinking has been denied by orthodox theologians and confessions over the centuries.

It seems fairly straightforward that Edwards held to and, in fact, was firmly convinced of the doctrine of total depravity.[65] The whole of human nature was infected and affected by the fall. No aspect of human nature was immune to the onslaught of sin. In terms of Edwards's anthropology, both the intellect and the will succumb to sin. It is not as if the will is perverted but the mind wishes it were otherwise. Nor is it the case that the intellect in depraved but the will wills differently. The whole man is overcome with sin.

Edwards's description of fallen men (and their internal inconsistencies) in his sermon on Matthew 11:16-19 is fairly indicative of his perspective.[66] And this relates to the question of whether Edwards held to some form of the doctrine of the super added gift. It would be good to consider what he says in this sermon at this point.[67] Edwards notes that the fall brought disequilibrium into the very nature of man. Prior to the entrance of sin into the world, man was comprised of a higher and a lower nature which existed in harmony. The different faculties of man consented with one another. But with the fall the higher nature is continually overturned by the lower nature.

What looks like an Edwardsean version of the *donum superadditum* may not be that at all. A brief survey of representative theologians will be conducted below to ascertain what the doctrine of the *donum* involves. That is, what makes it different from other accounts of the fall of Adam and Eve. Is it possible that what has been read as a form of the doctrine of the *donum*

---

65. Edwards' most famous sermon will be useful as an illustration in this regard. See "Sinners in the Hands of an Angry God," in *The Works of Jonathan Edwards/Vol. 22: Sermons & Discourses, 1739-1742* (Harry S. Stout, Nathan O. Hatch, and Kyle P. Farley, eds. New Haven, CT: Yale University Press, 2003), 400-435. Further, Edwards comments on the extent of the fall in his sermon "East of Eden," "He lost the vigor and strength of his faculties. His understanding was clouded and broken, and the whole man in all its faculties was but the ruins of what it before was," *WJE/17*, 334-335.

66. Edwards, *WJEB/2*, 918-929. The sermon is entitled "Wicked Men are Very Inconsistent with Themselves."

67. Edwards' comments here are consistent with his thoughts in his *Original Sin* treatise on the same subject. See *WJE/3*, 381-382.

resembles the *donum* formulation simply because both the traditional *donum* doctrine and other formulations are attempting to understand and explain the same reality, i.e., the fall? In other words, when Gerstner refers to Edwards's understanding of Adam pre-and post-fall, is he seeing similarities that arise because of the fact that the *donum* doctrine and other non-Roman Catholic (and non-Thomistic) formulations are analyzing the same thing? Both the traditional doctrine of the *donum superadditum* and non *donum* formulations will look alike in some ways because they are both *about the same thing*. In other words, both the *donum* and non-*donum* explanations are attempting to describe the same reality, and there may be semantic and conceptual overlap that falls short of identity. However, the use of similar or even identical terms does not equal identical conceptions. One can consider other doctrines. For instance, there are Roman Catholic, Lutheran, Reformed, and Wesleyan formulations of the doctrine of justification.[68] There is conceptual and linguistic overlap between the various formulations of the doctrine of justification even in the face of significant and essential differences. To answer the question of whether Edwards can fairly be said to hold to a doctrine of the *donum* requires an examination of Augustine, Thomas Aquinas, John Calvin, and Francis Turretin to provide a larger context.

It has been noted that Edwards stands in the "great tradition" of Christian orthodoxy and so this is not a test to determine whether any influence of Thomas Aquinas was had on Edwards. The question is not about whether Edwards read Thomas or whether he appreciated aspects of Thomas.[69] It needs to be said that Thomas Aquinas is an esteemed doctor of the church universal and so is part of the great orthodox tradition of Christian theology. While he may be fairly understood as a Roman Catholic theologian, his influence and value reaches far beyond the bounds of that ecclesiastical body. This is not just a contemporary sentiment. The great Protestant theologians of the Reformation and post-Reformation era read, critically appreciated and appropriated elements of Thomas's thought and these elements have entered into the "mainstream" of Reformed theological discourse.[70]

---

68. Of course there are more variations than these and there are variations *within* traditions.

69. It must be said, however, that most, if not all of Edwards' references to Thomas are far from complimentary. There is question as to whether or not Edwards had access to any of Thomas' works. It has been suggested that if Edwards had access to Thomas, it was through Edwards' grandfather's personal library. It is known that Solomon Stoddard had several of Thomas' works. Additionally, Thomas' *Summa Theologica* was catalogued at Yale during Edwards' time there. See the comments about this in Peter J. Thuesen's editorial introduction to *The Works of Jonathan Edwards: Vol. 26/The Catalogues of Reading* (New Haven, CT: Yale University Press, 2008), 63.

70. This is not to suggest complete agreement between Thomas and various

The upshot of all this is that one does not have to be a "Thomist" to critically appreciate and appropriate Thomas where he is deemed useful and helpful. What is being suggested here is that Thomas is one among several influential theologians from the past that Edwards probably drew upon either directly (through reading him) and indirectly (by reading theologians who had read and interacted with the Angelic doctor). To put it another way, elements of Thomas's thought end up becoming *common property* of the Western orthodox tradition. It has been said that Edwards was a member in good standing of the Enlightenment era "republic of letters." Perhaps it ought to be equally stressed that Edwards was equally at home within the Reformed consensual tradition. The question which is being entertained here is whether Edwards can be fairly classified as a sort of Thomist. For instance, it is recognized that there was a strain of Calvinistic-Thomism in such theologians as Jerome Zanchi and Peter Martyr Vermigli[71] so it is not out of the question that Edwards could be in that stream of Reformed thought.[72] But it is not even this larger question that is in view here. The concern of this study at this point is to ascertain whether Edwards's view of Adam as made in the image of God and as fallen ought to be understood as a variation of the doctrine of the *donum superadditum*.

Augustine's Understanding of the Adam's Nature

It seems wise before we look at Thomas Aquinas, to begin with the great African bishop, Augustine of Hippo Rhegius.[73] Augustine has much to say about Adam and Eve being created in the image of God. His thoughts on the topic are scattered throughout his writings, but the most salient observations are found in four sources: the commentaries on Genesis, the series of

---

Reformers and post-Reformation Reformed theologians. Martin Luther and John Calvin were fairly critical of the Scholastic tradition, although even they draw upon that tradition. The post-Reformation Reformed scholastics draw upon Thomas as one source among many. Additionally, there was a Calvinistic-Thomistic element in the post-Reformation scholastic era.

71. See Richard A. Muller, *Post-Reformation Reformed Scholasticism: The Rise and Development of Reformed Orthodoxy, ca. 1520- ca. 1725/Vol. 1: Prolegomena of Theology* 2nd Edition. (Grand Rapids, MI: Baker, 2003), 51ff, for comments about the continuation of the Thomist and other Medieval schools, amongst the Reformers and their descendants.

72. Hypothetically or theoretically Edwards could have identified himself with the Calvinistic Thomist school of men like Vermigli and Zanchi but there is no indication that he saw himself this way or intended to propagate its distinctives.

73. Aurelius Augustine, who served as bishop of the North African port of Hippo Rhegius, lived from AD 354 to AD 430.

replies to Pelagianism, his treatise on the Trinity, and finally in his magisterial *City of God*.[74] From these various sources a coherent picture of Augustine's theology of Adam as created in the image of God and as eventually fallen comes into view. This is not to suggest that there is no development of his thought on this topic. On the contrary, it is quite clear that there was development. For instance, Augustine initially understood Adam to be created in the image of the Son and then later repudiates that view to embrace the view Augustine has come to be known for: the so-called psychological model of the Trinity within the soul of man.[75]

Augustine understands man (and Adam as the father of the human race) to be created in the image of God and to be constantly dependent upon God for all things. While it would appear that there were vestiges of Neoplatonic thought in his theological anthropology, it would be a mistake to assume there was no change in his thinking as a result of his conversion to Christ and the Christian faith.[76] In Augustine is found both a stress on

74. Fresh translations of Augustine's works are regularly being made and this study's brief survey of Augustine on the image of God in Adam has benefitted from these. Augustine's commentaries on Genesis are now available as *On Genesis: On Genesis: A Refutation of the Manichees; Unfinished Literal Commentary on Genesis; and The Literal Meaning of Genesis* in *The Works of Saint Augustine: A Translation for the 21st Century*. Edmund Hill, trans. and ed. (Hyde Park, NY: New City Press, 2002). Augustine's understanding of the nature of the image in Adam undergoes solidification especially during his controversy with Pelagius and his followers as indicated in his works on that topic: *Punishment and Forgiveness of Sins* in *The Works of Saint Augustine: A Translation for the 21st Century: Answers to the Pelagians 1/23*. Roland J. Teske, trans. John E. Rotelle, ed. (Hyde Park, NY: New City Press, 1997); *Marriage and Desire* in *The Works of Saint Augustine: A Translation for the 21st Century: Answers to the Pelagians II/I/24*. Roland J. Teske, trans. John E. Rotelle, ed. (Hyde Park, NY: New City Press, 1998); and *Rebuke and Grace* in *The Works of Saint Augustine: A Translation for the 21st Century: Answers to the Pelagians IV/I/26*. Roland J. Teske, trans. John E. Rotelle, ed. (Hyde Park, NY: New City Press, 1999). Augustine's magisterial treatment of the Trinity can be found here: *On the Trinity* in *The Works of Saint Augustine: A Translation for the 21st Century*. Edmund Hill, trans. John E. Rotelle, ed. (Brooklyn, NY: New City Press, 1991). Augustine has further considerations of Adam and the image of God and the Fall in *The City of God Against the Pagans*. Cambridge Texts in the History of Political Thought series. R. W. Dyson, trans. and ed. (Cambridge: Cambridge University Press, 1998, 2001).

75. Augustine, *On the Trinity*, 9.1–18 [270–282], 10.1–18 [286–299], and 14.15 [383].

76. Augustine notes in his *Confessions* 7 and 8 that his reading of Platonic and Neoplatonic writers contributed to his conversion. In *City of God*, 8.9 Augustine notes that while Platonism fell short of Christianity, it was "nearest" to it. In *On Christian Doctrine* in *The Nicene and Post-Nicene Fathers: First Series* (J. F. Shaw, trans. Philip Schaff, ed., Grand Rapids, MI: Eerdmans, 1988), II.40.60, Augustine encourages Christians to affirm the truth discovered by Pagans, although he grants it will need to be recontextualized within the Christian faith. See Frederick Van Fleteren's entry on "Plato, Platonism"

the Plotinian chain of being with its hierarchical understanding of human nature[77] and a stress on the unity of the human nature so that his view of man is not a bare intellectualism. The will works in conjunction with and not in separation from, the intellect.[78] So while Augustine understands man to have a higher and lower aspect to his nature, he does not so separate them as to jeopardize the unity of the human nature. And he also does not conceive of the body as the prison house of the soul, a typical pagan view of his day.

---

in *Augustine Through the Ages*, 651–54, for further discussion of Augustine's familiarity with Plato and the Platonic tradition. Cornelius Van Til discusses Augustine's growth in Christian intellectual maturity and compares the presence of Platonic and Biblical thought together in him to Siamese twins where one will have to die in the process of their separation. Van Til understood Platonism's influence to wane while Biblical influence rose. See Van Til's syllabus *Christianity and Conflict*. At the end of his life Augustine admitted in his *Retractationes* that he was a little too free in offering praise to Plato and his disciples. However he still thought elements of Platonic thought could be made to square with Christian thought.

77. Augustine, *City of God*, 11.26 and *On the Trinity*, 15.2.11.

78. Augustine, *On the Trinity*, books XIII-XV. See also X.18, "Since, then, these three, memory, understanding, will, are not three lives, but one life; nor three minds, but one mind; it follows certainly that neither are they three substances, but one substance. Since memory, which is called life, and mind, and substance, is so called in respect to itself; but it is called memory, relatively to something. And I should say the same also of understanding and of will, since they are called understanding and will relatively to something; but each in respect to itself is life, and mind, and essence. And hence these three are one, in that they are one life, one mind, one essence; and whatever else they are severally called in respect to themselves, they are called also together, not plurally, but in the singular number. But they are three, in that wherein they are mutually referred to each other; and if they were not equal, and this not only each to each, but also each to all, they certainly could not mutually contain each other; for not only is each contained by each, but also all by each. For I remember that I have memory and understanding, and will; and I understand that I understand, and will, and remember; and I will that I will, and remember, and understand; and I remember together my whole memory, and understanding, and will. For that of my memory which I do not remember, is not in my memory; and nothing is so much in the memory as memory itself. Therefore I remember the whole memory. Also, whatever I understand I know that I understand, and I know that I will whatever I will; but whatever I know I remember. Therefore I remember the whole of my understanding, and the whole of my will. Likewise, when I understand these three things, I understand them together as whole. For there is none of things intelligible which I do not understand, except what I do not know; but what I do not know, I neither remember, nor will. Therefore, whatever of things intelligible I do not understand, it follows also that I neither remember nor will. And whatever of things intelligible I remember and will, it follows that I understand. My will also embraces my whole understanding and my whole memory while I use the whole that I understand and remember. And, therefore, while all are mutually comprehended by each, and as wholes, each as a whole is equal to each as a whole, and each as a whole at the same time to all as wholes; and these three are one, one life, one mind, one essence."

Having said that Augustine does not view the body with complete disdain, he does consider the soul to be superior to the body. In fact, the soul governs the body.[79] Augustine's rationale for this hierarchy is that humans share physical bodies with the beasts and so they have this in common. In other words, granted that humans were created to govern the creation under God's sovereign rule, what is it that distinguishes or differentiates man from beast? It is, of course, the reasoning abilities that man possesses and animals don't. But even here it needs to be noted that Augustine is not referring to a bare intellectualism as the reasoning capabilities of man include or involve the will.

Given this hierarchy of soul over body, it is not surprising, then, that for Augustine the soul is the locus of the divine image in man. It is with the soul that man directs his body and it is with the soul that he relates to God. It is the soul which reflects the image of God. In particular, man reflects the Trinitarian nature of the Biblical God. Augustine finds imperfect analogies of the Triune God in human nature (what he calls the *vestigia trinitatis*). In his classic work on the Trinity, *De Trinitate*, Augustine argues for multiple forms of what has come to be called the psychological model of the Trinity.[80] As Etienne Gilson points out,

> As he looks for analogies to help him sound this mystery, Augustine hesitates between several possible images of God in man. In the main, three held his attention: *mens, notitia, amor* is the first; *memoria sui, intelligentia, voluntas* the second; *memoria Dei, intelligentia, amor* the third.[81]

Augustine sought to explicate the oneness and threeness of God with his psychological model. And man's mind, knowledge, and love seemed to reflect the very Trinitarian nature of God in the human soul. Additionally, it should be noted that Augustine understood man to possess a *ratio superior* and a *ratio inferior*. The inferior reason involves such things as perception

---

79. Augustine, *City of God*, 11.26 and *On the Trinity*, 15.2.11.

80. The Western, Latin or Augustinian tradition is said to hold to the psychological model of the Trinity while the Eastern tradition holds to the social model, stemming ostensibly from the work of the Cappadocian Fathers (Gregory Nazianzus, Gregory of Nyssa, and Basil the Great). This is a debatable taxonomy. For criticism of this view of the various forms of Trinitarian theology, see Steven Studebaker, *Edwards' Augustinian Social Trinitarianism*, 78–99, and Lewis Ayres, *Augustine and the Trinity* (Cambridge: Cambridge University Press, 2010).

81. Etienne Gilson, *The Christian Philosophy of Saint Augustine*. (L.E.M. Lynch, trans. New York: Random House, 1960), 219.

and so is the basis for science and the superior reason is concerned with unchanging principles and so with wisdom.[82]

All of this serves as background to understanding Augustine's view of Adam and Eve as made in the image of God and how he wrestled with the Fall of the first couple. Does Augustine hold to a doctrine of the *donum superadditum* as John Gerstner suggests?[83] It is to this question that we now turn.

Adam and Eve in the Image of God and the Question of the Donum

Over against classical anthropology, Augustine held to a hierarchy of the soul over the body, but to a unity of the faculties. The intellect and will worked together. As Stephen Duffey notes,

> Augustine views the human person as structured hierarchically, with the soul superior to the body. Yet it would be rash to conclude that he simply adhered to Neoplatonic tendencies, to metaphysical dualism. The classical model of the person is that of a mixture or juxtaposition of soul and body. Its method of description and approach to ethical action rests on analysis and hierarchical evaluation of these components. The early Christian model, however, is that of unity and integration . . . For him the body is not the soul's prison. Nor is the soul's present bodily form divine punishment. Rather, God wills that humans be both body and soul and creates them thus. In the eschaton the whole person, body and soul, will be raised . . . If Augustine does not embrace Neoplatonic dualism, there is, nonetheless, a certain duality in his anthropology that is rooted in the hierarchical superiority of soul over body. Yet what Augustine sought was unity in the diverse dimensions of human being, a dynamic process of integration that gave proper value to all levels in subordination to God. The ideal is not escape from the body and the world, but reestablishment of inner equilibrium by unification of all one's levels of being, which includes the body's spontaneous submission to the soul.[84]

---

82. Stephen J. Duffey, "Anthropology," in *Augustine Through the Ages: An Encyclopedia*. Allan D. Fitzgerald, gen. ed. (Grand Rapids, MI: Eerdmans, 1999), 26.

83. Gerstner, *Rational Biblical Theology*, 2:316.

84. Duffey, "Anthropology," 26.

So while there is a hierarchical relation between the soul and body, there is integration of the psychological faculties.[85] The relation of the soul to the body and the inferior to the superior reason will enter into Augustine's treatment of Adam and Eve and the Fall.

Augustine is quite clear that Adam and Eve, though constituted by soul and body, did not suffer from the upheaval of passions that sinful human beings have experienced ever since the Fall. The body was subject to the soul and so there was harmony.

> This disobedience of the flesh, which is now found in this stirring, even if it is not permitted to carry out the act, did not exist then in those first human beings, when they were naked and were not embarrassed. The rational soul, the lord over the flesh, had not yet emerged as disobedient to its Lord, so it experienced the disobedience of its own servant, the flesh, with a certain sense of confusion and bother, and it certainly did not by its disobedience produce that feeling in God. After all, it is not something embarrassing or bothersome for God, if we do not obey him, for we are absolutely unable to diminish his sovereign power. But it is something embarrassing for us that the flesh does not obey our command, because this is the result of the weakness which we merited by sinning, and it is called the sin dwelling in our members. It is, however, sin in the sense that it is the punishment of sin. After the transgression was committed and the disobedient soul had turned away from the law of its Lord, its servant, that is, its body, began to have the law of disobedience in opposition to it, and those human beings were ashamed of their nakedness, when they noticed the stirring which they had not previously felt.[86]

The law of disobedience in the flesh, servant of the soul, is the result of the Fall. It was when Adam and Eve turned away from God that he turned away from them.[87]

How, then, did the Fall come about? For Augustine it came about in this way: Man, even in an unfallen state, was dependent upon God for his felicity and existence. Adam and Eve were never to think of themselves as

---

85. However, it needs to be remembered that for Augustine there is an inferior and superior reason so even here there is a kind of hierarchy. The inferior reason relates to perception, action, and knowledge of the mundane, changing world. This is science. The superior reason relates to unchanging principles (e.g., universals), and leads to wisdom via contemplation.

86. Augustine, *Punishment and Forgiveness*, II.19.33 [101].

87. Augustine, *City of God*, XVIII.15 [556].

autonomous, self-sustaining or self-governing creatures. Because they were created out of nothing, the first couple lacked the perfection supremely and solely possessed by God himself. Being mere creatures, Adam and Eve were constantly subject to the possibility of falling back into nothingness.[88]

While Adam and Eve were creatures subject to falling back into utter nothingness, Augustine holds that they were created in righteousness. It is not as if they were created in a neutral state and so had to be given the opportunity to chose right from wrong before having moral character. They were created upright. However, as already noted, though created upright, they were created with the potential, by virtue of being created out of nothing, of falling. How did this come about in Augustine's view of things? He tells us the Fall was the result of the poor use of free will.[89]

> He says, "If sin comes from the will, the will which commits sin is evil; if it comes from nature, nature is evil." I immediately reply: Sin does come from the will. Perhaps he is asking whether original sin also comes from the will. I reply: Of course, original sin also comes from the will, because this too was sown by the will of the first man so that it existed in him and was passed on to all. But with regard to this further statement, "If it comes from nature, nature is evil," I ask him to reply, if he can, to this: Just as it is clear that all evil actions come from an evil will, like the fruits from a bad tree, so let him state where the evil will itself, that is, the tree whose fruit is bad, comes from. If it comes from an angel, what was the angel itself but a good work of God? If it comes from a human being, what was the human being but a good work of God? In fact, since an angel's evil will comes from the angel and a human being's from a human being, what were these two before such evils came to be in them but God's good work and a good and praiseworthy nature? You see, then, evil arises from good, and there is absolutely nothing else but good from which it could arise. I mean: the evil will which was preceded by no evil, not evil deeds which come only from an evil will, as from a bad tree. But an evil will could arise from something good, not because it was made good by the good God, but because it was made out of nothing, not out of God.[90]

For Augustine the Fall is attributable to the misuse of free will. Evil, which is privation, arises from the good.[91]

---

88. R. W. Dyson, editor's introduction, *City of God*, xvi.
89. Augustine, *City of God*, XVIII.14 [555–556].
90. Augustine, *Punishment and Forgiveness*, II.28.48 [83–84].
91. Augustine, *On Genesis: The Literal Meaning*, VIII.14.31 [364].

More specifically, the misuse of free will arises from the appearance of pride. Adam's fall stems from the appearance of pride both in the internal disposition of the first parents and in their external act of eating from the tree of the knowledge of good and evil.[92] Adam and Eve would not have acceded to the serpent's temptation had they not already been entertaining thoughts of self-aggrandizement. The external act of eating the forbidden fruit was but the capstone of the superstructure begun in the foundation of the soul. But this gives rise to the question: how did evil arise out of the good? How is it that Adam and Eve began to give thought to a selfish assessment of themselves? If they were created upright and not merely neutral how is it that they turned on their Creator?

Here Augustine turns to a discussion of the first couple's relationship to their Creator and various kinds of grace made available to them in Paradise. One could argue that there are two foundations for Augustine's understanding of the Creator/creature relationship in the Garden of Eden. The first is the biblical foundation that man is by definition dependent for all existence and beatitude on God. There is nothing that man is, thinks, or does that is not dependent in some way on God. The second foundation relates to the Neoplatonic notion of the chain of being or the *analogia entis*.[93] The chain of being idea involves the notion that lower levels of being in the chain are dependent on higher levels of being which ultimately find their source in the highest level. In Christianized forms of the *analogia*, God provides existence to creation as a water fountain spills over when filled. In this scheme, Adam and Eve are dependent creatures by virtue of being lower on the chain of being than God. If God withdraws his care, the first couple would disappear and this is always potentially the case. Because they were made from nothing (*ex nihilo*) they are always in danger of slipping off the chain into nothingness. It is debatable how much influence the Neoplatonic scheme has on Augustine's view especially when one considers that it coincides at points with the very biblical notion of continuous dependence of the creature on the Creator. Augustine is quite right when he says, "Human nature, you see, did not receive the power to enjoy the state of bliss independently of God's control, because only God is able to enjoy blessedness and bliss by his own power independently of anyone else's control."[94]

Within this context of creaturely dependence on the Creator, Augustine discusses various graces made available to Adam and Eve. Taking

---

92. Augustine, *On Genesis: The Literal Meaning*, XI.5.7 [432]; *The City of God*, XIV.13 [608–609].

93. See J. Patout Burns, "Grace," *Augustine Through the Ages*, 391.

94. Augustine, *On Genesis: A Refutation of the Manichees*, II.15.22 [86].

into consideration the powerful psychological insight offered by Augustine that Adam and Eve fell internally before they ever ate from the tree of the knowledge of good and evil (a point Jonathan Edwards will also make in his analysis of sin and the imputation of Adam's sin to his posterity),[95] how does one account for this turn from God? How does a self-centered autonomous attitude arise in the first place if Adam and Eve were created righteous in first place? Keeping in mind what has already been said about Adam being created out of nothingness and so always potentially falling back into nothingness, Augustine discusses the why of the Fall in terms of the grace of perseverance.[96] On the one hand, although God knew how Adam would use his free will, he did not cause him to disobey his command. On the other hand, God did not provide the grace of perseverance in the good to Adam.[97] Augustine is clear that Adam did not possess the grace to not will evil (this is a grace which the saints in heaven will possess). But Augustine argues that Adam had the grace to persevere in the good *had he so willed it*. The grace which God did supply was enough to allow him to exercise free choice. "This help was, of course, such that he could abandon it if he willed to and could remain in it if he willed to, not such that it would make him will this."[98] In the same place Augustine goes on to explain the difference between the grace extended to the first Adam with that extended through the second Adam:

> This is the first grace which was given to the first Adam, but there is a more powerful grace than this in the second Adam. For the first grace brought it about that the man had righteousness if he willed to; the second, therefore, is more powerful, for it makes one even to will and to will so strongly and to love with such ardor that by the will of the spirit one conquers the pleasure of the flesh which has contrary desires.[99]

---

95. Edwards' inclusion of the internal state of Adam prior to eating of the forbidden fruit has caused no little confusion and debate in Reformed circles. It enters into the discussion of whether Edwards held to mediate or immediate imputation. For a detailed, but nevertheless helpful discussion of this matter, see John Murray, *The Imputation of Adam's Sin* (Phillipsburg, NJ: P&R Publishing, 1957).

96. Augustine, *Rebuke and Grace*, 10, 26 [126–127]; 11, 29 [129]; 31 [130–131]; 37 [134–135].

97. Augustine, *Rebuke and Grace*, 31 [130–131].

98. Augustine, *Rebuke and Grace*, 31 [130–131]. Parenthetically it should be noted that this grace offered by God to Adam in the garden of Eden appears much like the Wesleyan-Arminian doctrine of *prevenient grace* which enables a fallen sinner to either accept or reject the gospel with equal likelihood.

99. Augustine, *Rebuke and Grace*, 31 [131].

Adam fell because he did not exercise his free choice rightly, a free choice founded upon a grace that made it possible to fall or not fall with apparently equal probability. Of course this begs the question of just why it is that Adam failed to avail himself of the grace he had to exercise his free choice rightly. Augustine seems to be arguing that Adam fell because he fell. This does not appear to be a helpful explanation. On the one hand Adam had the grace to persevere in the good or not to persevere in the good. On the other hand, God withheld his grace to guarantee that Adam would persevere in the good. It is not clear what grace actually is in this context.

It is now appropriate to consider whether Augustine held to a doctrine of the *donum superadditum* or superadded grace. The ingredients to an answer are already at hand. They just need to brought together and analyzed with this question in view. First it needs to be noted that no creature, according to Augustine's way of seeing things, was capable of existing or operating without the presence and influence of God. There does not appear to be any sense of creatures (including Adam) being able properly to function in an autonomous fashion.[100] Of course, there appears to be a difference between functioning *simpliciter* and functioning properly. Or so it would seem. Augustine holds that man must be enabled by God to function properly and yet man is given a grace to potentially misuse his free choice (which he in fact goes on to do). So Adam is able, with the grace given him, to function properly or to function improperly. Either way there is some sense of grace at work in Paradise.

Second, the Holy Spirit is the gift given to Adam in the Garden prior to the Fall. Adam and Eve were not created neutral so that they would gain moral character through struggles with evil. They possessed righteousness and knowledge from the first. And unlike Augustine's interpreters who would shift the righteousness from the activity of God in Adam to a created disposition resident in man, Augustine does see the Holy Spirit as active in man from the beginning. Whatever is holy, true and good is the direct result of the work of the Holy Spirit in the mind and will of man.

The particular problem with the doctrine of the *donum superadditum* as traditionally understood is that Adam is considered in some sense complete without holiness, righteousness, and knowledge. In other words, when Adam falls he does not lose something intrinsic to himself, but the overlay of grace. Perhaps it would be helpful to articulate the problem looking at it from another direction. Typically, the doctrine of the *donum superadditum* is integral with a view of man's relation to God and eventual need for salvation which seems to fall far short of the biblical portrait. Man is made to

---

100. J. Patout Burns, "Grace," *Augustine Through the Ages*, 391–396.

experience the beatific vision, but this is understood as an optional extra that does not go to the heart of who and what man is considered in himself. Man (and Adam in particular) can choose to pursue the beatific vision or not. It is here that one can see that optional nature of the *donum*. Adam does not absolutely require it. He can function, albeit in a limited fashion, but properly nonetheless. The upshot of all this is that when Adam falls, he loses the *donum* but his essential nature remains intact *sans* the ability to pursue the beatific vision. Practically this means that human nature is not affected or infected by sin in the Fall.

It would seem that this optional nature of the *donum superadditum* would need to be present in Augustine's theology for there to be a doctrine of the *donum*. Admittedly he does affirm the presence of the Holy Spirit in the life of Adam and Eve prior to the Fall (and that creates problems but not the kind that arise from the presence of a *donum superadditum*),[101] but there is no sense of Adam functioning properly, though limitedly, after the Fall. The harmonious balance that existed prior to the Fall has gone and *in its place arises the problem of concupiscence*. The body wars against the spirit. These problems arise from the Fall. Another problem with the traditional *donum* doctrine is that while man is understood to function properly after the fall, there is ascribed to God what has all the appearance of a defective creation. That is, the passions are always potentially able to overrule the reason. In some sense the *donum* is given to provide this control of the reason over the body and its passions. Here it does appear that Augustine looks like he has a *donum* doctrine. However Augustine still lacks the idea that man can function adequately in the absence of the gift of the Holy Spirit (what is often referred to as the image of God in the narrow sense).

It must be admitted that Augustine does have a problem explaining, given the presence and activity of the Holy Spirit in the persons of Adam and Eve, how an autonomous fixation on self (i.e., pride) could arise in the first place. After all, God withdraws his presence in response to the first sin, not as the cause of it. Although that is the view one is driven to by Augustine's scheme. This is virtually the same problem Jonathan Edwards found himself with in his discussion of the Fall as well. How does one account for the Fall in the presence of righteousness, holiness, and knowledge (the activity of the Holy Spirit) and how does one avoid suggesting, as Augustine and Edwards do, that the Fall is either the result of a defective creature (even

---

101. The presence of the Holy Spirit at work in Adam and Eve before the fall creates the same problem for Augustine as it does for Edwards: how does one account for the fall in the presence of the Holy Spirit *before* the fall and the possession of a sinful nature? In other words, the ongoing battle with sin directed by the Holy Spirit in the life of a Christian cannot be read back into the pre-fall state of the Garden of Eden.

due to the mere fact that Adam was a creature) or the result of God withholding the appropriate grace or some combination of both?

It may be helpful to remind ourselves how this all relates to apologetics. It does so in this way. Apologists deal with human beings made in the image of God and it is necessary to know what man's nature is, as created, fallen, restored, and eventually glorified. How does an apologist approach an unbeliever who has properly functioning faculties as over against an unbeliever who experiences total depravity (as this has been traditionally understood)? So these are legitimate concerns of the apologist and not merely of the historical or systematic theologian.[102]

Thus far it has been shown how Augustine understood man as made in the image of God and how the Fall of Adam and Eve occurred. But does he articulate an unambiguous *donum superadditum* doctrine? At this stage in the historical survey the answer it is a cautious no. It also needs to be ascertained how Augustine relates to what has been seen of Jonathan Edwards. At this point the areas of agreement are these: both Augustine and Edwards understand that man is made in the image of God and that this image is reflective of the Trinitarian nature of God. The human faculties of knowledge, volition, and emotion are intersecting and are functions of one soul just as God is Father, Son, and Holy Spirit yet one God. Also, Augustine and Edwards see that the soul is superior to the human body. In other words, the image of God is primarily located in the human soul which may spill over in its effects to the body. So too Augustine and Edwards hold that Adam and Eve were created in holiness and righteousness and not mere neutrality. These two eminent theologians also agree the Holy Spirit was given to Adam and Eve before the fall. Additionally they agree that Adam's faculties were perverted by the fall. It is not the case for either Augustine or Edwards that removal of the Holy Spirit resulted in proper function of the human faculties. Augustine and Edwards can only be said to affirm a donum doctrine insofar as they each hold to God's giving the Holy Spirit to our first parents as the source of their holiness and righteousness.

There are several additional theologians which need to be examined. The next theologian to be considered provides what has come to be seen as the classical articulation of the *donum* doctrine. It is to Thomas Aquinas that this study now turns.[103]

---

102. The legitimacy of mentally sequestering these is questionable. Apologists are theologians and so ought to bring to bear in any given apologetic encounter the harvest of biblical, historical, and systematic theology.

103. The doctrine of the *donum superadditum* is usually traced to Alexander of Hales, *Summa Theologica*, 2.91.1, art. 3. See Bavinck, *Reformed Dogmatics*, 2:540–541 and Hoekema, *Created*, 38.

Thomas Aquinas, the Image of God, and the Doctrine of the Donum Superadditum

While Thomas was a prolific theologian, this study will limit itself to his discussion of the donum in his magisterial *Summa Theologica*.[104] It needs to be noted at the outset of this examination of Thomas's view of the image of God and the *donum superadditum* that he understood himself standing within the broadly Augustinian tradition.[105] For instance, with Augustine, Thomas understands the image in man to consist in a mirroring of the Triune nature of God. Thomas notes the possibility of understanding the image of God in man consisting in likeness to the Son alone, a view originally held by Augustine. Thomas considers this and rejects it.[106] Adam was created in the image of Triune God and not just in the image of one person of the Trinity. The image of God resides in the soul especially. While the body is affected by the image, it is in the soul that the image is found. Like Augustine, the mind, intellect, and will image forth the Father, Son, and Holy Spirit in a finite, imperfect way.

In this context it is reasonable to ask, what is the doctrine of the *donum superadditum* and what is its relationship to the image of God? Discussions of Thomas's doctrine within Reformed circles typically note that this doctrine reflects his nature/grace scheme and this seems to be borne out by the evidence.[107] What exactly does this mean? For Thomas, man as created has a higher and lower nature and the higher nature, understandably, is intended to govern the lower nature. The higher nature is comprised of the intellect and the lower nature is comprised of the will and lesser appetites.

> Since the soul is one, and the powers are many; and since a number of things that proceed from one must proceed in a certain order; there must be some order among the powers of the soul. Accordingly we may observe a triple order among them, two of which correspond to the dependence of one power on another; while the third is taken from the order of the objects. Now the

---

104. One reason for limiting the examination in this way, is that unlike Augustine and Edwards, but much like Calvin and Turretin, Thomas produced something approaching what is considered a more or less comprehensive systematic theology.

105. See Studebaker, *Edwards' Augustinian Social Trinitarianism*, 134. It is recognized that there are variations within the Augustinian tradition and that to be "in" the tradition does not mean a theologian slavishly attempts to follow Augustine. The Protestant Reformation is considered to be an Augustinian revival of sorts.

106. Thomas, *ST*, 1a.93.5 [1:472–473].

107. Specifically, I have in mind Herman Bavinck's treatment of the doctrine of the *donum* in his *Reformed Dogmatics/2: God and Creation* (John Bolt, ed. and John Vriend, trans. Grand Rapids, MI: Baker, 2004), 539–560, 571–574.

dependence of one power on another can be taken in two ways; according to the order of nature, forasmuch as perfect things are by their nature prior to imperfect things; and according to the order of generation and time; forasmuch as from being imperfect, a thing comes to be perfect. Thus, according to the first kind of order among the powers, the intellectual powers are prior to the sensitive powers; wherefore they direct them and command them. Likewise the sensitive powers are prior in this order to the powers of the nutritive soul.[108]

In one sense, man is complete on the natural plane. Man has sufficient capabilities to live, move, and have his being on the horizontal plane. In another sense, man's lower nature is always in danger of overwhelming and overpowering the higher nature. On the purely natural level we find what appears to be a tension. The natural man can function quite well apart from the *donum* in this created context. But the very nature of the natural man is always in danger, as created, of being thrown out of kilter. "In his original state man was divinely endowed with the grace and privilege that, so long as his mind was subject to God, the lower parts of the soul would be subject to his rational mind, and his body to his soul."[109] Thomas speaks of cardinal

---

108. Thomas, *ST*, 1a.77.4 [1:386]. "[C]um anima sit una, potentiae vero plures; ordine autem quodam ab uno in multitudinem procedatur; necesse est inter potentias animae ordinem esse. Triplex autem ordo inter eas attenditur. Quorum duo considerantur secundum dependentiam unius potentiae ab altera, tertius autem accipitur secundum ordinem obiectorum. Dependentia autem unius potentiae ab altera dupliciter accipi potest, uno modo, secundum naturae ordinem, prout perfecta sunt naturaliter imperfectis priora; alio modo, secundum ordinem generationis et temporis, prout ex imperfecto ad perfectum venitur. Secundum igitur primum potentiarum ordinem, potentiae intellectivae sunt priores potentiis sensitivis, unde dirigunt eas et imperant eis. Et similiter potentiae sensitivae hoc ordine sunt priores potentiis animae nutritivae." See 1a.78.1 for a discussion of the three kinds of soul: the rational, sensitive, and vegetative souls. See 1a.79.1 for Thomas' discussion of whether the intellect is the "power" of the soul.

109. Thomas, "[H]omini in prima sui institutione hoc beneficium fuit collatum divinitus, ut quandiu mens eius esset Deo subiecta, inferiores vires animae subiicerentur rationali menti, et corpus animae subiiceretur," *ST*, 2.164.1. Thomas notes that the submissiveness of the lower parts of the soul to the higher parts was not natural but the result of supernatural grace, "But the very rectitude of the primitive state, wherewith man was endowed by God, seems to require that, as others say, he was created in grace, according to Eccles. Vii.30, *God made man right*. For this rectitude in his reason being subject to God, the lower powers to reason, and the body to the soul: and the first subjection was the cause of both the second and the third; since while reason was subject to God, the lower powers remained subject to reason, as Augustine says. Now it is clear that such a subjection of the body to the soul and of the lower powers to reason, was not from nature; otherwise it would have remained after sin . . . ," "videtur requirere ipsa rectitudo primi status, in qua Deus hominem fecit, secundum illud Eccle.

virtues, which the natural man can exercise. These would include courage, excellence, honor, etc. But Thomas goes on to also discuss what he refers to as the theological virtues of hope, faith, and love. The natural virtues, as already noted, can be exercised by the natural man without the supernatural assistance of God. The same, however, cannot be said about the theological virtues. These virtues require the supernatural work of the Holy Spirit in the Christian in order for them to be evidenced. Related to this distinction between the cardinal and theological virtues, Thomas holds to a distinction between the natural and the supernatural man. That is, natural man can function quite adequately[110] on the natural plane, but if he is to achieve the ultimate purpose for his creation, which is to experience the beatific vision of God (*visio Dei*), man needs some sort of divine assistance. In other words, even before the fall, man needs grace.[111]

While both Thomas and Edwards seek, as Christian theologians are inclined to do, to understand the nature of creation and the fall, is it really the case that Edwards follows Thomas in his doctrine of the *donum superadditum*? It should be noted again that both theologians in their different times and places were attempting to wrestle with the nature of man as created and as fallen. Dealing with the same "raw materials" it should not come as any surprise that there may be some similarity in how the two theologians understand their subject. Having offered this caveat, some significant differences between the two men's views ought to be considered.

First, Thomas's doctrine is part of a larger system of doctrine that contains distinctly Roman Catholic elements. For instance, the doctrine of the super added gift is connected to the penitential system and the concept of merit included therein.[112] While it is possible to abstract certain elements to analyze them under close scrutiny it should not be forgotten that the treatment of Adam and Eve in Thomas's theology cannot be divorced from

---

VII, *Deus fecit hominem rectum*. Erat enim haec rectitudo secundum hoc, quod ratio subdebatur Deo, rationi vero inferiores vires, et animae corpus. Prima autem subiectio erat causa et secundae et tertiae, quandiu enim ratio manebat Deo subiecta, inferiora ei subdebantur, ut Augustinus dicit. Manifestum est autem quod illa subiectio corporis ad animam, et inferiorum virium ad rationem, non erat naturalis, alioquin post peccatum mansisset," *ST*, 1.95.1 [482–483].

110. See Hoekema, *Created*, 40. This is confirmed by Francis Turretin in his *Institutes*, cited below, where he cites a Scholastic maxim, "Naturals remained untouched, but the supernaturals only were lost," I.5.11.v.

111. Thomas, *ST*, 1a.95.1 [1:482–483]. Theological terminology can be problematic. If Thomas simply means that God exercised *benevolence* toward Adam in the garden, that would not be problematic. It seems that the word "grace" ought to be reserved for God's goodwill toward sinners.

112. See Bavinck, *Reformed Dogmatics*, 2:540.

his commitments elsewhere. This is not to dismiss Thomas out of hand. Thomas is an essential part of the great Christian tradition.

Second, there is no sense in Edwards, as there appears to be in Thomas, of the goal of humanity, fellowship with God, being in any sense an optional extra. Adam and Eve were created for fellowship with and worship of God and this was an integral part of their constitution. It was not an overlay.

Third, related to the above, there is no sense that fallen man can function adequately in Edwards whereas in Thomas it seems that natural man can, in fact, function on the horizontal plane sufficiently well. For Edwards, the loss of the presence of the Holy Spirit results in the loss of the integrity of human nature. For Thomas, the loss of the super added gift results in the natural man's inability to achieve the *visio Dei*, but it does not create any problems for man in his earthly pursuits.[113] For Edwards, there are noetic effects with sin. While Thomas affirms the entrance of sin onto the world's stage with the fall of the first couple, when it comes to detailed consideration of the reason of man, little effect seems to be felt from the fall.

The combined force of these differences suggests that Edwards did not specifically hold to any kind of doctrine of the donum superadditum. Before this historical survey is concluded, two additional theologians deserve consideration before we turn to consider how John Gerstner could have thought that Edwards did hold to a form of the super added gift. We turn now to consider the thought of John Calvin and Francis Turretin on the image of God in man as created and fallen.

John Calvin on the Image of God

A sense can be gathered of Calvin's understanding of the *imago Dei* in man from his *Institutes of the Christian Religion*.[114] Like Aquinas, Calvin is most appropriately understood as standing within the renewed Augustinian tradition. Adam was created in the image of the Triune God and reflects that reality in the very constitution of his nature. Additionally, while the body reflects the glory of God[115] the image is found "primarily" in the soul.[116] "For although God's glory shines forth in the outer man, yet there is no

---

113. This is so because concupiscence is a condition of the creature as creature and not a result of the Fall.

114. See John Calvin, *Institutes of the Christian Religion* Library of Christian Classics (Ford Lewis Battles, trans. and John T. McNeill, ed. Louisville: Westminster John Knox Press, 1961).

115. See Hoekema, *Created*, 42.

116. Hoekema, *Created*, 42.

doubt that the proper seat of his image is in the soul."[117] Calvin also believed that man's exercise of dominion over creation was not a part of the image. Given these initial observations, what does Calvin note about man's imaging of God?

Calvin understands Adam to be created with integrity and uprightness.

> The integrity with which Adam was endowed is expressed by this word, when he had full possession of right understanding, when he had his affections kept within the bounds of reason, all his senses tempered in right order, and he truly referred his excellence to exceptional gifts bestowed upon him by his maker.[118]

Unlike Edwards's interlocutor, Calvin does not see Adam as created in some sort of neutral state. In fact, Calvin makes a hermeneutical move that will be echoed throughout the Reformed community when he looks at the restoration of fallen man in redemption as providing some indication of what was lost in the fall. Turning to Colossians 3:10 and Ephesians 4:24, Calvin understands pre-lapsarian Adam to have possessed supernatural endowments of true knowledge, righteousness, and holiness.[119] Anthony Hoekema points out, Adam possessed " . . . faith, love of God, charity towards one's neighbor, and zeal for holiness and righteousness. In his original state man was capable of communicating with and responding to both God and other human beings."[120]

Hoekema goes on to note that Calvin understand these gifts of God to have been forfeited in the fall. That understandably leads to the question of whether, in forfeiting such gifts, fallen man also forfeited the image itself. There are passages in Calvin where that is exactly what he seems to affirm.[121] Calvin can speak about the image being obliterated or destroyed. However, he can also be found to use qualifiers that mitigate the total annihilation of the image. "Therefore, even though we grant that God's image was not totally annihilated and destroyed in him, yet it was so corrupted that whatever remains is frightful deformity."[122] Certainly Calvin did not think man's nature was unchanged by the fall. Adam lost the supernatural gifts and the remaining vestiges of the image were deformed or tarnished.[123]

---

117. Calvin, *Institutes*, I.15.3. That is, the soul is the primary seat of the image because it is spirit and therefore analogous to God who is incorporeal.

118. Calvin, *Institutes*, I.15.3.

119. Hoekema, *Created*, 43.

120. Hoekema, *Created*, 43.

121. Hoekema, *Created*, 43.

122. Calvin, *Institutes*, I.15.4.

123. In the language of Hoekema, *Creation*, 40 and 48, whereas Aquinas' view of

While the language of a broader and narrower image is absent in Calvin, it would seem that the substance of just such a distinction is present. And for Calvin redemption involved the gradual restoration of the fractured image of God in man.

In the end, does Calvin hold to the *donum superadditum*? Perhaps on a superficial reading of him he can be read that way. After all, Adam was said to possess *supernatural* gifts, specifically, true knowledge, righteousness, and holiness. If the only qualification for an understanding of the image of God to be labeled the superadded gift was that the image or elements of the image was of supernatural origin, then it could be arguably said that Calvin held to the *donum superadditum*.[124] It is true that Calvin believed the moral attributes of true knowledge, righteousness, and holiness were divine endowments. That is, man did not produce these qualities unaided by divine benevolence. However, Calvin's understanding of these supernatural gifts differs from the *donum* view in at least two ways. (1) True knowledge, righteousness, and holiness were not added attributes but integral to Adam's nature as created,[125] and (2) the remaining elements of the image were vitiated or corrupted by with the loss of supernatural endowments. Man was never intended to function without moral and spiritual integrity and when these characteristics were forfeited in the fall, his intellect and will were perverted.

How does Calvin relate to Edwards? They both agree that man is made in the image of the Triune God and that the soul is the primary seat of that image. They also agree that Adam and Eve were created in righteousness and holiness rather than being created in ethical equallibrium. Additionally, the loss of the narrow image resulted in the corruption of man's broader image.

Francis Turretin on the Image of God

It has recently been noted that John Calvin was not the only contributor to the Reformed tradition.[126] Certainly for Jonathan Edwards Calvin was

---

the fall resulted in Adam being "deprived," Calvin's view involved both *deprivation* and *depravation*.

124. This, it seems, is the substance of Arthur Bamford Crabtree's argument that by distinguishing between a narrower and broader aspect of the divine image, the Protestant tradition had reverted to or retained essential Roman Catholic elements in its theological anthropology. Crabtree, *Edwards' View of Man*, 22–24.

125. By "integral," it is not suggested that righteousness, holiness, and knowledge are purely products of human nature as such. It is readily agreed that these virtues were produced by the Holy Spirit as much prior to the Fall as they are afterwards in the work of redemption. But they are not an optional extra.

126. Richard Muller, *PRRD*, 1:30. See also his forthcoming *Calvin and the Reformed*

not the only influence on his theology. In fact, in personal correspondence with one of his former live-in pastoral interns, Edwards noted that his two favorite theologians were Peter Van Mastricht and Francis Turretin of Geneva.[127] In light of this favorable assessment of Turretin it would seem to make good sense to look at what he has to say about the nature of the pre and post fall image of God.

Turretin, in fine Scholastic fashion,[128] offers a thorough and thoughtful discussion of various elements of the creation of Adam (and Eve) and the nature of the *imago Dei* and its condition before and after the fall. For instance, the ninth question of the fifth topic (creation) was devoted to whether man could be said to have been created in a state of *puris naturalibus* ("pure nature").[129] It is to be remembered that John Taylor, Jonathan Edwards's nemesis in his treatise on original sin argued for Adam and Eve being created in a state of neutrality.[130] Arguments in favor of Adam being created in a state of neutrality are basically the same as those offered in Turretin's day for Adam's being created in a state of pure nature. Turretin opposed the teaching of a so-called pure nature.

The upshot is that Turretin opposed the doctrine of creation in a state of pure nature because (1) man was created in the image of God and therefore was morally upright and good; (2) he was created to glorify and worship God; (3) where two opposites belong to a subject, one or the other, must be in it; and (4) man in his estate of integrity was entire and innocent, in his fallen state a child of wrath, in his redeemed state a born again child of God, in his glorified state confirmed in righteousness.[131] Given the purpose of the creation of man it made no sense to hold to the notion of *puris naturalibus* or a neutral state. Turretin also notes that a state of pure nature is not posited in opposition to an impure state, but in distinction from gifts

---

Tradition: On the Work of Christ and the Order of Salvation (Grand Rapids, MI: Baker Academic, 2012).

127. Edwards made this comment to Joseph Bellamy which can be found in *The Works of Jonathan Edwards/Vol. 16:Letters and Personal Writings* (George S. Claghorn, ed. New Haven, CT: Yale University Press, 1998), 217.

128. Note that the term "Scholastic" is not used here or anywhere else throughout this dissertation in a derisive sense. This is not to suggest that certain Scholastics did not entertain unbiblical or unsound theological views, it is to simply recognize that with the ground breaking work of Richard Muller and his colleagues and students one can no longer use the expression as shorthand for dry and arid compromising rationalism. See Muller, *PRRD*, 1:34–37.

129. Francis Turretin, *Institutes of Elenctic Theology* (George Musgrave Geiger, trans. and James T. Dennison, ed. Phillipsburg, NJ: P&R Publishing, 1992), I.5.9 [1:462–464].

130. Edwards, *WJE/3*, 220–236.

131. Turretin, *Institutes*, I.5.9.v-vii.

and habits of a supernatural nature (i.e. righteousness and holiness) which comprise the doctrine of the *donum superadditum* of the Romanists which, he says, they hold "patronizing the integrity of free will and to make concupiscence natural in the first man."[132] Turretin continues by noting that God made man dependent upon him not only in the realm of being but also in the realm of behaving. In other words, God gave man a law written on the heart that reflected his own character. Additionally Turretin observes that man could not have been created lacking original righteousness as that is the very definition of sin so that Adam would have been created a sinner. Finally, Turretin notes that man may be either not righteous or not a sinner, but he cannot be neither righteous nor a sinner.[133] All of this is to say that Adam was not created in a morally or ethically neutral state in which he had to exercise libertarian free will in order to develop a habit of righteousness or sin. On the contrary, man was created upright.

Turretin next considers the nature of the *imago Dei*.[134] "As the image of God is the principal glory of man (by which he far excels other animals and approaches nearer to God), it becomes of the highest importance for us to know in what it most especially consists."[135] Turretin notes that the image does not involve participation in the divine essence nor does it essentially involve the corporeal body,

> Nor does it consist in any figure of the body or external bearing in which man resembles God . . . although we do not think that every relation of that image should be altogether denied of the body and see some rays of it glittering there . . . still it is certain that image shone in the body not so much formally as consequently and effectively (inasmuch as both the figure of man itself and the majesty resulting from it testify to the power of man over the rest of creatures, and thus of his having a soul fitted for contemplation and knowledge; and thus the proper seat of the divine image is the soul and not the body).[136]

If the divine image does not consist in a sharing in the essential divine nature nor in the physical body of man (considered in and of itself), then of what does it consist? According to the Genevan theologian,

---

132. Turretin, *Institutes*, I.5.9.viii. Turretin will give further consideration to the *donum superadditum* in a lengthy treatment of the subject.

133. Turretin, *Institutes*, I.5.9.ix-xi.

134. Turretin, *Institutes*, I.5.10.i-xxiii [1:464–470].

135. Turretin, *Institutes*, I.5.10.i.

136. Turretin, *Institutes*, I.5.10.v.

> This image consisted in gifts bestowed upon man by creation. These were not only essential or only accidental, but both at the same time: internal as well as external, by which he was placed in such a degree of nature, perfection and authority that no visible creature was either more like or more closely allied to God. It consists in three things most especially: (a) In his nature; (b) rectitude of nature; (3) the happy estate founded upon both. Antecedently in nature (as to the spirituality and immortality of the soul); formally in rectitude or original righteousness; consequently in the dominion and immortality of the whole man . . . [137]

Turretin thus sees the image consisting in the nature of the soul, then its rectitude, which results in the function of the image in dominion. He says, "the first part of the image, therefore, pertains to the substance of the soul and that too spiritual and incorruptible (or immortal intrinsically and as to its faculties, viz., the intellect and will and the liberty arising from both)."[138] It is the case that if the image of God in man did not consist in some sense in the substance of the soul, how could man be said to remain in the image even after the fall? Turretin also recognizes that one can speak of the image being partly conserved and partly lost. As he notes, "The former indeed, in the essence of the soul and in the gifts remaining after the fall; the latter, however, in depravity and pollution."[139] It appears as if Turretin is laying out the narrower or broader aspect of the image as later Reformed theologians came to discuss the matter and his distinction is also consistent with Edwards's distinction between the moral and natural image of God in man.

Regarding the moral image (to use Edwards's expression), Turretin explains it this way,

> To it [the soul-ed.] pertains rectitude and integrity, or the gifts bestowed upon man, usually expressed as original righteousness, which was created with man and bestowed upon him at his origin, embracing wisdom in the mind, holiness in the will, and rectitude and good order (*eutaxian*) in the affections. It bespeaks such a harmony among all his faculties that the members obey the affections, the affections the will, the will reason, reason the divine law, and thus man exists upright and innocent and without sin, but yet in a state always mutable, endowed with

---

137. Turretin, *Institutes*, I.5.10.vi.
138. Turretin, *Institutes*, I.5.10.vii.
139. Turretin, *Institutes*, I.5.10.vii.

a fourfold liberty: (a) from coaction; (b) from physical necessity; (c) from sin; and (d) from misery . . . [140]

As already noted Turretin grants different senses to the expression "image of God." He must do something like make the broad/narrow or natural/moral distinction with regard to the image in order to account for the fact that Scripture still sees man as made in the image of God even after the fall. "Adam after the fall had the image still (as also his posterity even now have), since they are said to be made after the image of God. Yet this must be understood only relatively (as to certain natural remains of the image) and not absolutely (as to spiritual and supernatural qualities which are evidently lost and must be restored to us by the grace of regeneration)."[141] From these remarks it can be seen that Turretin does indeed make a distinction between a "relative" and "absolute" possession of the image, or, to use his other terms, a distinction between "natural remains" and "spiritual and supernatural qualities."

Turretin devotes almost four densely packed pages to a consideration of the doctrine of the *donum superadditum* or superadded gift.[142] The question is whether the original righteousness so integral to an orthodox Reformed understanding of the image of God can be understood as natural or supernatural. The Genevan affirms that original righteousness was natural as over against Roman Catholicism. Close attention must be paid here as to how the terms "natural" and "supernatural" are being used in very specific and technical senses. Wishing to avoid terminological warfare, Turretin nevertheless must be precise.

> However because much logomachy is usually connected with this question (because of the multiple signification of the words natural and supernatural), we must speak of them first. Natural is taken in four ways: (1) originally and subjectively, drawn from nature concreated or born together with it (which is opposed to the adventitious); (2) constitutively and consecutively, constituting the nature of the thing or following and flowing from the principles of nature (such as are the essential part or properties of a thing which is opposed to the accidental); (3) perfectively, agreeing with the nature and adorning and perfecting it (opposed to that which is against nature); (4) transitively, which ought to propagated with the nature.[143]

---

140. Turretin, *Institutes*, I.5.10.viii.
141. Turretin, *Institutes*, I.5.10.xvi.
142. Turretin, *Institutes*, I.5.11.i-xvii [470–473].
143. Turretin, *Institutes*, I.5.11.ii.

In what sense, then, does Turretin understand original righteousness to be "natural"? It appears that Turretin holds that original righteousness was natural in both the original and perfective senses. He denies that any Reformed divines affirm that original righteousness was natural in either a constitutive or consecutive sense and notes that no Romanist denies that original righteousness was original and transitive. Original righteousness is certainly not natural in the fallen state. It takes a supernatural work of grace to restore righteousness. Turretin concludes, "But the question is-Is it natural with respect to the entire state, necessary to the perfection of the entire nature and pertaining to the native gifts of the entire man? For thus man is not considered simply physically as man, but theologically and morally as sound and entire."[144]

Turretin deals explicitly with the question of the *donum superadditum*. Here he notes that

> The Romanists hold original righteousness to be a supernatural gift, superadded to the native gifts and power of the entire man. Bellarmine explains the reason why they determine this to be so. There was in man naturally a contest between the flesh and the spirit, the reason and the appetite, from which flowed a certain disease and languor of nature, arising from the condition of the material. Therefore God added original righteousness as a "golden bridle," to repress that conflict and to cover like a precious garment their nakedness, and as a remedy to heal that weakness ("De gratia primi hominis," 5, 6 in *Opera* [1858], 4:23–29). This is the most common opinion among them although the Jansenists and others exclaim loudly against it. Whence arose this expression of the Scholastics: "Naturals remained untouched, but the supernaturals only were lost."[145]

Here in this paragraph can be seen the nub of the matter. The problem with the *donum superadditum* is not that it is a gift.[146] The problem is at least three-fold. First, there is the problem of a defective creation. As Turretin quotes Robert Cardinal Bellarmine, there was seen to be a conflict between the flesh and the spirit or the appetites and the reason inherent in man by virtue of his creation from material. Second, there is the unaffected nature of the essence of man according to this scheme. As the Scholastic maxim put it, "Naturals remained *untouched*, but the supernaturals only were lost" (emphasis added). Third, the problem with man as created was understood

---

144. Turretin, *Institutes*, I.5.11.iv.
145. Turretin, *Institutes*, I.5.11.v.
146. Turretin himself says as much at *Institutes*, I.5.11.xvi.

to be a metaphysical rather than a moral one. Turretin points this out in his concluding comments of the eleventh question, "Besides the habit infused by grace and acquired by practice, there is another connate and bestowed for the perfection of the creature. Nor is it confounded with natural power because the latter regards the constitution of nature in the genus of being; the former regards the perfection of the constituted nature in the genus of morals."[147] Ironically, the doctrine of the *donum superadditum*, especially as explained by Bellarmine, suggests a *sinful* Adam before the fall, and a *not so bad* fallen Adam after the fall.

Turretin also addresses the problem of sin and the nature of the fall of Adam. Sin consists in lawlessness and privation. Privation here refers to the lack of original righteousness that resulted from the fall. But sin is not mere privation.

> But this privation is not pure or simple, but corrupting; not idle, but energetic; not of pure negation, but of depraved disposition, by which not only is the due rectitude taken away, but also an undue unrectitude and a depraved quality laid down, infecting all the faculties. Just as a physical disease is not only a removal of the temper of the humors, but also a corrupt disposition and disorder (*dyskrasia*) of them, so sin (which holds the relation of a moral disease of the soul) is not only a negation of a good, but the possession of a corrupt disposition. Therefore inasmuch as it is the want of righteousness that ought to be in, it is well called privation; even so, inasmuch as it taints and corrupts the soul, it is called a corrupt quality and is usually described as a stain and disease … In this respect, some attribute a certain positive being to sin, not absolutely and physically (as if it was a subsistence having a physical entity and created by God), but both logically (because it is truly affirmed of the subject) and ethically (inasmuch as it is a corrupt habit infecting the moral faculties and the acts flowing from them). It is opposed to a mere nothing because it is one thing to do nothing, another to do badly; or to a simple privation, which deprives the subject indeed of the due rectitude without positing any contrary quality.[148]

With the Protestant tradition as a whole, Turretin therefore understood sin to involve more than the simple lack of righteousness. Why is this important? The Roman Catholic doctrine of the *donum superadditum* at one and the same time taught that natural man (unfallen man *sans* the *donum*) was able to function in the world adequately but that in order for man to achieve

147. Turretin, *Institutes*, I.5.11.xvii.
148. Turretin, *Institutes*, I.9.1.v-vi.

his highest end he needed divine assistance. That is, on the earthly plane, man was capable of living a reasonably complete life. The superadded gift was necessary in order for man to achieve beatitude. But failure to achieve beatitude apparently had no effect on man as he was in himself. Man was adequate without the *donum superadditum*. This means that privation was *merely* the absence of the *donum*. On the other hand, Roman Catholicism also taught that the *donum* was necessary to ensure the proper function of man's faculties. Due to the fact that man was made from matter he suffered a "languor" or internal conflict. The doctrine of the *donum* simultaneously affirms that man does not absolutely need the gift to adequately function in God's world and yet also that he does need it. But defining sin as privation is only partially correct. As Turretin notes, man's faculties prior to the fall were harmonious and it is only with the fall that they fall out of sync.

If Adam was created in the image of God and as such was created upright and with knowledge, righteousness and holiness, how then could he have fallen? The fact that Adam's posterity sin because they have an inherited proclivity toward sin (a habit) is understandable. But Adam and Eve had no such inherited disposition. First, echoing the thought of Augustine, Turretin notes that the fall involved not merely outward actions, but internal motion as well. In other words, the outward disobedience was an indication of internal defection.[149] And the whole person was involved in the fall. There was no "indirect" noetic effect.[150] In fact, since the intellect was the governor of the faculties it took the lead in the fall. The fall could not be laid at the feet of the will or the emotions alone.

> If it is further inquired what was the beginning or the first step of this sin, theologians do not agree. Some place it in sensuality, others in the will and others again the intellect. Although we do not think it should be zealously disputed about the order of the acts themselves or the first step of this sin (consisting of a complication of many acts, as we have already said, and among which an interval of nature rather than a long time intervened), yet we can safely assert that the first stage of this sin is not to be sought in external acts of inducement (which pertain to execution only) or in the internal acts (either of the appetite or the

---

149. Turretin, *Institutes*, I.9.6. Turretin also notes earlier that the sin involved in the fall was not merely that of the disobedience of the prohibition to eat from the tree of the knowledge of good and evil. The whole of the moral law (summarized in the Decalogue) was broken. "Thus here is, as it were, a complicated disease and a total aggregate of various acts, both internal and external, impinging against both tables of the law," *Institutes*, I.9.6.iii.

150. The idea that the fall involved the indirect total depravity of the intellect is from Gerstner, et al, *Classical Apologetics*, 243.

will), because in that state they were still subject to the intellect, the governing faculty (*to hēgemonein*). Rather we must rise to the acts of the directive faculty (to wit, of the intellect) to which belongs the judgment of the truth and falsity of things and on which the error and unbelief (holding the first place in that sin) properly fall. Now although man (not unwilling, but freely of his own accord) made that judgment, it does not follow that it was an act of the will and not of the intellect.[151]

It seems that Turretin rightly recognizes that the whole man Adam fell to temptation and sin. Since the intellect was the governing faculty it too was involved in the fall. It was not merely the misguiding influence of the will that tripped up the intellect. So the first sin, for Turretin, is characterized by unbelief as well as pride.

But how did the fall happen? According to the Genevan, unbelief formed because of "thoughtlessness."[152] Through thoughtlessness Adam took his mind off of the consideration of God's prohibition and his goodness. Thoughtlessness produced unbelief. "By this man did not have the faith in the word of God which he was bound to have, but shook it off at first by doubting and presently by denying; not seriously believing that the fruit was forbidden him or that he should die."[153] This doubt and denial which flowed from thoughtlessness yielded distrust in God and trust in the Devil. "Thus he made an erroneous judgment by which he determined that the object presented by the Devil was good for him. Hence presently his appetite and the inclination of concupiscence and its motions influenced the will to the eating of the fruit. At length the external action followed."[154] But what caused this thoughtlessness?

The Genevan theologian gives considerable consideration to the possibility of the fall.[155] Turretin divides the question into two parts. Granting that each question is "difficult to explain," he notes that he will deal with the possibility of the fall and its true cause.[156] No better exposition of the complexity of the fall can be offered here than Turretin's own words.

> Since men are corrupt, nothing is easier to conceive than why they sin daily. A depraved concupiscence can put forth no other than depraved and inordinate motions. But in an innocent man,

---

151. Turretin, *Institutes*, I.9.6.v.
152. Turretin, *Institutes*, I.9.6.ix.
153. Turretin, *Institutes*, I.9.6.ix.
154. Turretin, *Institutes*, I.9.6.ix.
155. Turretin, *Institutes*, I.9.7.i-xviii.
156. Turretin, *Institutes*, I.9.7.i.

while no error had place in his mind, nor did any disorder (*ataxia*) in his will (in whom was original righteousness) hinder a fall (and incompatible [*asystatos*] with it), it is most difficult to imagine in what way at length man in a state of integrity could fall.[157]

Turretin goes on to indicate that one explanation of the fall is that innocent man was inbuilt with "a headlong inclination to vice, from which arose the first sin . . . "[158] This is the view that would view concupiscence as part of the normal human condition and, in the Roman Catholic context, would call forth a doctrine of the superadded gift. Three reasons are offered for rejecting this view: (1) If a sinful inclination is in man by nature then God would be the author of sin; (2) the inclination to love and worship God is incompatible with an inclination to sin; and (3) all things in man at creation were good and the inclination to sin is not good since it is "repugnant to the law." "Hence it is evident that the mutability which was in Adam without any stain is not to be confounded with such an inclination to sin (which could not be but defective)."[159]

At the end of the day, Turretin believes that the possibility of the fall must lay with both mutability and free will.[160] Mutability is, as he notes, the cause *sine qua non*. As Turretin goes on to say, mutability must be divided into mutability *itself* which he deems suitable to the creature and the *act* of that mutability. Turretin distinguishes between the two this way, "The former denotes a power which could be inclined to evil, but was not yet inclined; the latter, however, designates the actual inclination to evil itself (condemned by the law of God) and the fountain of all sin."[161]

The proper cause of the fall, then, is the free will of man. Man allowed himself to be deceived by the Devil. Man "(who suffered himself to be deceived by the Devil and, Satan persuading though not compelling, freely departed from God). So neither as whole properly did he fall, nor as corrupt; but as imbued with a false idea, he corrupted himself and (the habitual knowledge implanted by God being neglected) received the error suggested by Satan."[162] Turretin avers that Adam had the ability to stand had he wished. Here Turretin, who echoes Augustine and will be later echoed by Edwards, discusses two kinds of assistance which could have been offered to

---

157. Turretin, *Institutes*, I.9.7.ii.

158. Turretin, *Institutes*, I.9.7.iii, attributes this view to ancient and modern Pelagians, Romanists, Socinians, and Remonstrants.

159. Turretin, *Institutes*, I.9.7.iii.

160. Turretin, *Institutes*, I.9.7.v-viii.

161. Turretin, *Institutes*, I.9.7.v.

162. Turretin, *Institutes*, I.9.7.vi.

Adam by God. First there is the help *without which* (*auxiliam sine qua non*) and second the help *by which* (*auxiliam quo*). The first involved the power to not sin and the second involved not only the power to not sin but also the will.[163] The first kind of assistance Adam possessed but the second form, which God did not owe to Adam, was in fact withheld.

John Gerstner is surely correct to be dissatisfied with this kind of distinction in the theology of Edwards. It is no more persuasive in Augustine or Turretin. As Gerstner notes, it is a mere labeling of something but not an explanation.[164] To note that Adam had the potential to withstand the temptation of the Devil, but not the actuality is to add little light to the conundrum of the fall.

What does Turretin say is the outcome of the fall? Turretin distinguishes between the moral and physical effects of the fall. The moral effects involved incurring the wrath and curse of God and the physical involved the miseries of this life and death. Usually included among the moral effects of the fall is the loss of the image of God in man. Here Turretin distinguishes between "gifts upright man received from God" or what he also calls "certain remains" and the "principal part of the image" which he defines as original righteousness.[165] It appears that Turretin, once again, is making the distinction often arising among Protestants between the broader and narrower image. Clearly Turretin views the moral image as more significant than the natural image. And unlike the standard Romanist position, the "certain remains" are indeed implicated in the loss of original righteousness.

Given that the fall involved the breaking of the whole law it could not help but have comprehensive effects.

> Hence it could not but shake off every habit of rectitude and devastate the conscience, so that no residuum was left except certain planks and rubbish of the unhappy shipwreck, allowed by God still to remain (both in order that from these the excellence of the former entire image might be recognized and to be a bond of external discipline in political society, to prevent the world from becoming a den of robbers; and that from these ruins he might erect a new work and form a new man after the same image in which we were at first created, Col. 3:10).[166]

---

163. Turretin, *Institutes*, I.9.7.vii.
164. Gerstner, *Rational Biblical Theology*, 2: 319–322.
165. Turretin, *Institutes*, I.9.8.ii-iii.
166. Turretin, *Institutes*, I.8.9.vii. Turretin goes on to describe the effects of the fall, " . . . As man is now born, so was Adam after the fall; for whatever he has by nature takes its origin from Adam himself. Now he is born with universal corruption, not only privative of good before received, but also positive of super-induced evil (whether as to

The fall for Turretin resulted in the near total obliteration of the *imago Dei*. But a near total obliteration is not a complete annihilation no matter how close Turretin comes to that view with his use of language. The truth of the matter is that Turretin echoes Calvin's language. The fall was devastating but not an utter destruction. There are "certain remains" and "certain planks and rubbish of the unhappy shipwreck." Turretin is simply trying to reflect the balanced language of Scripture which affirms the damage done to man because of the fall and yet recognizes that there are vestiges of the image that yet remain. However it should be noted that the "principal part" of the image (original righteousness or the moral image) was indeed lost and what remains (the natural image) is itself defaced. There are enough remains to build on, says Turretin, for the reconstruction of the image that occurs in regeneration and sanctification.

Summary of the Historical Survey

What is the result of this survey? Can it be legitimately argued that Jonathan Edwards held to some form of the *donum superadditum* doctrine? The evidence gathered from this selective survey suggests that Edwards did not hold to any form of the doctrine. The only unambiguous advocate of the doctrine was Thomas Aquinas. That there are similarities between ancient, Medieval, Reformation and post-Reformation era theologians should not be surprising. This reflects what has been called the "great tradition" of the Christian faith. There are aspects of the understanding of the nature of the image of God shared by all of these theologians. (1) They all understand the image to reflect the Trinitarian nature of God; (2) they all understand the image to involve broader and narrower aspects; and (3) they all understand the fall to have seriously affected Adam and his posterity through the loss of some aspect of the image.

However, Thomas stands out among the selected theologians reviewed here for his view of human nature before the fall and for his doctrine of the *donum superadditum*. The two are of a piece. Thomas apparently understood human nature as directly from the hand of God to involve a defect. This is undoubtedly not how he would phrase the matter, but for Thomas (as for Bellarmine in his work cited by Turretin) Adam had an internal conflict (*languor*) resulting from the fact that he was created from material. This conflict necessitated the supervenience or imposition of the superadded

---

blindness of mind or disorder [*ataxian*] of will); hence he is called not only blind, but blindness and darkness itself; he is said to be not only corrupt and sick, but "dead" (i.e., in a state of total impotence to good)," *Institutes*, I.9.8.x.

gift. On the one hand the gift or *donum* helps to prevent the overthrow of the higher faculties by the lower appetites (as concupiscence is not a result of sin but of being created out of matter) and on the other it aids or assists man to reach the goal for which he was created in the first place, namely achieving the beatific vision (*visio Dei*).

The details involved in the discussion of the nature of man as created, tempted, and as fallen can be complex and there is some semantic and conceptual overlap. For instance, both Thomas and Turretin speak of a harmony existing between reason, will, and the appetites and the potential for the harmony to become disordered. However, for Thomas that disorder is a concern prior to the fall and thus necessitates the *donum*. For Turretin the disorder of the faculties and appetites is the result of the fall. Edwards clearly agrees with Turretin over against Thomas in his understanding of where the disharmony occurs.[167]

A Return to a Consideration of Gerstner

This brings us back to the consideration of John Gerstner's claim that Edwards held to a form of the *donum superadditum*. Why did he take this view? There are three possibilities and they are not mutually exclusive. The first is that Gerstner views the *giftedness* of original righteousness as sufficient to suggest that Edwards holds a view akin to the traditional doctrine of the *donum*. The problem for Gerstner appears to be that original righteousness was not inherent or part of Adam's nature. But to recognize that original righteousness does not arise of itself from Adam's human nature is not to say that it is an optional extra or overlay. After all, the whole purpose for Adam's creation was that he commune with God and reflect God's character. That does not appear to be an afterthought. One could also note that the relation between the Holy Spirit and Adam was analogous to the Holy Spirit's operations in the regenerate saint. The Holy Spirit operates after the manner of a natural disposition but is not a natural disposition himself. In both cases, the Holy Spirit operates in an intimate manner without losing his own distinctive character or identity.

The second is that Gerstner had a rather positive assessment of the theology of Thomas Aquinas. This hardly makes Gerstner unique among Protestants. As already noted earlier in this chapter, among the second and third generation Reformers, there was a Reformed Thomistic school, exemplified in Girolamo Zanchi and Peter Martyr Vermigli and others. And it must be reiterated that criticism or agreement with one aspect of a theologian's

---

167. Edwards, *WJE*/17, 333–334.

work does not amount to complete support or rejection. Be that as it may, Gerstner not only evaluates Thomas more positively than many contemporary Protestants, he sees himself as following in the Thomistic tradition at specific points. And this is more than simply recognizing that Thomas is an integral part of the great Christian tradition.[168] Gerstner most clearly sees himself as upholding what he sees as Thomas's approach to apologetics. So it could be argued that one reason Gerstner may bring Thomas and Edwards together is that he favors both. Again it needs to be restated that the complexity of the subject of the image of God and the similarity of technical language, although used in analogous but different ways may feed into this.

Thirdly, Gerstner may be relying on the work of Arthur Bamford Crabtree.[169] Crabtree, whose work was surveyed in the first chapter, clearly argues that the Protestant Reformers (those of a Reformed persuasion) maintained the *donum superadditum* merely by upholding the distinction between a broad and narrow image and by holding that the broader image was in some sense maintained while the narrow image was lost.[170] Crabtree, like Edwards's nemesis John Taylor, holds to a view in which Adam and Eve were created in a state of neutrality. Edwards's distinction between the natural and moral/spiritual image lands Edwards within the confines of Catholicism

> This perfect integrity is sometimes expressed by saying that man was created in the image of God. Not only did he possess those *faculties* of understanding and will wherein he resembles the Godhead (the *natural* image) but his *exercise* of those faculties in humble love and obedience was a mirror of the divine glory (the *spiritual* image). This spiritual image depended upon the 'supernatural principles,' 'summarily comprehended in divine love' which dwelt in his heart in virtue of the 'divine communications and influences of God's Spirit.' In Edwards Calvinism thus turns full circle and returns to the Augustinian *adiutorium* and the Roman Catholic doctrine of nature and supernature.[171]

For Crabtree, Edwards's very distinction between a natural and spiritual image betrays him into the Roman Catholic camp. However Crabtree knows that Edwards is not unique within Protestantism for making this distinction which reflects the fact that man has both retained some

---

168. Which undoubtedly he is.
169. Crabtree, *Edwards' View of Man*.
170. Crabtree, *Edwards' View of Man*, 24–26.
171. Crabtree, *Edwards' View of Man*, 22–23.

elements of the image and lost others. But for Crabtree this recognition is a "contradiction."[172] Speaking of the Protestant theologians who preceded Edwards, Crabtree says

> They were thus betrayed into the apparent inconsistency of sometimes maintaining that the image is lost and sometimes that it abides. Often they sought to avoid this bewildering manner of speech by saying that while the image is essentially lost, some faint relics or sparks of it remain. This somewhat cloudy notion of a relic inevitably introduced much confusion into Protestant thought, and in the effort to dispel this, later theologians, both Lutheran and Reformed, began to distinguish between the *substantia* and the *dotes* of the image, the *substantia* representing the humanum and the *dotes* the added gift of righteousness. The doctrine now was that by the fall the *dotes* are lost and the *substantia* remains-which is of course the Roman Catholic doctrine in new dress![173]

While for Crabtree the suggestion that Edwards held to a *donum* was sign of contradictory theology, it seems to have been a positive attribute for Gerstner. Crabtree's description and assessment of the Protestant understanding of the image of God is facile and is based upon his belief that Adam was not

---

172. Crabtree, *Edwards' View of Man*, 24.

173. Crabtree, *Edwards' View of Man*, 25. Crabtree goes on to note, "This brings us directly to Edwards. As became a Reformed theologian he speaks only of the image, but he carefully distinguishes the spiritual or moral image which was lost at the fall from the natural image which still pertains to fallen man. The spiritual image, which is the mirror of God's moral excellency, consists on the 'moral excellency with which he was endowed.' The natural image consists in 'mans' reason and understanding, his natural ability, and dominion over the creatures,' i.e. the *humanum*. By the use of this distinction, which corresponds exactly to that between the *dotes* and the *substantia* of the image, he is able to express clearly the fact that man has lost his righteousness while retaining the essential attributes of human nature. He thus steps over the threshold of Catholic anthropology, and approaches the very centre when he goes on to speak of natural and supernatural principles. The natural principles are 'the principles of mere human nature, such as self-love, together with those natural appetites and passions which belong to the nature of man. The supernatural principles, which depend on 'divine communications and influences of God's Spirit' (the Augustinian *adiutorium*!) are 'spiritual, holy and divine, summarily comprehended in divine love.' At creation, the supernatural principles were 'given to possess the throne' and exercise complete dominion over the natural, but when at the fall God withdrew His gracious influences, the natural became at once the 'reigning principles.' And since the natural principles embrace not only the *faculties* of thought and will (the natural image) but also 'self-love,' man 'immediately set up *himself*, and the objects of his private affections and appetites, as supreme,' thereby partaking in an arrogant rebellion against God resembling that of Satan. Indeed, 'natural men are the image of the Devil. The image of God is razed out, and the image of the Devil is stamped upon them,'" *Edwards' View of Man*, 25–26.

created with original righteousness. Be that as it may, Crabtree provides us with one possible or probable source for Gerstner's own assessment that Augustine and Edwards embraced a doctrine of the *donum superadditum* (what is here called the *adiutorium*).[174] So it seems that between Gerstner's positive assessment of Thomas Aquinas and Crabtree's description of Edwards and his Protestant ancestors as upholding the *donum* doctrine, we find the roots of Gerstner's belief that Edwards follows Thomas in holding to a doctrine of the superadded gift.

Conclusion

In this chapter we have looked at Jonathan Edwards's understanding of the image of God in man and specifically have tried to ascertain whether he held to some form of the doctrine of the *donum superadditum*. After Edwards's understanding of man made in the image of God was considered, a brief historical survey was taken of four major theologians of the Christian tradition who could conceivably be recognized to have had an influence on Edwards. An examination of Augustine, Thomas Aquinas, John Calvin, and Francis Turretin revealed that the only clear exemplar of the doctrine of the superadded gift was Thomas and it was seen that there are significant differences between Thomas and Edwards so that no simple equation between the two can be made (Crabtree notwithstanding).

What does all this have to do with Edwards's apologetic? Much in every way. Every apologist has a view of the nature of man and his or her practice will reflect that view.[175] Apologetics is not a theologically neutral discipline. While there will be some conceptual and semantic overlap between various forms of Christian apologetics, a real life flesh and blood apologist defends a specific form of the faith. The desire to defend a minimalistic form of Christianity will undoubtedly yield a minimalistic faith. Jonathan Edwards's apologetic practice was not of the minimalistic kind. He defended and expounded specifically Reformed or Calvinistic doctrines. Reformed Christianity inasmuch as it is an expression of Christianity will have resonances with other forms of the faith. However, this semantic and conceptual overlap ought never to be confused with a generic or minimalistic defense of the faith or a defense of a generic or minimalistic faith.

---

174. Perhaps further evidence of Gerstner's reliance on Crabtree at this point is that Gerstner refers to the *donum superadditum* as an *adiutorium* as well. See Gerstner, *Rational Biblical Theology*, 2:316.

175. See the discussion about this in Ramm, *Varieties of Christian Apologetics*, 17–27.

Whether or not one can agree with everything Edwards said in his defense of various aspects of the faith, one must readily grant that his apologetic was a Reformed apologetic.[176]

Specifically, considering the contents of this chapter and how it relates to Edwards's apologetic, if one believes that man now exists as Adam did in the garden prior to the fall or believes that the fall does not have serious effects on the human intellect (as Thomas arguably thought), then apologetic encounters are more likely to take on a more intellectualistic approach. That is, the assumption may be that what is lacking in the thinking or worldview of the unbeliever is *sufficient* information and the apologist's job is to supply the said information. Edwards's nemesis in his treatise on original sin, John Taylor, believed that Adam was created in a neutral state and that his fall did not pass along the taint of original sin to his progeny. If there is no plenary depravity as a result of the fall, then apologetics takes on a different hue from what Edwards thought and practiced.

Intellectual arguments are legitimate. And Edwards answered intellectual attacks on the Christian faith throughout his career. However, he did not think that was sufficient. An apologist who accepts total depravity and serious noetic effects to sin and so understands that the whole person was implicated in the fall will target the whole person (intellect, will, and emotions) in an apologetic encounter. Edwards's distinction between speculative and spiritual understanding is key here. Intellectual arguments were one component of his apologetic armament. But they were not the only approach he took. If you consider his sermons as part of his apologetic arsenal, as well as treatises such as his *Religious Affections*, it will be readily apparent that the role of the Holy Spirit in preaching, witnessing, and in the apologetic encounter is key.

Intellectual assent to the truths of the Christian faith was not sufficient for salvation. Necessary, yes. Sufficient, no. Someone not only had to assent to truth, but also had to relish the truth. Speculative knowledge was necessary to faith. But saving faith must also include affiance or a trusting and resting in the Christ of the gospel as well as in the truth of the Scriptures. Edwards's apologetic reckoned with the whole person. While Edwards could answer apologetic questions and could respond to attacks on the Christian faith, he knew that it required the internal ministry of the Holy Spirit to turn his answers into true faith in the internal processes of a person.

---

176. One thinks of Edwards' defense of the Calvinistic doctrine of original sin or the Calvinistic doctrine of compatabilism. Edwards was creative in how he defended each of these perspectives but the perspective he was attempting to defend and explicate was Reformed and not something else.

The question of the *donum superadditum* is related to Edwards's apologetic as well and flows from what has already been said. This doctrine expresses the idea that man was at one and same time created with a natural tendency toward sin (concupiscence) and so needed a superadded gift to keep human nature in balance and also that man as fallen was fully competent to exercise his rational faculties in his fallen condition. Affirmation of such a doctrine would suggest that man only needs more information to come to faith in Christ. A little more information may tip the scales in the direction of conversion.

Jonathan Edwards clearly understood the lack of harmonious balance between the different powers of the human soul (faculties) to result *from* the fall, not as a constituent element of man being created as a finite creature. He also held that the essence of true religion was authentic and true religious affections. True religious affections involved truth held with approbation and delight.[177] To put it another way, true religious affections were tantamount to spiritual understanding. Spiritual understanding arose because of the internal work of the Holy Spirit causing the intellect to embrace truth taught in God's Word and the will to delight in God and the things of God. Edwards's understanding of man as created in the image of God and fallen and the elect being restored caused him to address both the intellect and the will so that they would work concurrently. The fall affected man's intellect and will and redemption restored both.[178]

In the next chapter Jonathan Edwards's understanding of how man possesses the knowledge of God will be examined.

---

177. More will be said about the nature of religious affections in the fourth chapter of this dissertation.

178. See Robert Davis Smart's *Jonathan Edwards' Apologetic for the Great Awakening* (Grand Rapids, MI: Reformation Heritage Books, 2011) for a helpful study of Edwards' defense of the awakening in the face of two opponents: rationalists and enthusiasts. Edwards attempted to formulate a truly Biblical anthropology and epistemology in the context of defending the revivals of the 18th century. More will be said about this in the next chapter.

3

Man's Knowledge of God

Introduction

WITH THIS CHAPTER WE continue to examine the larger question of whether Jonathan Edwards's theological anthropology coheres with Reformed scholar John Gerstner's portrait of him as a classical apologist.[1] The last chapter considered Edwards's understanding of man as created in the image of God as well as the nature of the fall into sin and effects thereof. Here we turn to the question of the nature of man's knowledge of God. Does man know God only from Scripture or does he know God from the constitution of his own nature and the world around him? These and related matters will be delved into as we attempt to assess Gerstner's argument that Edwards stood within the classical synthetic tradition of Christian theology and apologetics in which a natural theology is formulated apart from revelation that then serves as a foundation upon which to rear a specifically Christian theological superstructure.

Related to the above is the question of the relation of Christian theology and apologetics to pagan or non-Christian worldviews. Does the Christian theologian have anything to learn from non-Christian perspectives? It is the factual case that Christian theologians in the mainstream of the Christian tradition have sought to benefit and learn from their pagan neighbors. But how this is done is the question. Does the theologian take over,

---

1. By examining this question we do not mean to suggest that Jonathan Edwards was a presuppositionalist born out of season. He was not. However, inasmuch as Edwards was Reformed he will share certain characteristics with present day presuppositionalism. See K. Scott Oliphint's "Jonathan Edwards: Reformed Apologist," *WTJ* 57/1 (Spring 1995): 165–86.

wholesale, concepts and practices, worldviews, from non-Christian settings or does one evaluate before one assimilates? So given the fact that Christian theologians have attempted to use the insights of non-Christians, the question is this with regard to Jonathan Edwards: does his practice look more like Augustine and Calvin or more like Gerstner?[2] And what does all this have to do with the knowledge of God? Simply this: Christian theologians have often detected glimmers of natural revelation or reflection on natural revelation in non-Christian thinkers, indicating, at least to some extent, an awareness of God.

Did Jonathan Edwards understand man's natural knowledge of God to function as a pre-dogmatic foundation for a Christian theological superstructure? And did he think non-Christian worldviews evidenced any kind of truth? Our initial response to the first question is no. As will be unfolded below, it is our contention that while Edwards does use the traditional arguments for the existence of God in his various writings, this use fits better with the recent description of traditional Reformed uses of natural theology as described in the works of Michael Sudduth and Travis Campbell.[3] That is, Edwards does *not* use natural theology as such as a *pre-dogmatic foundation* for building a Christian theology. Rather, Edwards uses the traditional proofs for the existence of God *within* the context of formulating and expositing a specifically Christian theology and apologetic. Our response to the second question is a qualified yes. As will be seen, that is because Jonathan Edwards believed non-Christians were surrounded by natural revelation, special revelation, the residual traces of degraded special revelation, and types built into the universe. These account for whatever truth may be found in non-Christian religions.

How Edwards perceives man's knowledge of God is essential to understanding his apologetic practice. Does Edwards approach people as if they have never been exposed to either natural or special revelation? Does he think that Christians need to start from ground zero when they share the gospel with those who have never heard? Does Edwards think that apologetic arguments by themselves can bring someone into the kingdom of God? As happens to be the case, Edwards does think that non-Christians

---

2. Obviously the way the question is framed assumes that Augustine and Calvin differ from Gerstner at this point.

3. Specifically, discussion of the Reformed use of natural theology can be found in Michael Sudduth's *The Reformed Objection to Natural Theology* (Bristol, VT: Ashgate, 2010) and Travis Campbell's *The Search for Truth/Vol. 2: The Resurrection of Natural Theology/Part One: Ontological and Cosmological Arguments* (Unpublished manuscript, 2011).

have exposure to natural or special revelation. The Christian does not have to speak from or into a void.[4]

As we seek to wrestle with the contours of Edwards's understanding of man's knowledge of God, we will draw from various sources in the Edwards literary corpus. The chapter will proceed along the following lines: (1) First we will consider the exact nature of Gerstner's reading on Edwards's use of natural theology; (2) then we will provide a brief survey of the historical context in which Edwards approached the subject, specifically the nature and influence of deism in the Old World and the New; (3) next, an examination of Edwards's specific answers to the charges of deism will be conducted; (4) afterwards, we will consider Edwards's understanding of natural revelation and natural theology and how these relate to special revelation; and (5) finally, as with the previous chapter, we will look at how Augustine, Thomas Aquinas, Calvin, and Turretin addressed the matter of man's knowledge of God and ascertain their relation to Edwards's views. At the conclusion of this chapter it will be seen that while Edwards did reflect upon natural revelation and how it related to special revelation, he did not use natural theology as a neutral, autonomous pre-dogmatic foundation for Christian theology and apologetics.

John Gerstner on Natural Theology and Jonathan Edwards

It is no secret that the late John Gerstner had a high regard for what he called the classical synthetic Christian tradition, nor is it a secret that he thought Jonathan Edwards stood within the broad stream of that tradition.

> Unlike Karl Barth who believed that that which is philosophical is not Christian and that which is Christian is not philosophical, the Bible, the church in general and Edwards, very particularly, saw a perfect harmony. If this be so, Edwards is in harmony with the main historic position.[5]

---

4. At this point it may be helpful to point out that Reformed and non-Reformed apologists who embrace the classical method differ in their understanding of the method and the practice thereof. For instance, some Reformed classical apologists accept the reality of what Calvin calls the *sensus divinitatus* and factor that reality into their apologetic whereas Arminian apologists like William Lane Craig deny the existence of the *sensus* altogether. See Craig's comments to this effect in Steven B. Cowan and Stanley N. Gundrey eds., *Five Views on Apologetics* (Grand Rapids, MI: Zondervan, 2000), 285–87. Whether Reformed classical apologists properly reckon with the nature of Calvin's *sensus* is another question.

5. Gerstner deals at length with his view of the classical synthetic tradition and

What exactly is Gerstner referring to? It should be noted that Gerstner does appropriately see something in the history of Christian theology that could be understood as a classical synthetic tradition. However, the question remains open whether this reality is what Gerstner thinks it was and if it was, whether it was a good thing or not. In this section we will seek to first define or explain what the classical synthetic Christian tradition is and then we will seek to understand how Gerstner sees Edwards relating to this tradition. Before we do this we need to make an elementary distinction not always recognized. Whenever we examine historical matters, there is the *factual* question. Is the historian's description accurate to the facts? Then there is the *normative* question. Granted the accuracy of a given description of a historical reality, is what is described a good thing?[6]

What Gerstner refers to as the classical synthetic Christian tradition is the relationship of the church to culture and more specifically the relationship of Christian theology to non-Christian philosophy and other forms of learning. Gerstner is making both a factual and a normative assertion when he approves of the classical synthetic Christian tradition. He is affirming that what he describes has happened in history and *that it is a good thing* that it has happened. What is it that has happened? What Gerstner is pointing to is the practice of Christian theologians from the time of the early church fathers to benefit from pagan learning and insights into the world

---

Edwards' role in that in his *Rational Biblical Theology*, 1:21–79. Gerstner fails to note a careful distinction between philosophy as generically (or ideally or abstractly) conceived and specific philosophical schools. Francis Turretin in his *Institutes of Elentic Theology* (George Musgrave Geiger, trans. James t. Dennison, ed., Phillipsburg, NJ: P&R Publishing, 1992) notes this, "Philosophy is used either properly and in the abstract for the knowledge of things human and divine (as far as they can be known by the light of nature), or improperly and in the concrete for a collection of various opinions at variance with each other (which the philosophers of different sects held). In this latter sense, we acknowledge that it contains many errors and that it is of no use but of the greatest harm. Thus Paul condemns it (Col. 2:8). But in the former sense, its uses are many," I.13.IV (1:44–45). Turretin goes on to discuss in detail proper uses of philosophy for theology in sections V-XIV. Note that for Turretin philosophy is a handmaid of theology and is therefore subordinated to it, I.13.II.

6. To give an illustration, one can take a stand on the factuality of, say, the First Great Awakening, and another, though related, stand on its validity. Admittedly these often intertwine. But for sake of clarity and analysis it is useful and helpful to distinguish the two matters. See Richard Muller's comments on the tendency of church historians to make assessments of historical matters based upon their theology in James A. Bradley and Richard A. Muller, *Church History: An Introduction to Research, Reference Works, and Methods* (Grand Rapids, MI: Eerdmans, 1995), 11–25. For an example of one scholar who wrestles with these kind of questions relating to the First Great Awakening, see Robert Davis Smart, *Jonathan Edwards' Apologetic for the Great Awakening* (Grand Rapids, MI: Reformation Heritage Books, 2011), 37–91.

around us. This is easily illustrated in the thought of Augustine of Hippo. Augustine understood that God had not left himself without testimony outside of ancient Israel and sometimes pagan philosophers and statesmen or playwrights had gained insight into the human condition or the world around them. Augustine sought to encourage the Christian to benefit from such learning. All truth is God's truth no matter where it is found.

> Moreover, if those who are called philosophers, and especially the Platonists, have said aught that is true and in harmony with our faith, we are not only not to shrink from it, but to claim it for our own use from those who have unlawful possession of it. For, as the Egyptians had not only the idols and heavy burdens which the people of Israel hated and fled from, but also vessels and ornaments of gold and silver, and garments, which the same people when going out of Egypt appropriated to themselves, designing them for a better use, not doing this on their own authority, but by the command of God, the Egyptians themselves, in their ignorance, providing them with things which they themselves were not making good use of . . .[7]

However, because this truth is often found in the midst of serious misunderstanding or error, it has to be corrected. Augustine's insights are often referred to as the "plundering" or "spoiling of the Egyptians." Augustine drew from the biblical account of the departure of the children of Israel from Egypt in Exodus 3:21–22 and 12:35–36 where God caused the Egyptians to give to the Israelites precious items to take with them on their forthcoming journey. Just as the Israelites could benefit from the material wealth of the Egyptians, Christians could benefit from the intellectual wealth of pagans.[8] However, Augustine realized that this pagan learning had to be re-contextualized or "baptized" for it to have its true worth properly appreciated.[9] In

---

7. Augustine, *On Christian Doctrine*, in *The Nicene and Post-Nicene Fathers: First Series* (J. F. Shaw, trans. Philipp Schaff, ed., Grand Rapids, MI: Eerdmans, 1988): II.40.60 (2:554).

8. Cornelius Van Til frequently spoke of King Solomon using pagan servants and workers and using Lebanese cedars in the building of the Jerusalem Temple in a similar vein. Specifically Solomon allowed pagans to help with the resources and manual labor but operated under the divine blueprint. See his *Defense of the Faith* 3rd edition (Philipsburg, NJ: P&R Publishing, 1967), 223; *Survey of Christian Epistemology* (Philipsburg, NJ: P&R Publishing, 1969), 57; *Common Grace and the Gospel* (Philipsburg, NJ: P&R Publishing, 1972), 118–9; and *Christian Theistic Evidences* (Philipsburg, NJ: P&R Publishing, 1976), 64–5.

9. Similarly K. Scott Oliphint, in his *The Battle Belongs to the Lord* (Philipsburg, NJ: P&R Publishing, 2003), talks about the "twisted truth" found in unbelieving thought, that needs to be untwisted in order to be of use to the Christian, 163–73, especially 166

a similar manner, John Calvin in his *Institutes of the Christian Religion* notes that Christians ought to be grateful to God for the common gifts he gives to mankind which shine brilliantly even in those who are not believers.[10]

Factually, then, Christians have attempted to benefit from the riches of learning and wisdom and creativity found outside the church or Christian community. The question that arises in assessing this practice is whether this was a good thing or whether it was done well in any particular instance. The church father Tertullian, for instance, would seem to oppose this practice with his query "What has Jerusalem to do with Athens?"[11] However even Tertullian didn't completely forsake his pagan legal training when he became a Christian.[12] So as we seek to ascertain what it is that Gerstner understands as the classical synthetic Christian tradition, we desire to avoid simplistic assumptions that the Christian is to shun all non-Christian learning and thinking or that the Christian is to embrace all non-Christian culture without remainder.

This tradition of benefitting from the insights of pagan thought is in the mainstream and so would seem to be the *classic* Christian approach. But what kind of sifting or assessment process is to be implemented in the mining of gold from pagan mines? If truth discovered in pagan thought needs to be baptized, untwisted or re-contextualized, what does this process involve? It would seem that the Christian theologian must bring the totality of the Scriptures and the system of Christian doctrine to bear on any truth discovered in pagan thought. Gerstner refers to the classical relationship of Christianity to pagan thought as *synthetic*. That means that the tradition is a *combination* or *mixture* of Christian and pagan thought. But that view begs the question. How are Christian and non-Christian elements combined? If there is no careful thought given to how these elements are combined does

and 169.

10. John Calvin, *Institutes of the Christian Religion* Library of Christian Classics (Ford Lewis Battles, trans. John T.McNeill, ed., Louisville, KY: Westminster John Knox Press, 1965), II.2.15 (1:273-4).

11. Tertullian, *The Prescription Against Heretics* (*De praescriptione haereticorum*) in *The Ante-Nicene Fathers* (Peter Holmes, trans. Alexander Roberts and James Donaldson, eds. Grand Rapids, MI: Eerdmans, 1986), ch. 7 (3: 246). The full citation is: "What indeed has Athens to do with Jerusalem? What concord is there between the Academy and the church? What between heretics and Christians? Our instruction comes from "the porch of Solomon," who had himself taught that "the Lord should be sought in simplicity of heart." Away with all attempts to produce a mottled Christianity of Stoic, Platonic, and dialectic composition! We want no curious disputation after possessing Christ Jesus, no inquisition after enjoying the gospel! With our faith, we desire no further belief, that there is nothing which we ought to believe besides."

12. There is some dispute as to whether Tertullian actually was a lawyer or simply demonstrates knowledge of legal systems that any educated Roman would.

that not yield *syncretism* rather than synthesis? This is not an illegitimate question. Consider the role Gerstner sees, for instance, ancient Greek philosophy playing for Christian theology in the classical tradition. Citing approvingly from Clement of Alexandria's *Stromateis* Gerstner notes, "Probably no group was more characteristic of intellectual Christianity during the first half of third century than the Alexandrian school . . . This school continued and developed the theistic tradition of Plato and the Apologists."[13] The following is a citation from Clement which Gerstner seems to cite with approval:

> Thus philosophy was necessary to the Greeks for righteousness, until the coming of the Lord. And now it assists toward true religion as a kind of preparatory training for those who arrive at faith by way of demonstration . . . For God is the source of all good things, of some primarily, as of the old and new Testaments; of others by consequence, as of philosophy. But it may be indeed that philosophy was given to the Greeks. For philosophy was a schoolmaster to bring the Greek mind to Christ, as the law brought the Hebrews. Thus philosophy was a preparation, paving the way towards perfection in Christ.[14]

Ancient Greek philosophy[15] serves for the Gentile as a foundation upon which to build a Christian superstructure. In other words, ancient Greek philosophy serves as the equivalent of the Old Testament. What the Old Testament was for the Jewish church, pagan traditions serve for Gentile

13. Gerstner, *Rational Biblical Theology*, 1:25.

14. Gerstner cites Clement of Alexandra's *Stromateis* from the version included in Henry Bettenson, *Documents of the Christian Church* (New York: Oxford University Press, 1947; 2nd edition, 1986), 8–9. There is much that could be said about Gerstner's use of the citation and the citation itself. With regard to Gerstner, the citation appears to be made with his tacit approval as he offers it as evidence that there is a classical synthetic tradition and that it has an honorable pedigree. With regard to Clement it is true that he does distinguish God as the source of Scripture "primarily" and of philosophy "consequentially." But for this writer his suggestion that philosophy serves for the Greeks a parallel function that the law played for the Hebrews is problematic. There is only the slimmest connection between Clement on the one hand and Augustine on the other. Augustine and Calvin recognize that God expresses common grace in gifting pagans on the earthly plane, but they recognize that a sifting, cleansing and re-contextualization process is required which neither Clement nor Gerstner appear to evince here. Also note that Clement says that "philosophy was necessary to the Greeks for righteousness . . . " This would seem to suggest a view of common grace or natural revelation or human reflection thereon that is salvific. Gerstner nowhere qualifies Clement's statement or adds caveats.

15. Perhaps one could substitute one's preferred tradition for ancient Greek philosophy here as some theologians would like to do in other parts of the world. For instance, some theologians from Africa think that their tribal traditions are the equivalent of the Old Testament and have that much authority.

Christians. This, in bald terms, is what Gerstner understands as the synthetic element of the classical tradition.[16]

Jonathan Edwards, Deism, Natural Revelation, and Natural Theology

We now turn briefly to consider the historical setting in which Edwards wrestled with these questions of natural and special revelation. After that we will consider what Edwards thought about man's knowledge of God from nature and Scripture and how these are related to each other.[17]

Edwards did not think abstractly about these concerns. There was an historical context which drew out from Edwards a mature understanding of natural revelation or the light of nature and its relationship to special revelation. Specifically, Edwards ministered during an age when deism came to prominence, first in England, and then in the new world.[18] It is

---

16. It is important to reiterate what has already been noted, that there is a difference between Augustine's plundering of the Egyptians and Clement's philosophy serving as a preparation of the gospel. At the very least Clement fails to distinguish natural revelation given by God and concrete philosophical reflection on that natural revelation. That pagan philosophers have discovered elements of truth is not in doubt. That they understand these elements of truth aright is doubtful and even if they could understand these elements of truth aright it would not amount to a saving knowledge in any redemptive sense.

17. We go into some detail about the historical setting of Edwards' consideration of man's natural and supernatural knowledge of God because it assists in understanding the shape and color of his views. We further delve into the nature Edwards' response to deism to show what shape his apologetic concerns took. While it is inarguable that Edwards' apologetic takes the form of an eighteenth century approach, the content of his apologetic is more complex than the mere label "classical" would suggest. Edwards shares both continuity and discontinuity with the apologetic tendencies of his age. However, when all is said and done, one does not find him using theistic arguments as an autonomous pre-dogmatic foundation for a subsequently developed Christian theology. Note the words of Ava Chamberlain in her introduction to one of the Yale volumes dedicated to Edwards' Miscellanies, "Unlike the laditudinarian opponents of the Deists, however, Edwards' rational defense did not weaken his adherence to the fundamental doctrines of Reformed orthodoxy. He remains convinced of the rationality of these doctrines at least in part because he also uses a standard of rationality not shared by his opponents. He accepted the position first articulated by Locke that religious belief must conform to the principles of reason, but tempered it with the belief that divine, not human, reason was the ultimate standard of judgment. Consequently, he frequently presupposes not only the existence of God but the truth of the very doctrine that is the object of demonstration," *The Works of Jonathan Edwards/Vol. 18: The "Miscellanies" 501–832* (New Haven, CT: Yale University Press, 2000), 29.

18. See the following sources for background to the rise and advancement of Deism in the Old World and the New: Vere Chappell, ed., *The Cambridge Companion to*

now understood by Edwards scholars that deism was a major concern for him and a problem with which he wrestled in much of his writing.[19] Deism arose in England, as the Enlightenment as a whole did in Europe, as a response to the religious wars that resulted from the Protestant Reformation and Roman Catholic Counter-Reformation and from the persecution that followed in the wake of these conflicts.[20] Specifically in England, deism arose after exhaustion set in from the conflicts involving the toleration of Non-conformists in church and society. After the Interregnum of Oliver

---

Locke (Cambridge: Cambridge University Press, 1994); Frederick Copleston, *A History of Philosophy: Vol. IV: Modern Philosophy/From Descartes to Leibniz* (New York: Image/Doubleday, 1994); Frederick Copleston, *A History of Philosophy: Vol. V: Modern Philosophy/The British Philosophers from Hobbes to Hume* (New York: Image/Doubleday, 1994); Gerald R. Cragg, *The Church and the Age of Reason 1648-1789* (Baltimore, MD: Penguin Books, 1960); Gerald R. Cragg, *Freedom and Authority: A Study of English Thought in the Early Seventeenth Century* (Philadelphia: The Westminster Press, 1975); Gerald R. Cragg, *From Puritanism to the Age of Reason: A Study of Changes in Religious Thought Within the Church of England 1660-1700* (Cambridge: Cambridge University Press, 1950); Gerald R. Gragg, *Puritanism in the Period of the Great Persecution 1660-1688* (Cambridge: Cambridge University Press, 1957); Jonathan I. Israel, *Radical Enlightenment: Philosophy and the Making of Modernity 1650-1750* (Oxford: Oxford University Press, 2001); Jonathan I. Israel, *Enlightenment Contested: Philosophy, Modernity, and the Emancipation of Man 1670-1752* (Oxford: Oxford University Press, 2006); W. T. Jones, *A History of Western Philosophy: Vol. 3/Hobbes to Hume* (New York: Wadsworth, 1980. 2nd Edition); Peter Gay, *Deism: An Anthology* (Princeton: Princeton University Press, 1968); Peter Gay, *The Enlightenment: An Interpretation/The Rise of Modern Paganism* (New York: W. W. Norton & Company, 1966); Peter Gay, *The Enlightenment: An Interpretation/The Science of Freedom* (New York: W. W. Norton & Company, 1969); Herbert M. Morais, *Deism in Eighteenth Century America* (New York, 1960); John Redwood, *Reason, Ridicule, and Religion: The Age of Enlightenment in England 1660-1750* (London: Thames and Hudson, 1976); Henning Graf Reventlow, *The Authority of the Bible and the Rise of the Modern World* (J. Bowden, tr. Minneapolis, MN: Fortress, 1984);William M. Shea and Peter A. Huff, *Knowledge and Belief in America: Enlightenment Traditions and Modern Religious Thought* (Cambridge: Cambridge University Press, 1995); Richard B. Sher and Jeffrey R. Smitten, *Scotland and America in the Age of Enlightenment* (Princeton, NJ: Princeton University Press, 1990); Basil Willey, *The Eighteenth Century Background: Studies on the Idea of Nature in the Thought of the Period* (New York: Columbia University Press, 1941); Basil Willey, *The Seventeenth Century Background: Studies in the Thought of the Age in Relation to Poetry and Religion* (New York: Columbia University Press, 1967); and B. W. Young, *Religion and Enlightenment in Eighteenth-Century England: Theological Debate from Locke to Burke* (Oxford: Clarendon Press, 1998).

19. While Gerald R. McDermott's attempt to discover a "strange new Edwards" in Edwards' various *Miscellanies* who is more open to religious inclusivism is less than convincing, McDermott has persuasively demonstrated that deism is a major concern for Edwards. See his *Jonathan Edwards Confronts the Gods: Christian Theology, Enlightenment Religion, and Non-Christian Faiths* (New York: Oxford University Press, 2000), 17–51.

20. Deism, thus, is a specific variety of Enlightenment thought.

Cromwell, the pendulum swung toward moderation and rationalism. The English Civil War was religiously driven and many were tired of the results of "enthusiasm" and sectarianism. A premium came to rest on rationalism and the limits of human understanding.[21] On the one hand reason would become the arbiter of religious truth and at the same time awareness of the limits of human reasoning would prevent some of the extravagant claims of enthusiastic Non-conformists.[22] Deism was not merely the result of spiritual exhaustion however. Other streams flowed into the river deism. There was Latitudenarianism, Cambridge Platonism, Newtonian science, and the influence of the broader European philosophical scene.[23]

While Lord Herbert of Cherbury predates the actual rise of deism, he is often understood as the fountainhead and father of deism. Herbert first articulated five principles of natural religion in his book *De veritate* (*On Truth*) which became the hallmark of the movement. (1) God exists; (2) man's duty is to worship God; (3) practicing virtue is the true way of honoring God; (4) man is under obligation to repent of sin; and (5) there will be rewards and punishments after death.[24] Deism is typically traced to the work of John Toland and to a lesser extent Charles Blount. These and other writers and thinkers stressed the authority of natural religion and the role of reason. Edwards was familiar with the major deistic writers either directly through their own writings or through books on deism[25] and personally addressed the arguments of John Toland and Thomas Chubb in particular.[26] Regarding deism as a general movement (examined in conjunction

---

21. That is, human intellectual competence was both circumscribed and affirmed as fully competent within the limited sphere.

22. This can be seen in John Locke, *An Essay Concerning Human Understanding* (Alexander Campbell Fraser, ed., New York: Barnes & Noble Books, 2004; reprint of 1689 Original), especially book II, ch. III.

23. The French philosophical scene (including the influence of Voltaire) could not believe that truth was as particular as the Christian faith affirmed.

24. Lord (or Baron) Edward Herbert of Cherbury, *On Truth in Distinction from Revelation, Probability, Possibility, and Error* (Meyrick C. Carre, trans., Bristol, 1937), 58–60. A helpful summary of Herbert's common notions can be found in Cragg, *From Puritanism to the Age of Reason*, 137 and a more thorough treatment of Herbert and his contribution to the rise of Deism can be found in Willey, *The Seventeenth Century Background*, 121–132.

25 Edwards' secondary sources for information about deism would have included such works as John Leland's *A View of the Principal Deistic Writers* (3rd Edition., London, 1757) and Philip Skelton's *Ophiomaches; or, Deism Revealed* (London, 1747).

26. McDermott, *Edwards Confronts the Gods*, 35–37. For instance, Edwards reveals his familiarity with Thomas Chubb in Miscellanies 1213 and 1297, found in *The Works of Jonathan Edwards: Vol. 23/The "Miscellanies" 1153–1360* (Douglas A. Sweeney, ed., New Haven, CT: Yale University Press, 2004), 145–6 and 240–245 respectively, and

with Islam and Roman Catholicism concerning revelation), Edwards noted in his sermon "Light in a Dark World, A Dark Heart,"

> Another remarkable instance is that of the deists at this day in our land. They reject the Bible and all revealed religion, and hold that the Bible is a mere human book and Christ, a cheat; [that] God never gave any revelation of his mind any other wise than by the light of nature. This of late has made amazing progress in our nation. Deism has been growing in our nation for some time, till at length it has grown fashionable, [so that a] great part of the nation are become deists. [The] Bible is derided, Christ openly blasphemed, and all doctrines and miracles ridiculed in public houses and open streets. And 'tis surprising to see what darkness and confusion they have run into, having set up their own reason as a sufficient guide. 'Tis strange to see where their boasted light has led them. Some of 'em hold one thing, and others another, about another world and future state; and some deny any, but hold that men die like brutes.[27]

Gerald McDermott notes that Jonathan Edwards specifically sought to address two primary criticisms which deism leveled at orthodox Christianity: the rejection of special revelation and the scandal of particularity.[28] Taking these in reverse order, deism alleged that it was unreasonable that a benevolent God would limit his revelatory activity to such a small percentage of the world's population as suggested by the Bible and the Christian faith. Perhaps it was possible in the naïve world of ancient Israel and Rome or in the cloistered atmosphere of Medieval Europe to believe that God would show his

---

in his *Freedom of the Will* (Paul Ramsey, ed., New Haven: Yale University Press, 1957) where Chubb is one of Edwards' principle opponents. Edwards publically addressed deism in two sermons. The first was a lecture on 2nd Peter 1:19 which he delivered in August of 1737 and the other on Romans 2:5 sometime between August of 1731 and December of 1732. The Romans 2:5 sermon remains unpublished, but Gerstner notes in *Rational Biblical Theology*, 1:118, that "Indeed Edwards, incidentally, reveals the status of deists in his own mind when in an unpublished sermon in 1731 he referred to "robbers, pirates, and deists," with implied apologies to robbers and pirates for putting them in such company." The 2nd Peter sermon can be found in *The Works of Jonathan Edwards: Vol. 19/Sermons and Discourses 1734-1738* (M. X. Lesser, ed., New Haven, CT: Yale University Press, 2001), 704–733 and is titled "Light in a Dark World, A Dark Heart."

27. Edwards, "Light in a Dark World . . . ," *WJE/19*, 719. The brackets are in the text to indicate missing words supplied by the editors. Edwards continues on to recount the deist account of morality and the use of reason. We shall return to this sermon below. Parenthetically we note that Edwards criticizes the deistic trust in the sufficiency of its own reason to guide them in assessing Scripture and religion.

28. McDermott, *Edwards Confronts the Gods*, 17–33 and 71–86.

favor to only a small group of people, but in this modern age of expanded horizons and world exploration and greater familiarity with the various cultures of the world, it was no longer plausible to believe God would limit himself to only ancient Israel or to the Christian church. This problem of God limiting his saving intentions to a small percentage of the world's whole population came to be called the "scandal of particularity."

> The God who restricted salvation to a chosen few was especially associated by deists with the "partial and arbitrary" God of Calvinism. Herbert and his successors were enraged by the orthodox generally, and the Calvinists in particular, who seemed to promise eternal damnation to those who disagreed with them. Herbert himself raged that the "peremptory decrees" of Calvinism impugn God's justice (since they deny the means of salvation to so many) and goodness (since they imply a god that created people only to damn them, without their knowledge and against their will). Blount agreed that Calvinism denies God's goodness, and Toland, who tried to rehabilitate Druidism and showed interest in continental freemasonry, inveighed against Christian mysteries, of which the decrees of Calvinism were the most notorious.[29]

The second problem which Edwards attempted to address in deism was its rejection of special revelation. Proponents of deism argued that God's natural revelation of himself was sufficient to enlighten men of their duty to God. There was no need for any kind of Scriptural revelation whatsoever.[30] God loved all mankind equally and there was no need for redemption or for a revelation aimed at redemption. For Christianity to affirm the necessity of special revelation was in fact to suggest that God was not perfect and that his revelation given in nature and open to all men by use of their reasoning faculties was somehow defective. Related to this affirmation of the perfection and sufficiency of natural revelation was, not unexpectedly, a critique of the Bible. Scripture came increasingly under fire and so Edwards not only sought to address the criticisms of deism, and of the Enlightenment in general, but in many cases he sought to answer specific criticisms of various portions of Scripture.[31]

---

29. McDermott, *Edwards Confronts the Gods*, 26.

30. Edwards in Miscellanies 1297 specifically addresses the arguments against special revelation offered by Hobbes, Toland, the Earl of Shaftsbury, Dodwell, Chubb, Hume, and Lord Bolingbroke, *WJE*/19, 242–244.

31. For instance, Edwards defended the Mosaic authorship of the Pentateuch and Christ's prophetic fulfillment of various Old Testament promises and in numerous of his Miscellanies offered detailed refutation of biblical criticism. Edwards' defense of

How did Edwards answer these deistic criticisms of orthodox Christianity? There were in fact several planks in Edwards's platform to address deism.[32] The most basic response Edwards would offer would be to challenge the deistic assumption that man was in no need of redemption. Contrary to deistic views, man was not in a normal state. He was fallen and in need of salvation. Man's need of redemption would entail the necessity of specific revelation from God pointing man to a redeemer. Edwards would, of course, affirm natural revelation too.

> Mankind need means of certainty, clearness, and satisfaction in things that concern their welfare, in proportion to the importance of those things: whether there be a future state of happiness and misery, what that state is, what the will of God is, what are things which please him and make us the objects of his anger and hatred, whether there be any reconciliation after we have offended, and how it may be obtained. We see that God takes care of mankind and all other creatures, that usually they may not be without means, by foresight or something equivalent, of their own preservation and comfortable existence, and that in things of infinitely less importance. But it is exceeding apparent that, without a revelation, mankind must be forever in the most woeful doubt with respect to these things, and not only these things, but if they are not led by revelation and divine teaching into a right way of using their reason, in arguing from effects to causes,

---

the Mosaic authorship of the Pentateuch can be seen briefly in note 416 of his *Notes on Scripture* in *The Works of Jonathan Edwards: Vol. 15/Notes on Scripture* (Stephen J. Stein, ed., New Haven, CT: Yale University Press, 1998), 423–469 and in a longer, but unpublished treatise, "Defense of the Authenticity of the Pentateuch as a work of Moses" located in the Edwards Papers, Beinecke Library, Box 15, f. 1204. Edwards' "The Harmony of the Genius, Spirit, Doctrines, & Rules of the Old Testament & the New," is, unfortunately still unpublished and can be found in the Edwards Papers, Box 15, f. 1210. For more on the context of Edwards' defense of the Bible see Robert Brown's *Jonathan Edwards and the Bible* (Indianapolis & Bloomington, IN: Indiana University Press, 2002).

32. McDermott is to be commended for pointing students of Edwards to these elements in Edwards' apologetic against deism, *Edwards Confronts the Gods*, 55–129. Edwards does indicate a familiarity with the kind of argument offered by Bishop Butler in his *Analogy of Religion*, especially in Miscellanies 1340 where he notes at length that since there is mystery in the natural world so there is mystery in the supernatural revelation of the God of Scripture. However, it seems Edwards' point is legitimate and can't be said to be indicative of the whole of Edwards' apologetic approach as will be delineated in further detail below. See Jonathan Edwards, *The Works of Jonathan Edwards/ Vol. 23: The "Miscellanies" 1153–1360* (Douglas A. Sweeney, ed., New Haven, CT: Yale University Press, 2004), 359–76.

etc., they would forever remain in the most woeful doubt and uncertainty concerning the nature and the very being of God.[33]

Edwards's second response would be for him to affirm the idea of the *prisca theologica* or primitive theology.[34] That is, all people groups have in fact been exposed to special revelation which was given in ancient times and has filtered down to the present day. There is no culture or tribe that has not been privy to some form of redemptive revelation, albeit in corrupted form for having been passed down through the generations.[35]

A corollary of the *prisca theologia* for Edwards, if not exactly a third plank, was the fact that no people had ever developed a natural theology in the absence of the residue of Christian revelation. He would argue that all places where a natural theology was attempted were in fact places which had had the benefit of specifically Christian proclamation and which now experienced a decline in Christian knowledge. In other words, *natural theology in many instances was not a foundation for Christian theology but a clear declension from a clearer and fuller Christian theology*. Finally, Edwards would argue for typology in Scripture, history, and nature. Edwards saw Old Testament persons, events, and institutions typifying Christ and the Christian dispensation. This would not have made Edwards unique. What was unique was Edwards's extension of typology to history and nature. Edwards really believed that God built into mundane history and the world around him types which pointed those who could see and understand them to Christ and his redemption.[36]

> These types are words in persons, places, and things-they are found in every part of the creation. Hence there are sermons in the stones, flowers, and stars. God also speaks in history, both

---

33. Edwards, Miscellanies 1297, *WJE*/19, 240.
34. McDermott, *Edwards Confronts the Gods*, 71–109.
35. Edwards, Miscellanies 953, *The Works of Jonathan Edwards: Vol. 20/The "Miscellanies" 833–1152* (Amy Plantinga Pauw, ed., New Haven, CT: Yale University Press, 2002), 222–226. Edwards here interacts with Theophilus Gale's *Court of the Gentiles: Or A Discourse touching the Original of Human Literature, both Philologie and Philosophie, From the Scripture and the Jewish Church* (2nd Edition. Oxford, 1672). Miscellanies 986 details the corruption of this deposit of revelation in tradition, *WJE*/20, 309–11. McDermott points out that this reception of revelation and declension mirrors Edwards' larger view of history as involving the repetitive occurrence of reformation and revival, *Edwards Confronts the Gods*, 92.

36. This is another area where McDermott fails to convince in his *Edwards Confronts the Gods*. In addition to his attempt to make Edwards amenable to the salvation of non-Christians, he fails to note that this typology in nature is not obvious to the unbeliever. Rather, this typological reading of nature and history requires a regenerate heart and mind.

sacred and profane. He even speaks in the history of religions, heathen included. Indeed, every last atom of his creation pulsates with a divine melody.[37]

It would be beneficial to consider these planks of Edwards's response to deism in a little more detail before moving on to consider Edward's understanding of man's knowledge of God in its particulars.[38]

First, Jonathan Edwards understood man to be in a fallen state. The previous chapter serves as a demonstration of that point. As Edwards argued in his treatise on *Original Sin*, sin is prevalent and universal. Historically, the presence of sin is found at all times and geographically it is found everywhere. Such a pervasive and perpetual effect (sinfulness) requires just as pervasive and perpetual a cause-original sin.[39] Man is fallen and in need of redemption. Human beings need to be rescued from the just wrath of a holy God and they need to be rescued from themselves and the eternal and temporal consequences of the fall of Adam and Eve and sins each and every sinner commits. Edwards's main weapon in his arsenal to combat sin and win men and women to Christ was the sermon. It is no accident that Edwards is best known for his "fire and brimstone" sermon "Sinners in the Hands of an Angry God."[40] While "Sinners" is not the only sermon Edwards preached and if one based his or her understanding of the whole breadth and depth of Edwards's preaching on this one sermon one would have a skewed perspective,[41] it is nevertheless the case that this sermon was

---

37. McDermott, *Edwards Confronts the Gods*, 110–11. McDermott endeavors to show that these types were understandable by the unregenerate viewer but his concluding sentence of this citation seems to contradict his own efforts. Regarding the fact that divinely ordained types pulsate through every atom, McDermott notes that "[i]f the deists do not hear it, it is because they have stopped their ears."

38. A deeper consideration of these planks indicates that Edwards' apologetic is more complex than Gerstner's picture of Edwards leads us to believe. We are reminded that more than use of classical theistic arguments has been at play in this theater of action. We believe this does not so much refute Gerstner's portrait of Edwards *en toto* but that it indicates the need to refine and nuance the portrait considerably.

39. Jonathan Edwards, *The Works of Jonathan Edwards: Vol. 3/Original Sin* (Clyde A. Holbrook, ed., New Haven, CT: Yale University Press, 1970), 109–113.

40. Jonathan Edwards, "Sinners in the Hands of an Angry God" can be found in *The Works of Jonathan Edwards: Vol. 22/Sermons and Discourses 1739–1742* (Harry S. Stout and Nathan O. Hatch, eds., with Kyle P. Farley., New Haven, CT: Yale University Press, 2003), 404–435.

41. Edwards preached the whole gamut of biblical doctrine. One wonders what Edwards' reputation would be in the larger scene if his "Heaven is a World of Love" had been repeatedly published as has "Sinners in the Hands of Angry God" in various American literature anthologies. "Heaven is a World of Love" is the fifteenth and final sermon in his series that came to be known as *Charity and Its Fruits*, an exposition

not an aberration or a mistake. Edwards believed men and women, boys and girls were sinners in need of salvation and one way by which he could call sinners to repentance was by warning them of their fate should they fail to come to faith in Christ.[42]

> And let everyone that is yet out of Christ, and hanging over the pit of hell, whether they be old men and women, or middle aged, or young people, or little children, now hearken to the loud calls of God's Word and providence . . . Therefore, let everyone that is out of Christ, now awake and fly from the wrath to come.[43]

Second, Edwards accepted the concept of the *prisca theologia* or primitive theology. Edwards, of course, is not unique in holding this perspective. Most likely he learned it from Cambridge Platonists Ralph Cudworth and Theophilus Gale.[44] The doctrine of the *prisca theologia* taught that special revelation had been passed down from Adam and Eve (or, from Noah) to succeeding generations and that this revelation had thus spread to all people groups throughout the world. This was not a form of natural revelation but is founded in verbal revelation. Edwards embraced this idea and also noted that because of the oral nature of the transmission and because of the sinful nature of those transmitting the revelation it had filtered down to the present day in more or less corrupted forms. In other words, it was not redemptive. This *prisca theologia* serves the purpose of countering the idea that the specificity of Christianity is a scandal of particularity. It is not the case that only a small percentage of the world has been exposed to communication from God. On the contrary, God's revelation, albeit in corrupt and truncated form, has been dispersed throughout the world. So, in fact, one could say that there are five forms of divine communication circulating in the world: natural revelation, special revelation in its inscripturated form and

---

of 1st Corinthians 13. See Jonathan Edwards, *The Works of Jonathan Edwards: Vol. 8/ Ethical Writings* (Paul Ramsey, ed., New Haven: Yale University Press, 1989), 366-97.

42. Edwards has been painted as a nascent or inchoate religious inclusivist by such scholars as Anri Morimoto in his *Jonathan Edwards and the Catholic Vision of Salvation* (University Park, PA: Pennsylvania State University Press, 1995) and Gerald McDermott.

43. Edwards, "Sinners," *WJE*/22, 417-18.

44. For more on Ralph Cudworth, see Frederick J. Powicke, *The Cambridge Platonists: A Study* (Hamden, CT: Archon Books, 1971), 110-29. Cudworth's work which Edwards most likely drew upon was his *True Intellectual System of the Universe* (London, 1678). For more on the prisca theologia, see Daniel P. Walker, *The Ancient Theology: Studies in Christian Platonism from 15th-18th Century* (Ithaca, NY: Cornell University Press, 1972).

in a fallible and corrupt *prisca theologia* form, types in Scripture, history, and nature, as well as the general influence of the gospel in a fallen world.[45]

It is in this context that Edwards notes that no natural theology has ever been formulated in a vacuum. That is, it was Edwards's contention that everywhere natural theology had been formulated it was uniformly an evidence of declension. Rather than natural theology being the pure human reflection upon God's revelation of himself in nature without recourse to special revelation, natural theology had in fact been formulated only where Christianity had been influential and its influence had declined or been rejected. In other words, natural theology was neither sufficient to sustain one's relationship to God by itself nor had it ever really been formulated without drawing on Christian theological principles.[46] Speaking of man's awareness of where his true blessedness lay, Edwards noted

> Here we may see one instance wherein the revelation of Jesus Christ excels all human wisdom. It was a thing beyond the wisdom of the world, to tell wherein man's true happiness consisted. There was a vast variety of opinions about it amongst the wise men and philosophers of the heathen. There was scarcely anything that there was so great differences amongst them about. If I remember right, there were more than a hundred different opinions reckoned up about it, which shows that they were woefully in the dark, though there were many very wise men amongst them, men famed through all succeeding ages for their knowledge and wisdom. Yet their reason was not sufficient to find out men's true happiness.
>
> We can give reasons for it now it is revealed, and it seems so rational, that one would think the light of nature sufficient to discover it. But we, having always lived in the enjoyment of gospel light and being accustomed to it, are hardly sensible how dependent we are upon it, and how much we should be in the

---

45. It should be noted in passing that this is a more complex picture of the influence of different forms of divine revelation in the world than suggested by John Gerstner.

46. Jonathan Edwards, "Man's Natural Blindness in the Things of Religion," in *The Works of Jonathan Edwards* (Edward Hickman, ed., Carlisle, PA: Banner of Truth Trust, 1974), 2:253–54. While the whole sermon repays consideration, Edwards' comments about deism are worth consideration: "If human reason be the *only* proper means, the means that God has designed for enlightening mankind, is it not very strange, that it has not been sufficient, nor has answered this end in any one instance? All the right *speculative* knowledge of the true God, which the deists themselves have, has been derived from divine revelation."

> blind and dark about things that now seem plain to us, if we never had had our reason assisted by revelation.[47]

Nowhere in the world where the Christian message had not penetrated had a natural theology as such ever been developed. As a later Christian apologist put it, Edwards is arguing here that deistic natural theology "borrowed" heavily from Christian capital.[48] This *prisca theologia* also accounts for the presence of "twisted truth" in non-Christian religions.[49]

Edwards also developed a somewhat unique understanding of typology. The Christian tradition has always understood that certain persons, events, and institutions in the Old Testament pointed forward to and found their ultimate fulfillment and significance in the person and work of Jesus Christ in the New Testament. Edwards amply evidences this understanding of typology throughout his sermons and writings.

> We find by the Old Testament that it has ever been God's manner from the beginning of the world to exhibit and reveal future things by symbolical representations, which were no other than types of the future things revealed. Thus when future things were made known in visions, the things that were seen were not the future things themselves, but some other things that were made use of as shadows, symbols or types of the things.[50]

However, Edwards also held to a form of natural typology.

> 'Tis very fit and becoming of God, who is infinitely wise, so to order things that there should be a voice of his in his works instructing those who behold them, and pointing forth and showing divine mysteries and things more immediately appertaining to himself and his spiritual kingdom. The works of God are a kind of voice or language of God, to instruct intelligent beings

---

47. Jonathan Edwards, "The Pure in Heart," in *WJE/17*, 74.

48. This is the insight of Cornelius Van Til, a later Reformed theologian and apologist. See E. R. Geehan, ed., *Jerusalem and Athens: Critical Discussions on the Philosophy and Apologetics of Cornelius Van Til* (Phillipsburg, NJ: Presbyterian &Reformed Publishing, 1971), 17–18.

49. The *prisca theologia* is not natural revelation, nor is it *inscripturated* special revelation. It may be a medium of common grace. It may be in this sense and in this sense alone, inasmuch as whatever truth exists in pagan thinking comes from God, that Greek philosophy could be said to serve as a preparation for the gospel. But it itself is not redemptive. And given the corrupted nature of the *prisca theologia* it ought not be equated with or seen as equally authoritative to the Old Testament.

50. Jonathan Edwards, Miscellanies 1069 §1, in "Types of the Messiah," *The Works of Jonathan Edwards: Vol. 11/Typological Writings* (Wallace E. Anderson, Mason I. Lowance, Jr, eds. With David Watters, New Haven, CT: Yale University Press, 1993), 192.

in things pertaining to himself. And why should we not think that he would teach and instruct by his works in this way as well as others, viz., by representing divine things by his works, and so pointing them forth, especially since we know that God hath so much delighted in this way of instruction?[51]

Mundane or profane historical events and persons or elements of nature pointed to Christ and his redemption. For Edwards this was not an early form of reader response theory or the mere use of flowery metaphors under a heightened spiritual sensitivity.[52] No, God had built into nature and history these signs and their significances to be read there by the faithful. In other words, typology was not a mere subjective exercise but the reading off of nature and history what God had intended to be understood. This understanding of typology adds another layer of response to deism denying its central contention that natural revelation is perfect and sufficient to guide the reasonable man in his relationship with God.

Given what has been said so far, it should be clear that Edwards never thought that natural man was either in a position to properly understand or handle natural revelation and that in fact various attempts to formulate a natural theology borrowed from Christian theology and so natural theology, which is a fallible human reflection on God's natural revelation and not that revelation itself, could not serve as a "pre-dogmatic" foundation or

---

51. Edwards, entry 57 in the "Images of Divine Things" notebook, *WJE/11*, 67. The nexus of these two forms of typology, Scriptural and natural/historical, can be seen in Edwards' sermon series published as "The History of the Work of Redemption," *The Works of Jonathan Edwards, Vol. 9/A History of the Work of Redemption* (John F. Smith, ed., New Haven, CT: Yale University Press, 1989).

52. Edwards was acutely aware that he was in new territory by extending typology beyond inner-Biblical exegesis. "I expect by very ridicule and contempt to be called a man of a very fruitful brain and copious fancy, but they are welcome to it. I am not ashamed to own that I believe that the whole universe, heaven and earth, air and seas, and the divine constitution and history of the holy Scriptures, be full of images of divine things, as full as a language is of words; and that the multitude of those things that I have mentioned are but a very small part of what is really intended to be signified and typified by these things: but that there is room for persons to be learning more and more of this language and seeing more of that which is declared in it to the end of the world without discovering all. To say that we must not say that such things are types of these and those things unless Scripture has expressly taught us that they are so, is as unreasonable as to say that we are not to interpret any prophecies of Scripture or apply them to these or those events, except we find them interpreted to our hand, and must interpret no more of the prophecies of David, etc. For by the Scripture it is plain that innumerable other things are types that are not interpreted in Scripture (all the ordinances of the Law are all shadows of good things to come), in like manner it is plain by Scripture that these and those passages that are not actually interpreted are yet predictions of future events," in the "Types" manuscript, *WJE/11*, 152.

preparation for building a full scale Christian theology. That man was surrounded by natural revelation, inscripturated special revelation, the *prisca theologia* and God ordained types, Edwards had no doubt. But one searches in vain for an attempt by Edwards to build a full scale natural theology with no input from Christian revelation that would in turn serve to support a Christian theological superstructure as one would expect from the arguments offered by John Gerstner.[53] Rather, elements of natural theology (as Christian reflection on natural revelation) can be found in Edwards but they are always in the context of Scripture based Christian theology.

Having laid out this larger historical and theoretical framework for Jonathan Edwards's understanding of man's knowledge of God, and the relationship of natural and special revelation, we can now turn to look at specific features of Edwards's thought.

Jonathan Edwards on Man's Knowledge of God

It should be clear by this point that Jonathan Edwards did think that man has knowledge of God. Further questions arise as to when, where, and how man knows God. John Gerstner, for instance, seems to operate with very specific understanding of how man attains natural knowledge of God and sees Jonathan Edwards holding to a similar view.[54] Man's knowledge of God reflects his condition and relationship to the God he knows. Traditionally, for instance, in Reformed scholasticism, with which Edwards would have been intimately familiar,[55] man's knowledge of God is considered as either

---

53. See especially Gerstner in *Classical Apologetics* and his *Rational Biblical Theology*.

54. This will be delineated below, but for now it can be noted that Gerstner seems to hold to a *capacity innatism* with regard to man's natural knowledge of God as over against a *content innatism* model. Such a view entails than man is not concreated with actual knowledge of God but that man acquires such knowledge through inferential processes upon consideration of creation.

55. In personal correspondence Edwards noted his two favorite theologians were Francis Turretin and Peter Van Maastricht. Turretin was especially useful for polemical engagement with less consistent Christianity and Van Maastricht was the best all around theologian. These two theologians were Reformed Scholastics and while Edwards post-dates the high tide of Reformed Scholastic development, his theological formulations do reflect the influence of various Scholastic theologians. Admittedly Edwards does not write his theology in Scholastic form. That is, he does not present the state of the question (*status quaestionis*) followed by various objections which he then counters with his own positive formulation and answers to the objections offered. Nor does Edwards follow any given theologian slavishly. He is Reformed but independent minded. See Jonathan Edwards, Letter 73 to Rev. Joseph Bellamy, *The Works of Jonathan Edwards, Vol. 16/Letters and Personal Writings* (George S. Claghorn, ed., New

natural or supernatural and in its pre-fall and post-fall condition. This is then followed by a consideration of man as fallen, regenerate, and in heaven. On earth, man is a pilgrim (*viator*) and his knowledge reflects that condition (and so this form of knowledge is called a theology *in via* or "on the way"). Man is meant to know and love God and he will fulfill his purpose in heaven and this perspective ought to guide him along the way.[56] Knowledge of God can be fallen and therefore of little or no use or it can be regenerate and beneficial. We will follow this general Reformed scholastic schematization all the while recognizing that Edwards did not write in a Scholastic fashion and lived after the rise and decline of Reformed scholasticism.[57]

The first consideration is the nature of man's knowledge of God in his pre-fall and post-fall state. Adam and Eve knew God in a state of integrity and innocency in the Garden of Eden. It is well that our examination of Edwards's understanding of man's knowledge begin here as this follows the general trajectory of Scripture and the Reformed tradition and it makes sense epistemologically. That is, the knowledge of God that Adam possessed provides a baseline from which to assess the effects of the fall on knowledge of God as well as the effects of regeneration and consummation in the new heavens and new earth. While Adam and Eve were created good from the hand of the Creator, they were created mutable and had not achieved the state of confirmed righteousness. That reward was offered but the first couple fell far short of that and brought their posterity with them.[58]

Haven, CT: Yale University Press, 1998), 216–17.

56. See Jonathan Edwards' sermon, "The True Christian's Life a Journey Towards Heaven," in *WJE/17*, 427–46.

57. There are now many useful studies on Protestant scholasticism and its relation to both Medieval Scholasticism and the Protestant Reformation. Scholasticism, it is argued, was not a particular theological perspective (after all, Roman Catholic, Lutheran, Reformed, and Arminian theologians practiced the Scholastic method) but a method of doing academic theology. While Edwards was not a Scholastic in the strict and historical sense of the term, he certainly drank deeply at Protestant Scholasticism's well. See Heiko Oberman, *The Dawn of the Reformation: Essays in Late Medieval and Early Reformation Thought* (Grand Rapids, MI: Eerdmans, 1992) and Richard Muller's *Post-Reformation Reformed Dogmatics* 4 vols. (Grand Rapids, MI: Baker, 2003). For a very thorough study of Edwards' education and familiarity with Reformed Scholastic thought, see William Sparkes Morris, *The Young Jonathan Edwards: A Reconstruction* The Jonathan Edwards Classic Studies Series (Eugene, OR: Wipf & Stock, 2005), 103–28, 533.

58. In some sense this is a summary of material in the second chapter. It is important that we recognize the uniqueness of the Reformed understanding of the original constitution of our first parents. Adam and Eve were not created absolutely perfect nor is redemption a matter of simply returning to the pre-fall context of the Garden of Eden. For redemption being more than a return to the pristine conditions of the Garden of Eden, see Jonathan Edwards, "East of Eden," in *The Works of Jonathan Edwards/Vol. 17*:

What was Adam's knowledge of God in the Garden of Eden like? According to Edwards the knowledge of God which Adam and Eve possessed was reflective of their overall condition and relationship with God. There was not only knowledge of God but a full appreciation of and love toward God. Additionally, prior to the fall, all the powers of the human soul were in harmony and there was no internal strife between the intellect and will and the bodily appetites.

> And his soul was in a very perfect state, the faculties of it in full strength, not broken, impaired, and weakened and ruined, as they are now. The soul of man with regard to quickness and clearness of its faculties was then like the heavenly intelligences- as a flame of fire. The natural image of God that consists in reason and understanding was then complete.
>
> And man then had excellent endowments. His mind shone with the perfect spiritual image of God, being without any defect in its holiness and righteousness, or any spot or wrinkle to mar its spiritual beauty. God had put his own beauty upon it; it shone with the communication of his glory. And man enjoyed uninterrupted spiritual peace and joy that hence arose. His mind was full of spiritual light and peace as the atmosphere in a cool and calm day.[59]

In a word, our first parents were fully integrated individuals. This is not to suggest that their knowledge of God was exhaustive or that there was no room for growth. For indeed there must have been room for such growth just as there was possibility for declension (as was in fact actualized). Adam's knowledge of God was not identical or equivalent with God's knowledge of himself. Adam's knowledge was contingent or dependent on God's knowledge as his being was dependent upon God's own existence.

What does it mean to say that Adam's powers of the soul were unified or that his faculties were in harmony? It means that his mind worked properly as it was intended to work and that it worked in an environment conducive to its proper function and it is recognized that the God who created Adam and his ability to know also providentially upheld or preserved him and Eve in their ability to think. That is, in the Garden of Eden prior to the fall there was both proper function and the possibility for improvement and declension. Granted these points, what did Adam know about God and how did he know it?

Sermons and Discourses, 1730–1733. (Mark Valeri, ed. New Haven, CT: Yale University Press, 1999), 331–348. Man's knowledge of God is part and parcel of this larger reality.

59. Edwards, "East of Eden," *WJE/17*, 333–34.

Edwards would argue that Adam and Eve knew God personally as only creatures created to know and love him would. They knew him as their Lord and provider. Edwards would appeal to such biblical texts as Genesis 1–2 and Romans 1 where it is revealed that man has known God from creation. As cited just above, in his sermon "East of Eden," Edwards points out that prior to the fall, Adam and Eve had full and harmonious knowledge of God appropriate to the creature. Adam's knowledge of God in the Garden of Eden would have been based upon God's knowledge of himself but on the creature's level. In Edwards's Reformed heritage, God's knowledge would be said to be *archetypal* and man's would be *ectypal*.[60] That is, God's knowledge of himself and his creation is original and creative while man's knowledge is derivative and discovered. More specifically, Adam's knowledge of God was of three possible types: innate, implanted, or acquired.[61]

Edwards's theological predecessors would have shied away from the Platonic idea of *innate* knowledge.[62] This would not be a denial of the real knowledge of God possessed by Adam and Eve in the Garden of Eden which was not acquired. Rather, it was the assumption of Reformed theologians that the idea of innate knowledge contained within it the concept of human autonomy.[63] That is, humans would possess knowledge of God not revealed to them by God. However, Edwards would have been familiar with the concept of *implanted* knowledge.[64] That is, as the apostle Paul reveals in

60. While this language is not found in Edwards, it was standard Reformed fare Edwards would have been more than familiar with it. Those who read Edwards as leaning in a Platonic direction must reckon with the seriousness with which he views human sin. Platonism is inherently pantheistic or panentheistic and Edwards' stress on the break in the relationship between God and man at least complicates a simple equation of Edwards with Platonic or Neo-platonic thought. In other words, we must limit Edwards' Platonic looking language (assuming such appears in the Edwards corpus) by his acceptance of, support for, and dissemination of the biblical doctrine of sin. If God and man are identified with one another as pantheism or panentheism would suggest, then there would be no possibility of sin or both God and man would be evil.

61. See Muller, *PRRD*; 1: 270–310 for discussion of these standard theological distinctions. Reference to the Reformed Scholastics is not meant to suggest that Edwards was anymore a slavish follower of Scholasticism than he was of Calvin. It serves, however, as a reminder of the theological categories current in his day.

62. See Muller, *PRRD*, 1: 284–87. As will be explained below, what many theologians today mean by innate knowledge is best explained as implanted knowledge.

63. In addition to Muller's *PRRD*, 1:284–87, see Herman Bavinck's discussion of man's knowledge of God in Reformed thought in *Reformed Dogmatics: Vol. 2/God and Creation* (John Vriend, trans. John Bolt, ed., Grand Rapids, MI: Baker, 2004), 53–91, especially 54, and 59–68.

64. In the Latin of the Reformed Scholastics this would be known as *scientia insita*. This stands over against what will be explained below as *scientia acquisita* or acquired knowledge. For a full discussion of this see Muller, *PRRD*, 1:270–310.

Romans 1:18ff, man knows that God exists ever since the creation. A certain kind of knowledge of God is known by man, by Adam and Eve in particular, that is not acquired by inference from creation. Implanted knowledge is *immediate*. It is given by God directly as part of what it means to be human and made in the *imago Dei*. This would be close to what John Calvin in his *Institutes of the Christian Religion* referred to as the *semen religionis* or *sensus divinitatis*.[65]

This sense of divinity or implanted knowledge is not complete. Natural knowledge of God can also be *acquired*. Man knew God by implanted knowledge *and* by inference from the created order. This is mediated knowledge. That is, it comes to man through the ratiocinative or inferential process. Adam could look out over the lush environs of the Garden of Eden and deduce a benevolent Creator. But did Edwards think this was the sum total of the sense of divinity? Was the natural knowledge of God merely the result of human ratiocinative processes? To put it another way, was the *sensus divinitatis* a divinely ordained *capacity* to know God, a capacity that would be activated upon man's first perceptions of himself and the world around him? Or did Edwards think the *sense* was actually knowledge and not merely the capacity to know?[66] In other words, did Edwards think that Adam and Eve (and their posterity) actually know something about God and don't merely have a capacity that may or may not be used? This is a discussion that usually is carried forth under the rubric of natural knowledge of God being a *capacity innatism* or *content innatism*.[67] It is possible, on the capacity innatism model of the sense of divinity to have the potential of coming to knowledge of God without ever doing so. However, the content innatism model requires *both* that man have the in-built capacity to know

---

65. John Calvin, *Institutes*, I.3.1–3. For consideration of what the *sensus divinitatus*, *sensus numinis* or the *semen religionis* meant for the Reformed Scholastics, see Muller, PRRD, 1:285–86.

66. As noted above, John Gertsner's argument that Edwards was a classical apologist and that classical apologetics is the best method indicates his acceptance of *capacity innatism*. See *Classical Apologetics*.

67. This question lurks in the nearby bushes, casting its long shadow, but unfortunately without apparently being spotted, in the groundbreaking work of Alvin Plantinga in his *Warranted Christian Belief* in his discussion of the "Aquinas-Calvin model" and "extended Aquinas-Calvin model" (shortened to A/C model) of human natural knowledge of God, 167–289. Do not be thrown by the use of the term "innatism" as we believe it covers what the Reformed Scholastics would have understood by implanted natural knowledge of God. Travis Campbell, in his as yet unpublished volume *The Resurrection of Natural Theology*, 254, argues that Edwards holds to something like *capacity innatism* in that man can *come to* knowledge of God with the mind's a priori categories being brought to bear on the experience of a contingent world. See the next note and the comments about Turretin.

God and actually possess knowledge not acquired through inferential processes. Edwards would seem to hold that man possesses both the capacity to know God and actually has unacquired knowledge and that man can gain natural knowledge of God through a rational examination of himself and the world around him.[68]

So far we have only talked about the natural knowledge of God in man. But there was also supernatural knowledge provided by God to man in the garden. God verbally communicated with Adam and Eve in the Garden of Eden. Natural revelation is usually understood to be non-verbal. The Reformed tradition has typically understood special revelation to be concerned with redemption and Edwards would seem to concur with this consensus.[69] Edwards clearly understood that God communicated with Adam and Eve in the garden, especially giving the command to not eat from the tree of knowledge of good and evil. This exchange between God and Adam would not be natural revelation because it was verbal but it would not be redemptive. That is, Adam and Eve were exposed to both natural knowledge of God (natural revelation) and pre-redemptive and redemptive forms of special revelation.

Despite their full and harmonious knowledge of God from both natural and pre-redemptive special revelation, Adam and Eve defected from the cause of God in the world and there is no doubt Jonathan Edwards took this problematic reality with all seriousness. Does the fall into sin obliterate man's knowledge of God? Or does it complicate it some way? We will now turn to Edwards's understanding of fallen man's knowledge of God after which we will consider man's knowledge of God in a regenerate and then consummate state.

---

68. For a discussion of what the natural knowledge of God (Calvin's *sensus*) is with these concerns in view, see K. Scott Oliphint, "Using Reason by Faith," *WTJ* 73/1 (Spring 2011): 97–112. See below the discussion of Francis Turretin's understanding of man's natural knowledge of God being both implanted and acquired. Implanted knowledge would be intuitive and acquired knowledge would be discursive or dianoetical (i.e., inferred by ratiocinative process). It seems likely that Edwards is close to Turretin.

69. Jonathan Edwards, "General Observations § 15," *WJEB*, 2:461. "If human reason, by anything that has happened since the creation, be really very much corrupted; and if God is still propitious, and does not throw us off, but reserves us for that end for which he made us; it cannot be imagined that he would leave us to our reason as the only rule to guide us in this business, which is the highest end of life; for it is not to be depended upon; and yet we exceedingly need something that may be depended upon, in reference to our everlasting welfare." For a consideration of the pre-redemptive and redemptive forms of special revelation in John Owen and Geerhardus Vos, see Richard Barcellos, *The Family Tree of Reformed Biblical Theology* Reformed Baptist Academic Dissertation # 2 (Owensboro, KY: Reformed Baptist Academic Press, 2010).

Jonathan Edwards on Fallen Man's Knowledge of God

Did Edwards think that the fall of our first parents obliterated either their natural knowledge of God or the residue of God's verbal communication with them? Clearly he did not. Edwards affirmed both the noetic effects of the fall and that there remained real knowledge that fallen man possessed due to God's revelation of himself in nature, the memory of God's verbal communication with them in the Garden of Eden and new redemptive, post-fall special revelation. In other words, there is no point at which man was left to himself to conjure up truth about his Creator, Preserver, Governor, and now Savior.

There are two matters to keep clear as we consider the effects of the fall on man's knowledge of God. There are noetic effects of the fall and there is the purposeful limited creaturely way man knows anything including knowledge of God. The two of these are not the same even though the history of philosophical thought and even Christian theology indicates a repeated failure to distinguish the two. The fall has distorted and infected human knowing but the limitation of his creaturely status is not a problem per se. That human knowledge is finite is not the result of the fall but of man's creaturely status.[70] Whatever certain knowledge man has of God and the things of God is the result of both revelation and the gracious activity of the Holy Spirit. In Reformed Scholastic language, with which Edwards would have been intimately familiar, man's knowledge of God is built upon the principle of being (*principium essendi*) which is God himself and the external and internal principle of knowing (*principium cognoscendi externum et internum*) which are revelation and the internal witness of the Holy Spirit (*testimonium internum Spiritu Sancti*). While revelation was present in the Garden of Eden, it now takes a redemptive color and requires a corresponding radically corrective work of grace by the Holy Spirit in the individual man or woman.[71] Indeed, it can rightly be said that the origin of the fall was in man's inability to live with his epistemological limitations.

Jonathan Edwards affirmed each of these elements. He affirmed the distinction between God's omniscience and man's finite knowledge.[72] He

---

70. This is, of course, the practical results of what the Reformed Scholastics referred to as the archetype/ectype distinction. God's knowledge is his and man's knowledge is man's and when man thinks rightly he depends upon God's ectypal revelation of himself.

71. See Muller, *PRRD*, 1:430–50. See also Turretin's *Institutes* and the study of his thought on man's knowledge of God below.

72. Jonathan Edwards, Miscellanies 135 (mislabeled Miscellanies 150 in editions of Edwards' *Works* previous to the Yale Edition), in *The Works of Jonathan Edwards: Vol. 13/The "Miscellanies" a-500* (Thomas A. Schafer, ed., New Haven, CT: Yale University

also affirmed the fact of the noetic effects of the fall. Additionally he affirmed natural revelation, the residue of original verbal revelation and the ongoing redemptive revelation which God progressively gave in the biblical era. First, Edwards affirmed that God's knowledge was perfect, complete, and exhaustive. Conversely he also noted that man was limited in his knowledge even when man's knowledge was in process of restoration. Indeed, he argued in his sermon "Heaven is a World of Love," that the saints' knowledge and enjoyment of God in heaven will ever and always improve and grow.[73]

As noted previously, Edwards worked with the distinction in man's knowledge which he referred to as *speculative* or *notional knowledge* and *spiritual knowledge* or *understanding*.[74] One could have a notional or speculative understanding of, say, God and his Word without being attracted to them. However, one could not have a spiritual understanding of God and the things of God without also possessing speculative knowledge of God and Scripture. In other words, speculative knowledge was a necessary but insufficient condition of spiritual knowledge. This distinction will prove useful in understanding the noetic effects of sin and the practice of Edwards's apologetic. What accounts for the difference between speculative and spiritual knowledge in Edwards's thinking? Clearly it is not the presence of speculative knowledge. That is necessary and a given. What accounts for the difference is the attraction or repulsion of the will to the knowledge

---

Press, 1994), 295. Unfortunately Edwards appears to endorse the classic doctrine of the chain of being when he notes "Many have wrong conceptions of the difference between the nature of Deity and created spirits. The difference is no contrariety, but what naturally results from his greatness and nothing else, such as created spirits come nearer to, or more imitate, the greater they are in their powers and faculties. So if we should suppose the faculties of a created spirit to be enlarged infinitely, there would be the Deity to all intents and purposes, the same simplicity, immutability, etc."

73. Edwards, "Heaven is a World of Love," *WJE/8*, 366–97. Note that even though the saints' knowledge will increase it will never attain to the status or nature of God's own knowledge.

74. Edwards, *WJE/2*, 272. Edwards notes, "There is a distinction to be made between a mere notional understanding, wherein the mind beholds things in the exercise of a speculative faculty; and the sense of the heart, wherein the mind don't only speculate and behold, but relishes and feels. That sort of knowledge, by which a man has a sensible perception of amiableness and loathsomeness, or of sweetness and nauseousness, is not just the same sort of knowledge with that, by which he knows what a triangle is, or what a square is. The one is mere speculative knowledge; the other sensible knowledge, in which more than the mere intellect is concerned; the heart is the proper subject of it, or the soul as a being that not only beholds, but has inclination, and is pleased or displeased. And yet there is the nature of instruction in it; as he that has perceived the sweet taste of honey, knows much more about it, than he who has only looked upon and felt it."

possessed or to the object of the knowledge. The sinner knows God and hates him. The saint knows God and loves him.[75]

The fall did not destroy man's ability to know God. However, it did make it complicated and it made reconciliation between a holy God and sinful man impossible without the work of a theanthropic Mediator. Man can possess erroneous opinions and he can have various volitional (and emotional) reactions to these notions. But man also possesses true knowledge of God that he fights against and constantly endeavors to resist.

> There is a principle in his heart, of such a blinding and besotting nature, that it hinders the exercises of his faculties about the things of religion; exercises for which God made him well capable, and for which he gives him abundant opportunity.[76]

Man lives in God's world in which God reveals himself to man through nature (including the constitution of his own human nature), through the residue of pre-redemptive verbal revelation and redemptive special revelation, and in types in Scripture and nature. To put it another way, fallen man is surrounded on all sides with God and his revelation.

What does fallen man know? Man knows God in the manner exposited by Paul in Romans 1:18ff. Man knows that there is a God who possesses many divine excellencies. Edwards even believed that man knew that God was Trinitarian from nature as well as from Scripture.[77] Fallen man can know true things about God but he does not love God and the things of God. The sinner is repelled by God's holiness in particular. However, is it the case that Edwards only thought the difference between fallen and regenerate man's spiritual understanding was that the saint loved God and the sinner hated him? Is there any suggestion in Edwards that man's conceptual knowledge could be skewed as a result of this hatred? Yes, we believe so. In his treatise on the *Nature of True Virtue* Edwards waxes long and eloquent on how man can exercise a truncated virtue as a result of not taking God into view when thinking about the world. A man and his thinking and morals

---

75. We will go into greater detail about the relationship of the intellect and the will in the next chapter.

76. Jonathan Edwards, "Man's Natural Blindness," *WJEB* 2:247.

77. This is not a universally held view among Reformed theologians up to the time of Edwards, but it was his view. Edwards notes, "I think it is within the reach of naked reason to perceive certainly that there are three distinct in God, each of which is the same [God], three that must be distinct, really and truly distinct, but three, either distinct persons or properties or anything else; and that of these three, one is (more properly than anything else) begotten of the other, and that the third proceeds alike from both, and that the first neither is begotten nor proceeds," Miscellanies 94, *WJE/13*, 257.

can be cramped if he fails to reckon with the reality of God's existence and how that existence impinges on human morality and thinking.

> When I say, true virtue consists in love to Being in general, I shall not be likely to be understood, that no one act of the mind or exercise of love is of the nature of true virtue but what has Being in general, or the great system of universal existence, for its *direct* and *immediate* object: so that no exercise of love or kind affection to any one particular being, that is but a small part of this whole, has anything of the nature of true virtue. But that the nature of true virtue consists in a disposition of benevolence towards Being in general: though, from such a disposition may arise exercises of love to particular beings, as objects are presented and occasions arise.[78]

According to Edwards, such thinking, which fails to include God in the picture of the world, or any given element in the world, while it can have a kind of truthfulness, ultimately lacks proper proportion. Edwards speaks in terms of love to *being-in-general* but this is another way of speaking about God.[79]

Fallen man has true knowledge of God from various media and can potentially hold erroneous concepts of God or can possess true notions of him and is repulsed from God. Sinful man hates God. He hates God's power, knowledge, and holiness. He hates all God's attributes and excellencies. Edwards would say that fallen man can know true things about God but that these true notions by themselves cannot do him one iota of good.[80]

---

78. Jonathan Edwards, "The Nature of True Virtue," *WJE/8*, 541.

79. Jonathan Edwards, "Nature of True Virtue," *WJE/8*, 541. In this essay Edwards is arguing against the notion that man by nature has true benevolence. This moral sentiment theory was on the rise in Edwards' day and became popular in the Scottish Common Sense Realism school of philosophy and ethics. While Edwards does not deny the limited usefulness of fallen benevolence, ultimately only the regenerate saint can exercise true virtue toward God and his fellow man. Regarding the use of the expression "being-in-general" (*ens commune*) it should be noted that Edwards did not coin the expression and that its specific meaning has been disputed in Edwards scholarship. The expression has been taken to be a reference to God alone or to God and his creation together. Paul Ramsey, editor of *True Virtue*, holds that being-in-general refers to "God plus his ordered creation." Editorial introduction, *WJE/8*, 31. Ramsey here is agreeing with the argument of Norm Fiering's *Jonathan Edwards' Moral Thought and Its British Context* (Chapel Hill, NC: University of North Carolina Press, 1981), 326. Settling this dispute about the meaning of the expression being-in-general is beyond the purview of this study.

80. It should not be assumed that because Edwards thought sinful man could have true knowledge of God and the things of God and all the while hate them, that he thought sinful man had a cognitive grasp of the fullness and actual nature of God and the things of God. Quite the contrary, sinful man because he suppresses the truth in

> These things show how desperately prone mankind are to blindness and delusion, how addicted they are to darkness,-God now and then, by his instructions, lifts up some nations out of such gross darkness: but then, how do they sink down into it again, as soon as his hand is withdrawn! Like a heavy stone, which, though it may be forced upwards, yet sinks down again; and will continue to sink down lower and lower with a swift progress, if there be nothing to restrain it. That is the woeful tendency of the mind of man since the fall, notwithstanding his noble powers . . . [81]

These notions give rise to repulsion and rebellion. As Paul notes in Romans 1, man knows enough about God to be without excuse when brought before the righteous bar of divine judgment. Once again, there is no sense in which Edwards thinks there are people in the world somewhere somehow who have no awareness or knowledge of the God of the Bible. Yes, they may resist that knowledge. They may repress it and allow it to come out in idolatrous forms, but know God all men most certainly do. And yet this knowledge is not enough to save anyone. Salvation requires internal and external correction by God.[82]

Jonathan Edwards on Regenerate Man's Knowledge of God

Adam in the Garden of Eden had as full a knowledge of God as was needed for communion with God and existence in the world. Not only did he know God speculatively, he loved him as well. Adam possessed spiritual understanding or knowledge. At least Adam and Eve possessed this for a time. It is because of Adam's spiritual understanding of God and his will that the fall becomes inscrutable. How is it that a righteous man given all the blessings and benefits epitomized by the luxuriant surroundings of the Garden of Eden could not obey God? While the reasons for the fall may be ultimately

---

unrighteousness (per Paul in Romans 1) has a contorted and darkened intellectual apprehension even of those things he knows in some sense truly. In other words, sinful man does not know the truth *rightly*.

81. Edwards, "Man's Natural Blindness," *WJEB* 2:250.

82. Edwards' distinction between speculative and spiritual knowledge would seem to bear out this point. Speculative knowledge, primarily acquired, is the basis on which spiritual knowledge is given (graciously changing a sinner's disposition towards the speculative knowledge of God possessed). In other words, there needs to be *both* doctrinal knowledge and the sense of the heart wrought by the Holy Spirit. See Jonathan Edwards' sermon, "The Importance and Advantage of a Thorough Knowledge of Divine Truth," in *WJE/22*, 83–102. Note that speculative knowledge is not only *supplemented* by spiritual knowledge but is also *corrected* by it.

inexplicable, the reality of it is recognized by Jonathan Edwards. And so is the restoration of fallen man.

Jonathan Edwards's *raison d'être* was the salvation of the lost and the edification of the saints. Edwards understood his calling as a minister of the gospel to be one of proclamation and teaching with a view toward bringing fallen man to Christ and saints to further depths of spiritual vitality. For the saint to know God, meant that he or she also loved him. Again we see the notion of spiritual understanding at play. How is it that fallen man becomes regenerate man and what role does knowledge of God play in that transition? In this segment we want to consider the knowledge of God involved in the transition from wrath to grace and the knowledge of God involved in the Christian pilgrimage. It should be noted that Edwards's involvement in and support of the revivals known as the First Great Awakening come into play here as well.[83]

Consider what has already been said about the knowledge of God fallen man already possesses short of regeneration.[84] Man is created in God's image. While the fall damages the image it does not destroy or obliterate the image. Man lives in God's world. While man continually kicks against the goads of God's world he cannot run or hide from it. God surrounds man with natural revelation. This is revelation of who God is implanted within creation including the constitution of man. Again fallen man seeks to deny this but it is nonetheless present and clear. Then there are the arguments that further develop the ideas conveyed in natural revelation. The theistic proofs or arguments can be considered in this light. These can be formulated in a way consistent with Christian theism or not. But Edwards would grant the legitimacy of their use.[85] Edwards would also add the fact that there is a residue of verbal communication which is filtered down through the generations to all peoples and while now corrupt it still points to God in some fashion. And there is special revelation with its progressively unfolding drama of redemption. Additionally there are the types found in both Scripture and in nature and history that point to Christ and his saving

---

83. This will form the historical background of the next chapter but is relevant to our concerns here as well. As previously noted, an especially astute assessment of Edwards' defense of the awakening can be found in Smart, *Jonathan Edwards' Apologetic for the Great Awakening*.

84. These comments are directly relevant to apologetic practice.

85. Edwards also notes the limits of theistic arguments. For instance, the cosmological argument could yield multiple "gods" or, given the evil as well as good in the world, a good god and an evil god. See Edwards, Miscellanies 1350, *WJE/23*, 434–35. However, it should be noted that this entry is almost entirely taken up with citations from Samuel Clark's *A Discourse Concerning the Unchangeable Obligations of Natural Religion, and the Truth and Certainty of the Christian Revelation*.

work. Finally, there is the influence of the gospel or the Christian faith in the world, along with what Edwards referred to as the common operations of the Holy Spirit.[86] While only Scripture is potentially redemptive,[87] these other sources of the knowledge of God within access of fallen man mean that he has some knowledge of God and is without excuse when summoned before the divine assize.

As far as Jonathan Edwards was concerned, there was no man or tribe of men without exposure to some form of the knowledge of God.

> I think a little sober reflection on these things which appear among the Deists, weighing them together with the nature of things, may convince that a general renunciation of divine revelation, after the nations have enjoyed [it], would soon bring these nations to be more absurd, brutish and monstrous in their notions and practices than the heathens were before the gospel came among them. For . . . [t]hose nations had many things among them originally derived from revelation, by tradition from their own ancestors, the ancient founders of nations, or from the Jews, which led 'em to embrace many truths contained in the Scripture.[88]

Because of the various media of knowledge of God, even pagan philosophies and religions may grasp and grope after elements of truth. But these were never redemptive.[89] It was not the case, despite what deist writers

---

86. Edwards delves deeply into the distinction between the Holy Spirit's common operations and his saving operations. Edwards will talk about the Holy Spirit working *on* an individual and working *in* an individual. The one is temporary and the other abiding. For further consideration of this distinction, see Edwards, *WJE/2*, 276.

87. By "potentially redemptive" we mean that not all who hear the gospel outwardly are inwardly or effectually called. If Scripture were necessarily redemptive all who heard or read it would by virtue of that be saved.

88. Edwards, Miscellanies 1297, *WJE/23*, 244.

89. This is true despite the best efforts of Edwards scholars such as McDermott and Morimoto. Note the following comment by Edwards, "We don't know how long the remembrance of the revelation that God gave to Noah and his ancestors, might be continued among other branches of his posterity, besides the line of Jacob; or how long God continued to give new revelations to them, as he did to Job and Melchizedek. But by degrees other nations apostatized, and God withdrew this light from them. And corruption was become exceeding great and general in Abraham's time; which seems to have been the reason of God's calling Abraham, and separating him from the rest of the world, that divine revelation might be continued and upheld in his posterity. And 'tis probable that the true religion wholly ceased in all other nations in Moses's time, . . . after which time, till Christ's time, [Israel] only of all nations seemed to have been favored with divine revelation," Edwards, "Light in a Dark World," *WJE/19*, 711. If we combine what Edwards says here with his sermon "A Spiritual Understanding of Divine

might want to allege, that the Christian God was petty and vindictive given that so many stood outside the circle of his intimate communication. Nor was it the case that these other avenues of knowledge of God were sufficient for salvation. Only the Holy Spirit working with the Scriptures and the proclamation of the gospel could bring a fallen sinner to faith in Christ and thus to salvation.[90]

How does one come to faith in Christ and what role does knowledge of God play in that coming to faith? Edwards held that knowledge of God and the things of God were essential to conversion. And knowledge continued to be necessary for growth in the Christian life. Edwards's sermon "The Necessity of Christian Knowledge" is very clear about this point.

> Such is the nature of man, that nothing can come at the heart but through the door of the understanding: and there can be no spiritual knowledge of that of which there is not first a rational knowledge. It is impossible that anyone should see the truth or excellency of any doctrine of the gospel, who knows not what that doctrine is. A man cannot see the wonderful excellency and love of Christ in doing such and such things for sinners, unless his understanding be first informed how those things were done. He cannot have a taste of the sweetness and divine excellency of such and such things contained in divinity, unless he first have a notion that there are such and such things.[91]

Ordinarily, the Holy Spirit used speculative knowledge of God that has come to the unbeliever to bring them to faith. Faith arises in response to the external proclamation or exposition of God's Word. The knowledge of God that fallen man already possesses means that the preacher is not speaking into a void. The minister or the apologist is addressing someone who knows God after a fashion but who constantly fights with that knowledge. But the dissemination of information in preaching does not *by itself* save anyone. It is a necessary but not a sufficient condition. Sinful man, though knowledgeable of God is unwilling to come to Christ by faith. The secret regenerating work of the Holy Spirit is necessary to change the hard heart.

Things Denied to the Unregenerate," *WJE/14*, 70–96, we see that the idea that pagan possession of speculative truth would not be sufficient in Edwards' mind to save. For a direct response to McDermott's attempt to make pagan knowledge of God redemptive, see Greg D. Gilbert, "The Nations Will Worship: Jonathan Edwards and the Salvation of the Heathen," *Trinity Journal* 23 (2002): 53–76.

90. For one response to the attempt to make Edwards at least a latent inclusivist, see Jeffrey C. Waddington, "Must We Believe? Jonathan Edwards and Conscious Faith in Christ," *The Confessional Presbyterian* 6 (2010): 11–21.

91. Edwards, *WJE/22*, 88–89.

When the Holy Spirit changes the unregenerate heart, he uses the external proclamation of the Word (or the reading of it) but it is not the information *alone* that causes the change. The enlightening of the mind and the renewal of the will is the direct working of the Holy Spirit.[92]

Fallen man's transition from speculative to spiritual understanding involves the imparting of no new doctrine or information.[93] What does happen is that the Holy Spirit sweetly overcomes the resistance of the sinner to the Word of God. Typically this is understood to involve both the enlightening of the mind and the renewal of the will. But Edwards is very clear that no new doctrine (i.e., there is no new revelation) transmitted in the divine action of regeneration. The preacher or the lay Christian or the professional apologist is to share the gospel or answer questions brought to them, but this dissemination of information as such or the removal of confusion does not by itself cause regeneration. Again, these external acts are necessary but not sufficient. Edwards notes that God could have chosen to do things differently but has deigned to involve sinful, fallible creatures in the process of bringing sinners to faith in Christ.

What role does knowledge play in regeneration and conversion given that it is a necessary but insufficient condition of faith in Christ? Closing with Christ, to use Edwards's language, involves faith and faith involves, typically, knowledge, assent, and trust. Faith involves the whole soul of the individual. The intellect and the will together concur as one comes to Christ for salvation. Conrad Cherry has noted this about Edwards's understanding of faith,

> Faith may be compendiously termed affiance or trust, but it also contains in its very nature judgment regarding the reality of its object, a consent to that object as "good, eligible or desirable," and a dependence on, hope in, and venturing in practice on, the foundation of, the object. In faith, the powers of intellect and will tend to merge into one; strictly speaking, the various movements of the self in any act of faith are not distinct acts but are different modes of the same act.[94]

---

92. In the next chapter we will deal with the relationship of the intellect and will in the fall and in regeneration.

93. While this transition involves no new doctrine it does involve the *correction* of doctrine already received but until regeneration is suppressed. In other words, the movement from speculative to spiritual understanding is not a mere subjective change in the internal workings of the human will but also a enlightening of the mind as to what was present externally to the mind all along.

94. Conrad Cherry, *The Theology of Jonathan Edwards: A Reappraisal* (Indianapolis & Bloomington, IN: Indiana University Press, 1966), 17.

There is no such thing as "blind faith" for Edwards. How can one trust in a Christ one has never heard of? Notice here that faith in not bare knowledge or mere assent but also includes trust. Both assent and trust are acts of the will and are acts in response to an object in the intellect. As Edwards points out, God uses knowledge conveyed through ordinary means (preaching, catechesis, witnessing, theistic proofs, the apologetic encounter) to bring fallen man to salvation.

> There is no other way by which any means of grace whatsoever can be of any benefit, but by knowledge. All teaching is in vain, without learning. Therefore the preaching of the gospel would be wholly to no purpose, if it conveyed no knowledge to the mind.[95]

Growth in grace as the Christian navigates the pilgrimage from here to glory also requires continued growth in knowledge of God and the things of God. As noted earlier, Edwards in his sermon "The Necessity of Christian Knowledge" noted that the increase of knowledge through the study of God's Word and other good books is used by God to further a saint's sanctification.[96] New insights into Scripture come about not through new revelations or through somehow bypassing the ordinary study of God's Word. It is true that the Holy Spirit continually illuminates the mind of believers, but this is combined with the ordinary effort of actually reading the Bible and other helpful books in theology. A preacher may raise a point the saint had never thought of before or the same thing can happen by reading Scripture or good books of theology and Bible commentaries and the like. Again, the knowledge of God gained in biblical and theological and even secular study is a necessary but insufficient condition of growth in grace. And the increase of knowledge is a means to an end. It is intended to yield greater trust in Christ, a deeper walk with God, and a greater appreciation of divine grace. In other words, knowledge of God ought to yield love for God. As we shall see, this increase in Christian knowledge does not end in this life in the thought of Edwards.

---

95. Edwards, "Thorough Knowledge of Divine Truth," *WJE*/22, 87.

96. Edwards, "Thorough Knowledge of Divine Truth," *WJE*/22, 91. Particularly, Edwards notes that, "The things of divinity are things of superlative excellency, and are worthy that all should make a business of endeavoring to grow in the knowledge of them."

Jonathan Edwards on Man's Knowledge of God in the Consummation

Edwards believed that man's knowledge of and love for God would continuously increase in the new heavens and the new earth. This is the thrust of the sermon "Heaven is a World of Love."[97] Edwards noted that this was the fulfillment of the purpose for God's creation of the human race in the first place. God created man to have fellowship with him. He created man so that man would glory and enjoy him. As it turned out, God allowed the fall and planned for redemption in eternity to bring greater glory to himself and human satisfaction than would have been the case without the fall. Edwards would have been in agreement with the notion that the fall was a *felix culpa*. Edwards held that creation was for the purpose of redemption. And the dwelling of the saints with the Triune God in heaven was the culmination of the process begun at creation.[98]

Inasmuch as the saints are to be conformed to the image of the Son of God, Edwards believed this didn't cease with the passing of the saints into glory. A believer's knowledge of God and his love for him would increase over time, although never reaching a limit. However, the saints would never reach a point at which they either equaled God or lost their own identity. Edwards wanted to avoid any idea of heaven as a static place where nothing really ever happened. Since heaven was a world of love there would be no sin to contend with but there would be progress in understanding and loving God the Father, God the Son and God the Holy Spirit. This was Edwards's

---

97. See *WJE/8*, 366–97. Speaking of the saints love for God and each other in heaven, Edwards notes that, "They will have no dullness or unwieldiness, no corruption of heart to fight against divine love and hinder suitable expressions, no clog of a heavy lump of clay, or an unfit organ for an inward heavenly flame. They shall have no difficulty in expressing all their love. Their souls, which are like a flame of fire with love, shall not be a fire pent up but shall be perfectly at liberty. The soul which is winged with love shall have no weight tied to the feet to hinder its flight. There shall be no want of strength or activity, nor any want of words to praise the object of their love. They shall find nothing to hinder them in praising or seeing God, just as their love inclines. Love naturally desires to express itself, and in heaven the love of the saints shall be at liberty to express itself as it desires, either towards God or one another," 379. For further discussion of this sermon see Amy Plantinga-Pauw, "'Heaven is a World of Love': Edwards on Heaven and the Trinity." *CTJ* 30 (November 1995): 392–401 and Stephen J. Nichols's Heaven *on Earth: Capturing Jonathan Edwards' Vision of Living Between* (Wheaton, IL: Crossway, 2006). See also Jonathan Edwards, Miscellanies 777, *The Works of Jonathan Edwards, Vol. 18/The "Miscellanies" 501–832* (Ava Chamberlain, ed., New Haven, CT: Yale University Press, 2000), 427–34 for detailed discussion of the progressive nature of happiness (and so, knowledge and love) of the saints in heaven.

98. See Stephen R. Holmes, *God of Grace & God of Glory: An Account of the Theology of Jonathan Edwards* (Grand Rapids, MI: Eerdmans, 2001), 112–23.

version of the beatific vision or *visio Dei*. This is the goal or telos for all that God had created the universe for and all that went before in the Christian's life led to this point. God would dwell with his people and they would be his possession.

A Brief Historical Survey on Man's Knowledge of God

As with the previous chapter, we now examine the thinking of four giants of the theological world who predate Edwards to get a sense of where Edwards stands in the Christian tradition. Again we will follow a chronological order by first considering Augustine of Hippo, then Thomas Aquinas, followed by John Calvin, and concluding with a look at Francis Turretin.

Augustine of Hippo

Augustine has much to say about man's natural and supernatural knowledge of God and we will be drawing from various sources to gain a clear picture of Augustine's views on the subject.[99] Metaphysically, there exists a hierarchy of being between God at the top and matter at the bottom. This has been described as a three-tiered reality. God is at the apex of this hierarchy and bodies are at the bottom. The soul is therefore in the middle. As a composite being, man relates to the world of matter and to the spiritual realm.[100] While Augustine does not belittle the human body, it is the soul which images God and enables man to communicate with God and commune with him.

> And we indeed recognize in ourselves the image of God: that is, of the supreme Trinity. This image is not equal to God. Indeed,

---

99. For instance, we shall have recourse to Augustine, *Christian Doctrine* in *The Nicene and Post-Nicene Fathers: First Series* (J. F. Shaw, trans. Philipp Schaff, ed., Grand Rapids, MI: Eerdmans, 1988), 2: 513–97; *The City of God Against the Pagans* Cambridge Texts in the History of Political Thought (R. W. Dyson, tr. and ed., Cambridge: Cambridge University Press, 1998); *The Confessions of St. Augustine: Modern English Version* (Grand Rapids, MI: Baker, 2005); *Soliloquies* in *The Nicene and Post-Nicene Fathers: First Series* (Charles Starbuck, trans. Philipp Schaff, ed., Grand Rapids, MI: Eerdmans, 1986), 7: 531–60; *The Trinity* (Edmund Hill, trans. John E. Rotelle, ed., Brooklyn, NY: New City Press, 1991).

100. See Roland Teske's helpful discussion of Augustine's view of the soul in *Augustine Through the Ages: An Encyclopedia* (Allen D. Fitzgerald, gen. ed., Grand Rapids, MI: Eerdmans, 1999), 807–12. Augustine himself notes the distinction between God as uncreated and created souls in *City of God*, 11.26, and yet also notes that the soul is closest to God. Augustine notes in *The Trinity* 15.2.11, that "We could also define man like this and say, "Man is a rational substance consisting of soul and body." In this case there is no doubt that man has a soul that is not a body and a body that is not a soul," (403).

it is very far removed from Him; for it is neither co-eternal with Him, nor, to express the whole matter briefly, is it of the same substance as God. It is, however, nearer to God in nature than anything else made by Him, even though it still requires to be reformed and perfected in order to be a still closer likeness.[101]

Man has a body which connects him with other animals and a soul which allows him to interact with God his Creator. Augustine's epistemology relates closely to his metaphysics.

In his *Soliloquies*, Augustine states that all he desires to know is God and himself and nothing else.[102] To know God, one must turn inward from external distractions and then move upwards in consideration of God. In other words, the psychological and intellectual movement is from awareness and knowledge of the external world inwards to meditation on the soul and then ascent to a consideration of God. One comes to know God through contemplation of the individual soul.[103] Admittedly this is complicated by sin in the post fall world and so one needs Scripture and divine illumination to help to contemplate the God of all the universe. Augustine distinguishes between the *ratio inferior* (inferior reason) and the *ratio superior* (superior reason) which are powers of the human soul. The inferior reason deals with earthly external matters and the superior reason deals with matters of a divine nature.[104]

In a similar manner, Augustine distinguishes between *scientia* (knowledge) and *sapientia* (wisdom). By use of the inferior reason one gains knowledge of the mundane temporal world and this has real, though limited, value for Augustine. Man lives in the world and so this knowledge is useful. But the way man relates to God and the eternal is through contemplation and the acquisition of wisdom. By the inward turn, man's mind is illuminated by the light of God. By this light man is able to understand all else. Augustine's epistemology reflects the three-tiered nature of his ontology. For him there are three levels of vision or awareness: First there is *corporeal*

---

101. Augustine, *City of God*, 11.26 (483–4). Augustine also discusses the Trinitarian nature of the image of God in *The Trinity*, books 9–15.

102. *Soliliquies*, 1.2.7, "A. Behold I have prayed to God. R. What then wouldst thou know? A. All these things which I have prayed for. R. Sum them up in brief. A. God and the soul, that is what I desire to know. R. Nothing more? A. Nothing whatever," (539). As will be shortly seen, John Calvin picks up on this Augustinian theme in the introduction to his *Institutes of the Christian Religion*, 1.1.1.

103. See Robert Crouse, "Knowledge," in *Augustine Through the Ages*, 486–88. Specifically, Augustine argues for this ascent of the soul in pursuing knowledge of God in his *Explanations of the Psalms in The Nicene and Post-Nicene Fathers: First Series* (Philip Schaff, ed., Grand Rapids, MI: Eerdmans, 1988), 145.5.

104. Augustine, *The Trinity*, 13.1.1–2.

vision by which the body perceives things through the senses; second, there is *spiritual vision* in which the powers of the mind engage with the images of sensible things from the external world, and third, there is *intellectual vision* by which man comes to know God. And so the movement of human knowledge involves movement from sense perception to reflection on temporal things to intellectual contemplation of eternal verities.[105]

Augustine does affirm natural law so that he does possess some idea of natural revelation. Embedded within creation are what Augustine in his *Literal Interpretation of Genesis* calls *rationes seminales* which God has placed there to guide the development of creation.[106] These reflect the *rationes aeternae* or eternal ideas in the mind of God. As eternal and in the divine mind, these ideas are unchangeable and necessary and serve as the "exemplary cause and basic foundation of all created reality."[107] These eternal ideas serve as the basis for human knowledge. As already noted, man is a composite being and Augustine speaks of a *rationes hominis* or rational soul with its inferior and superior reason.[108]

Since wisdom is knowledge of God and universals and the human soul, man must in some way come to know these eternal verities. Augustine's understanding of how man comes to attain wisdom reflects what would now be classified as supernatural, special, redemptive revelation. With the exception of the teaching of the church (which is not infallible), man achieves wisdom via the mediation of the incarnation of the Son of God, the teachings of Jesus Christ, and the Bible more generally. Augustine also taught that faith was necessary for a man to obtain wisdom. In his *On Free Choice of the Will* he notes that faith is, among other things, assent to the truth found in Scripture.[109] As noted previously, sin interferes with the acquisition of wisdom. While faith may not be necessary for *scientia* it is most certainly necessary for *sapientia*. Man must be cleansed of his sin and live a righteous life in order to possess wisdom and know God.[110]

105. See Ronald. H. Nash's article on "Wisdom" in *Augustine Through the Ages*, 885–887 and his *The Light of the Mind: St. Augustine's Theory of Knowledge* (Lexington, KY: University of Kentucky, 1969).

106. Augustine, *On Genesis: A Refutation of the Manichees; Unfinished Literal Commentary on Genesis; and the Literal Meaning of Genesis* in *The Works of St. Augustine: A Translation for the 21st Century* (Edmund Hill, trans. and ed., Hyde Park, NY: New City Press, 2002), book 1.

107. Nash, "Wisdom," *Augustine Through the Ages*, 885.

108. We have already noted this distinction.

109. Augustine, *On Free Choice of the Will* (Indianapolis: Hackett Publishing, 1993), 1.2.4.

110. Augustine, *On Order* (Silvano Borruso, tr. and ed., South Bend: St. Augustine Press, 2007), 2.19.51.

Thomas Aquinas

Thomas has written extensively on man's knowledge of God, of both his natural and supernatural knowledge. We will be drawing primarily from his *Summa Theologia* and his *Summa Contra Gentiles*.[111] Thomas begins with the idea that since God is a spirit and has no corporeality that man cannot know him directly but only by his effects in creation. Thomas notes,

> Although we cannot know in what consists the essence of God, nevertheless in this science we make use of His effects, either of nature or of grace, in place of a definition, in regard to whatever is treated of in this science concerning God; even as in some philosophical sciences we demonstrate something about a cause from its effect, by taking the effect in place of a definition of a cause.[112]

Thomas rejects any form of innate ideas and therefore did not accept Anselm's ontological argument.[113] Man's knowledge begins with the senses.[114] However such knowledge does not end with the senses. The human mind abstracts universals from the percepts and these are the basis for knowledge.

There are certain things man can know about God from nature and that do not require supernatural assistance of any kind. There is also knowledge of God that man can possess only by means of supernatural revelation.

> There is a twofold mode of truth in what we profess about God. Some truths about God exceed all ability of the human reason.

---

111. Thomas Aquinas, *Summa Contra Gentiles: Book One: God* (Anton C. Pegis, trans. and ed., Notre Dame, IN: University of Notre Dame Press, 1975); *Summa Theologica: Complete English Edition in Five Volumes* (Fathers of the English Dominican Province, trans., Allen, TX: Christian Classics, 1948).

112. Thomas, *ST*, 1.1.7.

113. Thomas, *SCG*, 1.10–12.

114. See also *ST* 1.1.10, where he states, "Now it is natural to man to attain to intellectual truths through sensible objects, because all our knowledge originates from sense." Further, in *SCG*, 1.3.3, Thomas states, "That there are certain truths about God that totally surpass man's ability appears from the greatest evidence. Since, indeed, the principle of all knowledge that the reason perceives about some thing is the understanding of the very substance of that being (for according to Aristotle "what a thing is" is the principle of demonstration), it is necessary that the way in which we understand the substance of a thing determines the way in which we know what belongs to it. Hence, if the human intellect comprehends the substance of some thing, for example, that of a stone or triangle, no intelligible characteristic belonging to that thing surpasses the grasp of human reasoning. But this does not happen in the case of God. For the human intellect is not able to reach a comprehension of the divine substance through its natural power. For, according to its manner of knowing in the present life, the intellect depends on the sense for the origin of knowledge; and so those things that do not fall under the senses cannot be grasped by the human intellect except insofar as the knowledge of them is gathered from sensible things." See also *SCG*, 1.8.1 and 1.12.9.

Such is the truth that God is triune. But there are some truths which the natural reason also is able to reach. Such are that God exists, that He is one, and the like. In fact, such truths about God have been proved by the philosophers, guided by the light of natural reason.[115]

And there are aspects of knowledge that overlap these two categories. There are some things man can know about God from nature that are also revealed in Scripture. These Thomas called mixed doctrines. Thomas noted that not all men were capable of reasoning their way to God (for reasons of lack of interest, time, or ability) so God offered a more direct way to know him in his Word. But there were some men who were gifted with the ability to possess limited knowledge of God through the normal ratiocinative processes.

God can be known by his effects and so Thomas offers his "five ways" to move from effects in the world to a non-mundane cause outside the world.[116] It should be noted that the five ways are not offered to unbelievers in abstraction from the rest of theology. That that is how they have been used subsequently in apologetics there is no doubt. Thomas, however, offers his arguments in the context explicating his theology. The five ways involve movement from movement to an unmoved mover, from effects to a cause, from contingency to necessity, from imperfection to perfection, from the purposefulness of creation to a Creator. All of these move from some aspect of the created realm (an effect) to a cause outside the created realm. This natural knowledge of God was a limited knowledge. In other words, any man who reasoned in such a manner gained real but limited knowledge.

Thomas also argued that man was created with the desire and ability to gain knowledge[117] and that man's knowledge of God was *analogical*.[118]

---

115. Thomas, *SCG*, 1.3.2. "Est autem in his quae de Deo confitemur duplex veritatis modus. Quaedam namque vera sunt de Deo quae omnem facultatem humanae rationis excedunt, ut Deum esse trinum et unum. Quaedam vero sunt ad quae etiam ratio naturalis pertingere potest, sicut est Deum esse, Deum esse unum, et alia huiusmodi; quae etiam philosophi demonstrative de Deo probaverunt, ducti naturalis lumine rationis."

116. Thomas, *ST*, 1.2.3.

117. Thomas, *ST*, 2.66.5. Norman Geisler, in his *Thomas Aquinas: An Evangelical Appraisal* (Grand Rapids, MI: Baker, 1991), 90, offers this concise summary of Thomas on the question of *capacity* or *content innatism*: "Humans have an innate, natural capacity or form for the truth of first principles ingrained into our very nature by God. They have first principles in a kind of virtual and natural way as a precondition of all cognitive activity. And when this innate capacity is filled with the content of sense experience, we are able by conscious reflection to come to a knowledge of the very first principles, which as a fundamental part of our nature, enable us to have a consciousness of them." If Geisler is correct, then Thomas was a *capacity innatist*. In order for man to have natural knowledge of God, the first principles of thought must act on the data of experience.

118. Thomas, *SCG*, 1.29–35 and *ST*, .12–14.

That is, language used to talk about God was neither univocal nor equivocal. To illustrate the point, it can be said of both medicine and a man that they are healthy. While the word *healthy* is used in both instances, it is used in different ways. Medicine is said to be healthy because it causes or induces health. A man is said to be healthy when his body functions as it ought or in the absence of illness or disease. Given that God is not corporal and is transcendent, human language is limited in its ability to talk about God and the things of God. God is known from his effects and so language reflects that reality. Thomas sought to avoid the twin traps of univocity and equivocity. To say that language works in exactly the same way with man and God would lead to real complications. But to say that human language has nothing to say about God would create problems as well. Ascribing goodness to both God and man is not nonsensical. There is an analogy between the goodness of God and man. However God is simple and his essence is his existence where man is complex and his essence and existence differ. God simply *is* goodness itself and man can *possess* goodness. Ultimately man is created to attain to the beatific vision in heaven and this is an intellectual sight. Knowledge of God in this life is meant to train man for this eternal occupation.[119]

John Calvin

John Calvin, the reformer of Geneva, began his *Institutes of the Christian Religion* with one of the most cited statements, namely that man's knowledge of God and himself are inextricably intertwined. "Nearly all the wisdom we possess, that is to say, true and sound wisdom, consists of two parts: the knowledge of God and of ourselves. But, while joined by many bonds, which one precedes and brings forth the other is not easy to discern."[120] In other words, it was not possible for man to have any knowledge of God without also becoming acutely aware of his own condition and vice versa. There was no man or group of men who did not possess some sort of knowledge about the God who made man. Calvin unpacks the nature of man's knowledge of God under two categories. In addition to noting the interrelated nature of man's knowledge of God and himself, Calvin notes that we know God as both Creator and Redeemer, and that the knowledge of God as Creator is possessed by all men.[121]

---

119. Thomas, *ST*, 1.1.5.

120. John Calvin, *Institutes*, 1.1.1.

121. This is how the Battles translation of Calvin's *Institutes* divides the kind of knowledge man has of God. Book 1 discusses knowledge of God as Creator and books

Calvin points out that all men know God as Creator and calls this knowledge either the *sensus divinitatus* or the *semen religionis*.

> There is within the human mind, and indeed by natural instinct, an awareness of divinity. This we take to be beyond controversy. To prevent anyone from taking refuge in the pretense of ignorance, God himself has implanted in all men a certain understanding of his divine majesty. Ever renewing its memory, he repeatedly sheds fresh drops.[122]

This knowledge of God as Creator is possessed by all men but is of limited usefulness.[123] It accounts for the universal religiosity found among men of different cultures, eras, and geographical regions of the world. God's revelation of himself in creation (including his human creatures) is crystal clear but is limited by the sinful nature of human beings since the fall of Adam and Eve. Note that the natural knowledge of God which man possesses is revealed by God and not merely inferred by man.[124] It is natural knowledge because it comes through the medium of creation or nature. But it is revelation nonetheless for that.

Man's knowledge of God as Redeemer requires supernatural or special redemptive revelation.[125] In fact, ever since the fall, Calvin would argue, man does not know how to use even the revelation of God given through nature aright. Because of the fall, man takes clear revelation and perverts it to his own detriment. There are times when it appears that the fall obliterated the image of God in man and its correlative knowledge of God and at other times Calvin is not quite so radical or drastic. Sin infects the whole

---

2–4 discuss man's knowledge of God as Redeemer and how it is obtained from the Scriptures and nurtured in the life of the church.

122. Calvin, *Institutes*, 1.3.1.

123. Calvin, *Institutes*, 1.3.3. Calvin notes, "Men of sound judgment will always be sure that a sense of divinity which can never be effaced is engraved upon men's minds. Indeed, the perversity of the impious, who though they struggle furiously are unable to extricate themselves from the fear of God, is abundant testimony that this conviction, namely, that there is some God, is naturally inborn in all, and is fixed deep within, as it were in the very marrow." While this knowledge of God is inescapable, it is not sufficient to require man to worship God as he ought. A little later Calvin recognizes that, "[a]s experience shows, God has sown a seed of religion in all men. But scarcely one man in a hundred is met with who fosters it, once received, in his heart, and none in whom it ripens-much less shows fruit in season [cf. Ps. 1:3]. Besides while some may evaporate in their own superstitions and others deliberately and wickedly desert God, yet all degenerate from the true knowledge of him," 1.4.1.

124. The language Calvin uses is of divine revelatory *activity*. God "*sheds* fresh drops" of knowledge of himself, *implants, sows*, and *engrains*.

125. Calvin, *Institutes*, 1.6.1.

personality. There is no area that is protected from the ravages of the fall. However, man still knows God but actively works to repress that knowledge and that repression and hatred of God and the knowledge of him interferes with the proper function of the natural revelation of God which ought to yield adequate natural knowledge of God. To put the matter another way, God's revelation in nature is clear, but man's reception of that revelation is not. In fact, Calvin points out that man needs special revelation in order to properly understand the natural revelation of God. Calvin refers to this role of Scripture as Scripture's serving as "spectacles" which corrected the morally and epistemically blurred vision.

> Just as old and bleary-eyed men and those with weak vision, if you thrust before them a most beautiful volume, even if they recognize it to be some sort of writing, yet can scarcely construe two words, but with the aid of spectacles will begin to read distinctly; so Scripture, gathering up the otherwise confused knowledge of God in our minds, having dispersed our dullness, clearly shows us the true God.[126]

In other words, Scripture is both corrective and redemptive. While God in his benevolent providence has gifted unbelievers with wisdom and insight into this world, and Christians ought not to disparage such gifting on God's part, the brightest pagan falls infinitely short of heaven. With Augustine, Calvin affirms that Christians ought to benefit from the wisdom of the pagan and take that wisdom and baptize it into a Christian worldview.[127] However such knowledge will not save anyone. Redemption occurs through the internal secret energy of the Holy Spirit who takes the Word of God and applies it to the heart and mind of the individual.

> But even if anyone clears God's Sacred Word from man's evil speaking, he will not at once imprint upon their hearts that certainty which piety requires. Since for unbelieving men religion seems to stand by opinion alone, they, in order not to believe anything foolishly or lightly, both wish and demand rational proof that Moses and the prophets spoke divinely. But I reply: the testimony of the Spirit is more excellent than all reason. For as God alone is a fit witness of himself in his Word, so also the Word will not find acceptance in men's hearts before it is sealed by the inward testimony of the Spirit. The same Spirit, therefore, who has spoken through the mouths of the prophets must

---

126. Calvin, *Institutes*, 1.6.1.
127. See notes 6 and 9 of this chapter.

penetrate into our hearts to persuade us that they faithfully proclaimed what had been divinely commanded.[128]

This individual gains knowledge of God and his Word in the ministry of the church and under the external ministry of the Word in the church and the internal actings of the Holy Spirit, an unbeliever comes to faith in Christ. He comes to believe in the Scriptures as the true Word of God and he looks to Christ as the object of trusting faith.

The Christian then grows in the nurture and admonition of the Lord through the continued ministrations of the church, which is the believer's "mother."[129] The church cares for the flock of believers and the saints grow in conformity to their Lord and wend their pilgrim way to the celestial city. There in heaven the saints will behold God in all his glory as Father, Son, and Holy Spirit. There in heaven the knowledge of God will be perfect, albeit on a creaturely plane. The knowledge of God which the saints have in glory is what often goes under the name of the beatific vision or the *visio Dei*. Now the church knows by faith. Then it will know by sight. What that sight entails is an intellectual sight of God, creaturely spirits knowing and adoring the holy and righteous God.[130]

Francis Turretin

We now come to the concluding figure in our brief historical survey of man's knowledge of God. Turretin, professor at Calvin's Genevan Academy, gives a thorough treatment of this subject and we would do well to pause and consider his thought. Turretin makes the standard Reformed Scholastic distinction between God's comprehensive and exhaustive knowledge of himself and his creation (*archetypal* knowledge), God's revelation of himself to man (*ectypal* revelation), and man's knowledge of God (*ectypal* knowledge). God's knowledge of himself is the source of his revelation and man's knowledge of God.

> True theology is divided into: (1) infinite and uncreated, which is God's essential knowledge of himself (Mt. 11:27) in which he alone is at the same time the object known (*epistēton*), the

---

128. Calvin, *Institutes*, 1.7.4. Calvin is talking about the more narrow concern of the Holy Spirit witnessing to the divinity of Scripture, but the Holy Spirit must also enlighten and renew the fallen human heart before a man can exercise faith in Christ.

129. Calvin, *Institutes*, 4.1.1 and 4.

130. Calvin, *Institutes*, 4.17.18. For Calvin, the saints do not have to await the new heavens and new earth to have their minds lifted to the heavenlies. By faith, when the saints participate in the Lord's supper, their minds are there and then lifted up to heaven.

knowledge (*epistēmōn*), and the knower (*epistēmē*), and that which he decreed to reveal to us concerning himself which is commonly called archetypal; and (2) finite and created, which is the image and ectype (*ektypon*) of the infinite and archetypal (*prōtotypou*) (viz., the ideas which creatures possess concerning God and divine things, taking form from that supreme knowledge and communicated to intelligent creatures, either by hypostatic union with the soul of Christ [whence arises "the theology of union"]; or by beatific vision to the angels and saints who walk by sight, not by faith, which is called "the theology of vision;" or by revelation, which is made to travelers [viz., to those who have not yet reached the goal and is called "the theology of revelation" or the stadium).[131]

Man's knowledge of God is then said to occur in stages.[132] First is man's knowledge of God pre-fall. Here Turretin notes that Adam's natural knowledge of God (based in natural revelation) was complete (as complete as it can be on a creaturely level). There is also the suggestion, though not overly developed, that God's verbal communication with Adam and Eve constituted a pre-redemptive form of special revelation.

But Turretin is most concerned with man's knowledge of God after the fall. The lion's share of the discussion will deal with natural and supernatural knowledge of God subsequent to the fall and passing through the phases of unregenerate knowledge of God, regenerate knowledge, and heavenly creaturely knowledge of God. Turretin speaks of this life as a pilgrimage and so man's knowledge of God (specifically the saint's knowledge) is a knowledge on the way or *in via*.[133] Turretin speaks of man's knowledge of God using the language of "theology." Man is said to possess a natural theology and a supernatural theology.[134] Regarding theology in general, there are two types: false theology and true theology.[135] Sinful natural theology arises from a

---

131. Francis Turretin, *Institutes of Elenctic Theology* 3 vols (George Musgrave Geiger, trans. James T. Dennison, ed., Philippsburg, NJ: Presbyterian &Reformed Publishing, 1992), 1.2.6.

132. Turretin, *Institutes*, 1.2.9.

133. Turretin, *Institutes*, 1.2.6 where he notes that this theology is "of the stadium."

134. Turretin, *Institutes*, 1.2.7.

135. Turretin, *Institutes*, 1.2.5–6. "Theology is wont to be distinguished in diverse ways into true and false. The false and equivocally so-called (applied to an erroneous system concerning God and his worship) is of various kinds. First, that of the Gentiles which evidently has been manifold . . . Second, that of infidels and heretics . . . For although their theology may contain some truth, yet because the greater part is false and the errors fundamental, it is properly called "false" (the denomination being taken from the larger part)." When Turretin says that the designation "false theology" is equivocal,

corrupt man's reflection on natural revelation. Regenerate natural theology arises from the saint's reflection upon natural revelation. There is no sense here of a common natural theology which can serve as common ground between regenerate and unregenerate man. Of course natural revelation is common but how a man processes that revelation varies depending upon the spiritual state of the individual.[136]

Natural theology reflects upon God's revelation of himself in nature. This includes human nature itself. Turretin references Romans 1 in his exposition of natural revelation and the resultant natural theology.[137] Echoing John Calvin, Turretin notes that man has a sense of divinity and that this sense accounts for the universal religiosity of the human race.[138] But what is the nature of this sense? Does Turretin think that man has the capacity to possess knowledge of God or does he think man actually possesses knowledge of this sort? It seems clear that Turretin acknowledges that man is born with capacities or categories in the mind that cause him to come to belief in God upon conscious mental activity. Such categories as cause and effect and that the whole is greater than its parts are included here. In terms of the earlier terminology of *capacity innatism* or *content innatism*, Turretin clearly affirms *capacity innatism*.[139] It also seems possible that he affirms the

---

the term should be seen as applicable to the word "theology" and not to "false" as the closing comment in parentheses reveals.

136. Turretin, *Institutes*, 1.2.7, notes that natural revelation was "exquisite in Adam before his fall, but is highly disordered in corrupt man." Turretin, *Institutes*, 1.8–14, has an enlightening discussion of the relationship of faith and reason. Interestingly, right reason for Turretin is reason that is "sound and healed by grace" (*Institutes* 1.9.14). Reason as such can be considered in the abstract (its ideal form) and concrete. Several times in passing in his exposition Turretin makes it clear that right reason is regenerate reason and not some common neutral reason. This would cohere with the thesis of Paul Kjoss Helseth in *"Right Reason" and the Princeton Mind* (Phillipsburg, NJ: P&R, 2010) that the concept of right reason is redeemed reason. We will return to this subject in the fourth chapter.

137. Turretin, *Institutes*, 1.3.6.

138. Turretin, *Institutes*, 1.3.2, 5, 6.

139. Turretin, *Institutes*, 1.3.2. "The question is not whether natural theology (which is such by act as soon as a man is born, as the act of life in one living or of sense in one perceiving as soon as he breathes) may be granted. For it is certain that no actual knowledge is born with us and that, in this respect, man is like a smooth tablet (*tabulae rasae*). Rather, the question is whether such can be granted at least with regard to principle and potency; or whether such a natural faculty implanted in man may be granted as will put forth its strength of its own accord, and spontaneously in all adults endowed with reason, which embraces not only the capability of understanding, but also the first principles of knowledge from which conclusions both theoretical and practical are deduced (which we maintain)." This appears to be a clear affirmation of *capacity innatism* which edges ever so closely to *content innatism* without quite affirming it.

stronger claim of *content innatism* in that all men know God as much as they can from the natural revelation which he stamps upon his creation.[140]

Natural revelation is limited in its scope. It reveals that there is a God and it reveals some information about who God is, but in a post fall world, it is insufficient. Natural revelation may reveal to us that there is a great and awesome God to whom we owe absolute obedience and worship and whom we have offended, but it offers no succor to the guilty and polluted conscience.[141] Turretin points out that natural revelation reveals nothing about God's essentially triune nature, nor does it reveal the gospel whatsoever and natural revelation does not bring man to his purposed end. Man was meant to have fellowship with God and natural revelation and the consequent natural theology that arises from reflection does not lead man to the heavenly sight of God. A supernatural revelation is needed for that.

As already noted, Turretin offers the suggestion that God's verbal communication with Adam and Eve in the Garden of Eden was a form of special or supernatural revelation. But the onus of concern with supernatural revelation is redemption. The principle of sound theology (that is, knowledge of God) is revelation. Scripture reveals the essentially triune nature of God and the plan of redemption that culminates in the person and work of Jesus Christ and the pouring forth of the Holy Spirit on the church. To understand the word of God aright requires faith. The light of nature has limited and necessary usefulness, but faith is required to properly assimilate supernatural revelation. And so Turretin would be in agreement with the notion of the internal witness of the Holy Spirit as the *principium cognoscendi internum*. Turretin offers a thorough treatment of the relation of faith and reason and it is clear that while revelation may be supra rational, it is not anti rational. In Turretin's words, grace corrects nature, it does not

---

140. We say this because in *Institutes* 1.3.5 Turretin notes that natural law is "written upon each one's conscience." This implies actual knowledge, not simply the mere possibility. Later in 1.3.6 he says, "God has given to man both an innate and acquired knowledge." This may be a less than precise way of referring to first principles of knowledge (capacity innatism), but it seems Turretin skates fairly close the edge of affirming actual *innate* knowledge. If capacity innatism is correct, then it would seem that the precise way to describe the mechanics of natural theology would be to say that the first principles are innate but that the knowledge derived from the first principles being brought to bear on data is acquired. In other words, what is innate is not knowledge per se. Further, in 1.3.11, Turretin notes, "The mind of man is a *tabula rasa* not absolutely, but relatively as to discursion and dianoetical knowledge (which is acquired necessarily by inferring one thing from another); but not as to apprehensive and intuitive knowledge." It is this distinction between discursive and dianoetical knowledge on the one hand and apprehensive and intuitive knowledge on the other that is key to unlocking this puzzle.

141. Turretin, *Institutes*, 1.4.1–23.

destroy it.[142] However Turretin is equally adamant that reason as such is not the measure of revelation.

Man's knowledge of God from nature and Scripture is a dependent creaturely knowledge and remains that throughout the Christian pilgrimage and even into eternity in the new heavens and the new earth. In heaven the saints will see God and will have close fellowship with him. But the saints will never attain to the same knowledge or kind of knowledge that God has. Turretin reflects his Augustinian heritage as he notes that man will know and love God without the hindrances of sin which have beset man on earth.

Francis Turretin allows a limited place for natural theology, but note his careful distinction between true and false theology. There is no sense that natural theology provides a neutral foundation or pre-dogmatic basis on which a Christian theology can be built. Legitimate natural theology is developed by the regenerate saint and is included in an exposition of the full scope of God's revelation. Arguments can be offered for the existence of God, but these are offered within the context of a Christian theology and not outside of and leading into it.[143] There is no such thing as a neutral reason either. Reason can be considered in the abstract (i.e., ideal state) or in the concrete. But reason is either unregenerate reason or right reason.

Having looked at four major figures in the history of Christian thought on man's knowledge of God, we can now turn back for a brief consideration of Edwards.

Edwards and Man's Knowledge of God and His Apologetic

It may be worthwhile to remind ourselves what we have already had occasion to note before. Jonathan Edwards predates the age of apologetic self-consciousness and did not produce an apologetic manual.[144] We gain insight into his practice of apologetics by examining specific attempts to wrestle with unbelief or less consistent belief. We also gain insight into his apolo-

---

142. Turretin, *Institutes*, 1.9.

143. Turretin, *Institutes*, 3.1.2–5. Turretin offers arguments for the existence of God building off the intuitive knowledge which all men possess by virtue of its implantation by God.

144. Given this reality, the best one can say about Gerstner's argument that Edwards was a classical apologist is that *he may have happened to have been one*. If Edwards was a classical apologist in the Gerstnerian sense, it could be (1) a historical accident. That is, Edwards is a classical apologist because he predates apologetic self-consciousness and so saw no better option and was a child of his times. Or, and this is more likely, (2) Edwards reflects some aspects of classical apologetic method and also reflects elements that do not fit the mold.

getic by looking at how he understands man as made in the image of God. We learn, too, by considering his views of man's natural and supernatural knowledge of God.

Already this far into our study we have reason to believe that Edwards understood that man possessed both natural and supernatural knowledge of God by virtue of being created in the image of God. To image God man would need to know his God.

> And his soul was in a very perfect state, the faculties of it in full strength, not broken, impaired, and weakened and ruined, as they are now. The soul of man with regard to quickness and clearness of its faculties was then like the heavenly intelligences-as a flame of fire. The natural image of God that consists in reason and understanding was then complete. And man then had excellent endowments. His mind shone with the perfect spiritual image of God, being without any defect in its holiness and righteousness, or any spot or wrinkle to mar its spiritual beauty. God had put his own beauty upon it; it shone with the communication of his glory. And man enjoyed uninterrupted spiritual peace and joy that hence arose. His mind was full of spiritual light and peace as the atmosphere in a cool and calm day.[145]

Man also knows God because the world in which he lives is suffused with revelation from God about his greatness, goodness, righteousness, and holiness. God has also, since the fall, spoken into the world he created by giving redemptive verbal or special revelation. But Edwards brings more to the table. Beyond the standard Reformed affirmation of natural and special revelation, Edwards affirmed a natural typology through which God communicated to those with eyes to see. Additionally, Edwards held to and used the *prisca theologia* idea.

What does all this mean? First, there is no sense in which man exists in a vacuum. It is not as though man has to reason his way to God from the ground up with no materials but his own reason from which to build.[146] Edwards's comments about the failure of deism to prove the thesis that God intended for human reason to be a sufficient vehicle for knowing him ought to give the lie to any idea that Edwards was a bald autonomous rationalist.

> But it is exceeding apparent that, without a revelation, mankind must be forever in the most woeful doubt with respect to these

---

145. Edwards, "East of Eden," *WJE*/17, 333–4.

146. This would be the problem of John Gertsner and *capacity innatism* mentioned earlier in that there is no sensus divinitatis but rather all natural knowledge of God is inferred from creation through ratiocinative processes.

things, and not only these things, but if they are not led by revelation and divine teaching into a right way of using their reason, in arguing from effects to causes, etc., they would forever remain in the most woeful doubt and uncertainty concerning the nature and very being of God.[147]

This is not to say that man does not use his reason in seeking to know and understand his God. But there is a difference between using reason as a medium through which revelation may come to a man and he therefore possesses knowledge and reason serving as a source or origin of divine knowledge. While it is true that Edwards thought that arguments for God's existence were useful, these very arguments themselves built upon and developed out of revelation in nature and the constitution of the world and man's own structure as God created them.[148] Most likely, Jonathan Edwards's use of theistic arguments reflect an understanding of man's natural knowledge of God close to those explicated by Francis Turretin.[149] That is, man's natural knowledge of God is *both* intuitive and discursive. Arguments for the existence of God build off the intuitive knowledge of God (Calvin's *sensus*), unpacking what is implicit in the intuitive knowledge. Edwards, like Turretin, walks a razor's edge with regard to the *capacity/content innatism* discussion. This can be said. No man lacks natural knowledge of God. But no one is saved by possession of this knowledge.

Second, God's revelation in nature (the "light of nature") was never redemptive in the sense that knowledge derived from it alone was sufficient for one's salvation. The same could be said about the *prisca theologia*. This ancient, primitive knowledge of God's early special revelation given to our first parents and passed down from generation to generation was corrupted along the way and so may have accounted for similarities between Christianity and other faiths and philosophies and it may have accounted for how these other worldviews contained elements of truth, but none of these were salvific.[150] At best they prepared the ground (*praeparatio evangelicae*) for

147. Edwards, Miscellanies 1297, *WJE*/23, 240.

148. See the discussion above of how Turretin used arguments for God's existence. Turretin attempted to use theistic arguments to develop *dianoetical* or discursive knowledge of God that was derived from intuitive knowledge. Michael Sudduth's *The Reformed Objection to Natural Theology* details this matter at length.

149. This would distinguish Edwards' use of theistic arguments from John Gerstner's classical method in which the arguments *do serve* as a pre-dogmatic foundation for an explicitly Christian superstructure. God, argues Gerstner, must be proved to exist philosophically before it can be determined that he has communicated with his creation.

150. The *prisca theologica* and types are not redemptive in themselves because redemptive knowledge is spiritual knowledge. In his sermon "A Spiritual Understanding

the gospel. Additionally, the types God had built into nature and history, and which pointed to Christ and the church, were not accessible to the unregenerate eye.

Not even special revelation was redemptive without the ministry of the Holy Spirit. That is, mere exposure to the Bible and a knowledge of its contents were not sufficient to bring someone to faith in Christ. Knowledge of Scripture and its center in Christ was necessary but not sufficient for conversion. Edwards himself said that a man could be an accomplished theologian and know all the intricacies of doctrine without loving God and the things of God.[151] Here we see the significance of Edwards's distinction between speculative and spiritual understanding. As previously noted, speculative knowledge of Scripture and the gospel was needed to bring a man to salvation, but it was the Holy Spirit who enabled fallen man to love these truths.[152] The work of the Holy Spirit did not convey new doctrine but it changed a man's disposition or orientation to the doctrine already learned. Whereas the unregenerate theologian might be able to recount the details of a theological question, the saint could appreciate the spiritual significance of the question and its relation to God. "There is a distinction to be made between a mere notional understanding, wherein the mind only beholds things in the exercise of a speculative faculty; and the sense of the heart, wherein the mind don't only speculate and behold, but relishes and feels."[153] The doctrine under consideration would not just inhabit the understanding but would attract approval and love. To be more accurate, the unbeliever did

---

of Divine Things Denied to the Unregenerate," Edwards spelled out his distinction between the common and saving operations of the Holy Spirit, "natural men may have that knowledge which may have some influence on their lives. Their conscience thereby has the greater advantage, for although their understandings are not savingly enlightened, yet their consciences are enlightened: for it's impossible but that a man that knows and is versed in the study of divinity, should know his duty better, and know better what is sin," WJE/14,70–96. Regarding types in particular, Edwards noted that types are "dark resemblences; though there be a resemblance, yet the image is accompanied with darkness, or hiding of the light. The light is beyond the substance," Notes on Scripture. 288, WJE/15, 247–48. See Douglas A. Sweeney's unpublished lecture, "Jonathan Edwards and the World Religions: A Response to Gerald McDermott," 1–8.

151. See the previous note.

152. There is an error which needs to be clearly avoided. Speculative knowledge is not merely supplemented by a change of attitude when it transitions to spiritual knowledge. On the contrary, speculative knowledge is taken up and *corrected* and the objects of spiritual knowledge (God and the things of God) are seen for what they *truly* and *rightly* are, namely glorious and beautiful and lovel. In other words, the transition from speculative to spiritual knowledge does make God and the things of God lovely, beautiful, and glorious. God and the things of God were that before the transition. But now man sees God and the things of God for what they really and truly just are.

153. Edwards, *Religious Affections*, WJE/2, 272.

not merely possess speculative knowledge of God and the things of God, he also possessed a *distaste* or repulsion for God and his Word. It was not the mere absence of vigorous affections. It was the presence of malevolent affections with the speculative knowledge. While speculative knowledge was necessary for salvation it was not decisive. The deciding factor was the change of heart (which includes what is traditionally called the mind).

Apologetics, like preaching and teaching, was therefore a means to an end and not an end in itself. False motives and erroneous ideas do need to be corrected. But it was only as the Holy Spirit took up these correctives and changed the heart and mind of an individual with regard to his relationship to God and these truths that regeneration would ever occur. In other words, the Holy Spirit would work internally on the unregenerate heart using what had been revealed in the Word or taught in a lesson or preached in a sermon.

In all this there is no sense in which special revelation is subservient to natural revelation or that natural knowledge of God was sufficient to save an individual. Natural revelation does not even serve as a sufficient basis for man's relationship to God. As Edwards contended, everywhere where men attempted to formulate a natural theology it always happened in a land where the gospel had already been proclaimed and was subsiding from memory. In other words, the deists could not construct their natural theology or practice their natural religion without borrowing from Christianity.

No man ever came to faith in Christ without knowledge of Christ drawn either directly from the Scriptures or indirectly from them through the testimony of the church in preaching or in writing or by personal witness. In contrast to some Evangelical theologians in this day, Edwards never thought the bits and pieces of revelational truth that unbelievers might possess ever did them any good if it was not followed up with clear exposure to Scripture and the ministry of the Holy Spirit. And Edwards did not confuse the common operations of the Holy Spirit with his saving work. These were key distinctions in Edwards's thought.[154]

This brings us to a consideration of how the human heart works in both the fall and in regeneration. It is to that consideration that we now turn in the next chapter.

---

154. This needs to be said because scholars such as Gerald McDermott, Michael McClymond, and Amos Yong teach otherwise. In these writers, the work of the Holy Spirit is decoupled from the work of Christ and his Word (they themselves advocate this decoupling and seek to find aporias in Edwards to allow for it). Wherever the Spirit is at work it must be a redemptive work. See Edwards' Miscellanies 819, *WJE/18*, 530–31, for Edwards' view that coming to faith in Christ (or as Edwards would put it, a "closing with" or "adhering to" Christ) is necessary for salvation.

4

The Relation of Intellect and Will: A Unity

Introduction

THUS FAR THIS STUDY has sought to examine Jonathan Edwards's theological anthropology and apologetic to ascertain whether John Gerstner's view that Jonathan Edwards was a classical apologist *simpliciter* is accurate. Edwards's view of man as created in the image of God has been considered as well as his views of natural and special revelation. Now the study will turn to an examination of his views on the various powers of the human soul. John Gerstner, has essentially argued that Jonathan Edwards held to a form of faculty psychology

> The mind comes first and the heart second. "Such is the nature of man, that no object can come at the heart but through the door of the understanding: and there can be no spiritual knowledge of that of which there is not first a rational knowledge." . . . [T]he fallen heart of man certainly does not follow the enlightened dictates of the understanding. If the heart is good it will respond favorably to the truth. If the heart is evil it will respond unfavorably to the truth.[1]

---

1. John Gerstner, *The Rational Biblical Theology of Jonathan Edwards* (Powhatan, VA & Orlando, FL: Berea Publications & Ligonier Ministries, 1992), 2:267. Without getting ahead of ourselves, Gerstner's note of Edwards' recognition of an order or *taxis* in the internal workings of the human soul is not *by itself* problematic. Also, inasmuch as this citation reflects an Augustinian *primacy of orientation* it is also correct. However, as will be seen below, the distinction between mind and heart or the equation of them with the intellect and will is questionable. Gerstner cites a line from Edwards' sermon "The Importance and Advantage of a Thorough Knowledge of Divine Truth," which can be found in *The Works of Jonathan Edwards/Vol. 22: Sermons and Discourses,*

Further, in his co-authored *Classical Apologetics*, Gerstner goes so far as to say that the noetic effects of sin are "indirect."[2] Such an assertion makes the most sense in the context of a hierarchical, reified faculty psychology. This chapter will seek to examine Edwards's views on the nature of the human soul. It will be shown that, contrary to Gerstner, Edwards in fact embraced what has been called "the unitary operations of the human soul."[3] Edwards moved away from the stratified prioritization of the will to the intellect or of the intellect to the will which we find in much of the theological anthropology of Edwards's day and in his tradition.

This chapter will begin (1) with a brief description of John Gerstner's view of the primacy or priority of the intellect, (2) will continue with an examination Edwards's discussion of the relationship of the will to the intellect in the historical context of the Great Awakening. Here it will be seen that in trying to walk a fine line between rationalism and enthusiasm, Edwards argued for distinctions regarding the powers of the human soul without separation. Further, (3) consideration will be given to the three schools of thought within the Christian tradition: the Thomistic-intellectualist, Scholastic-voluntarist, and the Augustinian-voluntarist schools and their exemplars in order to ascertain where Edwards fits in this scheme.[4] Ex-

---

1739–1742 (Harry S. Stout, Nathan O. Hatch, with Kyle P. Farley, eds. New Haven, CT: Yale University Press, 2003), 88–89.

2. R. C. Sproul, John Gerstner, and Arthur Lindsley, *Classical Apologetics: A Rational Defense of the Christian Faith and a Critique of Presuppositional Apologetics* (Grand Rapids, MI: Zondervan/Academie Books, 1984), 243–44. Actually, the authors do not indicate who has written which chapters or segments of the book. Given this fact, whenever reference is made to Gerstner as the author of this book it should be kept in mind that this is a co-authored publication. Gerstner specifically notes, "Something is wrong with the heart-not the mind-which needs the nonrational, super-rational revelation of divine majesty." "Jonathan Edwards," it is said, "taught total depravity totally. He was also very sensitive to the way that depravity of the heart always tries to make the mind its flunky. In spite of this indirect noetic influence of sin, the mind as an instrument survives and is utterly indispensible . . . " Conclusively, it is maintained that "classic Reformed orthodoxy saw the noetic influence of sin not as direct through a totally depraved mind, but as *indirect* through a totally depraved heart." For a thorough critique of this idea of an indirect noetic influence of sin, see K. Scott Oliphint, "Jonathan Edwards: Reformed Apologist," *WTJ* 57/1 (Spring 1995): 165–86. Interestingly, Charles Hart in his *Thomistic Metaphysics: An Inquiry into the Act of Existing* (Englewood Cliffs, NJ: Prentice-Hall, 1959), 378–9, also argues for an indirect noetic influence of sin based upon the theory of sin as privation.

3. It is not clear who first coined the expression "unitary operations of the human soul." Both Paul Helseth and this writer came to the expression independently of one another and yet our understanding of the term is virtually synonymous.

4. This tri-fold scheme comes from Norman Fiering's *Jonathan Edwards' Moral Thought and Its British Context* (Chapel Hill, NC: University of North Carolina Press, 1981), 262–71.

amination of the concept of "right reason" will be appropriate at this point as well. The traditional reading of the concept of "right reason" would seem to cohere with an intellectualist faculty psychology. However, recent scholarship has called into question the reigning assessment of "right reason" and has significant bearing on this study.[5] Additionally, (4) this study will involve itself in a critical evaluation of not only Gerstner's assessment of Edwards but also Alvin Plantinga's consideration of the relationship of the intellect to the will in his *Warranted Christian Belief*.[6] Plantinga offers one of the best considerations of Edwards on this subject. The results of this critical interaction with Plantinga will allow the reader properly to assess Gerstner's assertion about the "indirect" nature of total depravity according to the mind of Jonathan Edwards. Finally, (5) this chapter will conclude with how Edwards's concern with the unified operations of the human soul related to his apologetic efforts.

Gerstner on "Indirect" Total Depravity

In 1984 John Gerstner coauthored *Classical Apologetics* which was simultaneously a critique of the presuppositional apologetics of Cornelius Van Til and an affirmation and exposition of what the authors classified as the classical method of defending the Christian faith.[7] Jonathan Edwards is mentioned throughout the volume as illustrative of the classical tradition. However it is Gerstner's affirmation of the *primacy* or *priority of the intellect* that is of concern at this point.

> ... Primacy of the intellect refers not to a *priority of excellence* but to a *priority of order*. Primacy of intellect means that we must think about God before we can actually know him. Primacy of intellect does not mean that the intellect is of a higher order or excellence than the God whom we discover by means of it. This would be a blasphemous notion.[8]

---

5   Specifically, the work of Paul Helseth has been ground-breaking in this area. See his *"Right Reason" and the Princeton Mind: An Unorthodox Proposal* (Philippsburg, NJ: P&R Publishing, 2010).

6. Alvin Plantinga, *Warrented Christian Belief* (New York: Oxford University Press, 2000). Plantinga offers one of the most fascinating discussions of the relationship of the intellect and will in contemporary literature. And he is wise to draw upon the insights of Edwards.

7. Sproul, Gerstner, and Lindsley, *Classical Apologetics*.

8. Sproul, Gerstner, and Lindsley, *Classical Apologetics*, 227. Ordinarily one would take an author at his word when he denies priority of excellence. However, further discussion below will show that more than priority of order is involved in Gerstner's

What does it mean to say that the intellect has priority in the operations of the human soul? Later in this chapter different schools of thought within the Christian tradition will be examined in order to help us understand where Jonathan Edwards fits in the discussion. For now this can be said: the primacy of the intellect view holds that the intellect rules or governs the other faculties or powers (will and emotions) of the human soul in a hierarchically valued manner. There are various ways to understand this so it would be well to attend to what Gerstner says.

At the outset Gerstner states that he is arguing for a *chronological priority* of the intellect. That is, the will cannot act blindly. In order for the will to either approve or reject something, *that something* must be held as an object in the mind for consideration. And so the intellect has priority over the will in this sense at least. This chronological view of the priority of the intellect is not particularly controversial. Evidence can be offered from the pen of Jonathan Edwards affirming just such a chronological priority.

> So the sacraments of the gospel can have proper effect no other way, than by conveying some knowledge. They represent certain things by visible signs. And what is the end of signs, but to convey some knowledge of the things signified? Such is the nature of man, that nothing can come at the heart but through the door of the understanding: and there can be no spiritual knowledge of that which there is not first a rational knowledge. It is impossible that anyone should see the truth or excellency of any doctrine of the gospel, who knows not what that doctrine is. A man cannot see the excellency and love of Christ in doing such and such for sinners, unless his understanding be first informed how those things were done. He cannot have a taste of the sweetness and divine excellency of such and such things contained in divinity, unless he first have a notion that there are such and such things.[9]

---

defense of the primacy of the intellect. Additionally, priority of the intellect relates the intellect to the will in this discussion and not the human intellect to the divine intellect. Gerstner is correct to note that suggesting that the human intellect is greater than the God who made it would be blasphemy.

9. Edwards, *WJE/22*, 88–89. Regarding chronological priority of faculties within the human soul, Cornelius Van Til also affirms such a view in his *Introduction to Systematic Theology* (William Edgar, ed. Phillipsburg, NJ: Presbyterian &Reformed Publishing, 1974), 34–36, where Van Til compares the relation of the intellect, will, and emotions to the relations of the three persons of the Triune Godhead. Just as there can be said to be ontological equality or parity between the Father, Son, and Spirit but economic subordination of the Son to the Father for the redemption of the lost, so there is an equality or parity between the intellect, will, and emotions but an economic subordination of the will to the intellect. It will be argued below that something like Van Til's economic

There seem to be two options about this: either the will is "informed" by the intellect and so is attracted to or repulsed by the intellect's object or the two operate concurrently. B. B. Warfield has helpfully reminded us that when a person comes to faith in Christ, that faith must have content on which to work. According to Protestant orthodoxy, it is not the case that a person is regenerated and acquiesces to the gospel without having been previously exposed to information about the gospel. The use of the word "previously" does not have to be pressed too hard. It is possible that upon the first presentation of the message of the gospel that the Holy Spirit sovereignly works his secret sweet energy and both reveals knowledge of the gospel to the intellect and moves the will to love and embrace it. More often than not, however, the message of the gospel is sewn over time in a series of occurrences and the Holy Spirit regenerates a man or woman using information previously received. Whether the information is received by the intellect and later the Holy Spirit causes a person to love and embrace it or the Holy Spirit works with the proclamation of the Word and at the time of the proclamation causes a person to embrace the gospel, the will does not respond blindly. Nor does the Holy Spirit normally give both content to the intellect and cause the will to be drawn to that content at one and the same time without the use of human instrumentality.

Where Gerstner and his colleagues may run into trouble is by valuing the intellect above the will as if both were not the creation of an all wise and all loving God. Gerstner seems to operate with a hierarchical faculty psychology that Edwards himself was moving away from as he sought to explain and defend the Great Awakening in his day. This hierarchical view of the powers of the human soul comes to the surface in the idea of the indirect nature of the noetic effects of sin. What does it mean to say that the effects of sin on the intellect are "indirect"?[10] It would appear that there is more than chronological priority involved in Gerstner's primacy of the intellect. The idea of indirect noetic effects of sin suggests that the intellect is untouched, in and of itself, by the fall, but is infected by means of a corrupt will. The intellect functions quite normally subsequent to the fall, as it was created to govern the rest of the faculties, but is overpowered by the will acting out of its proper sphere.

While it cannot be demonstrated conclusively, this view looks quite like a view criticized by Archibald Alexander, founding professor at Princeton Theological Seminary, back in the mid 19th century. Alexander, arguing

---

subordination view may be at work in Edwards' thought as well.

10. K. Scott Oliphint and Paul Kjoss Helseth have both addressed the idea of indirect noetic effects of sin. For Oliphint, see "Edwards: Reformed Apologist," 180 and for Helseth, see *"Right Reason" and the Princeton Mind*, 18.

for the unified operations of the human soul, faulted the view which held that the intellect was a natural faculty and the will a moral faculty and so only the will was infected by the fall.

> If men are unaffected with the truth known, it must be because they do not know it aright...Did any man ever see an object to be lovely and not feel an emotion corresponding with that quality? And what unconverted man ever beheld in Christ, as represented in Scripture, the beauty and glory of God? Hence that doctrine is not true which confines depravity or holiness to the will, and which considers the understanding as a natural and the will as a moral faculty. The soul is not depraved or holy by departments; the disease affects it, as a soul; and of course all faculties employed in moral exercises must partake of their moral qualities.[11]

The idea that the noetic effects of sin are indirect stems from a legitimate concern, however faulty the formulation may ultimately be. The fall has not utterly destroyed the intellect, anymore than it has the will. And there is a tendency to confuse postmodern skepticism with the Christian doctrine of the noetic effects of sin. The whole soul of man is fallen, intellect and will (and emotions if these are distinguished from the will), but the intellect is still functional in some sense. However, to place the powers of the soul in a hierarchy is unnecessary.

The fall infected every power or faculty of the human soul. One defect of a hierarchical faculty psychology is tendency to treat each power as a self-contained agent. The British philosopher John Locke commented on this tendency

> These powers of the mind, viz. of perceiving and of preferring, are usually called by another name. And the ordinary way of speaking is, that the understanding and will are two faculties of the mind; a word proper enough, if it be used, as all words should be, so as not to breed any confusion in men's thoughts, by being supposed (as I suspect it has been) to stand for some real beings in the soul that performed these actions of understanding and volition. For when we say the will is the commanding and superior faculty in the soul; that it is or is not free; that it determines the inferior faculties; that it follows the dictates of the understanding, &c.,-though these and the like expressions, by those that carefully attend to their own ideas, and conduct

---

11. Archibald Alexander, *Thoughts on Religious Experience* (Carlisle, PA: Banner of Truth Trust, 1989), 63. This is cited in Helseth, *"Right Reason" and the Princeton Mind*, 31–32.

> their thoughts more by the evidence of things than the sound of words, may be understood in a clear and distinct sense-yet I suspect, I say, that this way of speaking of faculties has misled many into a confused notion of so many distinct agents in us, which had their several provinces and authorities, and did command, obey, and perform several actions, as so many distinct beings; which has been no small occasion of wrangling, obscurity, and uncertainty, in questions related to them.[12]

It is true that the best treatments of faculty psychology in the Scholastic tradition did not deem the faculties to be reified, but the tendency exists all the same. It is important that the positive point be stressed. It is a specific unified individual person that thinks, wills, and feels. There are not three persons-in-miniature vying for control internally in the mind of a man or woman. It is either a regenerate man or an unregenerate man who thinks, wills, or feels as he does. Gerstner and his colleagues would have been better served in this discussion, had they considered, among other things, the historical context in which Jonathan Edwards formulated his mature understanding of the unified operations of the human soul.

Edwards on the Intellect and Will in the Great Awakening

In order properly to understand Edwards at this point, it is essential that we grasp his own historical context for it is here that we will clearly see the contours of his views as they are compared and contrasted with those of his theological opponents. The social context into which Edwards spoke was, of course, the age of the Great Awakening. But what was it about the Great Awakening that could be of interest to our discussion? It is the fact that the nature of the human soul and all its various powers was at the heart of many of the debates of that era. The basic question was whether the Great Awakening in its day was a legitimate work of God or the work of excited passions or (worse still), the work of the Devil. Jonathan Edwards, in endeavoring to defend the awakenings that occurred in his parish in Northampton and across the colonies, attempted to plow a middle row between two extremes (the "two great armies") of rationalism on the one hand and unbridled enthusiasm on the other. What this meant was that he challenged the regnant faculty psychology of his day in order to pioneer a path toward a better understanding of the human personality or soul or mind. In other words, Edwards was not conducting an abstract examination of the human soul.

---

12. John Locke, *An Essay Concerning Human Understanding* (Alexander Campbell Fraser, ed. New York: Barnes & Noble Books, 1689 [2004]), II.21.6 (178).

He was endeavoring to deal with two extremes in the Awakening that he deemed problematic.[13] Jonathan Edwards was trying to develop an approach to the interaction of the various powers of the soul which emphasized their harmonious or unified operations. He neither confused nor conflated the intellect and the will, nor hermetically compartmentalized them.[14] As we have already seen with regard to true religious affections, the intellect and will worked together. The human soul comprised a "dispositional complex." Edwards was dealing with rationalists like Charles Chauncy on the one hand and enthusiasts like James Davenport on the other. In other words, true religion comprised neither light without heat or heat without light.[15]

It has already been mentioned that Edwards was trying to break new ground, as it were, by fashioning a new way to understand the human soul wherein he could avoid the faculty psychology he had inherited. What was so bad about the faculty psychology after all? The kind of faculty psychology that Chauncy defended (in support of rationalism and his criticism of the Great Awakening) posited a hierarchical chain or gradation of the faculties in which the most valued (reason) was at the top of the hierarchy and those less valued (such as the emotions) were at the bottom. The reason controlled the will and the passions and any effort to appeal to the will by bypassing the reason was deemed wrong.[16] For Chauncy, the pastors of the awakening were preaching so as to appeal merely to the emotions while skirting the intellect.

---

13. See Stephen J. Stein, introduction to Conrad Cherry's *The Theology of Jonathan Edwards: A Reappraisal* (Bloomington & Indianapolis, IN: Indiana University Press, 1966 [1990]), xii. These extremes would be rationalism and emotionalism.

14. Stein, introduction, *Theology of Jonathan Edwards*, xii.

15. John Smith tells us, "The first point to be stressed is that Edwards, for all his ability to draw clear distinctions, nevertheless struggled to preserve the unity and integrity of the self and to avoid compartmentalizing the human functions and powers. This means that despite his rather sharp distinction between the understanding, affections, and will, we must not overlook the extent to which these initial distinctions are overridden in the course of the argument. The entire discussion shows a moving back and forth between analysis and synthesis; clarity demands distinctions within the self and between its powers, but the integrity of the self requires that its faculties or capacities be related to each other so as to preserve unity." Introduction, *The Works of Jonathan Edwards: Vol. 2/Religious Affections* (John E. Smith, ed. New Haven, CT: Yale University Press, 1959), 11–12.

16. Chauncy here begs the question. A concern for the affections, Edwards would aver, is not a "bypassing" of the reason, something Edwards himself would disapprove. Another fascinating treatment of the affections can be found in Kelly M. Kapic's study of Puritan theologian John Owen's "anthroposensitivity" in *Communion with God: The Divine and the Human in the Theology of John Owen* (Grand Rapids, MI: Baker Academic, 2007), especially 35–66. This is not to say that Owen would agree with Edwards or the arguments set forth here. However, Kapic notes that while Owen relied upon the psychological insights of Aristotle, the Aristotelian input was greatly modified by

> You must not lay too great stress upon the *workings* of your *passions* and *affections*. These will be excited, in a less or greater degree, in the business of religion: And 'tis proper they shou'd. The passions, when suitably move'd, tend mightily to awaken *reasonable powers*, and put them upon a lively and vigorous exercise. And this is their proper use: And when address'd to, and excited to this purpose, they may be of good service: whereas we shall mistake the right use of the passions, if we place our religion only or chiefly, in the *heat* and *fervor* of them.[17]

According to Chauncy, true religion consisted in the supremacy of reason. On the other hand, enthusiasts such as James Davenport saw true religion as residing in the passions apart from the use of reason.[18] Edwards had to respond to both groups by fashioning a new understanding of the human soul all the while using language that seemed more at home in the context of traditional faculty psychology.

Is faculty psychology problematic because it makes distinctions between the intellect and the will? Or is it problematic because it prizes one faculty or power or capacity over another? Didn't Edwards himself make distinctions among the various powers of the human soul? Yes, he did. This is partly because distinctions are not problematic in themselves and because distinguishing language is hard to avoid if we are going to talk meaningfully about the soul or *anything whatsoever*. That is, to make distinctions is not necessarily to make one part of a distinction more significant than another. To recognize difference in function is not to value one function over another. We make a distinction between our right leg and our left, but to ask which is more important seems either mistaken or silly. And to examine something closely involves the act of making distinctions. *This* thing is different from *that* thing. To say that *A* is different from *B* is not the same thing as to say that *A* is more important than *B*. To make distinctions is legitimate and there are legitimate distinctions to be made regarding the powers of the soul. Thinking and willing are different kinds of powers, although by no means are they to be separated. Nor is it possible to avoid this kind of language if we are going to talk specifically about the soul doing *this*

Owen's biblical commitment to the unified human nature and total depravity.

17. This assessment is the point that is challenged by Edwards with his definition of the affections involving both the understanding and the will. See more fully Chauncy's sermon "Enthusiasm Discovered and Caution'd" in Alan Heimert and Perry Miller's *The Great Awakening: Documents Illustrating the Crisis and Its Consequences* (Indianapolis, IN: The Bobbs-Merrill Company, 1967), 228–256. This citation is from 248.

18. See Davenport's "Confession and Retractions," Heimert and Miller, *Great Awakening*, 257–262. See especially 260 where Davenport addresses impressions or impulses.

or doing *that*. So Edwards had to speak, so it seems, in terms of the relations of the intellect and the will, even if he didn't conceive of them in terms of a hierarchical faculty psychology. The issue for Edwards was not distinction, but the problem of separation and valuation. The powers of the soul worked together and it was one soul, one dispositional complex, one self, who did these different things.

Edwards's View in the Context of the Christian Tradition

As we endeavor to understand Jonathan Edwards's notion of the unified operations of the human soul, it might be helpful to consider various ways in which the intellect and will are understood to relate to one another.[19] What is discussed here is not intended to be exhaustive, but rather suggestive only. Putting the matter as simply as possible, there are two general ways to understand the relationship between the intellect and will, together with some significant variation within these two broad perspectives. These two categories are *intellectualism* and *voluntarism*.

Intellectualism

The first way to understand the relationship between the intellect and will is "intellectualism." One way to differentiate within this perspective is to talk in terms of either an *absolute* or a *functional* intellectualism. In absolute intellectualism the intellect or reason is the *governing* faculty or power of the

---

19. Norm Fiering illustrates the complexity of the problem by referring to a 1703 *Athenian Oracle* article entitled "How Does the Understanding Move the Will?" in which eight different variations are discussed. See his *Jonathan Edwards' Moral Thought*, 267. See also Allen Guelzo's *Edwards on the Will* (Middletown, CT: Wesleyan University Press, 1989); John Smith's introduction to Edwards' *Religious Affections* in *WJE/2*, 1–83; Conrad Cherry, *The Theology of Jonathan Edwards*, Heimert and Miller's *The Great Awakening: Documents Illustrating the Crisis and Its Consequences*; Daniel Walker Howe, *Making the American Self: Jonathan Edwards to Abraham Lincoln* (New York: Oxford University Press, 2009); James Hoopes, *Consciousness in New England: From Puritanism and Ideas to Psychoanalysis and Semiotic* (Baltimore, MD: Johns Hopkins Press, 1989) and his "Calvinism and Consciousness From Edwards to Beecher," in *Jonathan Edwards and the American Experience* (Edited by Nathan Hatch and Harry Stout. New York: Oxford University Press, 1988), 205–25; Allyn Lee Ricketts' *The Primacy of Revelation in the Philosophical Theology of Jonathan Edwards* (PhD diss. Westminster Theological Seminary, 1995); Steven Studebaker, *Jonathan Edwards' Social Augustinian Trinitarianism: A Criticism of and an Alternative to Recent Interpretations* (PhD diss. Marquette University, 2003); Robert Davis Smart, *Jonathan Edwards' Apologetic for the Great Awakening* (Grand Rapids, MI: Reformation Heritage Books, 2011), and the two previously noted articles by K. Scott Oliphint.

human soul and the will is considered blind and is seen as a slave of sorts to the intellect. Historically, this kind of thinking (i.e., where the intellect is given priority over the will) can be seen in what Norman Fiering has labeled "Thomistic-Intellectualism."[20] The Thomistic-Intellectualist school, which has typically been traced back to Thomas Aquinas, held that the will was blind and followed the last dictate or judgment of the "practical intellect."[21] In other words, it is the intellect or judgment that shows the will what is to be accepted or rejected. As such, the will can never be guilty of moral error or corruption.[22] "The will itself is never culpable in the case of moral error, since it only follows the judgment of the intellect. The will as the rational appetite is supposed to govern the lower sensitive appetites, although it may happen that unruly vehement appetites from below will obscure rational judgment and thus influence choice wrongly."[23] Accordingly, without information from the intellect, "the will is not the will, but a confused appetite."[24] To summarize the Thomistic-Intellectualist tradition, we can say with regard to the relationship between the intellect and the will in the human soul, there is a *primacy of the intellect* in the absolute sense since the will is itself blind. The will, then, must be ruled, governed, or directed by the faculty of the understanding.[25] There is, then, an implied denigration of the will and the other powers.

---

20. Fiering, *Edwards' Moral Thought*, 264–67.

21. Fiering, *Edwards' Moral Thought*, 264. Fiering notes, "The intellectualist position was often represented by the dictum that the choice of the will is determined by the last judgment of the practical intellect. For those belonging to this school of thought, the will itself was assumed to be inherently blind, lacking in cognitive function entirely, moving only as an aspect of intellect."

22. Fiering, *Edwards' Moral Thought*, 264.

23. Fiering, *Edwards' Moral Thought*, 264.

24. Fiering, *Edwards' Moral Thought*, 265.

25. See Thomas Aquinas, *Summa Theologica* (Fathers of the English Dominican Province, trans., New York: Benzinger Brothers, 1948), 1a.77.4 (386), "Now the dependence of one power on another can be taken in two ways; according to the order of nature, forasmuch as perfect things are by their nature prior to imperfect things; and according to the order of generation and time; forasmuch as being imperfect, a thing comes to be perfect. Thus according to the first kind of order among the powers, the intellectual powers are prior to the sensitive powers; wherefore they direct them and command them." For an attempt by a later day Thomist to read Thomas as affirming indirect noetic effects of sin, see Hart, *Thomistic Metaphysics: An Inquiry into the Act of Existing*, 378–79. For a thorough treatment of Thomas' view of psychology, see Robert Pasnau, *Thomas Aquinas on Human Nature* (Cambridge: Cambridge University Press, 2002), 143–70 and 330–60.

Another possibility within *this* tradition would be something like *functional* intellectualism.[26] While it is recognized that the will is dependent upon the intellect to provide an object to which it is either attracted or repulsed, the will is neither blind nor enslaved to the intellect. According to functional intellectualism, neither the intellect nor the will has an ontological priority or primacy over the other, but in operations, the intellect provides the idea or object to which the will responds. In many ways the relation between the intellect and will[27] reflects the relationship between the Father, Son, and Holy Spirit in the Trinity. As Calvin so clearly pointed out, while the Father, Son, and Holy Spirit are equally divine as to their being, the Son and the Spirit are functionally subordinated or differentiated in the history of redemption. "Indeed, although the eternity of the Father is also the eternity of the Son and the Spirit, since God could never exist apart from his wisdom and power, and we must not seek in eternity a *before* and *an after*, nevertheless an observance of an order is not meaningless or superfluous, when the Father is thought of as first, then from him the Son, and finally from both the Spirit."[28] Therefore, ontological equality *and* functional or economical subordination or differentiation are both true. Applying these qualifications to the working of the human soul, one could say that the intellect and will (or intellect, will, and emotions) are ontologically equal although each has different functions. Therefore, the priority of the intellect is one of functional order according to this scheme, and not a primacy of importance. Absolute intellectualism, on the other hand, sees the intellect as governing or ruling over the will, and therefore understands sin as affecting the will but not the intellect. In contrast, functional intellectualism, sees sin as affecting both the intellect and the will. And whereas absolute intellectualism sees regeneration as correcting the will, bringing the affections into line (whether as seen as an aspect of the will or as a separate power),

26. See note 9 on Van Til about this.

27. Or the intellect, will, and emotions. Van Til recognized that his Trinitarian insight was still legitimate whether one embraced a bipartite or tripartite division of the powers of the soul. See *IST*, 36.

28. John Calvin, *Institutes of the Christian Religion* Library of Christian Classics (Ford Lewis Battles, trans. John T. McNeill, ed., Louisville, KY: Westminster John Knox Press, 1961), 1.13.18. Calvin, in the next section, goes on to note, "Therefore, when we speak simply of the Son without regard to the Father, we well and properly declare him to be of himself; and for this reason we call him the sole beginning. But when we mark the relation that he has with the Father, we rightly make the Father the beginning of the Son," 1.13.19. See the helpful discussion of the matter in Gerald Bray, *The Doctrine of God* Contours of Christian Doctrine Series (Downers Grove, IL: Inter Varsity Press, 1993), 197–224. Sang Lee also addresses Edwards' approval and expansion of Calvin's views in his introduction to *The Works of Jonathan Edwards: Vol. 21/Writings on the Trinity, Grace, and Faith* (New Haven, CT: Yale University Press, 2003), 20f.

functional intellectualism understands regeneration as correcting both the intellect and the will so that there is a proper functioning of both and that neither will end up governing the other. Ultimately, absolute intellectualism (consciously or unconsciously) denigrates the will while functional intellectualism recognizes a *taxis* to the unified powers of the dispositional complex, but not a *superiority* of one power over another.

Voluntarism

The other broad tradition regarding the relation of the will to the intellect is voluntarism. Norman Fiering, in his book *Jonathan Edwards' Moral Thought and Its British Context*, has divided voluntarism into two streams. The first stream he labels "Scholastic-Voluntarism." The Scholastic-Voluntarists held to a *self-determining* will, not even influenced by the faculty of understanding. It might be said that in comparison to the Thomistic-Intellectualist position, the Scholastic-Voluntarist school advocated a *primacy of the will*.

> The leading competing point of view, the Scholastic-voluntarist, also had its origins in the Middle Ages, if not earlier, and is often associated with the name of Duns Scotus. The Scholastic-Voluntarists maintained that human beings retain a freedom of will beyond the freedom of unconstrained intellectual judgment and action. It is questionable, according to this group, that human freedom could be distinguished from the freedom (or lack of it) of animals if one went along with the intellectualists. For the choices of animals, too, when they are not subject to external constraints, are governed by internal necessities only, rather than mechanical causation. Man's freedom, then, must consist in a liberty to will in opposition to any preceding influences of the soul. Any internal necessities, including those of reason, may be considered restrictions on freedom nearly as much as external compulsions.[29]

The second form of voluntarism delineated for us by Fiering is labeled "Augustinian-Voluntarism." For this school of thought, the will involved the tendency, trajectory, or "orientation" of the whole human personality and

---

29. Fiering, *Edwards' Moral Thought*, 266–67. Fiering cites Humphrey Ditton's comments about the freedom of the will in his *A Discourse Concerning the Resurrection of Jesus Christ* (3rd edition, London, 1722), that "The Resolutions of the understanding, even the most sound and positive ones impose no manner of Necessity on the will: For even the *last Dictate* itself is but one of the Prerequisites to Action, and leaves the Will an intire and perfect Dominion over its own Act; which it may therefore either proceed to exert, or may suspend and forebear, by its own native Liberty . . . ," 90.

not just the "mental faculty" in abstraction.[30] According to this scheme, the will is *oriented* either to God or to self. "Finally, we come to the Augustinian-voluntarists, for whom the concept of will encompassed not just the idea of a mental faculty but also the entire tendency or orientation of the personality. The term 'heart' was used almost interchangeably with that of 'will,' since the meaning of 'will' was enlarged to include the whole soul."[31] Here we find a *primacy of orientation*-in the case of the regenerate it is a primacy of grace whereas for the unregenerate it is a primacy of sin.[32] As I have indicated above, the preceding description of possible ways of understanding the relationship of the intellect to the will is not exhaustive. Hopefully, however, it will provide the reader with an introduction to some of the different ways in which this relation has been conceived.

"Right Reason" and the Unified Operations of the Human Soul

Closely related to the question of the primacy or priority of the intellect or will is Edwards's use of the language and concept of "right reason." For many years the use of such language has been assessed as evidence of a rabid or bald rationalism. If this assessment is correct, it would add weight to Gerstner's reading of Edwards as an unqualified intellectualist. First, does Edwards ever use the language? If so, what does he mean by it and what function does such a concept have in his theological anthropology? Secondly, what is the background to his use of such language and conceptuality?

Jonathan Edwards does speak in terms "right reason" and rationality.[33] Edwards, in agreement with the mainstream of consensual Christian tradition affirms that one of the traits of human nature that distinguishes man from brutes is his possession of reason and the ability to think.

---

30. Fiering, *Edwards' Moral Thought*, 268.

31. Fiering, *Edwards' Moral Thought*, 268. John Owen, a fellow Augustinian with Jonathan Edwards, described the heart in Scripture as the "whole rational soul," *Pneumatologia: A Discourse Concerning the Holy Spirit* (London: 1674), 181, cited in Fiering, *Edwards' Moral Thought*, 268.

32. See Augustine, *The Works of Augustine for the 21st Century: Vol.5/ The Trinity* (Edmund Hill, trans. John Rotelle, ed., Brooklyn, NY: New City Press, 1991), 9.2.9–16 (276–80).

33. A search of the *Jonathan Edwards Center at Yale University* website yields 19 occurrences of the expression "right reason" in the Edwards' literary corpus. The lion's share of these references has in view ideal reason or reason in the abstract. In other words, reason as God intended it to properly function. See http://edwards.yale.edu/archive. Accessed 17 September 2011.

> Our business should doubtless much consist in employing those faculties, by which we are distinguished from the beasts, about those things which are the main end of those faculties. The reason why we have faculties superior to those of the brute given us, is, that we are indeed designed for a superior employment. That which the Creator intended should be our main employment, is something above what he intended the beasts for, and hath therefore given us superior powers. Therefore, without doubt, it should be a considerable part of our business to improve those superior faculties. But the faculty by which we are chiefly distinguished from the brutes, is the faculty of understanding. It follows then, that we should make it our chief business to improve this faculty, and should by no means prosecute as a business by the bye. For us to make the improvement of this faculty a business by the bye, is in effect for us to make the faculty of understanding itself a by-faculty, if I may so speak, a faculty of less importance than others: whereas indeed it is the highest faculty we have. God hath given to man some things in common with the brutes, as his outward senses, his bodily appetites, a capacity for bodily pleasure and pain, and other animal faculties: and some things he hath given him superior to the brutes, the chief of which is a faculty of understanding and reason. Now God never gave man those faculties whereby he is above the brutes, to be subject to those which he hath in common with the brutes. This would be great confusion, and equivalent to making man a servant to the beasts. On the contrary, he has given those inferior powers to be employed in subserviency to man's understanding; and therefore it must be a great part of man's principal business, to improve his understanding by acquiring knowledge.[34]

Other animals act by instinct but man also reasons. However Edwards does not think of man's ability to reason in hermetical separation from his whole character or nature. If intellectualism or rationalism is defined as a position that recognizes that man can reason then Edwards is a pure intellectualist. But that is a simplistic or reductionistic definition. To be concerned with the fact that man reasons is not necessarily a sign of rationalism or intellectualism. An intellectualistic anthropology arises when the intellect is understood to act as a free floating faculty unaffected by the whole character of a person.[35]

---

34. Jonathan Edwards, *WJE/22*, 90.

35. Note that the idea of the intellect "governing" the other faculties is *not by itself* an indication of intellectualism. It would be a necessary but not a sufficient condition of intellectualism.

The appearance of the concept and language of "right reason" in Edwards's theology is no sure sign that he is an absolute intellectualist in the sense John Gerstner affirms. Edwards does offer arguments in his apologetic/polemical treatises that build on reason or what reason would affirm. For instance, even a cursory reading of the outline of Edwards's *The End for Which God Created the World*[36] indicates a division of the text into two basic sections, one on what reason teaches about God's end in creation and the other details what Scripture reveals about the subject. A *prima facie* reading of this text might suggest to the reader that Edwards thinks reason can *equally serve as a foundation* of his theology *along with* Scripture. But that would be an erroneous reading. While Edwards does believe reason supports his thesis in *The End*, it is not unaided reason or unregenerate reason or neutral reasoning. It is reason as it ought to properly function.[37]

Edwards notes at the beginning of his discourse on *The End* that he will attempt to address skeptics who question God's end in creation by means of reason. This could mean he will attempt to deal with unbelievers in an autonomous fashion using neutral principles of rationality, or, it could mean he is attempting to stand on the ground of the unbeliever to show them that their own principles fail to support them.

> And in the first place, I would observe some things which reason seems to dictate in this matter. Indeed, this affair seems properly to be an affair of divine revelation. In order to be determined what was aimed at or designed in the creating of the astonishing fabric of the universe which we behold, it becomes us to attend to and rely on what he has told us who was the architect that built it. He knows best his own heart, and what his own ends and designs were in the wonderful works which he has wrought. Nor is it to be supposed that mankind, who, while destitute of revelation, by the utmost improvements of their own reason, and advances in science and philosophy, could come to no clear and established determination who the author of the world was, would ever have obtained any tolerable settled judgment of the end which the author of it proposed to himself in so vast, complicated, and wonderful a work of his hands. And though it be true that the revelation which God has given to men, which has been in the world as a light shining in a dark place, has taught men how to use their reason (in which regard, notwithstanding

---

36. Jonathan Edwards, *The Works of Jonathan Edwards/Vol. 8: Ethical Writings* (Paul Ramsay, ed. New Haven, CT: Yale University Press, 1989), 400–536.

37. That is, it is reason as it is ideally understood or as it functions imperfectly in the regenerate.

> the nobleness and excellency of the faculties which God had given them, they seemed in themselves almost helpless); and, though mankind now, through the long continual assistance they have had by this divine light, have come to attainments in the habitual exercise of reason, which are far beyond what otherwise they would have arrived to: yet I confess it would be relying too much on reason to determine the affair of God's last end in the creation of the world, only by our reason, or without being herein principally guided by divine revelation, since God has given a revelation containing instructions concerning this matter. Nevertheless, as in the disputes and wrangling which have been about this matter, those objections, which have chiefly been made use of against what I think the Scriptures have truly revealed, have been from the pretended dictates of reason- I would in the first place soberly consider a few things, what seems rational to be supposed concerning this affair; and then proceed to consider what light divine revelation gives us in it.[38]

In other words, Edwards can divide his study of *The End* into two sections because he operates with a notion of reason or "right reason" that is not mere intellectualism but understands reason within the context of the unified operations of the human soul.[39] To put it another way, right reason is reason cleansed and restored in conjunction with a restored will/affections. Reason supports Edwards's thesis in *The End* that God's ultimate end in creation is his own glorification because reason has been restored and functions (albeit imperfectly this side of the new heavens and new earth) properly.

Jonathan Edwards, then, manifests the Reformed understanding of "right reason" as either ideal reason or concretely as regenerate reason.[40]

---

38. Edwards, *WJE/8*, 420–21.

39. It should be noted that reason is not detached from the will nor abstracted from its role in the dispositional complex when *The End* is read in conjunction with its sister discourse, *The Nature of True Virtue*. When reason is contemplated in the light of *True Virtue* it becomes apparent reason cannot be neutral or amoral. In *True Virtue* Edwards argues that true virtue is virtue that takes God into the picture. While there is a virtue of a sort practiced by the unregenerate, it falls far short of ethics that seeks to honor and glorify God. Given Edwards' views about the unified operations of the soul and his exposition of the nature of true virtue involving "consent to being in general" (which is a philosophical way of expressing the view that God must be the ultimate motive, goal, and standard of ethical living) it is not likely that he would conceive of reason in neutral terms. His thinking about reason would follow a similar path in that true reason must be subject to God and his Word. A review of what Edwards believes "reason dictates" shows that reason cannot function autonomously or neutrally. See Edwards, *WJE/8*, 537–627.

40. Paul Kjoss Helseth has made a cogent argument for this on the part of exemplary Old Princeton theologians in his *"Right Reason" and the Princeton Mind*. In that

For Edwards the reason is one power of the human soul along with the will and these work together.[41] The soul is not made up of individual agents within that either act harmoniously or at odds with one another. The one individual man or woman thinks, acts, and feels. Either the whole soul is fallen and unregenerate or it is regenerate and in the process of restoration.[42] Given that Edwards does not embrace a notion of the intellect as a reified power of the human soul unaffected by the character of the said soul, how did Edwards come to hold his view of right reason?

As Helseth and others have shown, the concept of "right reason" goes back to ancient Greece and has entered the Christian mainstream in two forms.[43] The first thing to note is that reason was understood to involve more than pure rationalism. Truth existed in conjunction with the good, and the beautiful.

> What, then is "right reason"? In short, "right reason" is "not merely reason in our [modern] sense of the word, it is not a dry light, a nonmoral instrument of inquiry . . . [Rather] It is a kind of rational and philosophical conscience which distinguishes man from the beasts and which links man with man and with God." As a philosophical concept that was born in Ancient Greece and later assimilated "by the early Church Fathers and redefined in the Christian context of sin and grace," it denotes at once "a mode of knowing, a way of doing, and a condition of being" that is invested with "unique meaning" by two "controlling" assumptions. In the first place, the concept assumes-in stark contrast with the fractured worldview that came to reign in the Age of Reason-that we live in a rationally ordered and organically integrated universe that is comprised of truth that is simultaneously intellectual and moral as well as natural and supernatural in nature. To put it differently, the concept affirms what Herschel Baker calls a "sacramental" as opposed to "secular" view of the universe, and thus it champions the notion

---

volume Helseth uses Edwards as an example of the Reformed understanding of right reason as regenerate reason, see especially 18-19.

41. How these powers work together will be the subject of the section where we interact with the views of Alvin Plantinga below.

42. This is not to suggest that either the regenerate or the unregenerate are completely consistent. Scripture and experience teach otherwise.

43. Helseth, *"Right Reason" and the Princeton Mind*, 196-209. Helseth interacts with the following sources: Herschel Baker, *The Wars of Truth: Studies in the Decay of Christian Humanism in the Earlier Seventeenth Century* (Cambridge: Harvard University Press, 1952); Douglas Bush, *Paradise Lost in Our Time: Some Comments* (Ithaca, NY: Cornell University Press, 1945); and Robert Hoopes, *Right Reason and the English Renaissance* (Cambridge, MA: Harvard University Press, 1962).

that the right way for human beings to lay hold of the truth that comprises this organically integrated universe is through the use of an "organic epistemology." Since "Beauty, goodness, [and] love" are according to this view a "part of truth," it follows that reasoning itself is rightly regarded as an act of the whole soul that includes "faith, intuition, [and] feeling, as well as the more strictly rational processes."[44]

Therefore reason was not understood to operate after the mode of mathematics alone.[45] The idea of reason was more expansive than it has been since the Enlightenment. One form of right reason, usually associated with Thomas Aquinas and so of a more intellectualistic stripe, conceives of right reason as neutral reason.[46] The other form, much more Augustinian, understands the soul to be a unified substance.[47] That is, while the soul may think, will, and feel it is one soul that does all these things and for the soul to think, will, and feel rightly, it must be rightly related to the truth it knows. The ultimate truth is God himself and so for the soul to know truly requires that the soul be in a right relationship with God. Since the fall this has been impossible apart from grace. In this Augustinian form of right reason, reason can only rightly relate to God through the gracious activity of the Triune God.[48]

This Augustinian view of right reason can be seen in the exemplary Reformed Scholastic theologian Francis Turretin who has left a helpful discussion of the role of reason in Christian theology.[49] Turretin distinguishes

---

44. Helseth, *"Right Reason" and the Princeton Mind*, 197–98. Helseth cites Bush, Hoopes, and Baker in this quotation.

45. The technical name for the view of reason as operating after the manner of mathematics is *"more geometrico."* For a discussion of this view of reason see Robert Brown, *Jonathan Edwards and the Bible* (Bloomington & Indianapolis, IN: Indiana University Press, 2002).

46. Whether this is a fair and accurate assessment of Thomas is a question of some interest and significance but remains outside the purview of this study. This stream is called by Helseth the "Christian humanist" stream, *"Right Reason and the Princeton Mind*, 199.

47. Helseth labels this stream "Christian antihumanism," *"Right Reason" and the Princeton Mind*, 203.

48. Helseth points out that examples of Augustine's holistic psychology can be found in several places in his literary corpus: *The Confessions of Saint Augustine* (Grand Rapids, MI: Baker), 7.10.17; *The City of God Among the Pagans* (R. W. Dyson, trans. and ed., Cambridge: Cambridge University Press, 1998), 12–14; and *On the Trinity*, 8–13, *"Right Reason" and the Princeton Mind*, 203n92. Helseth cites a few others and cites from the *Nicene and Post-Nicene Fathers* series.

49. Francis Turretin's discussion of reason can be found in his *Institutes of Elenctic Theology* (George Musgrave Geiger, trans. James T. Dennison, ed. Philippsburg, NJ:

THE RELATION OF INTELLECT AND WILL: A UNITY 167

between abstract and concrete reason. Abstract reason is ideal reason.[50] But no human being possesses abstract reason. Reason is only instantiated as concrete reason and so can be found in two forms: regenerate or unregenerate reason. Only the redeemed possess regenerate reason and this is right reason. Right reason is sound reason and cleansed reason.

> When we allow a certain judgment to reason in things of faith, we do not mean reason as blind and corrupted by sin (in which sense we confess the natural man cannot receive the things of God [1 Cor. 2:14] and that "the carnal mind [*phronēma*] is enmity against God," Rom. 8:7), but we speak of reason as sound and healed by grace (in which sense "the spiritual man is said to judge all things" [1 Cor. 2:15], and Paul often appeals to the judgment of believers, 1 Cor. 10:15; 11:13; Heb. 5:13, 14).[51]

It is not perfect reason as that is the possession of the saints in glory alone. Even then it will be perfected reason on the creaturely level. This discussion of reason, it should be remembered, is held within the context of the distinction between archetype and ectype (pilgrim) theology and reflects that distinction in its details.

In the end while Jonathan Edwards does exhibit a confidence in human reasoning powers uncommon today, he does not hold to a notion of right reason which is neutral.[52] Rather, Edwards has confidence in human reasoning powers because they were created by God for the purpose of glorifying God and when regenerated can begin to fulfill that purpose. Reason does not function on its own but is an integral part of a dispositional complex that exhibits an orientation bent in on itself or bent away from itself towards God.[53]

Presbyterian &Reformed Publishing, 1993), 1.8.1–1.13.14 (1:23–48). Turretin is one of two of Edwards' favorite theologians. The other was Peter Van Mastricht.

50. Turretin, *Institutes*, 1.8.1 (24).

51. Turretin, *Institutes*, 1.9.14. Similar comments can be found throughout this discussion. In 1.9.10, Turretin notes that "Reason as corrupt and in the concrete may be at variance with theology, but not reason as sound and in the abstract . . ." In 1.9.12 Turretin allows reason a "judgment of discretion" because it is "reason enlightened by the Holy Spirit" and "always judges according to Scripture as the first and infallible standard."

52. Is it possible that confidence in reason as created by God to glorify him and as restored to properly fulfill that function, is misread as confidence in human reason as omni-competent due to the critical influence of Kantian and post-Kantian philosophy?

53. More will be said about the soul as a dispositional complex below.

Alvin Plantinga's Consideration of Edwards on the Intellect and Will

While this study is an examination of whether Jonathan Edwards's anthropology coheres with the picture of Edwards as a classical apologist as argued by John Gerstner, any consideration of Edwards on the relationship between the intellect and will needs to consider the meticulous examination of the subject presented by the distinguished Christian philosopher Alvin Plantinga. In 2000 Plantinga offered an account of how Christian belief acquires warrant (if, in fact, Christian belief is true) in the culmination of his warrant series, *Warranted Christian Belief*.[54] Key to his discussion of warranted Christian belief is the presentation and explanation of what Plantinga calls the Aquinas/Calvin model (hereafter A/C model) and the *extended* A/C model.[55] The A/C model is initially comprised of Plantinga's version of the *sensus divinitatus*,[56] which is then extended to include explicitly Christian belief with three elements: the Bible, the internal instigation of the Holy Spirit and faith.[57] Faith, for Plantinga, involves both the intellect and the will and in chapters eight and nine of *WCB* he goes into some detail as he discusses the cognitive and volitional elements of faith and how they relate to one another.

Of interest is Plantinga's examination of Jonathan Edwards's understanding of the relationship between the intellect and the will that occurs in chapter nine of *WCB*, where Plantinga examines the "testimonial model." Plantinga wants to know what distinguishes mere belief from faith:

> According to the model, these beliefs enjoy justification, rationality, and warrant. We may therefore say with Calvin that they are "revealed to our minds." There is more, however; they are also "sealed upon our hearts." What could this latter mean, and how does it figure into the model? Given that these truths are revealed to our minds, what more could we need? Why must they also be sealed upon our hearts? To answer, suppose we ask whether one could hold the beliefs in question but nevertheless fail to have faith. The traditional Christian answer is, "Well

---

54. Alvin Plantinga, *Warranted Christian Belief* (Oxford: Oxford University Press, 2000), hereafter referred to as *WCB*. The previous two volumes in the trilogy are *Warrant: The Current Debate* (Oxford: Oxford University Press, 1993) and *Warrant and Proper Function* (Oxford: Oxford University Press, 1993).

55. Discussions of these can be found on 168–90 and 199–323 respectively in *WCB*.

56. Plantinga's treatment of the *sensus* is problematic, but need not detain us here. See K. Scott Oliphint's review of *WCB* which will be referenced below.

57. See Plantinga's discussion on 242ff in *WCB*.

yes: the demons believe and they shudder" (James 2:19); but the demons do not have faith. What distinguishes the Christian believer from the demons? According to the model, the shape of the answer is given in the text just mentioned: the demons *shudder*. They *believe* these things, but *hate* them; and they also hate God. Perhaps they also hope against hope that these things aren't really so, or perhaps believe them in a self-deceived way. They know of God's power and know that they have no hope of winning any contest of power with him; nevertheless they engage in just such a contest, perhaps in that familiar self-deceived condition of really knowing, in one sense, that they couldn't possibly win such a contest, while at some other level nevertheless refusing to accept this truth, or hiding it from themselves. Or perhaps the problem here is not merely cognitive but *affective*: knowing that they couldn't possibly win, they insist on fighting anyway, thinking of themselves as courageously Promethean, as heroically contending against nearly insuperable odds, a condition, they point out, in which God never finds himself, and hence a way in which they can think of themselves as his moral superior. The devils also know of God's wonderful scheme for the salvation of human beings, but they find this scheme-with its mercy and suffering love-offensive and unworthy. No doubt they endorse Nietzsche's notion that Christian love (including the love displayed in incarnation and atonement) is weak, whining, resentful, tergiversatory, and in general unappealing.[58]

Plantinga is also concerned to hypothesize how the intellect and will interrelate, and so he asks which of the faculties of the mind has priority, or which comes first? While his discussion is interesting in its detail and consideration of several possible angles, it seems to neglect a key factor in the reading of Jonathan Edwards. Plantinga himself doesn't think that there is any good reason to believe that either faculty has priority or primacy,[59] but he does see Edwards as having affirmed some type of priority for the intellect.[60] Although Plantinga undoubtedly offers one of the more intricate discussions of the matter, he arguably misconstrues Edwards. It appears he reads Edwards as some sort of absolute "intellectualist."

---

58. Plantinga, *WCB*, 290–91.

59. On 308 of *WCB* Plantinga indicates that he can't determine, due to the complexity of the interrelationships of the intellect and will (or, to use his terminology, "dependency relationships") which, if either, has priority. He has reiterated this viewpoint in personal email correspondence as well.

60. Plantinga, *WCB*, 301.

> [A]ccording to Edwards, which comes first, affection or intellection? Love for God or knowledge of God? I think Edwards's answer is that it is knowledge. I think he thinks that one first perceives the beauty and loveliness of the Lord, first comes to this experiential knowledge, and then comes to develop the right loves and hates: love for the Lord, for the great truths of the gospel, hatred for sin: "all gracious affections do arise from some instruction or enlightening of the understanding"; "Gracious affections do arise from the mind's being enlightened, rightly and spiritually to understand or apprehend divine things." What he means here, I think, is that this experiential knowledge of God and his qualities comes first; then there is a consequent raising of the affections. "Truly spiritual and gracious affections . . . arise from . . . some new view of Christ in his spiritual excellencies and fullness." His idea, I think, is that the regenerated person perceives the beauty and loveliness of the Lord and of the great things of the gospel and then, naturally enough, comes to love them. It is the perceiving that comes first; in this respect, therefore, intellect is prior to will.[61]

Developing a suggestion made by K. Scott Oliphint in his review of *WCB*,[62] it will be demonstrated that Edwards's concern to tread a new path (i.e., to move away from the hierarchical faculty psychology of his day) by affirming the unified, mutually interrelated operations of the human soul (the "dispositional complex") may account for the missing element in Plantinga's assessment of Edwards on the intellect and will. In other words, while Plantinga's examination of the relationship between the will and intellect is to be commended, he nevertheless misses Edwards's major point, which was a *rejection* of a hierarchical faculty psychology. Additionally, Plantinga seems to think that the "affections," which Edwards frequently speaks about, are something akin to emotions. As it turns out, the affections, as it will hopefully be shown, involve *both* the intellect *and* the will.

---

61. Plantinga, *WCB*, 301. Plantinga cites Edwards' *Religious Affections* throughout this citation. I say Plantinga "appears" to read Edwards as an intellectualist, as the citation above bears out, but Plantinga himself does not directly affirm faculty psychology as such. Later remarks in *WCB* suggest some voluntarist leanings (what looks like a "see-sawing") in Plantinga even though the final conclusion is that Plantinga himself is a "concurrentist."

62. K. Scott Oliphint, "Review: Epistemology and Christian Belief," in *WTJ* 63/1 (Spring 2001), 151–82. See especially 159–60. See also Oliphint's fuller treatment of these issues in "Jonathan Edwards: Reformed Apologist," in *WTJ* 57/1 (Spring 1995), 165–86 (especially 170–75) and "Jonathan Edwards on Apologetics" in *The Legacy of Jonathan Edwards: American Religion and the Evangelical Tradition*. D. G. Hart, Sean Michael Lucas, and Stephen J. Nichols, eds. (Grand Rapids, MI: Baker, 2003), 131–46.

Therefore, the goal of this segment of the current chapter is *not* to reject Plantinga's use of Edwards altogether, but to correct, to enhance and more carefully nuance what he has accomplished so that it might cast light on the question of whether Edwards's theological anthropology coheres with the picture drawn by John Gerstner of Jonathan Edwards as a classical apologist. What is offered here is a *suggestive* correction. Plantinga's assessment of Edwards is slightly askew and it will be shown *how* and *why*. Plantinga reads Edwards as a more or less straightforward intellectualist when in fact Edwards stressed the unity and harmony of the distinct powers or operations of the dispositional complex (the human soul). The center of this dispositional complex, if it may be put that way, just *is* the affections. So it is this that stands at the heart of Plantinga's misunderstanding of the relation of the intellect and will. Plantinga's instincts, though, are sound in looking to Jonathan Edwards to provide helpful insights into the discussion of this relationship. What is so important about asking about whether the intellect or will comes first? It seems that the issue of priority involves three elements: (1) Recognizing the *distinction* of powers within the dispositional complex, whether it can be done or not. (2) Making a *value judgment* or creating a *hierarchy* out of these distinctions. In other words, is there any reason to set one power above another? And (3) *reifying* the powers or faculties so as to create *de facto* autonomous individual agents within a single soul.[63] In the end, with the corrections suggested here kept in mind, it just may be that Plantinga is closer to Edwards's own position than he realizes.

Plantinga's assessment of the intellect/will issue and his use of Edwards will be examined in light of what has been seen thus far. After looking at Plantinga's assessment of Edwards, some possibilities will be considered as to how we can understand the relation of the intellect and will, by providing some parameters for a proper understanding of Edwards. In the end, it will be shown that Jonathan Edwards and Alvin Plantinga *may not be that far apart in their understanding of how the intellect and will function together.* In other words, if this thesis is correct, the difference between Plantinga and Edwards is merely one of degree. That is, Edwards can be understood as either a concurrentist, a functional intellectualist, or an Augustinian voluntarist because of his move away from faculty psychology and his stress on the unified powers of the dispositional complex.[64] Edwards is, in fact, none

---

63. A concern, as seen in the citation given above, raised by John Locke in his *Essay Concerning Human Understanding*, II.XXI.5 and 6. Edwards' rejection of autonomous faculties in his *Freedom of the Will* involves a similar concern.

64. Edwards will refer to the dispositional complex as the "whole soul" at various places in his corpus. One such place is his M.A. *Quaestio* where he discusses the nature of the faith that justifies. Edwards' definition of justifying faith raises a whole host of

of the foregoing, although his perspective embraces elements of each. This study will bring to bear on Plantinga's discussion an assessment of Edwards that more carefully considers his views on the subject.[65]

Plantinga's own Assessment of the Intellect and Will

Alvin Plantinga discusses the relationship of the intellect and will in chapters eight and nine of *WCB* where he deals with that relationship with regard to the occurrence of faith that he outlines in the extended A/C model. According to Plantinga, faith involves both cognitive and affective aspects. What does this mean? Plantinga is endeavoring to make the point that faith is more than strictly an intellectual exercise (i.e., faith is more than just knowledge *that* God exists and assent to that knowledge).[66] If sin has both cognitive and affective elements, then so too does faith.[67] It is not necessary to reproduce Plantinga's discussion of the relationship of the intellect and will here except to note that he explores various "dependency relations" in which either the intellect or the will has priority and he concludes that he cannot determine which has priority.[68] In light of this Plantinga is a "concurrentist" with regard to the relationship between the intellect and will. Neither intellect nor will has priority.

---

questions, but that is a study for another day. See *The Works of Jonathan Edwards: Vol. 14/Sermons and Discourses, 1723–1729.* (Kenneth J. Minkema, ed., New Haven, CT: Yale University Press, 1997), 60–66.

65. For instance, Plantinga fails to indicate any awareness of the historical context in which Edwards developed his views of faculty psychology nor does he demonstrate familiarity with the long standing scholarly discussion of the issue.

66. See note 59. Just prior to the citation presented earlier, Plantinga cites John Calvin's definition of faith: " . . . Christian belief is produced in the believer by internal instigation of the Holy Spirit, endorsing the teachings of Scripture, which is itself divinely inspired by the Holy Spirit. The result of the work of the Holy Spirit is *faith*- which, according to both John Calvin and the model, is "a firm and certain knowledge of God's benevolence towards us, founded upon the truth of the freely given promise in Christ, both revealed to our minds and sealed upon our hearts through the Holy Spirit," *WCB*, 290.

67. See chapter seven of *WCB* on sin and its cognitive effects.

68. Plantinga, *WCB*, 303.

Plantinga's Assessment of Jonathan Edwards on the Intellect and Will

Plantinga's extended discussion gives rise to an examination of Jonathan Edwards's own consideration of the matter. Plantinga rightly sees that Edwards is in harmony with Calvin in his assessment that true religion is more than correct belief.[69] Plantinga quite well sums up the fact that faith is more than proper notions.

> The person with faith, however, not only believes the central claims of the Christian faith; she also (paradigmatically) finds the whole scheme of salvation enormously attractive, delightful, moving, a source of amazed wonderment. She is deeply grateful to the Lord for his great goodness and responds to his sacrificial love with love of her own. The difference between the believer and the devil, therefore, lies in the area of *affections*: of love and hate, attraction and repulsion, desire and detestation. In traditional categories, the difference lies in the orientation of the *will*. Not primarily in the *executive* function of the will (the function of making decisions, of seeking and avoiding various states of affairs), though of course that is also involved, but in its *affective* function, its function of loving and hating, finding attractive or repellant, approving or disapproving. And the believer, the person with faith, has the right beliefs, but also the right affections. Conversion and regeneration alters affection as well as belief.[70]

Plantinga quite properly recognizes Edwards's emphasis on the religious affections. As Edwards puts it, "True religion, in great part, consists in holy affections."[71] But we must ask whether Plantinga recognizes that such a perspective does not rule out the cognitive element of true affections.[72] Plantinga then examines how Edwards understood the relationship of the intellect to the will.[73] Plantinga sets up the question in terms of which is prior, "which, if either, is primary?"[74] Is it the case that someone first sees that God is altogether lovely, and then comes to love him afterwards? Or is it that a person loves the things of God and God himself and then comes to *see* that they are lovable? Does the Holy Spirit reveal truth to our intellects

---

69. Plantinga, *WCB*, 294.
70. Plantinga, *WCB*, 290–91.
71. Edwards, *WJE/2*, 95. Cited in Plantinga, *WCB*, 294.
72. I will return to this point below.
73. Plantinga devotes nine pages to his discussion of Edwards on the intellect and will, *WCB*, 295–304.
74. Plantinga, *WCB*, 295.

and then conform our affections to the truth perceived? Or does our failure to love the gospel require correction before we can see the truth of it? Or, as Plantinga notes, is it a matter of the Holy Spirit *simultaneously* correcting both the intellect and will so that we come to see the loveliness of the "great things of the gospel" and God himself and love him all at once? Plantinga rightly connects this with the question of the nature of sin. "This question, of course, is connected with a correlative question . . . is sin primarily a matter of intellect, of blindness, of failing to see or believe the right things, thus leading to wrong affection and wrong action, or is it primarily a matter of the wrong affections, of loving and hating the wrong things?"[75]

Initially Plantinga reads Edwards as affirming the priority of the intellect in that the believer first perceives the beauty and amiableness of God and then the affections follow in natural order. Edwards does say that "[k]nowledge is the key that first opens the hard heart and enlarges the affections, and so opens the way for men into the kingdom of heaven."[76] Edwards makes similar remarks to the effect that the affections arise "from the mind's being enlightened." But Plantinga finds this problematic in that this priority of the intellect doesn't mesh well with Edwards's view that "what lies at the bottom of sin is *hardness of heart*."[77] Hardness of heart, as Plantinga understands it, is essentially having the wrong affections and failing to have the right ones. "It is less a failure to *see* something than to *feel* something."[78] This suggests to Plantinga that the gift of faith and regeneration involves the redirection of the will *and then* the acquisition of knowledge, although he concedes that acquiring faith could still be seen as a kind of knowledge that is *prior*.

Plantinga goes on to unpack this thought by considering whether sin is *indeed* a malfunction or dysfunction of the will that requires a repair by being granted a kind of knowledge. Sin is indeed and "fundamentally" a malfunction of the will but what comes "first" in regeneration is enlightenment. As Plantinga says, "Then revealing would be prior to sealing, with respect to faith, even though what needs repair is, at bottom, will rather than intellect."[79]

But Plantinga does note some diffidence in Edwards about this. While we have seen that Plantinga sees in Edwards some sort of priority of the intellect to the will in regeneration (even though at bottom, it is the will that needs correction), Plantinga sees Edwards as holding to the priority of neither the

---

75. Plantinga, *WCB*, 295.
76. Edwards, *WJE/2*, 266 and cited in Plantinga, *WCB*, 296.
77. Plantinga, *WCB*, 296, emphasis his.
78. Plantinga, *WCB*, 297.
79. Plantinga, *WCB*, 297.

intellect nor the will elsewhere. Here Plantinga notes Edwards's notion of the "sense of the heart" which Plantinga rightly realizes, is not limited to the will since it involves understanding as well. Edwards notes that with the "sense of the heart" a clear demarcation cannot be made between understanding and the will "as acting distinctly and separately, in this matter."[80]

Related to the above Plantinga discusses Edwards's notion of the "new simple idea" and he understands this to be a form of cognition or perception. The "new simple idea" spawns spiritual understanding which Plantinga sees as a form of *experiential* understanding. The analogy is often used of the difference between knowing *that* honey is sweet by learning about it and tasting the sweetness of honey and then understanding *how* or *in what way* it is sweet. The first form of knowledge is second-hand whereas the second form, the tasting of honey, is first-hand knowledge. Even though Jonathan Edwards is known as the master of the "interior life" as Plantinga tells us,[81] he ultimately reads him as an intellectualist of sorts. Plantinga says,

> ... according to Edwards, which comes first, affection or intellection? Love of God or knowledge of God? I think Edwards's answer is that it is knowledge. I think he thinks that one first perceives the beauty and loveliness of the Lord, first comes to this experiential knowledge, and then comes to develop the right loves and hates-what he means here, I think, is that this experiential knowledge of God and his qualities comes first; and then there is a consequent raising of the affections-his idea, I think, is that the regenerated person perceives the beauty and loveliness of the Lord and of the great things of the gospel and then, naturally enough, comes to love them. It is the perceiving that comes first; in this respect, therefore, intellect is prior to will.[82]

It would be good for us to ask whether Plantinga has completely and accurately understood Edwards here. Does Edwards hold to the priority of the intellect? And if he does, what does *he* mean by this? Or, is it, as the discussion of the sense of the heart seems to suggest, that Edwards affirms the priority of neither? Plantinga seems to understand Edwards as an intellectualist because he misunderstands the nature of the affections.

---

80. Edwards, *WJE/2*, 272, cited by Plantinga, *WCB*, 297.

81. Plantinga, *WCB*, 294.

82. Plantinga, *WCB*, 301. Plantinga may indicate his misreading of Edwards on the nature of the affections here. The affections ought not to be understood apart from intellection. The affections involve both the intellect and the will in tandem or simultaneously.

The affections cannot be reduced to emotions or passions.[83] As John Smith tells us in his introduction to the Yale edition of Edwards's *Religious Affections*,

> There is a further preliminary distinction; and although it occupies but a paragraph, it is of pivotal importance. 'The *affections* and *passions*,' he says, 'are frequently spoken as of the same,' but there are good grounds for distinguishing them. Passions he describes as those inclinations whose 'effects on animal spirits are more violent' and in them the mind is overpowered and 'less in its command.' The self becomes literally a 'patient,' seized by the object of passion. With the affections, however, the situation stands quite otherwise. These require instead a clear understanding and a sufficient control of the self to make choice possible. This distinction enabled him to criticize and reject a great many revival phenomena, especially those of a pathological sort, and to dissociate the heart religion he advocated from hysteria, the excesses of bodily effects and enthusiasm. His contemporaries paid insufficient attention to his distinctions. They thought he was defending revivalism in the sense of religious passions at the expense of the intellect, whereas he was developing a conception of affections accompanied by understanding.[84]

Was Edwards an Intellectualist, a Voluntarist, or a Concurrentist?

Edwards was not pioneering the avoidance of the use of distinctions, but he was trying to look at the powers of the soul as *working together*. He was trying to move away from the valuation of one faculty over another. In the proper operation of the powers or capacities of the soul, it was possible for the intellect or understanding to be enlightened with little or no impact on the will (perhaps some forms of speculative science or Plantingian analytic philosophy might fall into this category) and conversely it may have been possible to move the will with little or no impact or engagement of the understanding.[85] Edwards recognizes these possibilities, but in the exercise of

---

83. Plantinga may be setting up a false antithesis here. The question of which comes first, relates to the intellect and will. The affections are, by definition, the will either in response to or in concurrence with the intellect.

84. Smith, introduction, *WJE*/2, 14–15.

85. This seems to be the position of the enthusiasts in their understanding of true religion, whereas the former was the understanding of religion from the perspective of the rationalists.

true religious affections, *both* the intellect *and* the will were involved. In conversion, it is not a matter of the intellect working without the will nor is it a matter of the will working without the intellect. They work *together*. Each is necessary and both are essential. After all, how could the will be attracted to or repulsed by something without being held in view?[86] I suppose it is possible to construe the operation of the will so that it performs perceptive or cognitive or speculative functions. But then the question would shift from the relationship of the intellect to the will, to the relationship of the cognitive to the volitional functions of the will. My point is that we would still have to reckon with questions of *taxis* in the dispositional complex, whether it is the relation of one power or faculty to another or the relations of functions within one faculty. The issue, then, is not about the making of distinctions. To repeat, for Edwards, the problem is not the making of distinctions but the separation of powers to such an extent that they become *compartmentalized*. Additionally, the problem involves the *hierarchical valuation* of the intellect over the will as can be found in Chauncy, or the converse elevation of the will over the intellect in the enthusiasm of a Davenport. True affections involve an idea to which the will responds with heightened awareness. Edwards is not attempting to abolish the proper distinctions made between the intellect and the will. In other words, he is not trying to *conflate* or *confuse* them. He is simply attempting to show their unity. And unity implies *harmonious* difference and harmonious *differentiation*.

Edwards's distinction between speculative or notional understanding and spiritual understanding (another name for the "sense of the heart") may help to get at his concern to stress the unity (but not *identity*) of the powers of the human soul. One could understand Edwards in an intellectualist sense since true religious affections, or spiritual understanding, or the sense of the heart, involve an object being perceived by the understanding and the will being attracted to or repulsed from it (i.e., manifesting affections). While there may be priority in some sense, it is *not* a priority of value nor is it a primacy in the sense that *that* word is usually used (i.e., primacy implies more significance or importance than something that doesn't have it). To use Plantinga's language, there are "dependency relations" between the intellect and the will, and it is possible to have speculative knowledge of the great things of the gospel without having a spiritual knowledge of them. But it is not possible to have a spiritual knowledge, the sense of the heart, or true affections, without speculative understanding.

> There is a distinction to be made between a mere notional understanding, wherein the mind only beholds things in the exercise

86. This may beg the question about what "in view" means.

> of a speculative faculty; and the sense of the heart, wherein the mind don't only speculate and behold, but relishes and feels. That sort of knowledge, by which a man has a sensible perception of the amiableness of and loathsomeness, or of sweetness and nauseousness, is not just the same sort of knowledge with that, by which he knows what a triangle is, and what a square is. The one is mere speculative knowledge, the other sensible knowledge, in which more than the mere intellect is concerned; the heart is the proper subject of it, or the soul as a being that not only beholds, but has inclination, and is pleased or displeased. And yet there is the nature of instruction in it; as he that has perceived the sweet taste of honey, knows more about it, than he who has only looked upon it and felt of it.[87]

To the rationalists, Edwards would say that you can't have *true* religion without having the will engaged and to the enthusiasts he would say that you can't have true *religion* without having the intellect engaged. Edwards could be understood as an intellectualist, but that seems to imply a valuation he would not accept and it fails to take cognizance of his concern to stress the unity of powers of the human soul. Edwards may sound like an intellectualist and that may conflict with his *perceived* emphasis on the affections, but that misunderstanding only seems possible if one presupposes some sort of faculty psychology with its concomitant hierarchical valuation that Edwards was himself trying to avoid and it evinces a misunderstanding of affections.[88]

Jonathan Edwards could also be understood as a voluntarist as he has indeed been so understood by many scholars who recognize his desire to transcend faculty psychology. Both Allen Guelzo and Norman Fiering see him in the voluntarist tradition, albeit qualified in an Augustinian way. The will is not blind nor is it obligated to follow the dictates of the understanding. With his own Augustinian and Reformed tradition he understood that it was the orientation of the individual that determined what was primary, grace or sin.

But as has already been seen, Edwards could be understood to conform to the concurrentist model that Plantinga seems to embrace. Edwards sometimes finds it hard to distinguish the acts of the intellect and will in

---

87. Edwards, *WJE/2*, 272.

88. Plantinga seems to think that Edwards' emphasis on the *heart* is in contradistinction to the intellect, but if Edwards is understood aright at this point, the heart includes both the intellect and the will since true religious affections involve both and true religious affections appear to me to be synonymous with spiritual understanding and the sense of the heart. The heart is not the source of emotions only. In other words, the heart *just is* the dispositional complex.

his sense of the heart. This would seem to suggest the same view Plantinga comes to at the end of his own discussion of the subject.

So which model best describes Jonathan Edwards on this issue? It can be seen how Edwards could be understood as a functional intellectualist or an Augustinian voluntarist or maybe even as a Plantingian concurrentist. Each view is attractive in turn because each touches upon an element of truth in Edwards's own position. While Edwards makes room for the use of the intellect that moves the will a little or not at all, and while he recognizes that the will can be moved without the light of understanding, *true religion consists in both functioning together*. If the intellectualist label must be used, Edwards would certainly *not* be understood as an absolute intellectualist since *that* is best exemplified in the person of Charles Chauncy, whom Edwards clearly opposed. Given Edwards's Trinitarian views and the analogical nature of the human soul or personality to the Trinity, he could be classified as a *functional* or *economic* intellectualist, as long as it is kept in mind what that entails. However, Edwards can also be seen as a voluntarist, but most definitely not of the Scholastic variety. The will is not free from the influences of the whole personality of the individual. While Edwards, along with the Augustinian-voluntarist tradition, recognized that the will did not necessarily follow the last dictate of the intellect, it does in the exercise of true religion, since true affections arise at the sight of the loveliness of God and the great things of the gospel. With the Augustinian-voluntarist school Edwards most assuredly affirmed that there was a *primacy of the orientation* in an individual human being.[89] For Edwards, there is neither primacy of the intellect nor of the will in the practice of true religion, where true religious affections are in evidence. And it is possible for Edwards to be described as a concurrentist in that he sometimes found it hard to distinguish between the intellect and the will in the sense of the heart. However, Edwards didn't always find that distinction hard to make.

> God has indued the soul with two faculties: one is that by which it is capable of perception and speculation, or by which it discerns and views and judges of things; which is called the understanding. The other faculty is that by which the soul does not merely perceive and view things, but is some way inclined with respect to the things it views or considers; either is inclined to 'em, or is disinclined, and averse from 'em; or is the faculty by which the soul does not behold things as an indifferent unaffected spectator, but either as liking or disliking, pleased or displeased, approving or rejecting. This faculty is called by

---

89. It should be noted that the *primacy of orientation* is not the same as the primacy of the will, which is what Plantinga understands a concern with affections to entail.

various names: it is sometimes called the *inclination*: and, as it has respect to the actions that are determined and governed by it, is called the *will*: and the *mind*, with regard to the exercises of this faculty, is often called the *heart*.[90]

Edwards doesn't fit comfortably into either the intellectualist or the voluntarist school as we have understood them up to this point. To label him as either a functional intellectualist or an Augustinian voluntarist seems to assume the very priority that he would reject. Jonathan Edwards, rather, affirms *elements of both*. He affirms the functional priority of the intellect in the rising of true religious affections *and* he affirms that the will is not enslaved to the intellect, both the intellect and the will reflect their orientation in sin or grace. They either work properly under the rule and reign of grace or improperly under the rule and reign of sin. To affirm the functional priority of the intellect in perceiving an object or in holding an idea to which the will then responds (or as the concurrentist model would affirm, both operate simultaneously) is not to imply that one is more important than the other. In a highly significant way, to try to affirm the greater significance of the intellect viz-a-viz the will or vice versa is closely akin to trying to affirm the greater significance of either unity over diversity (oneness or threeness) or vice versa in the Holy Trinity. Neither properly comes first nor last in importance, even though we do recognize the distinction.[91] As has been repeatedly noted throughout this essay, Edwards affirms the dispositional complex. The dispositional complex involves *both* distinction *and* unity, difference in function and equality of importance. It is not wrong to make distinctions. If distinctions can't be made, learning grinds to a halt before an amorphous undifferentiated mass or a blooming, buzzing chaos. Edwards talked meaningfully about the human soul, affirming *both* the distinction of powers and unity of essence (i.e., in Trinitarian language, diversity *and* unity of powers).

---

90. Edwards, *WJE/2*, 96. Note the fluidity or flexibility of terminology in this citation. At the conclusion Edwards notes that the mind, with regard to the faculty of the will, is called the heart. What is interesting is that mind is not equated with or limited to the intellect or understanding.

91. Gregory Nazianzen's comments about thinking of the three whenever he thinks of the one and vice versa has resonance in this discussion of the unified operations of the human soul.

How Plantinga Misses the Point

So how, then, does the apparent lack of historical context effect Plantinga's use of Edwards?[92] Plantinga seems unaware of Edwards's effort to transcend faculty psychology with its hierarchical valuation of faculties. He seems to be unfamiliar with the fact that Edwards was trying to walk a middle road between the two extremes of rationalism and enthusiasm that valued one of the powers of the soul to the detriment of the other. Or, if Plantinga is aware of it, perhaps he disagrees with Edwards or finds him unconvincing or misguided. How would Edwards come across *that* way if he isn't already being read through the lens of faculty psychology, as he surely was in the eyes of Charles Chauncy? Plantinga does read Edwards as a sort of intellectualist with the priority of the intellect in the workings of true affections. That would be true after a fashion, as long as it was understood that Edwards was trying to move away from faculty psychology although not away from making legitimate distinctions of the powers of the human soul. We can speak of a "priority" of the intellect as long as that priority is understood in terms of taxis or functional order and not primacy of importance.

Plantinga also seems to equate the affections with emotions, although this connection is not always clear or hard-and-fast. On the related matter, Plantinga recognizes that sin, for instance, can be understood as *blindness*, as a not seeing God or the great things of the gospel as the truly lovely things they are. But sin is also a *willful* blindness. It *is* a hatred of the loveliness of God and his attributes. *We* are responsible for our failure to see. We can distinguish the powers of the soul, but we cannot separate them. And we should not consider the intellect or the will more important than the other. After all, God made us with both. Admittedly sin has wreaked havoc in this area just as it has in others. We sinful human beings tend to prize one power over the other. We still struggle with the same extremes Edwards faced.

What are the Consequences?

So what is the difference between Edwards and Plantinga? If this study has been correct in its assessment of both Plantinga and Edwards, the difference *may* be minimal in practical effect. Nevertheless, it may be significant in that Plantinga's discussion would have benefitted from the historical awareness of the context of the Great Awakening and Edwards's desire to transcend faculty psychology, and from a correction of what might be a

---

92. Refer to the section on Edwards' formulation of a unified operation of the human soul in the context of the Great Awakening treated earlier in this chapter.

misunderstanding of what the affections are. The way Plantinga asks the question, "which comes first" suggests that he doesn't realize that for Edwards, the affections involved both the intellect and the will. Yes, the intellect precedes occurrence of the affections or is simultaneous with them. Either option is possible for Edwards as long as both are understood to be involved in the exercise of true religious affections.

Is there much difference between Plantinga the concurrentist and Edwards? Sometimes the impression is given that Plantinga thinks Edwards should have been a voluntarist given his emphasis on the affections and is then surprised with Edwards's functional priority of the intellect. But, given that Edwards did admit that even he could not always distinguish the acts of the intellect and will in the sense of the heart, it would have to be said that he and Plantinga come within a hair's breadth. So is there *much* significant difference between Plantinga and Edwards? Probably not. Is there *any* difference at all? Yes. When all is said and done, Plantinga appears to come to a position close to, if not exactly identical with, Edwards, through exhausting all possible angles as he sees them. Plantinga is closer to Edwards than he appears to realize and *that* may be the result of his lack of awareness of or at least his failure to mention his awareness of, the historical context in which Edwards formulated his thoughts on the relation of the intellect and will with his concern to stress the unity of the powers of the human dispositional complex *as expressed* in his doctrine of the affections. While Alvin Plantinga has offered an extremely lively and fascinating discussion of the relation of the intellect to the will, it appears that he could have saved himself a lot of trouble had he been fully aware of the trajectory of Edwards's thought and the historical context in which that was articulated.

The time has been taken to consider Alvin Plantinga's examination of Jonathan Edwards on the relationship of the intellect to the will because it helps us to evaluate John Gerstner's assessment of Edwards as a classical apologist who affirmed an absolute intellectualist faculty psychology.

Edwards on the Unified Operations of the Human Soul and His Apologetics

John Gerstner has argued that Jonathan Edwards was a classical apologist who held to an intellectualist faculty psychology. Certainly Edwards used traditional arguments for God's existence (for instance, a negative form of the ontological argument)[93] and he was a convinced believer in the cause

---

93. Edwards' negative ontological argument is an argument for the impossibility of nothing. Edwards first articulated this argument in his personal notebook "Of Being"

and effect relationship[94] and he valued laws of logic and logical analysis.[95] But there is no sense in which these functioned outside the existence of God. How could such a God-entranced theologian like Edwards ever argue for the existence of God from the presumed non-existence of God? Additionally, as has been noted earlier in this study, Edwards does not use classical arguments as a pre-dogmatic foundation of theology but in the very context of his Biblically informed Reformed theology.[96]

Edwards's affirmation of the unified operations of the human soul works against Gerstner's intellectualist faculty psychology. The argument here is not against a *taxis* in the relationship of the intellect to the will. There can be a chronological priority of the intellect to the will or a simultaneity. But there is no suggestion that the intellect is by-passed. Edwards, despite mischaracterizations, was no enthusiast. The whole person is fallen in Adam and restored in Christ. The whole person is involved in redemption. To affirm the importance of the intellect is not the same as to treat it as hermetically sealed off from the rest of the soul. To affirm a *taxis* in the relationship of the intellect to the will is also not to form a hierarchy of value in which one faculty is more esteemed than another. To affirm that the intellect as well as the will is a moral faculty is not to denigrate the intellect. It is simply to recognize, as Edwards did, that the heart or dispositional complex is the center of human nature and all aspects of the dispositional complex are fallen or restored. Edwards affirms the significance of both the intellect and the will.

Gerstner's affirmation that Edwards was an intellectualist is not without some basis in the Edwards corpus. However, it should be noted that Edwards was (1) affirming the importance of the intellect, but (2) not arguing for the primacy or priority of the intellect over the will in terms of hierarchical valuation. Also Edwards was formulating his view of the unified operations of the human soul against the backdrop of a previously developed grammar of theological anthropology. Edwards did not reject distinction between the powers of the soul. Thinking is different from willing which is different from feeling. But it is one person who exercises these different powers. So with Gerstner we agree that Edwards affirmed the importance of

---

which is found in *The Works of Jonathan Edwards/Vol. 6: Scientific and Philosophical Writings* (Wallace Anderson, ed. New Haven, CT: Yale University Press, 1980), 206–7.

94. Edwards notes that if the cause/effect relationship is denied, as it was by David Hume, it would be nearly impossible to demonstrate God's existence. See his remarks in *WJE/1*, 420.

95. Countless references to confirm this could be offered, but one will suffice: "On the Mind," *WJE/6*, 313–93.

96. We shall return to this matter in the final chapter of this dissertation.

the intellect but against him we deny that Edwards placed the intellect at the apex of a hierarchical chain.

A corollary of all this is that Edwards most assuredly did not work with a notion that the intellect was indirectly affected by sin. As already noted, that view comes perilously close the view criticized by Archibald Alexander.[97] It is not the case that the intellect is a natural faculty (unaffected by the fall), while the will, being a moral faculty, is so affected. In the fall the intellect is darkened and the will is perverted. Each faculty may be affected in ways consistent with its nature, but it is affected nonetheless. In regeneration the intellect is enlightened and the will is renewed.

Edwards's distinction between speculative and spiritual understanding helps us to understand how his view of the unified operations of the human soul would interface with his apologetic. Speculative understanding (for instance, knowledge of Christian doctrine) is a necessary condition for spiritual understanding but not a sufficient condition.[98] Spiritual understanding involves the presence of speculative understanding plus a disposition of love and attraction towards the knowledge possessed or towards the realities embraced in the speculative knowledge.[99] Specifically, one could know that Christ died on the cross to satisfy divine justice and this would be classified as speculative understanding or knowledge. But when one sees that Christ died on the cross so that God's condemnation of himself has been reversed and so loves God in Christ, that would count as spiritual understanding. As Edwards regularly pointed out, spiritual understanding added no new doctrine to what was known speculatively. But the attitude or disposition of the heart is changed toward the object of knowledge.

This distinction enters into Edwards's practice of apologetics this way: Edwards offered arguments for a given position or against a certain position knowing that the arguments by themselves could not *cause* regeneration or faith in Christ. However, as with preaching and evangelism, the Holy Spirit could take the knowledge presented and use it in bringing a person to faith.

> Such is the nature of man, that nothing can come at the heart
> but through the door of the understanding: and there can be

---

97. See note 11.

98. It may be of some value to explore the concepts of *necessary condition* and *primacy* or *priority*. The activity of the intellect is a necessary condition of true religious affections but that does not entail primacy or priority in the valuational sense.

99. As noted previously at points throughout this study, the transition from speculative knowledge to spiritual knowledge is no *mere supplementation* nor is it a matter of the intellect getting a firm grasp on an extra-mental reality but not liking it. No, the transition involves both a correction of the intellect's apprehension of the nature of its object and a correction of the will's reaction to the object.

> no spiritual knowledge of that which there is not first a rational knowledge. It is impossible that anyone should see truth or excellency of any doctrine of the gospel, who knows not what that doctrine is. A man cannot see the excellency and love of Christ in doing such and such things for sinners, unless his understanding be first informed how those things were done. He cannot have a taste of the sweetness and divine excellency of such and such things contained in divinity, unless he first have a notion that there are such and such things.[100]

After all, as Edwards was keen to point out, faith was no blind leap into the dark. The acquisition of speculative knowledge could precede regeneration by some period of time or it could occur at the same time as regeneration. Either way, the intellect is involved along with the will in the experience of the new birth. So it is not as if Edwards thought that piling arguments on top of arguments or evidence on top of evidence could *cause* regeneration but that the Holy Spirit could use such arguments in the process of bringing a person to faith in Christ.

Conclusion

Jonathan Edwards was a Reformed apologist who affirmed the importance of the intellect but not at the expense of the will or by undermining the unitary operations of the human soul. While he inherited a tradition that embraced various hierarchical faculty psychologies (intellectualists and voluntarists can be found among the ranks of Reformed theologians), Edwards himself moved away from them towards a view stressing the unified powers of the soul. In the historical context of the Great Awakening Edwards formulated a view that avoided the pitfalls of rationalism on the one hand and enthusiasm on the other.

The intellect and the will are equally moral faculties which are fallen in Adam and restored in Christ. To argue for the parity of the intellect and will is not to deny their distinctiveness but to deny the legitimacy of valuing one power of the soul over another. Nor is it correct to say that the fall indirectly affects the intellect. The mind is darkened and the will is perverted. In regeneration the intellect is enlightened and the will is renewed.[101] In

---

100. Edwards, *WJE/22*, 89.

101. That is, the sinful mind now sees rightly what before it apprehended but did not fully grasp. Now the mind is enlightened and the will is made to love the object it now properly sees. God and the things of God are not made lovely, beautiful, and good by the change in man but the change in man makes it possible for him to see what was true all along but not fully known or appreciated.

preaching, evangelism, and apologetics, information transfer by itself will not cause someone to come to faith, although information transfer is necessary. Conversion, then, involves both knowledge and a love of the object of that knowledge. Jonathan Edwards preached, evangelized and defended the faith knowing and affirming this truth.

5

Edwards's Apologetic and Anthropology & Summation of the Whole

Introduction

THE DISSERTATION UP TO this point has endeavored to examine and critically assess the theological anthropology of Jonathan Edwards with a view to considering how this anthropology coheres with his apologetic methodology. Specifically, the question has been raised whether Edwards's doctrine of man is consistent with the picture painted of Jonathan Edwards by John Gerstner that he was the epitome of the classical apologist. This study has conducted this examination by considering in turn Edwards's understanding of man as made in the image of God, of man's knowledge of God, and of the relation of man's intellect to his will. In this chapter an attempt will be made to examine five of Edwards's apologetic ruminations. It will be argued that Edwards practiced an *eclectic* apologetic sans apologetic self-awareness. In other words, Edwards was a child of his training and times. At times Edwards appears to follow a classical approach to the defense of the faith, and at other times he seems to depart from it.[1]

---

1. For instance, Edwards appears to practice a classical method of apologetics with his acceptance and powerful use of the principle of causality. At one point in his *Freedom of the Will*, Edwards notes that if we reject the notion of cause and effect we have cut ourselves off from the only means for proving the existence of God. See Jonathan Edwards, *The Works of Jonathan Edwards/Vol. 1: Freedom of the Will* (Paul Ramsey, ed. New Haven, CT: Yale University Press, 1957), 181–83 and 259–60. However, Edwards is wise enough to avoid a common error by noting, as he does, that God is not to be included within the earthly chain of causes and effects. Also, Edwards uses the standard proofs for God's existence (ontological, cosmological, and teleological) in his sermon on Romans 1:20 (now known as "The Being and Attributes of God Seen in the Work

Then the results of the description of Edwards's apologetic practice will be brought into proximity with the results of the previous chapters to determine whether there is any coherence between Edwards's theological anthropology and his apologetic. It will be demonstrated that Edwards was Reformed in his anthropology and that he was an eclectic by training and ad hoc in his apologetic practice. This does not mean that he was thoughtless. It simply suggests that Edwards was *not a self-conscious devotee of the classical apologetic method* per se. Edwards used what is subsequently called the classical method where it was useful in his own mind and it sufficiently cohered with Scripture. At other times he departed from the classical method. In the final analysis, Edwards was the scion of the Reformed and Catholic tradition in which he was reared and trained and which he consciously embraced as his own.

Outline

We will begin this chapter by (1) juxtaposing two assessments of Edwards's way of defending the faith, (2) move to a consideration of the context in which Edwards used what are usually considered traditional theistic arguments, and (3) conclude the initial part of this chapter with an assessment of whether Edwards used traditional arguments to construct a pre-dogmatic foundation for Christian theology. It is the argument of this segment that while Edwards used classical or traditional arguments to demonstrate the existence of God, he did *not* do so from a neutral or autonomous vantage point. In the latter segment of this chapter we will (4) reconnoiter the ground that has been traversed in the previous chapters and bring the results into relation with the conclusions of the first part of this chapter. At the end of the day, we will see that Jonathan Edwards was a more complex thinker than John Gerstner has allowed. It will be seen that Gerstner is not completely wrong. Rather his portrait of an intellectualist Jonathan

---

of Creation" and accessed on 3.25.12 at www.edwards.yale.edu/archives. The sermon is classified as sermon 706 in series II, 1743, in *WJE online* volume 61). However, these are used in a sermon and not in a context divorced from Scripture. Additionally, Edwards notes in Miscellanies 1350 that one problem with the use of traditional theistic arguments, specifically, the idea that like begets like (i.e., that effects resemble their causes), is that there is not only evidence of design in the world but there is also evidence of evil which would naturally suggest a good and an evil god. In this Miscellany Edwards is interacting with and citing Samuel Clarke's *A Discourse Concerning the Unchangeable Obligations of Natural Religion, and the Truth and Certainty of the Christian Religion* (London: 1706). See Jonathan Edwards, *The Works of Jonathan Edwards/Vol. 23: The "Miscellanies" 1153–1360* (Douglas A. Sweeney, ed. New Haven, CT: Yale University Press, 2004), 435.

Edwards will need to be nuanced and corrected at points as a result of this study. Jonathan Edwards was a Reformed pastor-theologian who practiced an eclectic approach to apologetics which reflects his training in general and the Reformed Scholastic approach to philosophy in particular. (5) Finally, an evaluative assessment of the coherence of Edwards's theological anthropology and apologetic will be offered which shows appreciation for his Reformed and biblical convictions and his desire to defend the Christian faith and also appreciates aspects of his creative work and notes weaknesses as well. In the end Jonathan Edwards attempted to be a faithful servant of God's Word to his people and yet was fallible.

Two Perspectives on Jonathan Edwards and Apologetics[2]

John Gerstner has argued that Jonathan Edwards was committed to an intellectualist approach to the Christian faith in general and the defense of the faith in particular. Specifically, Edwards was committed to a classical model of apologetics. First one must demonstrate philosophically that there is a God and then one considers whether this God has communicated with his creation after which the Bible is then examined as to whether it is just such a divine communication. Typically the Bible is determined to be divinely inspired via the route of historical veracity. In other words, the Bible is deemed at a minimum to be historically accurate and it is ascertained that Scripture evidences miraculous activity in attestation of divine spokesman and this is most clearly indicated in the person of Jesus Christ and his resurrection. Antecedently Christ offers attestation of the divine inspiration of the Old Testament. So Gerstner thinks Edwards fits within this overall perspective.

> While the church rests on special revelation, special revelation rests on common revelation. A person is in the world before he enters the church. He must be persuaded that there is a God before he can entertain a special revelation from God. Theistic proofs naturally and logically precede Christian evidences. A person may believe that there is a God without believing in Christ. He cannot believe in Christ without believing in God (John 14:2). He must be persuaded that there is a God before he can be persuaded that Christ is the Son of God (Matt. 16:16).[3]

---

2. It is not intended to suggest that there are only two perspectives on Edwards and apologetics, but that on *this* question, these two perspectives offer up different answers.

3. John Gerstner, *The Rational Biblical Theology of Jonathan Edwards* (Powhatan, VA & Orlando, FL: Berea Publications & Ligonier Ministries, 1991), 1:22.

It would appear the Christian apologist must argue from the perspective of neutrality, meticulously building, plank by plank, a case for the God of the Christian faith. The question is, does Edwards fit this model?

> This introduction is meant to show that Jonathan Edwards was an eighteenth-century apologist in that classical age of apologetics. More idealistic, comprehensive, and demonstrative in his argumentation than the Westminster divines, Bishop Butler or William Paley, Edwards, there can be no doubt, belonged in that tradition which is the general tradition of the Bible and the church.[4]

More specifically, does the *mere presence* of *any* of these elements constitute Edwards a classical apologist in Gerstner's sense? Before attempting to answer this question, we need to consider an alternative perspective on Edwards.

Ava Chamberlain, editor of the eighteenth volume of the Yale edition of Edwards's *Works* offers another take on Edwards and his apologetic method,

> In the miscellanies of the 1730s, especially in the entries on "Christian Religion," Edwards constructs a defense of the rationality of the Christian faith against the deist critique. Unlike the latitudinarian opponents of the deists, however, Edwards' rational defense did not weaken his adherence to the fundamental doctrines of Reformed orthodoxy. He remains convinced of the rationality of these doctrines at least in part because he uses a standard of rationality not shared by his opponents. He accepted the position first articulated by Locke that religious belief must conform to the principles of reason, but tempered it with the belief that divine, not human, reason was the ultimate standard of judgment. Consequently, he frequently presupposes not only the existence of God but the truth of the very doctrine that is the object of demonstration.[5]

---

4. John Gerstner, "An Outline of the Apologetics of Jonathan Edwards: Part One: The Argument from Being," *BSac* 133/529 (January 1976): 6.

5 Ava Chamberlain, editor's introduction, *The Works of Jonathan Edwards/ Vol. 18: The "Miscellanies" 501–832* (New Haven, CT: Yale University Press, 2000), 28. Chamberlain goes on to suggest that Edwards uses "circular reasoning" in such Miscellanies as 519 as well using classical theistic proofs in Miscellanies 587, 650, 651, and 749. She notes, "For Edwards, a conviction of the truth of Christianity was finally grounded not in human reason but in the perception of divine excellency conveyed by the new spiritual sense. This higher form of conviction was ultimately unavailable for public discussion, for to the unredeemed, who lack the perception of excellency, talk about it is "foolishness" and "words without a meaning" (No. 683)," 29.

Chamberlain evidences why the question of the nature of Edwards's apologetics is complex. She notes that Edwards presupposes the Christian God when he argues for him.[6] And she notes that even though he might agree *formaliter* with John Locke that revelation must be subject to reason it is God's reason and not human reason that sets the bar. This, in a nutshell, may be the conundrum of the Edwards scholar. On the one hand Edwards presupposes God in his argumentation for God *and* on the other he agrees with aspects of the thought of a contemporary Enlightenment philosopher. Edwards agrees with Locke, but not quite so.

Who is correct? In order to answer that question we will need to revisit Edwards's treatment of reason and consider the context of his use of classical theistic arguments. Does Edwards reason in the abstract from a position of neutrality (principles of logic which would properly function with or without the Scriptural God)? Again, does the presence of elements typically understood to be integral to the classical model of apologetics constitute Edwards a classical apologist?

Elements of Edwards's Apologetic and Their Context

Noting that Edwards never wrote an apologetics manual, his actual defense of the faith can be pieced together from various sources within his literary corpus. In particular, we will examine five examples of his apologetic reasoning drawn from his semi-private notebooks, a sermon, and a major treatise. First we will consider his negative ontological argument for the non-existence of nothing in his "Of Being." Second we will look at the unpublished sermon outline of Romans 1:20 now known as "The Being and Attributes of God Seen in the Work of Creation." Thirdly we will examine his comments about how to argue for God's existence in *Freedom of the Will*. Fourthly we will consider "Miscellanies" 1340 with its consideration of mystery in special revelation. Fifth and finally we will assess *Notes on Scripture* entry 416 in which Edwards defends the Mosaic authorship of the Pentateuch.[7]

---

6. It should be noted that Chamberlain is no presuppositionalist.

7. These can be found, respectively, in Jonathan Edwards, *The Works of Jonathan Edwards/Vol. 6: Scientific and Philosophical Writings* (Wallace E. Anderson, ed., New Haven, CT: Yale University Press, 1980), 202–7; *WJE Online* at www.edwards.yale.ed/archives; *WJE*/1:182; *WJE*/23: 359–756; and *The Works of Jonathan Edwards/Vol. 15: Notes on Scripture* (Stephen J. Stein, ed. New Haven, CT: Yale University Press, 1998), 423–69. Note that Gerstner uses each of these in his portrayal of Edwards as a classical apologist. See his "Outline of the Apologetics of Jonathan Edwards," *BSac* 133/529 (January 1976): 4–11.

Of Being

"Of Being" is an entry in Edwards's semi-private notebooks dating from about 1723. A similar expression of the negative ontological argument can be found in his "On the Mind" as well.[8] Edwards's negative ontological argument argues that it is impossible that nothing can exist, but that there must be something that does in fact exist and that something is God.

> But here we are run up to our first principle, and we have no other to explain the nothingness or not being of nothing by. Indeed, we can mean nothing else by "nothing" but a state of absolute contradiction. And if any man thinks that he can think well enough how there should be nothing, I'll engage that what he means by "nothing" is as much something as anything that ever [he] thought of in his life; and I believe that if he knew what nothing was it would be intuitively evident to him that it could not be. So that we see that it is necessary some being should eternally be. And 'tis more palpable contradiction still to say that there must be being somewhere, and not otherwhere; for the words "absolute nothing" and "where" contradict each other. And besides, it gives a great shock to the mind to think of pure nothing in any one place, as it does to think of it at all; and it is self-evident that there can be nothing in one place as well as another, and so if there can be in one, there can be in all. So we see this necessary, eternal being must be infinite and omnipresent.[9]

Edwards concludes his entry on being by offering these observations,

> A state of absolute nothing is a state of absolute contradiction. Absolute nothing is the aggregate of all the absurd contradictions in the world, a state wherein there is neither body, nor spirit, nor space: neither empty space nor full space, neither little nor great, narrow nor broad, neither infinitely great space nor finite space, nor a mathematical point; neither up nor down, neither north nor south (I don't mean as it is with respect to the body of the earth or some other great body, but no contrary points nor positions nor directions); no such thing as either here or there, this way and that way, or only one way. When we go about to form an idea of perfect nothing we must shut out all these things. We must shut out of our minds both space that has

---

8. "On the Mind," is also found in *WJE/6*, 313–93. This series of entrees dates from about the same time period.

9. Edwards, *WJE/6*: 202.

> something in it, and space that has nothing in it. We must not allow ourselves to think of the least part of space, never so small, nor must we suffer our thoughts to take sanctuary in a mathematical point. When we go to expel body out of our thoughts, we must be sure not to leave empty space in the room of it; and when we go to expel emptiness from our thoughts we must not think to squeeze it out by anything close, hard and solid, but we must think of the same that the sleeping rocks dream of; and not till then shall we get a complete idea of nothing. A state of nothing is a state wherein every proposition in Euclid is not true, nor any of those self-evident maxims by which they are demonstrated; and all other eternal truths are neither true nor false. When we go to inquire whether or no there can be absolutely nothing we speak nonsense. In inquiring, the stating of the question is nonsense, because we make a disjunction where there is none. "Either being or absolute nothing" is no disjunction, no more than whether a triangle is a triangle or not a triangle. There is no other way, but only for there to be existence; there is no such thing as absolute nothing. There is such a thing as nothing with respect to this ink and paper. There is such a thing as nothing with respect to you and me. There is such a thing as nothing with respect to this globe of earth, and with respect to this created universe. There is another way besides these things having existence. But there is no such thing as nothing with respect to entity or being, absolutely considered. And we don't know what we say, if we say we think it possible in itself that there should not be entity.[10]

Edwards notes that very often if we affirm the possibility of the existence of nothing we in fact affirm the existence of something. Nothing, Edwards tells us, is what sleeping rocks dream of! We may try to explain what we mean by nothing and as soon as we attempt a description of nothing it then morphs into something.

> In our historical sampling of ontological arguments, we bypassed Jonathan Edwards (until now), for we consider his work on Anselm's argument to be superior to most others, and, indeed, to constitute the ultimate proof. According to Edwards, we have an idea of being and we cannot have even an idea of nonbeing ... This is the other side of Anselm's coin. Anselm, at least implicitly, shows that we cannot *not* think of being. Anselm shows that being must be; Edwards that nonbeing must not-cannot-be. If nothing *is*, it is not nonbeing. If being is not, it is not being.

10. Edwards, *WJE/6*: 206–7.

> Since nonbeing cannot be, it cannot be conceived; just as, since being cannot not be, its nonbeing cannot be conceived.[11]

Arguably, this negative ontological argument offered here by Edwards could be understood, to use anachronistic language, as a form of an argument for the impossibility of the contrary. That is, it is impossible that nothing should exist. The very notion of nothing precludes affirming anything positive about it. Further, the argument's context is in a semi-private notebook in which Edwards is performing a thought experiment,[12] although he will later publically express such sentiments in his *Freedom of the Will*.[13] Edwards is not, in this context, combating unbelief but thinking about reality and how it relates to God. John Frame in his review of Gerster, Sproul, and Lindsley's *Classical Apologetics* notes potential pitfalls of this argument.

> A brief look now at the authors' theistic proofs. Their ontological argument, following Jonathan Edwards, is virtually Parmenidean: We have an idea of being; in fact, we can think of nothing else than being. Nonbeing is unthinkable. Thus being must be eternal, omnipresent, limitless in all perfections-in other words, God. There is an obvious objection to this, however, which the book doesn't even mention. However infinite being may be, our idea of being extends to finite being as well. Therefore, if "being" is divine, then finite beings are part of the divine being. In other words, without some modifications, the argument proves pantheism . . . [14]

Frame's point is well-taken if Edwards is aiming to demonstrate the existence of all being. However it seems that he is ruminating on the existence of *necessary* being as opposed to *contingent* being. By definition creation did

---

11. R. C. Sproul, John Gerstner, and Arthur Lindsely, *Classical Apologetics: A Rational Defense of the Christian Faith and a Critique of Presuppositional Apologetics* (Grand Rapids, MI: Zondervan/Academie Books, 1984), 105–6. It should be noted that Anselm in his consideration of what later came to be called (by Immanuel Kant) the ontological argument was reflecting on the nature of infinity and not the nature of being as such.

12. Specifically, the two citations presented here serve as bookends for an exposition of Edwards' *theistic idealism*. Edwards does not deny the existence of extra-mental reality (or objective reality) but notes that reality is what it is because it is primarily in the mind of God. Truth for Edwards is agreement of our ideas with the ideas in God's mind. Related to his theistic idealism is Edwards' embrace of continuous creationism and occassionalism.

13. Edwards, *WJE*/1, 186.

14. John Frame, "Book Review: *Classical Apologetics*," *WTJ* 47 (Fall 1985):279–99. This has been reprinted as an appendix in Frame's *Cornelius Van Til: An Analysis of His Thought* (Philipsburg, NJ: Presbyterian &Reformed Publishing, 1995), 401–22 which is cited here. This quotation is from 419.

not have to exist and so Edwards's argument for the impossibility of nothing would not seem to necessarily yield pantheism.[15]

Is this a good argument? It would seem that it gains its cogency for Edwards from the fact that he already knows from natural and supernatural revelation that there is a God whose existence is absolutely necessary. Given the God of Scripture, it could not be any other wise. In other words, Edwards is drawing out the negative implications of the truth of revelation given by God himself. This is not a stand-alone argument. What's more, the argument considered in and of itself achieves little other than proving the necessary existence of God. While this is no minor detail, it tells us nothing about God's will for the human race or about his plan of redemption. Edwards's negative ontological argument, at best, builds on one aspect of God's being which is true and gives reason enough for us to worship God. But by itself this kind of argument is not likely to lead someone to faith.[16]

Given Jonathan Edwards's understanding of fallen human nature, this negative ontological argument could be used in an exposition of the greatness of the God of the Bible or in a discussion of some aspect of God's nature as Edwards in fact uses it in *Freedom of the Will*. But it would not function as a pre-dogmatic foundation of a specifically Christian theology. It would function to show the impossibility of the contrary. That is, given that the Triune God of Scripture has revealed himself to the human race, *it cannot not be true* that it is impossible that there should be nothing rather than something. But it would take regeneration to bring an unbeliever to the point of not only intellectually accepting the validity and soundness of this argument but also appreciating the God whose existence the argument seeks to prove. At the end of the day, the negative ontological argument may be a reasonable argument, but it is only reasonable on the assumption that the God of the Bible exists and that reason is subject to him.

---

15. Edwards has been considered a pantheist by some. Admittedly his language is unguarded at times. However, given his affirmation of human sin, this would seem to mitigate the pantheistic color of some of his language. Given what is said here, does this mean that Edwards collapses the basic Creator/creature distinction? His argument in *Freedom of the Will* for the necessity of cause and effect distinguishes between eternal being and being that "begins to be." See Edwards, *WJE*/1, 181.

16. We do not mean to suggest that a *particular* apologetic argument needs to argue for *every* truth revealed in God's Word. That would be a tall order indeed.

Romans 1:20 Sermon: "The Being and Attributes of God Seen in the Work of Creation"

Jonathan Edwards first preached this sermon on Romans 1:20 in July of 1743.[17] Unfortunately this sermon only exists in outline form, although it is arguably a fairly full outline.[18] Jonathan Edwards understands himself to be unpacking the sense of the verse. In this sermon Edwards seeks to show how the invisible attributes of God, related to his eternal nature, are clearly evident from creation. The sermon is as it were a series of arguments *arising from* the revelation given in creation (the "light of nature") and confirmed in this text of special revelation that is not merely probable but demonstrably certain.[19]

The series of arguments that comprise the sermon can be broadly characterized as traditional and even classical and evince little that is new.[20] It cannot even be said that one argument yields to another but that Edwards provides a concatenation of arguments for the existence of God and that these are in some sense spelling out what the light of nature reveals. Edwards holds that these evidences of God in creation are clear.[21] Edwards begins with an argument for the fact that there is some cause for the existence of the world and that this cause is one. Additionally there is something that has existed from eternity. The world is not eternal itself so there must be a cause of the world that is eternal.

Edwards develops these thoughts with a consideration of the evidences for the contingency of the world: namely that world is of a fading nature, both of its greater and lesser parts. Not only is there diminution in creation, there is also increase as well. Edwards then discusses the fact that the world must have had a beginning in time and so it was produced by another. Here he discusses the impossibility of an infinite regress or the impossibility of

---

17. It appears to have been repreached in August 1756 according to notations on the sermon manuscript. It is possible, given the length of the outline, that this was a series of sermons. Edwards might take a single "sermon" and preach it over two or more consecutive occasions. See Wilson Kimnach's introduction to the sermon volumes in *The Works of Jonathan Edwards/Vol. 10: Sermons and Discourses, 1720–1723* (Wilson Kimnach, ed., New Haven, CT: Yale University Press, 1992), 3–258.

18. When the sermon is formatted to fill two columns on landscape paper and is set at 12 point font, it takes up 84 pages of text. However it is comprised of incomplete and somewhat disjointed sentences and hints of arguments.

19. Edwards, Romans 1:20 sermon, left column, page 3.

20. The main exception to this generalization is Edwards' comments about the beauty of creation requiring an intellect cause. Edwards, Romans 1:20 sermon, right column, page 21.

21. Edwards, Romans 1:20 sermon, left column, page 2.

an eternal succession of moments.[22] Edwards provides illustrations of this principle with consideration of the revolutions of the sun and the succeeding generations of men.

Edwards then offers discussion of the dependency of the world. He points out that there are two kinds of existence, necessary and contingent.[23] That which is necessarily existent needs no cause but non-necessary existents do need a cause. Edwards then notes that the necessary cause for the existence of the world must be a personal being "that acts by will & choice."[24] This then leads into a presentation of the teleological argument. He points out that the various parts of the world indicate or evidence themselves to be "disposed & ordered to various Ends & uses that they are designed for."[25] Of course, he argues, if these parts of the world evidence design there must be a cause of the design and so there is a Designer "who disposed 'em to those Ends."[26] Related to Edwards's use of the teleological argument is his articulation of something like the *anthropic principle*.[27] That is, "the earth [was] made for habitation" and all the elements combine and converge to provide for the environment in which man will live and even the minutest change in this environment would have made man's existence impossible.[28] As he unpacks this evidence of divine intention and handiwork Edwards makes use, however briefly, of an aesthetic argument. Not only does creation point to a Creator by the intricacy and intentionality and directedness of its mechanics, but creation ought to cause one to wonder and marvel at the workmanship (not to say craftsmanship) of the world.[29] Edwards spends several pages considering the beauty and functionality of different elements of creation such as a tree leaf and parts of the human body.[30] For Edwards the most obvious parts of the world which point to divine "contrivance" are

---

22. Here Edwards looks as if he were offering an argument similar to the well-known *Kalam cosmological argument* which attempts to prove that the world began in time because it is impossible to traverse an infinite series of numbers. Or, to put it another way, one cannot subtract from or add to an infinite series of numbers. This would seem to preclude movement and change whatsoever. For a contemporary exposition of this theistic argument, see William Lane Craig, *The Kalam Cosmological Argument* (Eugene, OR: Wipf & Stock, 2000).

23. Edwards, Romans 1:20 sermon, right column, page 13.

24. Edwards, Romans 1:20 sermon, left column, page 18.

25. Edwards, Romans 1:20 sermon, right column, page 18.

26. Edwards, Romans 1:20 sermon, left column, page 19.

27. Edwards, Romans 1:20 sermon, beginning at left column, p. 20.

28. Edwards, Romans 1:20 sermon, right column, page 21.

29. Edwards, Romans 1:20 sermon, right column, page 22.

30. Edwards, Romans 1:20 sermon, page 22ff. Edwards resembles William Paley and his discussion of one finding a watch and inferring a watchmaker from that fact.

the faculties of the human soul.[31] Their operations "immensely exceed all that of machines that are seen."[32]

Having looked at some length into the teleological evidence for the existence of a divine cause of the world, Edwards then turns to a consideration of the clarity of this evidence. Edwards notes the evidence of God's existence from nature is not merely probable, but "demonstrative."[33] Part of this clarity stems from the manifold nature of it. Everywhere one turns, one is faced with God, not only in the big picture, but in the details of creation. The detailed and intricate nature of creation argues for a Creator who is infinitely wise and powerful. And Edwards suggests that the creation of this infinitely wise and powerful Creator matches and even surpasses the "contrivance & design as much as the most curious machine of the most exquisite workmanship."[34] Citing the Roman statesman and orator Cicero, Edwards notes that life in creation is above and beyond mere mechanics and evidences a vital principle which "surely shows demonstratively a Living Cause[,] a fountain of life."[35] Additionally, Edwards argues that the similarity or uniformity of various creatures argues against an accidental cause of creation.[36] In fact, according to Edwards, "Chance produces diversity[,] because it is blind [and] can't have Respect to a pattern."[37]

Regarding the evidence of creation, Edwards notes that "we see nothing[,] we can turn our Eyes on nothing[,] we hear no sound[,] we taste nothing[,] we smell nothing[,] we feel nothing[,] we understand nothing[,] we Consid[er] nothing but what is a demonstra[tion] of the being of a G[od]."[38] Edwards mentions that Cicero and Seneca both note that no nation is so barbarous that there is not some notion of God among them. "All men have implanted in them an opinion concerning the Gods[,] neither is there any nation so destitute of civility & morality that doth not believe there be some Gods."[39] Edwards here is articulating the insight of John Calvin that all men

---

31. Edwards, Romans 1:20 sermon, left column, page 30ff.
32. Edwards, Romans 1:20 sermon, left column, page 31.
33. Edwards, Romans 1:20 sermon, left column, page 32.
34. Edwards, Romans 1:20 sermon, right column, page 35.
35. Edwards, Romans 1:20 sermon, right column, page 36.
36. Edwards, Romans 1:20 sermon, right column, page 37.
37. Edwards, Romans 1:20 sermon, left column, page 38. Edwards is, of course, not arguing that there is not a diversity of creatures, but that, for instance, they propagate in similar ways which suggests a pattern which in turns suggests a pattern maker.
38. Edwards, Romans 1:20 sermon, left column, page 45.
39. Edwards, Romans 1:20 sermon, left column, page 49.

have a *sensus divinitatis* or *semen religionis*. It is no doubt perverted and twisted, but it cannot be ignored, avoided, or ultimately denied.[40]

Answering the complaints of atheists that God cannot be seen, Edwards responds that these atheists might as well deny the existence of the souls of their neighbors.[41] Edwards points out that other souls are known by their effects and are not seen directly and so it is with God himself. Edwards draws the conclusion from all this that atheists and other critics of Christianity and the belief in God hold to their views because of the blindness brought about by the fall.[42] Indeed such men are little different from the brutes. And so if there is a God he is undoubtedly the fountain of all happiness and the one to whom we owe submission. Indeed, Edwards goes on to encourage unbelievers to turn from their blind sinful thoughts about the God whom they have despised and been an enemy to.[43]

What is one to make of this sermon? John Gerstner argues that it is clear evidence that Edwards was a classical apologist of an undoubted sort.[44] It needs to be admitted, as already noted, that there is little here that is not amenable to a classical apologetics assessment. The various arguments offered do have a longstanding classical pedigree. Admittedly Edwards looks like a Thomas Aquinas, or a William Paley or a Bishop Butler at points. Specifically, Edwards sounds like Thomas when he argues that God is known from his effects, he sounds like Paley when he notes the marvelous contrivances of creation pointing to a Creator, and he resembles Butler when he notes that the unseen world is analogous to the observable natural world. There can be little doubt that Edwards was influenced by the classical Christian tradition. However, before drawing the conclusion that Jonathan Edwards is simply or merely a classical apologetics exemplar, consider these points.

First, not to overlook the obvious, Edwards is offering these arguments in the context of a sermon on Romans 1:20. These arguments are not being presented to the unbeliever in a vacuum.[45] In fact, it could be argued

40. Edwards uses the expression "sense of a deity" here in Romans 1:20 sermon, right column, page 50.

41. Edwards, Romans 1:20 sermon, right column, page 51ff. Edwards seems to anticipate the more detailed discussion along the same lines of Alvin Plantinga in his *God and Other Minds: A Study of the Rational Justification of Belief in God* (Ithaca, NY: Cornell University Press, 1990).

42. Edwards, Romans 1:20 sermon, left column, page 55.

43. Edwards, Romans 1:20 sermon, left column, page 57. The manuscript outline appears to repeat itself at this point, an indication that this was a series of sermons rather than one single unit.

44. Gerstner, "Outline of the Apologetics of Edwards," *BSac*,133/530 (April 1976): 101.

45. Undoubtedly Edwards did *not* assume that everyone in his congregation

that this sermon was preached to an overwhelmingly Christian audience. Additionally, Edwards is offering what he takes to be an extended exposition of Paul's comments in the passage in question. Specifically, "*For his invisible attributes,* namely, his *eternal power* and *divine nature, have been clearly perceived,* ever since the creation of the world, *in the things that have been made.* So they are without excuse."[46] One can say that Edwards's use of classical arguments stems from his understanding of what Paul here says. The invisible God is known through the clearly perceived effects of his work in creation and providence. For good or ill, Edwards understands himself to be expositing this verse.

Second, Jonathan Edwards clearly affirms the *sensus divinitatis*. That is, man knows God because he has been created in the divine image and lives in God's world. God's invisible attributes, namely his eternal power and divine nature, are clearly seen in the things that have been made, and that includes human nature itself. Edwards cites Cicero and Seneca, sources used by John Calvin in his classic articulation of the *sensus*. Men from different ages and cultures uniformly evidence a belief in some sort of God. Edwards notes that this results from either the light of nature or tradition (the so-called *prisca theologia*) or both. The *sensus* accounts for the ubiquity of human religiosity.

But the question arises as to how the *sensus* functions for Edwards. Does Edwards operate with a *capacity innate* model or *content innate* model? Clearly a Reformed classical apologetics tends toward the *capacity innate* model. That is, Reformed classical apologetics would understand that God has implanted in man *the principles or categories by which he can come to know* God but not that God has actually conveyed content to human beings. *Content innatism* holds that God has not only supplied the principles for knowing him but has also conveyed revelatory knowledge. The evidence in Edwards's Romans 1:20 sermon could be read to lean in either direction. On the one hand, the mere presence of classical arguments could lead one to think that Edwards is a *capacity innatist*. That is, arguments are necessary to come to belief in God. On the other hand, elsewhere Edwards argues that belief in God does not require arguments.[47] How do we account for the

---

was a regenerate believer. However, at least the initial preaching of this sermon was to a predominantly Christian audience. The subsequent preaching of the sermon to Stockbridge Indians would probably involve a significantly different setting, but not necessarily so.

46. Romans 1:20, emphasis added. The italicized expressions appear to provide the biblical basis for Edwards' approach to preaching the text.

47. In *Freedom of the Will*, Edwards argues that arguments for the existence of God are made necessary because of the weakness of the human mind. Otherwise God's

presence of theistic arguments if God implants in man not only the capacity to know him but has actually revelationally conveyed knowledge of his existence? Is it possible that what looks like Edwards's *capacity innatism* is actually a form of *content innatism* in which Edwards offers the arguments to clarify and articulate what may initially be inchoate? In other words, theistic arguments could serve to unpack what is already present in the natural knowledge of God implanted in man. Conversely, what do we say about a form of *capacity innatism* in which the principles *always* yield their proper, though limited results?

Third, and this follows from what has already been said, Edwards does not offer the arguments as a neutral pre-dogmatic foundation for developing a more thoroughly articulated Christian theology but as part of an exposition of the biblical text and of Christian theology in general. Edwards is not, in other words, pretending he is not a Christian nor does he pretend to be impartial in his examination of the evidence. The evidence, he argues, is demonstrative and clear. As Ava Chamberlain argued in a citation noted earlier in this chapter, even where Edwards appears as a most typical eighteenth century apologist he assumes the God of Scripture and no other.

Does this make Edwards's arguments persuasive? It seems that whatever strength his arguments have it is because they assume the biblical worldview as background. Since the Triune God of Scripture is who he has revealed himself to be in nature and Scripture, it is this God and not another that Edwards presupposes in his use of the various arguments put forward in the Romans 1:20 sermon.[48] Since the Scriptures reveal that God had a purpose for creating, then it should not come as a shock that creation exhibits signs of purpose or teleology. Since God declares that he is one then it should not come as a surprise that there is only one necessary being who is both one and three. Since the Scriptures declare that the heavens declare the glory of God it makes complete sense that creation reflects its Creator right down to the very minutest details of its diverse mechanics. Having said this, it is debatable that the arguments by themselves, shorn of their biblical sermonic context would carry as much weight. But Edwards understood this because he affirmed the fall and the noetic effects of sin. In order for the unregenerate sinner to come to faith in Christ and believe the Scriptures and subordinate theistic arguments, the Holy Spirit would have to work a radical change.

existence would be self-evident. See *WJE*/1,181–82.

48. That Edwards is thoroughly Trinitarian in his views about God has been amply and ably demonstrated in recent years. In other words, God, for Edwards, is not an "undifferentiated monad"!

Freedom of the Will

John Gerstner has primarily built his case for Jonathan Edwards being a classical apologist upon Edwards's "programmatic statement"[49] in his *Freedom of the Will* to this effect

> We first ascend, and prove *a posteriori*, or from effects, that there must be an eternal cause; and then secondly, prove by argumentation, not intuition, that this being must be necessarily existent; and then thirdly, from the proved necessity of his existence we may descend and prove many of his perfections *a priori*.[50]

Gerstner argues that this statement is programmatic because it sums up in brief compass how Edwards views the apologetic task. That is, Edwards views it *classically*. (1) The Christian must argue for and demonstrate the existence of God from general, universally shared philosophical principles. (2) Additionally, one must then prove by further argumentation that this philosophically demonstrably existent God exists necessarily. (3) Finally, by even further argumentation, one must deduce this philosophically demonstrably necessarily existent God's perfections. (4) Gerstner adds as an addendum the examination of the revelation of this God communicated to man.[51]

Is Edwards doing here what Gerstner argues he is doing? On the surface it appears that Edwards is following the well-worn path of classically demonstrating God's existence *seriatim* through successive philosophical arguments. But does further consideration hold up this assessment? Let's consider this a little more. First, consider the context of the citation in *Freedom of the Will*. Edwards is discussing the reality of cause and effect relationships. There is no such thing as a causeless effect.[52] Things do not

---

49. Gerstner, "Outline of the Apologetics of Jonathan Edward": 6.

50. Edwards, *WJE/1*,182. Gerstner goes on to provide a brief outline of his "Outline" as follows: "Therefore, the discussion in this series will first consider his doctrine of the Eternal Cause and how he finds that Cause from an empirical a posteriori observation of the universe. Then the discussion will follow his argumentation from that doctrine that the Eternal Being must necessarily so be; and some of the a priori deductions of the perfections of this necessarily existing Eternal Cause will be indicated briefly. That will be followed by a study of Edwards' argument that this eternally and necessarily existing perfect Being has revealed Himself in the Sacred Word," "An Outline of the Apologetics of Jonathan Edwards," 6–7.

51. It is obvious that Edwards does not discuss special revelation per se in the citation from *Freedom of the Will* and so it is referred to here as an addendum.

52. This comes pretty close to a classic example of a tautology. By definition, an *effect* is the product of a preceding act or *cause*. More specifically, things that "begin to be" require causes. Also note that in the immediate context of this citation, Edwards argues for cause and effect relations because of the fact that this principle is implanted

just appear out of the blue. Edwards is suggesting that the principle of cause and effect which we see operate in this world points ultimately to a cause of the universe as a whole. Also remember that Edwards is arguing for a Calvinistic compatibilism between divine sovereignty and human responsibility. Strictly speaking Edwards is involved not so much in apologetics as polemics. He is not addressing atheists per se but professing Christians who reject Calvinism and deists.

Beyond these contextual observations there is more that can be said. Edwards is often understood to be an empiricist and that is no doubt true. However, it would be more accurate to say that Edwards trusted in his sense perception because the God of Scripture created sense perception to work properly so that one could draw conclusions from the world around him.[53] What's more, Edwards would include the study of Scripture within the purview of *a posteriori* examination. In other words, Scripture is an *effect* of God's revelatory activity. And we come to know what Scripture says in an a posteriori way, through careful examination of its contents. So a move from effect to cause is a perfectly legitimate way of describing the process of arguing for God's existence from a reading of the Bible. One of the characteristics of Edwards's form of empiricism, if indeed it can be called that, is that he includes within the scope of observation not only natural revelation but also special revelation.

Secondly, Edwards says that we must demonstrate the necessary nature of God's existence via argumentation and not merely from intuition. Edwards may have his negative ontological argument in mind here. Notice, however, that Edwards does not deny intuition, that is, probably the *sensus divinitatis* or implanted sense of divinity. Rather he says this is not sufficient for the purposes of demonstration. Remember that Edwards is not arguing in a vacuum here. He is saying that God's necessary existence, a knowledge of which is given by God himself in the *sensus*, needs to be more fully spelled out or articulated and the use of argumentation assists with that effort. Specifically, the human mind may be too weak to see the self-evident nature of God's existence.[54]

Finally Edwards notes that once the eternal and necessary existence of God is determined, drawing out what is known inchoately in the *sensus divinitatis*, one can then prove in an *a priori* fashion many of God's perfections. This would seem to make sense given the biblical reality of God's

---

in man by God and because of the weakness of the human mind.

53. It should go without saying by this time that Edwards understood sense perception to be effected by the fall with the rest of human nature.

54. Edwards, *WJE/1*, 181. It should be noted that for something to be self-evident does not require that it be facilely evident to everyone.

simplicity.⁵⁵ If, for instance, God is necessary, that means he cannot not be. How could he cease to be? This could happen by means of disintegration. But if God is simple he cannot disintegrate as that would require parts that become detached or that could be gained or lost. The same can be said about eternality. This is a function, if it may be put that way, of his simplicity. There is no before or after with God as he is in himself.

When all is said and done, while it looks like Edwards is arguing with the standard weaponry of classical apologetics, he does not argue from an ostensibly neutral vantage point. It is true that Edwards uses traditional arguments to explicate or articulate more fully what is in fact revealed in Scripture, but Scripture is included in the mix. It is not the case that Edwards is trying to prove these truths apart from Scripture. That is an impossible task. Edwards himself notes that men relying solely on their own reason would end up believing in evil and good gods.⁵⁶ Historically he notes that in fact men have not reasoned their way to the biblical God by their own wits but instead have landed themselves in various forms of idolatry and darkness.

This very insight points us to the fact that Edwards affirmed that God implanted knowledge of himself in all men, but that men suppress that knowledge in sin. Edwards held that it would be necessary to draw out the fuller implications of this implanted knowledge through the use of argumentation. But this argumentation does not ignore the teaching of Scripture. Natural revelation may provide the origin of knowledge of God and arguments draw out the implications but this is all done within the context of biblical revelation.

Edwards admittedly offers little in the way of new insights or apologetic arguments here. He tends to pass on what he has inherited from his forebears and what he has learned from his own context and study. But there is no desire for him to argue as if Christianity was untrue or untried. There is no place to stand outside of God's theater of natural and special revelation.

Miscellanies 1340⁵⁷

We turn for our fourth consideration to Edwards's observations in Miscellanies 1340. In this entry Edwards addresses the relation of human reason

---

55. While it is popular in our day for scholars to assert that Edwards did not whole-heartedly affirm divine simplicity, there are hints of his affirmation of that essential doctrine in his Romans 1:20 sermon.

56. See Edwards' comments to this effect in *WJE/23*, 435.

57. Edwards, *WJE/23*, 359–76. This entry is also available (from the Hickman/Banner of Truth edition of the text) with a brief introduction by K. Scott Oliphint

and revelation, especially as revelation contains mysteries. As with many other Miscellanies entrees, Edwards attempts to address the deist rejection of special revelation and the over-valuation of human reason (or natural revelation). Edwards regularly combats a high estimation of undirected human reason and here points out that there is no such thing in reality as undirected human reason. Attempts to build a religion or morality apart from special revelation inevitably landed one in an epistemological fog and more so in a morass of darkness. Even the best and brightest of the world's philosophers and wise men have been unable to ascertain the nature of reality and the nature of the only God who is.

> And so innumerable other such like mysteries and paradoxes are involved in the notion of an infinite and eternal intelligent Being, insomuch that, if there never had been any REVELATION by which God had made known himself by his word to mankind, the most speculative persons would, without doubt, have forever been exceedingly at a loss concerning the nature of the Supreme Being and First Cause of the universe. And that the ancient philosophers and wiser heathen had so good notions of God as they had, seems to [be] much more owing to tradition, which originated from divine revelation, than from their own invention, though human reason served to keep these traditions alive in the world, and led the more considerate to embrace and retain the imperfect traditions which were to be found in any parts remaining; they appearing, after once suggested and delivered, agreeable to reason.[58]

Edwards particularly has in his scope Matthew Tindal's *Christianity as Old as the Creation*.[59] More specifically Edwards goes after the argument of Tindal that undirected reason[60] not only is competent to judge whether a pretended revelation[61] is indeed revelation but that it has the competence to judge of each and every doctrine within the said revelation.[62]

---

in *Christian Apologetics: Past & Present: Vol. 2/From 1500* (William Edgar & K. Scott Oliphint, eds. Wheaton, IL: Crossway, 2011), 219–38.

58. Edwards, *WJE/23*, 372.

59. Matthew Tindal, *Christianity as Old as the Creation* (London: [No publisher noted],1730).

60. Undirected reason is human reason ostensibly undirected by natural or special revelation.

61. At this point Tindal seems to be following the direction of John Locke.

62. Edwards appears to be arguing that one must begin with presuppositions which have not been demonstrated by argumentation. In other words, one must begin *somewhere*. This would relate to the Reformed Scholastic notion of *principia*, foundational

> Great part of Tindal's arguing, in his *Christianity as Old as the Creation*, proceeds on this ground: that seeing that reason is the judge whether there be any revelation, or whether any pretended revelation be really such, therefore reason without revelation, or undirected by revelation, must be the judge concerning each doctrine and proposition contained in that pretended revelation; which is an unreasonable way of arguing.[63]

Edwards will have none of this. He begins by discussing the nature of knowledge and how human reason judges of the truth of propositions either directly by intuition or self-evidence or by connecting propositions which are derived from intuition or connected in some way to intuited truth with those that are not.

> By REASON I mean that power or faculty an intelligent being has to judge of the truth of propositions, either immediately, by only looking on the propositions, which is judging by intuition and self-evidence; or by putting together several propositions which are already evident by intuition, or at least whose evidence is originally derived from intuition.[64]

Edwards attacks Tindal's notion that each and every doctrine found in an ostensible revelation must be weighed in the balances by undirected human reason. Edwards criticizes both the idea that reasoning works this way and the idea that human reason is truly undirected and can function without divine direction in any case whatsoever. He also deals with human dependency on testimony as well.

> So that general truth, that the testimony of our memories is worthy of credit, can be proved only by reason. And yet what numberless truths are there which we have no other way, and cannot be known to be true by reason considering the truths in themselves, or any otherwise than by the testimony of our

---

principles that form the bedrock of a worldview. Additionally, Edwards may also be arguing against Tindal's apparent attempt to require *epistemological atomism*. That is, there can be no distinction between basic and non-basic beliefs or there can be no mutual influence of one doctrine found in Scripture upon another (what the later Reformed apologist Cornelius Van Til referred to as "limiting concepts").

63. Edwards, *WJE/23*, 359.

64. At this point in the introduction of Miscellanies 1340 Edwards looks like he is affirming and defending some form of epistemological foundationalism. To use more recent terminology, foundationalism holds that beliefs must be either *properly basic* or derived from or refer back to properly basic beliefs in order to be warranted or justified. Edwards seems to be arguing for this distinction against Tindal's suggestion that all beliefs are *non-basic*, *WJE/23*: 359.

memory, and an implicit faith in this testimony. So that the agreed testimony of all we see and converse with continually is to be credited, is a general proposition, the truth of which can be known only by reason. And yet how infinitely numerous are the propositions do men receive as truth that can't be known to be true by reason viewing them separate from such testimony, even all occurrences, and matters of fact, persons, things, actions, works, events, and circumstances, and all existence that we are told of in our neighborhood, in our country, or any part of the world that others tell us of, that we han't seen ourselves.[65]

All of this yields a fairly lengthy consideration of mystery in divine revelation. It is here with Edwards's consideration of the *reasonably expected* mystery present in divine revelation that he comes closest to the apologetic method of Bishop Butler in his *Analogy of Religion*.[66]

> To apply this to the case in hand: if the difficulties that attend that which is recommended by good proof or testimony to our reception as a divine revelation, and this revelation is attended with difficulties, but yet with difficulties no greater nor of any other nature than such as (all things considered) might reasonably be expected to attend a revelation of such a sort, of things of such a nature, and given for such ends and purposes, and under such circumstances; these difficulties not only are not of weight sufficient to balance the testimony or proof that recommends it, but they are of no weight at all as objections against [it]. They are not reasonably to be looked upon as of the nature of arguments against it. But, on the contrary, they may with good reason be looked upon as confirmations, and of the nature of arguments in its favor.[67]

However, there are some differences that may prove significant.

To begin with, and to state the obvious, Butler was an Anglican Arminian whereas Edwards was a Congregationalist Calvinist. This is not to deny overlap of apologetic method *at this one point*, but to suggest that their distinctive theological backgrounds and commitments ought not to be ignored. So then is it really the case that Butler and Edwards share the same method? Yes and no. However, before that question can be answered we

---

65. Edwards, *WJE*/23, 361.

66. Joseph Butler, *Analogy of Religion Natural and Revealed to the Constitution and Course of Nature* (London: [No publisher noted], 1736).

67. Edwards, *WJE*/23, 366.

need to return to Edwards's ruminations in Miscellanies 1340 after which the Butler/Edwards connection can be revisited.

Edwards rejects Tindal's suggestion that undirected human reason ought to attempt to assess each and every doctrine discovered within a purported divine revelation. He rejects both the attempt to by-pass the basic/non-basic relation between beliefs and he rejects Tindal's epistemological atomism. Edwards also dismisses the attempt to avoid reliance on testimony, be that the testimony of another person or the testimony of the human senses. If we proceed with such radical or drastic skepticism, all or virtually all human knowledge would be obliterated. To go through life in this fashion is to fail to reckon with the epistemological antinomies and paradoxes humans run up against in the world of science and experience. If humans experience the limits of human reasoning about such mundane things, should not such finitude be expected when confronted with divine revelation?

Edwards's point is that humans confront epistemological conundrums as a matter of course and so this is no reason for humans to reject divine revelation. If God is who he has said he is, then we should expect to find anomalies. This is not to argue for the irrationality of divine revelation, but the finitude of human reasoning. God is a divine being who is transcendent[68] and so the nature of his being and ways in the world are bound to surpass human attempts at comprehensive or exhaustive understanding. Edwards is not arguing for the unknowability or unintelligibility of God, but he is arguing that God is God and creation is not God. The Latin Reformed Scholastic expression for this reality is *finitum non-capex infiniti*.[69] The presence of mystery in Scripture is not evidence *against* its divine origin but *in favor* of its divine provinence.[70]

Edwards ends his ruminations on reason and revelation by pointing out that man can understand what is revealed although he may not be able to understand all that is entailed in such a revelation.[71] Edwards also notes that objections to divine revelation because of the presence of mystery fails to account for the possibility that future generations may yet gain

---

68. It should go without saying that Edwards also affirms the transcendent God's imminence in the world.

69. That is, "the finite cannot comprehend the infinite." See Richard Muller, *Post Reformation Reformed Dogmatics: The Rise and Development of Reformed Orthodoxy, ca. 1520 to ca. 1725/ Vol.1: Prolegomena to Theology* (Grand Rapids, MI: Baker, 2003), 221–69. This is, of course, a shorthand way of referring to the archetype/ectype or Creator/creature distinction.

70. Edwards, *WJE/23*, 366.

71. Edwards, *WJE/23*, 374.

understanding of things now shrouded in mystery.[72] Edwards further notes that another error in objections to divine revelation because of mystery is the unfounded presupposition that God's revelation is given to satisfy human intellectual curiosity. Such is not the case. Finally, Edwards considers again the fact that as there are conundrums in the system of nature so there are conundrums in the system of revelation. Neither system is destroyed by the mere presence of mystery. God is behind both.[73]

What is one to make of all this? First, it is no doubt true that God's revelation of himself and his redemptive will would contain much that surpasses human understanding. Were it otherwise would be to assume or affirm human omniscience. Edwards walks a fine line here in affirming both the reasonableness of revelation and its supra-mundane nature. In order for revelation to be a form of communication it must be intelligible. However, this does not mean that it will be fully comprehensible on a prima facie reading. Scripture is both intelligible and intellectually challenging. As Edwards points out, some of the challenges may be due to the limitations of the current state of human knowledge or they may be the result of the permanent limitations of human knowledge as such.

Second, we agree that Edwards is correct to challenge the notion that human reason can function aright apart from divine revelatory direction. Human reason was never intended to properly function in this manner. From creation God intended both natural revelation and special revelation to mutually reinforce each other. There is no point at which God intended his human creatures to think on their own. This was true before the fall in the Garden of Eden and it is most certainly true after the fall and the introduction of sin and its noetic effects. Edwards frequently noted several things about fallen man's attempt to think without God's direction: (1) As already noted, man was not created to function this way. (2) Since the fall, man cannot function this way. (3) In fact, those who have attempted to understand God apart from divine revelation and who have attempted to order their moral lives accordingly, end up in gross ignorance or rely upon God's natural revelation and the corrupt vestiges of his special revelation.

72. Edwards, *WJE/23*, 375.

73. Edwards, *WJE/23*, 374–76. Edwards notes "For such a system (or Bible) of the word of God is as much the work of God as any other of his works, the effect of the power, wisdom and contrivance of a God whose wisdom is unsearchable and whose nature and ways are past finding out. And as the system of nature and the system of revelation are both divine works, so both are in different senses a divine word. Both are the voice of God to intelligent creatures, a manifestation and declaration of himself to mankind. Man's reason was given him that he might know God and might be capable of discerning the manifestations he makes of himself in the effects and external expressions and emanations of the divine perfections," 374.

> And that the ancient philosophers and wiser heathen had so good notions of God as they had, seems to [be] much more owing to tradition, which originated from divine revelation, than from their own invention, though human reason served to keep these traditions alive in the world, and led the more considerate to embrace and retain the imperfect traditions which were to be found in any parts remaining; they appearing, after once suggested and delivered, agreeable to reason.[74]

In other words, the deistic attempt to formulate a natural theology/religion from reason alone fails on all counts. Given this failure of ostensible undirected human reason, the presence of mystery serves as no impediment against the reality of divine special revelation.

Does Edwards follow Bishop Butler at this point? It seems that with regard to the recognition of an analogy between the system of nature and the system of revelation that there is some similarity. However, at least one point of difference would be that Butler does not start with Scripture whereas Edwards's whole point is to explain the presence of mystery in revelation. In other words, while Butler tries to move from experience in this mundane world to the possibility or probability of similar experience in the next world, Edwards moves from the given of Scripture and the presence of mysteries in special revelation backwards to the presence of similar kinds of mysteries in science and the experiences of this life. The difference may be subtle, but it is a difference nonetheless. Edwards's argument can be said to yield a unity of natural and special revelation because behind them both stands the same Trinitarian God. It can also be noted that Edwards does not argue in terms of probability. Natural and special revelation provide certain knowledge.[75]

Notes on Scripture Entry 416

As was noted earlier in this chapter, John Gerstner argues that Jonathan Edwards was an exemplar of the classical apologetic method that involved a demonstration of God's existence[76] from philosophical sources followed

---

74. Edwards, *WJE/23*, 372.

75. Edwards references Butler ten times throughout his literary corpus. For instance, see his comments concerning the *Analogy of Religion* in *The Works of Jonathan Edwards: Vol. 21/Writings on Trinity, Grace, and Faith* (Sang Huyn Lee, ed. New Haven, CT: Yale University Press, 2003), 298.

76. Clearly Edwards assumes the existence of the Trinitarian God of Scripture and does not argue for a generic deity which is typical for the classical method.

by an examination of the Bible with the goal of proving that it is a revelation of the God demonstrated to exist from philosophical argumentation via a probabilistic historical veracity. With this model of the classical apologetic method in view it would be useful to examine one of Edwards's attempts to defend a traditional view of the Bible. In *Notes on Scripture* entry 416 Edwards seeks to defend the Mosiac authorship of the Pentateuch in the face of rising Enlightenment critical biblical scholarship.[77]

Stephen J. Stein, the editor of the Yale edition of the *Notes on Scripture*, offers a very helpful synopsis of Edwards's effort:

> The longest single entry in the series, No. 416, entitled "Whether the PENTATEUCH was written by MOSES" (see fig. 1), joins the debate generated by the judgments of Thomas Hobbes (1588–1679) and others who attacked the Mosaic authorship of the first five books of the Hebrew Bible. In a chapter of *Leviathan* (1651) dealing with "the Number, Antiquity, Scope, Authority, and Interpreters of the Books of Holy SCRIPTURE," Hobbes argued that the conventional identification of the Pentateuch as "the five Books of *Moses*" did not automatically provide sufficient reason to conclude that he wrote them, for often the names of books mark content rather than authorship, as, for example, in the book of Ruth. On the basis of internal evidence, Hobbes concluded that "the five Books of *Moses* were written after his time," though when was not clear. Edwards's defense of Mosaic authorship included an argument based on the internal witness of Scripture. He assumed the correctness of the ancient testimony linking Moses with the writing of the precepts delivered on Mount Sinai. His task, however, was to establish that Moses wrote the balance of the Pentateuch. Edwards posited a necessary link between history and law in the Pentateuch. The history of God's dealings with ancient Israel served as an essential "preamble," or rationale, for the legal codes; Moses would not have trusted the memory of those events to oral tradition. Therefore he also recorded in writing the great acts of God. Furthermore, Edwards cited references throughout the Old Testament that he regarded as further confirmation of Moses's authorship of the entire Pentateuch and as proof that a written record containing both precepts and history existed from the time of Moses. Such record-keeping, he pointed out, was common among ancient

---

77. A similar unpublished manuscript appears to continue the discussion. See Stein's comments at 15n2 in *WJE/15*. Note that Edwards recognizes some "post-Mosaica" elements in the Pentateuch but he does not think these mitigate his argument whatsoever. See Edwards, *WJE/15*, 466–69.

nations. The existence of the Book of the Law in the period before the Babylonian captivity was, in Edwards' judgment, further proof of the Pentateuch's antiquity and evidence against any notion of possible "forgery" by a later hand.[78]

At the outset it should be noted that in this entry Edwards does not argue from the standpoint of neutrality endeavoring to pile up evidences of divine activity. Rather he argues from the internal evidence of the Pentateuch and the Old Testament as a whole that Moses is the author of the first five books of the Bible. One could rightly argue without any exaggeration that Edwards practices here a form of inner-biblical exegesis. Edwards is impressive in his familiarity with the details of the Scriptural text and all throughout the entry Edwards argues *from* the assumption of divine revelation, not *to* it.

As Stein has indicated, Edwards defends Mosaic authorship of the Pentateuch on the basis of two internal arguments. First, Edwards argues for the inextricable intertwining of law and history in the Pentateuch.

> 'Tis the more likely that the history of the Pentateuch should be a part of that which was called the law of Moses, because it is observable that the words law, doctrine, statute, ordinance, etc., as they were used of old, did not only intend precepts, but also promises, and threatenings, and prophecies, and monuments, and histories, or whatever was revealed, promulgated, and established, to direct men in or enforce their duty to God ... And 'tis probable that when we read of the great things of God's law (Hosea 8:12), and the wondrous things of God's law, that thereby is not only intended precepts and sanctions, but the great and wondrous works of God recorded in the law. 'Tis evident that the history is as much of an enforcement of the precepts (and is so made use of), as the threatenings, promises, and prophecies; and why then should it not be included in the name of the law as well as they? There is something of history, or a declaration of the great acts or works of God, in that [which] is by way of eminency called the "law," viz. the Decalogue, in that there is a declaration of the two greatest works that the history in the Pentateuch gives an account of, viz. the creation of the world and the redemption out of Egypt out of the house of bondage. The latter is mentioned in the preface, and both in the 4th commandment in Deuteronomy 5:6–15.[79]

---

78. Stein, editor's introduction, *WJE*/15, 14–15.
79. Edwards, *WJE*/15, 430–31.

It is not as though Moses was responsible for the promulgation of the law but that some later redactor created the history surrounding the legal pronouncements. Second, this inextricable intertwining of law and history is familiar to later biblical writers throughout OT history as is evidenced in the various books. It is not as if only the bare laws were known nor are there signs of an evolving encrustation of history forming around the laws. The two go hand-in-hand at the beginning and are known to co-exist throughout the history covered in the OT.[80] Edwards does note toward the end of entry 416 that a similar awareness of the close connection between law and history in the Pentateuch was known to the Gentiles as well through contact between various Gentile nations and the Jews. In other words, as already indicated, Edwards draws on the *prisca theologica* tradition here.[81] However the weight of the case does not fall on the *prisca*, which is brought in near the end of the entry as confirming evidence.

Jonathan Edwards does meticulously examine the internal biblical evidence for the Mosaic authorship of the Pentateuch and confirms it with his detailed overview of later OT use of the Pentateuch.[82] Edwards does refer to "common sense" or "reason" being able to understand what is there in the text. But he does appear to be careful in distinguishing between the objective evidence in the text (evidence for Mosaic authorship and later OT familiarity with that fact) and the subjective awareness of it. In other words, properly functioning reason would see what ought to be so obvious. But as Edwards recognizes elsewhere and proclaims clearly himself, fallen man does not reason properly and only the regenerate see what is in front of them in the biblical text. There is a careful balancing of the objective and subjective here. The internal work of the Holy Spirit does not create the evidence of Mosaic authorship. That is in the text. But the work of the Holy Spirit enables an otherwise recalcitrant reader to recognize with joy what lies before his eyes in the Bible.

Edwards gives ample evidence for the fact that starting *from* the divine authorship of the Bible (and that is really what his argument about Mosiac

---

80. Edwards, *WJE/15*, 443. Edwards then cites 12 pages worth of passages that indicate later Israelite awareness of both the intertwining nature of law and history and that Moses authored the Pentateuch.

81. Edwards, *WJE/15*, 456–67.

82. One could plausibly argue that Edwards foreshadows the argument of Martin Noth in *The Deuteronomistic History* (Sheffield, UK: Sheffield Academic Press, 1981), that the author of the Deuteronomy writes a book that casts a shadow over the rest of the OT historical books, even the whole of the OT. Of course Edwards holds to the Mosaic authorship of the whole of the Pentateuch and would say that it is not surprising that the foundational books of the OT cast a shadow over the rest of the OT as that is the divine intent.

authorship is all about since the OT and the NT attribute the Pentateuch to Moses) does not preclude close examination of the textual evidence. What it does mean is that the Bible itself is the standard and judge of what is true.

Preliminary Conclusions

In the foregoing part of this chapter five of Edwards's apologetic considerations were described and given an initial assessment. Edwards's negative ontological argument, his exposition of Romans 1:20, his brief discussion of proving the existence of God in *Freedom of the Will*, his consideration of the presence of mystery in special revelation, and his defense of the Mosaic authorship of the Pentateuch were given consideration. What do these reveal about Edwards's approach to the defense of the faith? First, Edwards was *not* the pioneer of some *new* well-defined apologetic method. Edwards's arguments are classical in the sense that they build on the mainstream tradition of defending the Christian faith. The also reflect the classical Christian tradition in their *eclecticism*. As with many of his Reformed Scholastic and Puritan forebears, Edwards drew from various philosophical sources which he found helpful.[83] This eclecticism reflects the conviction that no single philosophical school had captured the sum total of biblical truth. After all, philosophy was understood to be the handmaiden of theology. The question of whether these roles were ever reversed will be considered later in this chapter.

Second, there is no unambiguous evidence that Edwards intended to argue from the ground up for the Christian faith in these readings. It is one thing to use traditional arguments in the midst of an exposition of some aspect of the Christian faith, but it is quite another to try to reach Christian theism from a foundation of autonomous shared convictions that would be true whether the God of Scripture existed or not. In other words, Edwards did not argue for a "god" before arguing for the Triune God of Scripture. This is key. For instance, Edwards never said that the principle of cause and effect would be operative apart from the operations of God, but that the principle is indicative of God's existence and is one means of demonstrating

---

83. Once again, this eclecticism reflects both Edwards' education and his wide-ranging reading habits. Edwards, as has already been noted, was a member of the transatlantic "republic of letters" and so endeavored to keep up with the latest currents of thought in Great Britain and Europe in order to both refute error and harness what was useful. See William Sparkes Morris, *The Young Jonathan Edwards* The Jonathan Edwards Classic Studies Series (Eugene, OR: Wipf & Stock, 2005), Norman Fiering, *Jonathan Edwards' Moral Teaching and It's British Context* (Chapel Hill, NC: University of North Carolina Press, 1981), and Gerald McDermott and Michael McClymond, *The Theology of Jonathan Edwards* (New York: Oxford University Press, 2011).

his existence. Given that the Bible clearly presents God as Creator of all things outside of himself, the principle of cause and effect is valid with regard to creation. Edwards was wise enough to know that God, as uncaused, was not himself covered by the principle as to his own existence.[84] Having said that, the principle did explain how God ordinarily worked providentially in this world.[85]

Third, and related to the second point and to Ava Chamberlain's comments referenced earlier, Edwards presupposed the God of Scripture in his argumentation and while he may have adapted some traditional apologetic arguments, these were never used in a vacuum. Edwards's sermon on Romans 1:20 is a good case in point. Whatever argumentation appears in the sermon is building upon and drawing out what has been revealed in God's natural revelation. At least that is what Edwards thought he was doing. This raises the question of whether these arguments are sound. It seems that their cogency is drawn from the reality of the biblical God and the world which he brought into existence. Given the biblical datum that God is eternal and necessarily existent, the possibility of nothing existing is impossible. Given that God has revealed aspects of his divine nature and moral government in creation (including human nature), can it be said that arguments drawing out the implications of this natural revelation are illegitimate? Given that the God of Scripture has revealed himself to his creation, is it not realistic and something one ought to expect that there would be mysteries in that revelation given the Creator/creature distinction? And would not the Bible internally provide evidence of its own veracity when it attributes a book or books to a specific author? God is a God of truth.

It has not been the purpose of this chapter to evaluate the cogency of the various apologetic arguments Edwards used. The concern was instead to see if Edwards was doing what John Gerstner has said he was doing, which was, in essence, building a pre-dogmatic foundation for the rearing of an eventual Christian theistic superstructure. That is, was Jonathan Edwards endeavoring to defend the Christian faith by first arguing for a generic theism upon principles shared by believers and unbelievers alike? For example, that there are laws of logic that work apart from their recognition by humans is undoubtedly true. That unbelievers ought to use them rightly is also true. But did Edwards think unbelievers consistently used logic is highly

---

84. See Edwards, *WJE/1*, 181.

85. See Edwards, Miscellanies 1263, for a full treatment of the ways of God with his creation, at *WJE/23*, 201–12.

unlikely.[86] Did Edwards think that laws of logic functioned apart from the existence of the biblical God and/or did he argue like they did? Not at all.[87]

From a consideration of the foregoing, the least that can be said is that the conscious classical apologetic commitment is missing. What's more, the manner in which the various elements function in Edwards's arguments don't always fit a classical use. More will be said below after the various strands of this study have been woven together.

Recapitulation of the Whole Study

In the first chapter we were introduced to John Gerstner's portrayal of Jonathan Edwards as a practitioner of the classical method of apologetics. In the first volume of *The Rational Biblical Theology of Jonathan Edwards* Gerstner devotes some 79 pages to positioning Edwards within the mainstream of the classical apologetics tradition.[88] Gerstner offers the classical tradition in opposition to both Neo-Orthodoxy and Presuppositionalism. One of the hallmarks of the classical tradition, both in terms of theology in general and apologetics in particular, was its acceptance and use of various philosophical tools. While there has been a stream in the Christian tradition that questions the validity of secular philosophy, the mainstream has not been so quick to dismiss its value. Philosophy is understood by this mainstream as the *ancilla* or handmaiden of theology. Gerstner suggests that philosophy was to the Gentile world what the Old Testament was to the Hebrews. This raises questions about the validity of philosophy, the relation of philosophy to theology, the nature and uses of human reason, the nature of natural and special revelation, etc. Edwards, it is argued, stands within the mainstream of this classical theological and apologetic tradition. The purpose of this study has been

---

86. Consideration of this point needs to be careful, as the Reformed faith has never affirmed that the noetic structure of the human mind was utterly obliterated. That would incapacitate the human race altogether. That we affirm total depravity is not the same as affirming absolute or utter depravity. Even the 20th century Reformed apologist Cornelius Van Til understood this point. In his analogy of the noetic effects of sin to a slanted buzz saw he noted that the saw still "worked" in some sense. But it did not work properly or as it was intended by God.

87. Consider the fact that Edwards was a Trinitarian theistic idealist. That is, in response to the materialism of Thomas Hobbes, Edwards argues that the extra mental world is based in God's mind and so God is the only true substance in the world. Gerstner notes Edwards' idealism, but does not seem to allow it to color his treatment of Edwards as a theologian or apologist. If one did not know better, one might come away from reading Gerstner and think Edwards was a Scottish common sense realist.

88. Gerster, *Rational Biblical Theology* 1:1–79.

to seek to nuance and correct Gerstner's general assertion that Edwards was a classical apologist *simpliciter*. The picture is far more complex.

The second chapter was devoted to Jonathan Edwards's understanding of man as the image of God. Specifically, Gerstner's suggestion that Edwards held to some form of the doctrine of the *donum superadditum* was given consideration. The presence of such a doctrine in Edwards's theological anthropology while not completely determinative of the question of whether he was a classical apologist, would point in the direction of his being so. After all, the classical apologist *par excellence*, Thomas Aquinas, articulated a full-blooded *donum* doctrine. In general terms, it was seen that Jonathan Edwards held to the traditional Reformed understanding of Adam and Eve as created good, with a holy disposition and that they were created in the image of God. Unlike other traditions of the Christian faith, Adam and Eve were not understood to be created neutral. They were created in holiness, righteousness, and knowledge. This image is understood by Edwards in two senses.[89] Reflecting man's analogical relationship to God, man has a natural and a moral image. The natural image would involve man's rationality and relationality, etc. The moral image would be man's reflection of God's character on a human scale. One could say that the natural image provides the preconditions of the moral image. As with the Reformed tradition in general, Edwards affirmed that the fall involved the loss of the moral image and the corruption of the natural image.

A consideration of the question of whether Edwards held to some form of the *donum superadditum* doctrine was given as the presence of such a doctrine would be consistent with a classical view of apologetics even if was not by itself fully determinative. The doctrine of the *donum* suggests that man was created in a natural state and that God superadded a gift of moral rectitude. Man could function quite adequately without the *donum* but if he were to achieve the purpose for which he was created, to achieve the beatific vision, he would need this supplementation. Given that the *donum* was an added layer and not constitutive of man's nature or character, its loss would be serious but not wholly destructive. Man without the *donum* could function adequately in this world but without redemption could not achieve the beatific vision.

The Reformed position recognized a broad and a narrow aspect to the image. Edwards, while using the language of a natural and moral image rather than the broad and narrow language, was in accord with this standard view. Man was never intended to function without the moral image.

---

89. These two senses correspond more or less to the traditional broad and narrow definitions of the *imago Dei*.

While Edwards could distinguish between the natural and moral image they were integral to one another. Additionally, there is no sense in Edwards that fallen man, *sans* moral image, can function adequately, except in the limited sense of functioning in this world in society. The loss of the moral image involved the corruption of the natural image. This would be a major difference between the Reformed and traditional Roman Catholic *donum* doctrine. It was suggested that John Gerstner may have partially accepted the judgment of Arthur Bamford Crabtree who argued that Edwards, and the Reformed tradition more generally, had returned to the doctrine of the *donum superadditum* with the broad and narrow image distinction. The difference with Crabtree came down to this: for Crabtree the recourse to the broad/narrow image distinction was a dead end.[90] For Gerstner it was a legitimate move and provided further evidence that Edwards stood within the mainstream of the classical apologetic tradition.[91] The problem, as already noted, was that Edwards recognized that the natural (broad) image was corrupted with the loss of the moral (narrow) image. The only sense in which Edwards could be said to hold to a *donum* doctrine is his view that the moral image was a result of the presence and activity of the Holy Spirit in the life of Adam and Eve before the fall.

The relation of the discussion of the image of God to apologetics may easily get forgotten. The point of the thing is that man was not created neutral and was not left neutral by the fall. Created upright and good, man fell into the degradation and mire of sin. This means that when the Christian does apologetic work he or she is not addressing a person who functions properly nor with no bias. Man was created to commune with God and now naturally despises God. Man is not able to respond positively to the gospel/apologetic encounter without the supernatural work of the Holy Spirit. Edwards clearly understood that man was fallen and that he is not able to assess an apologetic argument with equanimity.

In the third chapter of this study Edwards's understanding of natural and special revelation was examined. Relative to the question of revelation is Edwards's estimation of philosophy and its relation to theology. Jonathan Edwards affirmed the existence of natural revelation, which he frequently referred to as the "light of nature." Quite obviously he also affirmed special revelation. In the midst of his debates with various and sundry deists Edwards noted that natural revelation was not sufficient for man to practice

---

90. See Arthur Bamford Crabtree, *Jonathan Edwards' View of Man: A Study in Eighteenth Century Calvinism* (Wallington, Surrey: The Religious Education Press, LTD., 1948), 22–27.

91. See Gerstner, *Rational Biblical Theology*, 2:316–19.

acceptable piety towards God.[92] Sole reliance upon natural revelation was problematic for several reasons. First, natural revelation was never meant, in God's providence and the unfolding plan of redemption, to be sufficient unto itself. Second, man exists now, subsequent to the fall, in a fallen state, and so cannot rightly interpret natural revelation. Edwards would agree with Calvin's assessment that Scripture provides the clarifying lenses through which the light of nature may be properly understood. Third, addressing the scandal of particularity, Edwards built upon the tradition of the *prisca theologica* or primitive or pristine theology.[93] The *prisca theologica* is, strictly speaking, neither a species of natural revelation nor special revelation. It is, rather, the corrupt residue of special revelation passed down through the generations. Edwards's point is that deists who claim that natural revelation is sufficient to frame a God-honoring religion are wrong because they rely for the assessment not upon natural revelation per se but the truncated residuals of divine special revelation.

Related to this is Edwards's consideration of secular philosophy and its relation to theology and the authority of Scripture. With the Reformed Scholastics and the mainstream of the Christian tradition, Edwards appreciated the benefits of philosophy all the while remaining wary of specific proposals. That is, philosophy as the love of and search for wisdom, was a worthy endeavor considered as an ideal (or in the abstract). But specific philosophical schools often conflicted with one another and sought to formulate views without recourse to special revelation. Given this reality, Edwards was an eclectic in his use of various philosophical views. Beneficial philosophical views could properly be seen as an element of either common grace or as an instance of the workings of the *prisca theologica* or some combination of both. [94]

92. Numerous Miscellanies entrees, some of which are referenced in chapter three of this study, indicate Edwards' familiarity with the deist movement. Edwards also publically addressed deism in two sermons. The first was a lecture on 2nd Peter 1:19 which he delivered in August of 1737 and the other on Romans 2:5 sometime between August of 1731 and December of 1732. The Romans 2:5 sermon remains unpublished, but Gerstner notes in *Rational Biblical Theology*, 1:118, that "Indeed Edwards, incidentally, reveals the status of deists in his own mind when in an unpublished sermon in 1731 he referred to "robbers, pirates, and deists," with implied apologies to robbers and pirates for putting them in such company." The 2nd Peter sermon can be found in *The Works of Jonathan Edwards: Vol. 19/Sermons and Discourses 1734–1738* (M. X. Lesser, ed., New Haven, CT: Yale University Press, 2001), 704–733 and is titled "Light in a Dark World, A Dark Heart."

93. Edwards' apologetic response to deism and these specific answers are detailed throughout Gerald McDermott's *Jonathan Edwards Confronts the Gods* (New York: Oxford University Press, 2000).

94. If one must categorize Edwards philosophically he would be a Trinitarian

In the fourth chapter consideration was given to the relation between the intellect and the will and Edwards's views about faculty psychology. Space was given to the historical context of the formulation of Edwards's views in the midst of the First Great Awakening reminding us that no views are formed in a vacuum. Edwards, it was contended, moved away from the hierarchical faculty psychology prevalent in his day in which either the intellect or the will was given predominance (thus giving rise to various schools of thought such as the Thomistic-intellectualist, the Scotistic-voluntarist, and the Augustinian-voluntarist schools) in his desire to formulate a biblical psychology which avoided the intellectual extreme of rationalism on the one hand and emotional excesses of fanaticism on the other. A careful examination was made of Christian philosopher Alvin Plantinga's use of Edwards in wrestling with this question in his *Warranted Christian Belief*.[95] Plantinga found Edwards at times sounding an intellectualist note and at others a more voluntaristic note. At the end of the day Plantinga opted for an intellectualist Edwards. The conclusion of this study was that Edwards was closer to Plantinga than he himself may have realized. Edwards could be categorized as either a concurrentist or as economic intellectualist. Either the intellect and will work concurrently or the intellect precedes the will in a proper functioning psychology and epistemology but that this suggests no superiority of one faculty over another. Both the intellect and will are necessary components of a properly functioning soul. This consideration of Plantinga helped us in assessing John Gerstner's assertion that the noetic effects of sin are "indirect" by way of the will. That is, the intellect functions properly but that the will is what varies between the unregenerate and the regenerate. This formulation appears problematic as it fails to square with Edwards's own view and seems to retain a preserve of uninfected human nature.[96]

---

theistic idealist.

95. Alvin Plantinga, *Warranted Christian Belief* (New York: Oxford University Press, 2000).

96. One could conceivably understand the speculative knowledge/spiritual knowledge distinction to be a matter of *mere volitional change* in the knower. This would require one to see the transition from speculative to spiritual knowledge to be one of *simple supplementation*. The intellect functions properly but the will does not and the transition from speculative to spiritual knowledge is the retention of speculative knowledge unchanged but supplemented by a corrected will. In fact, the transition involves *both* the correction of the intellect so that it apprehends extra-mental realities like God and the things of God aright (that is, sees God as truly and rightly lovely and beautiful and glorious because that is just what God is) and sees so them *as they really are* and renews the will so that it responds to extra-mental realities (like God and the things of God) as it should.

Related to the question of the intellect and will is Edwards's understanding of "right reason." Following on the work of recent reconsideration of the history of reception of the concept of right reason, with a more intellectualistic strain on the one hand and a more holistic strain on the other, it was determined that Edwards stood squarely within the holistic stream. That is, Edwards understand human reason to be the good creation of an all-wise God but that sin had infected its proper function. Reason cannot properly function in its fallen condition but must be restored in regeneration. Reason could be understood, as articulated by one of Edwards's favorite theologians, Francis Turretin, in the abstract and in the concrete. In the abstract or ideal condition reason is meant to function properly under God and his revelation. However reason does not function in the abstract but only in the concrete. Therefore reason is either fallen or regenerate and right reason is regenerate reason. Edwards often considers reason in its ideal form but does not consider any fallen sinner as possessing the ideal form. While Edwards may argue that certain truths should be apparent to right reason or common sense this is not an appeal to neutral reason but an appeal to reason as it should function or as it has begun to function in regenerate souls.

In this fifth and final chapter five apologetic arguments or reflections offered by Edwards were considered. Strictly speaking three of the Edwardsean texts are from the semi-private notebooks ("Of Being," "Miscellanies" 1340, and Notes on Scripture 416) so that they are not public apologetic treatises per se. Arguably *Freedom of the Will* and the *Romans 1:20 sermon* are fully public documents and so their apologetic force is much more obvious. However the three notebook entries are nonetheless full of apologetic significance. In the "Of Being" entry Edwards argued for a negative ontological argument. It is impossible that nothing should be. It was argued that while Edwards could be guilty of arguing for pantheism, it is more likely that he was arguing for necessary being, not all being as such. If God is a necessary being then it seems reasonable that there is zero possibility of non-existence. This is not a merely rationalistic argument since Edwards is assuming the biblical God in the background.

In his sermon on Romans 1:20 Edwards exposits the text and in the midst of doing that offers a concatenation of standard arguments for the existence of God. Edwards does not present these as autonomous or free standing arguments. He is developing Paul's comments that God's invisible attributes are seen in the things that have been made. Edwards expatiates on the cosmological argument, the teleological argument, and others.[97] The point is that these are drawing out and building on revelation given by God in nature and are not merely autonomous human attempts to prove God's existence out of thin air. Edwards is seeking to draw out what is given in and with the creation. A consideration was given to the capacity innate versus content innate models of understanding how one comes to know God through creation. Given Edwards's views that even the triune nature of God can be known from nature, it is not possible that he would argue for a vague theism.

In *Freedom of the Will* Edwards is defending Calvinistic compatibilism.[98] There is no such thing as an uncaused effect. There is no such thing as libertarian free will. The will is effected by the disposition of the human soul. A person does as he is. God has built into creation the principle of cause and effect and it can be used to lead us from creation back to God. But does Edwards think that this cause and effect principle stands whether or not the God of Scripture exists? Not likely. After all, even revelation itself is an effect that requires a cause because that is how the Triune God of the Bible has constituted the world. Nor is there something suspect about a *posteriori* reasoning. One can reason by induction or deduction under the authority of God's Word or autonomously.

We saw that Edwards discusses the existence of mystery in divine revelation in *Miscellanies 1340*.[99] Edwards argues that given the existence of mystery in mundane science we should not be surprised to see mystery in Scripture. There is some resemblance here to Joseph Butler's method. But not completely so. Edwards also argues that given the nature of the God of Scripture (i.e., the Creator/creature distinction) it should not be surprising that human beings find conundrums in the Bible. Of course there are no real inconsistencies, but given the vast chasm that exists between God and his human creation puzzles and paradoxes would not be out of place. The argument stands whether or not there is an analogy between the book of nature and the book of revelation. However given that the same Triune God stands behind both books it would not be surprising that there are some shared characteristics.

---

97. See 197–201 above for a discussion of Edwards' use of traditional arguments in the context of expositing the text of Romans 1:20.

98. See 202–04 above.

99. See 204–10 above.

Finally, Edwards's defense of the Mosaic authorship of the Pentateuch in *Notes on Scripture entry 416* was examined.[100] Here Edwards does not appeal to external standards of logic or evidence but argues internally from the details of the text of Scripture that in the Pentateuch the law and history are inextricably intertwined and that this close connection was seen and understood at various points along the way as the books of the Old Testament were written. From beginning to end, in both the OT and the NT Moses is understood to be the author of the first five books of the Bible. Given that this is what the Scriptures themselves claim, Edwards's defense of Mosaic authorship is indirectly an argument for the divine authorship and veracity of the claims of Scripture.

Final Conclusions

So was Jonathan Edwards a model exemplar of a classical apologist? John Gerstner says yes. But the picture that has come into focus here is more complex. There is more to the picture than meets the eye. The answer to the question would have to be a yes and no or a no and yes. Consider the description that has been offered of what classical apologetics is. It is a two part apologetic in which the existence of God (or a "god") is proved by recourse to secular philosophy (i.e., rules of logic or structures in the universe that function regardless of the real existence of the God of the Bible) and sometimes the nature of man is considered and whether such a god as can be proved by neutral rationality can communicate with his human creation. Once this initial assessment has been made then the Bible is examined to determine whether it is in fact a revelation from God to man. This assessment usually seeks to prove the probability of the Bible's divine origins through demonstrating its historical veracity and trustworthiness.

However, is it true that the presence of some of these elements in Jonathan Edwards's apologetic constitutes him a classical apologist? In one sense since Edwards was not completely original in his apologetic approach it comes as no surprise that he resembles all sorts of other apologists. Scholars have noted in passing that in some ways he looks just like other 18th century defenders of the faith.[101] Edwards was not seeking to pioneer some new earth-shattering apologetic method. To even speak of a self-conscious

---

100. See 210–14 above.

101. Josh Moody has suggested this in his *Jonathan Edwards and the Enlightenment: Knowing the Presence of God* (Lanham, MD: University Press of America, 2005), 155–57, and more recently McDermott and McClymond in their *Theology of Jonathan Edwards*, 26, 40–59.

awareness of apologetic method is probably anachronistic. One notable distinction, for instance, between Jonathan Edwards and John Gerstner is that Edwards uses arguments at hand without a full-blooded commitment to a "classical apologetic" method.[102] Edwards is in this sense a child of his times. The development of apologetic schools is arguably a post-Edwardsean development. However, this is not to say that Edwards was not addressing real and serious apologetic issues. On the contrary, Edwards defended the faith at those points in his day where it was being attacked.[103]

Looking at the description of the classical method just given above, it could be suggested that Edwards used classical arguments. Indeed he did. However there is a difference between *happening* to use an argument at hand (good, bad, or indifferent) which has frequently been used by apologists in the history of the Christian church and being ideologically committed to only using certain kinds of arguments or using them within the context of a well-defined and articulated apologetic method. Additionally it could be argued that there is a significant difference between presenting apologetic proofs as confirmation of Scripture and the faith and offering them as originating proofs (i.e., as the non-dogmatic foundation of Christian theology). Once again it needs to be noted that Edwards reflects both his Reformed Scholastic heritage (eclecticism) and his own era (the Enlightenment concern with the natural sciences). But one could also argue that Edwards's Reformed and biblical theological commitments served as a mitigating force regarding the less felicitous aspects of classical arguments.

For instance, does Edwards endeavor to prove the existence of a vague divinity? One could say that his negative ontological argument comes right up to the edge. But even here it needs to be noted that the God he believes is necessarily existent and so could not not exist is the Triune God of Scripture. As previously noted, Edwards affirmed with Augustine that God left signs of his Trinitarian being in nature as well as Scripture. So at that point there is no attempt by Edwards to prove the existence of a generic deity. Additionally, for Edwards God is a communicative being who desires to extend his own glory through redemption and this must involve revelation. God must display his attributes and this display must be seen and so praise and glory returned to him by the creature. Edwards's God is no undifferentiated and uncommunicative monad.

Related to the above it must be remembered that Edwards was committed to a fully articulated covenant theology. God is Trinitarian and

---

102. It should go without saying that Edwards also lacks the anti-presuppositional bias of Gerstner as well.

103. One is reminded of the statement attributed to Martin Luther that if we man the battlements at every point but where the attack is occurring we fail at every point.

God's beauty and glory is communicated to creation through the persons and works of the Son and the Holy Spirit. In other words there is no obvious separation between Edwards's fully Trinitarian federal theology and his apologetics. While Edwards's federal theology may not always be at the forefront, it is most certainly the case that it is at work in the background. The God Edwards seeks to defend with sometimes traditional arguments *just is* the Triune God of Scripture: Father, Son, and Holy Spirit.

Regarding the nature of man, Edwards is clearly within the Augustinian stream by affirming man's incapacity to save himself. Gerstner appreciates Edwards's high view of the human mind with its acute reasoning capacities. Edwards does have a deep appreciation for the human mind. However this should not be interpreted to mean that the intellect is somehow exempt from the noetic effects of the fall. Man is a whole-souled creature and sin permeates to all levels of his being. The intellect and will are infected by sin. Saying this does not require that sin infects the intellect and will in exactly the same way. They are each infected in ways related to how they each function. But sin does not merely indirectly affect the intellect. Nor does regeneration *indirectly enlighten* the mind.[104] Man was made in the image of God and when he fell he lost the moral image *and* the natural image was corrupted. This is not to suggest that the intellect is obliterated. It is to say that it does not function properly as it was intended by God. It is only because of God's common grace that man can function at all in a serendipitous way.

Jonathan Edwards understands that man is made in the image of God and so not only is God fully capable of communicating revelation to man in nature and Scripture, man is capable of receiving revelation. The fall has now added the redemptive element for sure. This is no minor matter. But the subjective correction that man now requires does not negate the objective reality of the Triune God's existence nor does it negate the evidence for God in nature and Scripture. God has communicated himself and this requires an internal make-over for fallen man to now be receptive to that communication. Apologetics relies on both the objective evidence for God's existence in nature and Scripture and the arguments that can be used to draw out the implications of that and it requires the subjective change necessary for man to see God's communication. Actually, for Edwards, saving faith involved both seeing and savoring God and the things of God.

While Edwards could talk about right reason and the way reason ought to function and he could talk about common sense, there is no hint

---

104. It seems altogether appropriate that if sin affects the intellect indirectly then so too does regeneration.

that he thought the sinful human mind could reason rightly. God has revealed himself in nature and Scripture and reason rightly functioning will see and savor that revelation and the God who has revealed it. But because of the fall only the elect in time will come to see and savor God and his revelation. And they will do that because of the internal regenerating and sanctifying work of the Holy Spirit in conjunction with the Word he himself has inspired.

Edwards is famously known for his concern for the subjective aspects of the Christian faith. But he was equally concerned to uphold the objective aspects as well. God is God and his Word is what it is apart from the human perception of it. However, proper human perception is key as well. And so Edwards was also concerned with addressing the increasingly critical attacks on the Bible that were part and parcel of the rising Enlightenment age. As seen in his *Miscellanies 1340* and his *Notes on Scripture* entry 416 Edwards was concerned to address specific criticisms head on. However one does not find Edwards arguing for probabilities even here. Given the Creator/creature distinction Edwards tells us that mystery is no proof that the Bible is not from God. The mind of man is not the measure of truth. Man can arrive at truth through careful thought. But careful thought in the end requires supernatural regeneration. As Edwards was quick to point out, while brilliant minds have existed from time immemorial, brilliant minds have made brilliant hash of God's nature and man's nature and the need for redemption. Fallen man exists in a fog which only the Holy Spirit and the Word can dissipate. But to recognize the necessity of the internal work of the Holy Spirit does not negate the apologetic need to deal with specific criticisms, whether they be of the Christian faith in general or the biblical text in particular.[105]

---

105. Robert Brown in his *Jonathan Edwards and the Bible* (Indianapolis & Bloomington, IN: Indiana University Press, 2002) has made the suggestion that in the face of the rising tide of Enlightenment and deistic biblical criticism that Edwards shifted from a more traditional Reformed emphasis on the necessity of the internal work of the Holy Spirit to a more evidentialist approach dealing with the particulars of biblical criticism. However this is not proven inasmuch as Brown has failed to show the incompatibility between affirming the divine nature of Scripture and the necessity of regeneration for a proper understanding of God's Word and an intricate investigation and defense of the details of Scripture against attack. To use a more recent illustration of the compatibility of these two aspects of apologetics, consider that Cornelius Van Til served on the same faculty at Westminster Theological Seminary with the likes of E. J. Young and Ned B. Stonehouse. As far as this writer is aware, these men supported each other. Van Til noted that he dwelt on the philosophical issues involved in apologetics and that his comrades on the faculty in the Biblical studies departments dealt with Christian evidences. This is simply to say that a concern with the necessity of affirming the *principium essendi* and *principium cognoscendi internum et externum* does not

Was Jonathan Edwards's theological anthropology consistent with his apologetic practice? It seems so. He understood the objective and subjective elements of the Christian faith. While he has a high view of human reason, it is not a view that thinks fallen reason is or ought to be autonomous. That is, human reason was created to function under the authority of God and his Word. Edwards understood that both the intellect and will were damaged in the fall and are restored in redemption. But man was meant to be subservient to God in both creation and redemption. Apologetics seeks to vindicate God's good name and to win the sinner/critic for Christ. Like preaching and teaching and evangelism, apologetics is a means to an end. That end is the glory of God and the salvation of man.

Jonathan Edwards was not a presuppositionalist apologist born out of season. However, there are areas of overlap that seem to have escaped the notice of John Gerstner. It is this writer's view that major advances have occurred in the field of apologetics since the time of Edwards. One such advance is the self-conscious nature of the discipline. It is not as if apologists from the different schools do things absolutely differently. That is surely not the case. But we are better off being sensitive to epistemological issues and how the Scriptures bear on these. Edwards may have used some classical arguments in his apologetic endeavors, but he lacks the zeal for the classical method that Gerstner himself evidenced. What's more, Edwards does in fact show some leanings in a presuppositional direction. But that is not surprising. Inasmuch as he was a Reformed theologian he would manifest such things.

It would be wrong to conclude from this study that John Gerstner was wide of the mark in his understanding of Jonathan Edwards in general or with regard to the more specific matter of apologetics. Gerstner properly has a reputation as a learned and thoughtful student of Edwards. We gladly stand on his shoulders for much of our appreciation of Edwards. For instance, Gerstner helpfully upheld Edwards's orthodoxy, his Calvinism and covenantal theology, and Edwards's Biblicism and supernaturalism. With regard to Edwards's understanding of human nature, Gerstner was correct to see Edwards's high regard for human reason. Here we join hands with John Gerstner in his robust rejection of neo-orthodoxy or any attempt to recreate Edwards in the mold of neo-orthodoxy with its apparent under appreciation for the human intellect. The human mind is fallen. But it is restored in redemption and is one characteristic that distinguishes humans from animals. However, to possess a true regard or a high regard for reason does not necessitate intellectualism.

---

preclude detailed defense of the details of Scripture.

As we can critically appropriate the insights of John Gerstner, so too Jonathan Edwards is an apologist from whom we can learn much. Inasmuch as Edwards points us in a biblically faithful direction in his understanding of theological anthropology and apologetic practice, we should learn from him and adopt and adapt his views and methods. Where he falls short of a faithful biblical and sound theological understanding we can learn what paths to avoid.

Bibliography

Alexander, Archibald. *Thoughts on Religious Experience.* Carlisle, PA: Banner of Truth Trust, 1989
Ames, William. *The Marrow of Theology.* Translated from the 3rd Latin edition and edited by James D. Eusden. Grand Rapids, MI: Baker, 1968.
Augustine. *The City of God Against the Pagans.* Cambridge Texts in the History of Political Thought series. Translated and edited by R. W. Dyson. Cambridge: Cambridge University Press, 1998, 2001.
———. *The Confessions of St. Augustine: Modern English Version.* Grand Rapids, MI: Baker, 2005.
———. *Explanations of the Psalms* in *The Nicene and Post-Nicene Fathers: First Series.* Edited by Philip Schaff. Grand Rapids, MI: Eerdmans, 1988.
———. *Marriage and Desire* in *The Works of Saint Augustine: A Translation for the 21st Century: Answers to the Pelagians II/I/24.* Translated by Roland J. Teske. Edited by John E. Rotelle. Hyde Park, NY: New City Press, 1998.
———. *On Christian Doctrine* in *The Nicene and Post-Nicene Fathers: First Series.* Translated by J. F. Shaw. Edited by Philip Schaff. Grand Rapids, MI: Eerdmans, 1988.
———. *On Genesis: On Genesis: A Refutation of the Manichees; Unfinished Literal Commentary on Genesis; and The Literal Meaning of Genesis* in *The Works of Saint Augustine: A Translation for the 21st Century.* Translated and edited by Edmund Hill. Hyde Park, NY: New City Press, 2002.
———. *On the Trinity* in *The Works of Saint Augustine: A Translation for the 21st Century.* Translated by Edmund Hill. Edited by John E. Rotelle. Brooklyn, NY: New City Press,1991.
———. *Punishment and Forgiveness of Sins* in *The Works of Saint Augustine: A Translation for the 21st Century: Answers to the Pelagians 1/23.* Translated by Roland J. Teske. Edited by John E. Rotelle. Hyde Park, NY: New City Press, 1997.
———. *Rebuke and Grace* in *The Works of Saint Augustine: A Translation for the 21st Century: Answers to the Pelagians IV/I/26.* Translated by Roland J. Teske. Edited by John E. Rotelle. Hyde Park, NY: New City Press, 1999.
———. *Soliloquies* in *The Nicene and Post-Nicene Fathers: First Series.* Translated by Charles Starbuck. Edited by Philipp Schaff. Grand Rapids, MI: Eerdmans, 1986.

Ayres, Lewis. *Augustine and the Trinity.* Cambridge: Cambridge University Press, 2010.
Ayers, Michael. *Locke: Vol. 1, Epistemology.* London: Routledge, 1991.
Baker, Herschel. *The Wars of Truth: Studies in the Decay of Christian Humanism in the Earlier Seventeenth Century.* Cambridge: Harvard University Press, 1952.
Bahnsen, Greg. *Van Til's Apologetic: Readings and Analysis.* Phillipsburg, NJ: Presbyterian and Reformed Publishers, 1998.
Barnett, Das Kelly. *The Doctrine of Man in the Theology of Jonathan Edwards.* Th.D. diss., Southern Baptist Theological Seminary, 1943.
Barcellos, Richard. *The Family Tree of Reformed Biblical Theology.* Reformed Baptist Dissertation Series # 2. Owensboro, KY: Reformed Baptist Academic Press, 2010.
Bavinck, Herman. *Reformed Dogmatics/2: God and Creation.* Edited by John Bolt and translated by John Vriend. Grand Rapids, MI: Baker, 2004.
Bercovitch, Sacvan. *The Puritan Origins of the American Self.* New Haven, CT: Yale University Press, 1975.
Berkeley, George. *The Works of George Berkeley, Bishop of Cloyne.* 9 vols. Edited by A. A. Luce and T. E. Jessup. London: Thomas Nelson, 1948-57.
Berkouwer, G. C. *Man: The Image of God.* Studies in Dogmatics Series. Translated by Dirk W.Jellema. Grand Rapids, NY: Eerdmans, 1962.
Bettenson, Henry. *Documents of the Christian Church.* New York: Oxford University Press, 1947; 2nd edition, 1986.
Biehl, Craig. *The Infinite Merit of Christ: The Glory of Christ's Obedience in the Theology of Jonathan Edwards.* Jackson, MS: Reformed Academic Press, 2009.
Boa, Kenneth and Robert Bowman, *Faith Has Its Reasons.* Colorado Springs, CO: NavPress, 2001.
Bogue, Carl W. *Jonathan Edwards and the Covenant of Grace.* Jonathan Edwards Classic Studies Series. Eugene, OR: Wipf & Stock, 2008.
Bombaro, John. "Dispositional Peculiarity, History, and Edwards's Evangelistic Appeal To Self-Love." *WTJ* 66 (2004): 121-57.
_____. "Jonathan Edwards's View of Salvation." *WTJ* 65 (2003): 45-67.
Bray, Gerald. *The Doctrine of God.* Contours of Christian Doctrine Series. Downers Grove, IL: Inter Varsity Press, 1993.
Brown, Robert E. "Edwards, Locke, and the Bible." *Journal of Religion* 79 (July 1999): 361-84.
_____. *Jonathan Edwards and the Bible.* Bloomington and Indianapolis, IN: Indiana University Press, 2002.
Bush, Douglas. *Paradise Lost in Our Time: Some Comments.* Ithaca, NY: Cornell University Press, 1945.
Butler, Diana. "God's Visible Glory: The Beauty of Nature in the Thought of John Calvin and Jonathan Edwards." *Westminster Theological Journal* 52 (Spring 1990): 13-26.
Butler, Joseph. *The Analogy of Religion, Natural and Revealed.* London: J. M. Dent, 1906.
Caldwell, Robert N. *Communion in the Spirit: The Holy Spirit as the Bond of Union in the Theology of Jonathan Edwards.* Studies in Evangelical History and Thought. Eugene: Wipf & Stock, OR/Paternoster, 2006.
Calvin, John. *Institutes of the Christian Religion.* Edited by John McNeill and translated by Ford Lewis Battles. 2 vols. Library of Christian Classics Series. (Louisville, KY: Westminster John KnoxPress, 1960)
Campbell, Travis. *The Search for Truth/Vol. 2: The Resurrection of Natural Theology/Part One: Ontological and Cosmological Arguments.* Unpublished manuscript, 2011.

Campbell-Jack, W. C. and Gavin McGrath, Editors. C. Stephen Evans, Consulting Editor. *The New IVP Dictionary of Apologetics*. Downers Grove, IL: IVP, 2006.

Carse, James. *Jonathan Edwards and the Visibility of God*. New York: Charles Scribner's Sons, 1967.

Chai, Leon. *Jonathan Edwards and the Limits of the Enlightenment*. Oxford: Oxford University Press, 1998.

Chamberlain, Ava. "Self Deception as a Theological Problem in Jonathan Edwards's 'Treatise Concerning Religious Affections'." *Church History* 63 (December 1994): 541-56.

Chappell, Vere, Editor. *The Cambridge Companion to Locke*. New York: Cambridge University Press, 1994.

Cherry, Conrad. *The Theology of Jonathan Edwards: A Reappraisal*. Bloomington and Indianapolis, IN.: Indiana University Press, 1966.

Clapper, Gregory S. "Finding a Place for Emotions in Christian Theology." *Christian Century* : 409-11.

Clark, M. L. *Paley: Evidences for the Man*. Toronto, ON: University of Toronto Press, 1974.

Clark, R. Scott. *Recovering the Reformed Confession. Our Theology, Piety, and Practice* Phillipsburg, NJ: Presbyterian and Reformed Publishing, 2008.

Clarke, Samuel. *A Discourse Concerning the Being and Attributes of God, the Obligations of Natural Religion, and the Truth and Certainty of the Christian Revelation*. London: 1711.

Copan, Paul. "Jonathan Edwards's Philosophical Influences: Lockean or Malebranchian?" *Journal of the Evangelical Theological Society* 44 (Spring 2001): 107-24.

Copleston, Frederick. *A History of Philosophy*. 9 vols. Paramus, NJ: Newman Press, 1971.

Cowan, Steven, ed. *The Five Views of Apologetics*. Grand Rapids, MI: Zondervan, 2000.

Crabtree, Arthur Bamford. *Jonathan Edwards' View of Man: A Study in Eighteenth Century Calvinism*. Wallington, Surrey: The Religious Education Press, LTD, 1948.

Cragg, Gerald. *Freedom and Authority: A Study of English Thought in the Early Seventeenth Century*. Philadelphia: The Westminster Press, 1975.

———. *From Puritanism to the Age of Reason: A Study of Changes in Religious Thought within the Church of England, 1660-1700*. London: Cambridge University Press, 1950.

———. *Puritanism in the Period of the Great Persecution 1660-1688*. Cambridge: Cambridge University Press, 1957.

———. *Reason and Authority in the Eighteenth Century*. Cambridge: Cambridge University Press, 1964.

Craig, William Lane. *The Kalam Cosmological Argument*. Eugene, OR: Wipf & Stock, 2000.

Crisp, Oliver. *Jonathan Edwards and the Metaphysics of Sin*. Burlington, VT: Ashgate, 2005.

———. "Jonathan Edwards' Ontology: a critique of Sang Lee's dispositional account of Edwardsian metaphysics," *Religious Studies* 46 (2010): 1-20.

Cunliffe, Christopher. *Joseph Butler's Moral and Religious Thought: Tercentenary Essays*. Oxford: Clarendon Press, 1992.

Cudworth, Ralph. *The True Intellectual System of the Universe*. London, 1678.

Danaher, William. *The Trinitarian Ethics of Jonathan Edwards.* Louisville, KY: Westminster John Knox Press, 2004.

Davidson, Bruce W. "Reasonable Damnation: How Jonathan Edwards Argued for the Rationality of Hell." *Journal of the Evangelical Theological Society* 38 (March 1995): 47-56.

Davidson, Edward H. "From Locke to Edwards." *Journal of the History of Ideas* 24 (1963): 355-72.

Delattre, Roland Andre. *Beauty and Sensibility in the Thought of Jonathan Edwards: An Essay in Aesthetics and Theological Ethics.* Jonathan Edwards Classic Studies Series. Eugene, OR: Wipf & Stock, 2006.

Descartes, René. *A Discourse on Method.* London: 1949.

Dever, Mark. *Richard Sibbes and the Truly Evangelical Party in the Church of England.*

Dowey, Edward Q., Jr. *The Knowledge of God in Calvin's Theology.* Grand Rapids, MI: Eerdmans, 1974.

Dulles, Avery. *A History of Apologetics.* Philadelphia: Westminster Press, 1971.

Edgar, William and K. Scott Oliphint, Editors. *Christian Apologetics: Past & Present.* Wheaton, IL: Crossway, 2009-10, 2 vols.

Edwards, Jonathan. *The Blessing of God: Previously Unpublished Sermons of Jonathan Edwards.* Edited by Michael D. McMullen. Nashville, TN: Broadman and Holman, 2003.

_____. Edwards Papers. Beinecke Rare Book and Manuscript Library. Yale University. New Haven, CT.

_____. George S. Claghorn Papers. Montgomery Library. Westminster Theological Seminary. Glenside, PA.

_____. *The Glory and Honor of God: Volume 2 of Previously Unpublished Sermons of Jonathan Edwards.* Edited by Michael D. McMullen. Nashville, TN: Broadman and Holman, 2004.

_____. *Jonathan Edwards: Representative Selections.* Edited by Clarence H. Faust and Thomas H. Johnson. New York: American Book Co., 1935.

_____. *The Salvation of Souls: Nine Previously Unpublished Sermons on the Call of Ministry and the Gospel.* Edited by Richard A. Bailey and Gregory A. Wills. Wheaton, IL: Crossway Books, 2002.

_____. *Selected Writings of Jonathan Edwards.* Edited by Harold P. Simonson. Prospect Heights, IL: ,1970.

_____. *Selections from the Unpublished Writings of Jonathan Edwards.* Edited by Alexander Grosart. Ligonier, PA: Solid Deo Gloria, 1992.

_____. *Treatise on Grace and Other Posthumously Published Writings.* Edited by Paul Helm. Cambridge: James Clarke, 1971.

_____. *The Works of Jonathan Edwards, Vol. 1: Freedom of the Will.* Edited by Paul Ramsey. New Haven, CT: Yale University Press, 1957.

_____. *The Works of Jonathan Edwards, Vol. 2: Religious Affections.* Edited by John E. Smith. New Haven, CT: Yale University Press, 1959.

_____. *The Works of Jonathan Edwards, Vol. 3: Original Sin.* Edited by Clyde A. Holbrook. New Haven, CT: Yale University Press, 1970.

_____. *The Works of Jonathan Edwards, Vol. 4: The Great Awakening.* Edited by C. C. Goen. New Haven, CT: Yale University Press, 1972.

_____. *The Works of Jonathan Edwards, Vol. 5: Apocalyptic Writings.* Edited by Stephen J. Stein. New Haven, CT: Yale University Press, 1977.

_____. *The Works of Jonathan Edwards, Vol. 6: Scientific and Philosophical Writings.* Edited by Wallace E. Anderson. New Haven, CT: Yale University Press, 1980.

_____. *The Works of Jonathan Edwards, Vol. 7: The Life of David Brainerd.* Edited by Norman Pettit. New Haven, CT: Yale University Press, 1985.

_____. *The Works of Jonathan Edwards, Vol. 8: Ethical Writings.* Edited by Paul Ramsey. New Haven, CT: Yale University Press, 1989.

_____. *The Works of Jonathan Edwards, Vol. 9: A History of the Work of Redemption.* Edited by John F. Wilson. New Haven, CT: Yale University Press, 1989.

_____. *The Works of Jonathan Edwards, Vol. 10: Sermons and Discourses, 1720-1723.* Edited by Wilson H. Kimnach. New Haven, CT: Yale University Press, 1992.

_____. *The Works of Jonathan Edwards, Vol. 11: Typological Writings.* Edited by Wallace E. Anderson and Mason I. Lowance, Jr., with David Watters. New Haven, CT: Yale University Press, 1993.

_____. *The Works of Jonathan Edwards, Vol. 12: Ecclesiastical Writings.* Edited by David D. Hall. New Haven, CT: Yale University Press, 1994.

_____. *The Works of Jonathan Edwards, Vol. 13: The "Miscellanies," a-500.* Edited by Thomas A. Schafer. New Haven, CT: Yale University Press, 1994.

_____. *The Works of Jonathan Edwards, Vol. 14: Sermons and Discourses, 1723-1729.* Edited by Kenneth J. Minkema. New Haven, CT: Yale University Press, 1997.

_____. *The Works of Jonathan Edwards, Vol. 15: Notes on Scripture.* Edited by Stephen J. Stein. New Haven, CT: Yale University Press, 1998.

_____. *The Works of Jonathan Edwards, Vol. 16: Letters and Personal Writings.* Edited by George S. Claghorn. New Haven, CT: Yale University Press, 1998.

_____. *The Works of Jonathan Edwards, Vol. 17: Sermons and Discourses, 1730-1733.* Edited by Mark Valeri. New Haven, CT: Yale University Press, 1999.

_____. *The Works of Jonathan Edwards, Vol. 18: The "Miscellanies," 501-832.* Edited by Ava Chamberlain. New Haven, CT: Yale University Press, 2000.

_____. *The Works of Jonathan Edwards, Vol. 19: Sermons and Discourses, 1734-1738.* Edited by M. X. Lesser. New Haven, CT: Yale University Press, 2001.

_____. *The Works of Jonathan Edwards, Vol. 20: The "Miscellanies," 833-1152.* Edited by Amy Plantinga Pauw. New Haven, CT: Yale University Press, 2002.

_____. *The Works of Jonathan Edwards, Vol. 21: Writings on the Trinity, Grace, and Faith.* Edited Sang Hyun Lee. New Haven, CT: Yale University Press, 2003.

_____. *The Works of Jonathan Edwards, Vol. 22: Sermons and Discourses, 1739-1742.* Edited by Harry S. Stout and Nathan O. Hatch, with Kyle P. Farley. New Haven, CT: Yale University Press, 2003.

_____. *The Works of Jonathan Edwards, Vol. 23: The "Miscellanies," 1153-1360.* Edited by Douglas A. Sweeney. New Haven, CT: Yale University Press, 2004.

_____. *The Works of Jonathan Edwards, Vol. 24 A & B: The "Blank Bible".* Edited by Stephen J. Stein. New Haven, CT: Yale University Press, 2006.

_____. *The Works of Jonathan Edwards, Vol. 25: Sermons and Discourses, 1743-1758.* Edited by Wilson H. Kimnach. New Haven, CT: Yale University Press, 2006.

_____. *The Works of Jonathan Edwards, Vol. 26: The Reading Catalog.* Edited by Peter J. Thuesen. New Haven, CT: Yale University Press, 2008.

_____. *The Works of Jonathan Edwards.* 2 vols. Edited by Edward Hickman. Edinburgh/Carlisle, PA: Banner of Truth, 1974.

_____. *The Works of Jonathan Edwards Online.* New Haven, CT: The Jonathan Edwards Center at Yale University, 2005. http://edwards.yale.edu/archive/ (accessed 2012).

Elwood, Douglas J. *The Philosophical Theology of Jonathan Edwards.* New York: Columbia University Press, 1960.

Erdt, Terence. *Jonathan Edwards, Art, and the Sense of the Heart.* Amherst, MA: University of Massachusetts Press, 1980.

Fesko, John V. *The Doctrine of Justification: Understanding the Classic Reformed Doctrine.* Phillipsburg, NJ: Presbyterian and Reformed Publishing, 2008.

Fiering, Norman. *Jonathan Edwards's Moral Thought and Its British Context.* Chapel Hill, NC: University of North Carolina Press, 1981.

_____. *Moral Philosophy at Seventeenth-Century Harvard: A Discipline in Transition.* Chapel Hill, NC: University of North Carolina Press, 1981.

_____. "The Rationalist Foundations of Jonathan Edwards's Metaphysics." In *Jonathan Edwards and the American Experience.* Edited by Nathan O. Hatch and Harry S. Stout, 73-101. New York: Oxford University Press, 1988.

_____. "Will and Intellect in the New England Mind." *William and Mary Quarterly* 3rd Series 29 (1972): 515-558.

Fitzgerald, g Allan D., en. ed. *Augustine Through the Ages: An Encyclopedia.* Grand Rapids, MI: Eerdmans, 1999.

Flavel, John. *The Works of John Flavel.* Carlisle, PA: Banner of Truth, 1968.

Frame, John. "Book Review: *Classical Apologetics*," *WTJ* 47 (Fall 1985): 279-99.

Fuller, Randall. "Errand into the Wilderness: Perry Miller as American Scholar," *American Literary History* 18/1 (2006): 102-28.

Gale, Theophilus. *Court of the Gentiles: Or A Discourse touching the Original of Human Literature, both Philologie and Philosophie, From the Scripture and the Jewish Church.* 2nd Edition. Oxford, 1672.

Gay, Peter, Editor. *Deism: An Anthology.* Princeton, NJ: Princeton University Press, 1968.

_____. *The Enlightenment.* 2 vols. New York: W. W. Norton & Company, 1966.

Geehan, E. R., Editor. *Jerusalem and Athens: Critical Discussions on the Philosophy and Apologetics of Cornelius Van Til.* Phillipsburg, NJ: P&R, 1971.

Geisler, Norman L. *The Baker Encyclopedia of Christian Apologetics.* Grand Rapids, MI: Baker, 1998.

_____. *Thomas Aquinas: An Evangelical Appraisal.* Grand Rapids, MI: Baker, 1991.

Gerstner, John. "An Outline of the Apologetics of Jonathan Edwards." *Bibliotheca Sacra* 133 (1976): 3-10, 99-107, 195-201, 291-98.

_____. *John Gerstner: The Early Writings.* Morgan: Soli Deo Gloria, 1997.

_____. "Jonathan Edwards." *Eternity* 39 (Jan 1998): 36-37.

_____. "Jonathan Edwards and the Bible." *Tenth* 9 (1979): 1-90.

_____. *Jonathan Edwards, Evangelist.* Morgan: Soli Deo Gloria, 1995.

_____. "Jonathan Edwards: Insights That Shaped History." *Fundamentalist Journal* 4 (April 1985): 43-44.

_____. "Jonathan Edwards on the Bible and Reason." Sound Recording. Philadelphia: Westminster Media, 1979.

_____. *Jonathan Edwards: A Mini-Theology.* Wheaton, IL: Tyndale House Press, 1987.

_____. "Jonathan Edwards on Natural Theology." Sound Recording. 1975.

_____. *Jonathan Edwards on Heaven and Hell*. Carlisle: Banner of Truth, 1980.
_____. *The Rational Biblical Theology of Jonathan Edwards*. 3 vols. Powhatan, VA/ Orlando, FL: Berea/Ligonier, 1991-93.
_____. *Reasons for Faith*. New York: Harper & Brothers, 1960.
_____. "Scottish Realism, Kant and Darwin in the Philosophy of James McCosh" PhD Diss. Harvard University, 1945.
_____. *Steps to Salvation: The Evangelistic Message of Jonathan Edwards*. Philadelphia: Westminster Press, 1960.
_____. *The Theology of Jonathan Edwards*. Sound Recordings. Grand Rapids, MI: Institute of Theological Studies, 1986.
_____ and Jonathan Gerstner. "Edwardsean Preparation for Salvation." *Westminster Theological Journal* 42 (Fall 1979): 5-71.
Gibson, Michael O. "The Integrative Philosophy of Jonathan Edwards: Empiricism, God, Being, and Postmillennialism." *Westminster Theological Journal* 64 (Spring 2002): 151-61.
Gilbert, Greg D. "The Nations Will Worship: Jonathan Edwards and the Salvation of the Heathen." *Trinity Journal* 23 (2002): 53-76.
Gilson, Etienne. *The Christian Philosophy of St. Augustine*. Translated by L. E. M. Lynch. New York: Random House, 1960.
Godhes, Clarence. "Aspects of Idealism in Early New England." *Philosophical Review* 39 (1930): 537-55.
Guelzo, Allen. *Edwards on the Will*. Middletown, CT: Wesleyan University Press, 1989.
Gura, Phillip F. *Jonathan Edwards: America's Evangelical*. New York: Hill and Wang, 2005.
Hall, Richard A. S. "Did Berkeley Influence Edwards? Their Common Critique of the Moral Sense Theory." In *Jonathan Edwards's Writings: Text, Context, Interpretation*. Edited by Stephen J. Stein, 100-121. Bloomington: Indiana University Press, 1996.
Haratounian, Joseph. *Piety Versus Moralism: The Passing of New England Theology from Edwards to Taylor*. Studies in Religion and Culture: American Religion Series, no. 4. New York: Henry Holt & Co., 1932.
Haykin, Michael A. G. *Jonathan Edwards: The Holy Spirit in Revival: The Lasting Influence of the Holy Spirit in the Heart of Man*. Darlington, UK: Emmaus/ Evangelical Press, 2005.
Heimert, Alan and Perry Miller, Editors. *The Great Awakening: Documents Illustrating the Crisis and Its Consequences*. Indianapolis, IN: Bobbs-Merrill, 1967.
Helm, Paul. "John Locke and Jonathan Edwards: A Reconsideration." *Journal of the History of Philosophy* 7 (January 1969): 51-61.
Helseth, Paul. "The Apologetical Tradition of the OPC: A Reconsideration," *WTJ* 60/1 (Spring 1998): 109-29.
_____. "B. B. Warfield's Apologetical Appeal to 'Right Reason': Evidence of a 'Rather Bald Rationalism'?," *SBET* 16 (Autumn 1998): 156-77.
_____. "B. B. Warfield on the Apologetic Nature of Christian Scholarship: An Analysis of His Solution to the Problem of the Relationship Between Christianity and Culture," *WTJ* 61/1 (Spring 2000): 89-111.
_____. "Christ-Centered, Bible-Based, and Second-Rate? 'Right Reason' as the Aesthetic Foundation of Christian Education," *WTJ* 69/2 (Fall 2007): 383-401.

———. "'Re-imagining' the Princeton Mind: Postconservative Evangelicalism, Old Princeton, and the Rise of Neo-Fundamentalism," *JETS* 45/3 (Spring 2002): 427-50.

———. *"Right Reason" and the Princeton Mind*. Phillipsburg, NJ: P&R Publishing, 2010.

———. "'Right Reason' and the Princeton Mind: The Moral Context," *JPH* 77/1 (Spring 1999): 13-28.

———. "'Right Reason' and the Science of Theology at Old Princeton Seminary: A New Perspective," *The Confessional Presbyterian Journal*, forthcoming.

Hart, Charles. *Thomistic Metaphysics: An Inquiry into the Act of Existing*. Englewood Cliffs, NJ: Prentice-Hall, 1959.

Herbert of Cherbury, Edward. *On Truth in Distinction from Revelation, Probability, Possibility, and Error*. Translated by Meyrick C. Carre. Bristol, UK, 1937.

Hobbes, Thomas. *Leviathan*. Edited by Richard Tuck. Cambridge Texts in the History of Philosophy. Cambridge: Cambridge University Press, 1991.

Hodge, Charles. "Jonathan Edwards and the Successive Forms of New England Theology." *Biblical Repertory and Princeton Review* 30 (October 1858): 585-620.

Hoekema, Anthony. *Created in God's Image*. Grand Rapids, MI: Eerdmans, 1986.

Hollifield, E. Brooks. *Theology in America: Christian Thought from the Age of the Puritan to the Civil War*. New Haven, CT: Yale University Press, 2003.

Holmes, Stephen R. "Does Jonathan Edwards Use a Dispositional Ontology?: A Response to Sang Hyun Lee" in *Jonathan Edwards, Philosophical Theologian*. Edited by Paul Helm and Oliver Crisp. Burlington, VT: Ashgate, 2003, 99-114.

———. *God of Grace and God of Glory: An Account of the Theology of Jonathan Edwards*. Grand Rapids, MI: Eerdmans, 2000.

Hoopes, James. *Consciousness in New England: From Puritanism and Ideas to Psychoanalysis and Semiotic*. Baltimore, MD: The Johns Hopkins University Press, 1989.

———. "Jonathan Edwards's Religious Psychology." *Journal of American History* 69 (March 1983): 849-65.

Hoopes, Robert. *Right Reason and the English Renaissance*. Cambridge: Harvard University Press, 1962.

Horton, Michael S. *Covenant and Salvation: Union with Christ*. Louisville: Westminster John Knox Press, 2007.

Howe, Daniel Walker. *Making the American Self: Jonathan Edwards to Abraham Lincoln*. New York: Oxford University Press, 2009.

Hume, David. *Enquiries Concerning the Human Understanding and Concerning the Principles of Morals*. 3rd ed. Edited by P. H. Nidditch. Oxford: Oxford University Press, 1975.

———. *A Treatise of Human Nature*. 2nd ed. Edited by P. H. Nidditch. Oxford: Oxford University Press, 1978.

Hutchinson, Frances. *An Essay on the Nature and Conduct of the Passions and Affections with Illustrations of the Moral Sense*. 3rd ed. Gainesville, GA: Scholars Facsimiles and Reprints, 1969.

Israel, Jonathan I. *Enlightenment Contested: Philosophy, Modernity, and the Emancipation of Man 1670-1752*. Oxford: Oxford University Press, 2006.

———. *Radical Enlightenment: Philosophy and the Making of Modernity 1650-1750*. Oxford: Oxford University Press, 2001.

Jones, W. T. *A History of Western Philosophy: Vol. 3/Hobbes to Hume.* New York: Wadsworth, 1980. 2nd Edition.

Kant, Immanuel. *Critique of Practical Reason.* Translated and edited by Mary Gregor. Cambridge Texts in the History of Philosophy. Cambridge: Cambridge University Press, 1997.

_____. *Critique of Pure Reason.* Translated by Norman Kemp Smith. New York: St. Martin's Press, 1968.

Kapic, Kelly M. *Communion with God: The Divine and the Human in the Theology of John Owen.* Grand Rapids, MI: Baker Academic, 2007.

Kidd, Thomas S. *The Great Awakening.* New Haven, CT: Yale University Press, 2007.

Kling, David W. and Douglas A. Sweeney, Editors. *Jonathan Edwards at Home and Abroad: Historical Memories, Cultural Movements, Global Horizons.* Columbia, SC: University of South Carolina Press, 2003.

Knight, Janice. *Orthodoxies in Massachusetts: Rereading American Puritanism.* Cambridge, MA: Harvard University Press, 1994.

LaShell, John K. "Jonathan Edwards and the New Sense." *Reformation and Revival* 4 (Summer 1995): 87-98.

Laurence, David. "Jonathan Edwards, John Locke, and the Canon of Experience." *Early American Literature* 15 (1980): 107-23.

Lee, Sang Hyun. *The Philosophical Theology of Jonathan Edwards.* Princeton, NJ: Princeton University Press, 2000.

_____, Editor. *The Princeton Companion to Jonathan Edwards.* Princeton, NJ: Princeton University Press, 2005.

_____ and Allen C. Guelzo, Editors. *Edwards in Our Time.* Grand RapidsMI: Eerdmans,1999.

Leland, John. *A View of the Principal Deistic Writers.* 3rd Edition., London, 1757.

Lesser, M. X. *Jonathan Edwards: An Annotated Bibliography, 1979-1993.* Westport, CT: Greenwood Press, 1994.

_____. *Jonathan Edwards: A Reference Guide.* Boston: G. K. Hall, 1981.

_____. *Reading Jonathan Edwards: An Annotated Bibliography in Three Parts, 1729-2005.* Grand Rapids, MI: Eerdmans, 2008.

Lewis, Paul. "The Springs of Motion: Jonathan Edwards on Emotions, Character, and Agency." *Journal of Religious Ethics* : 275-97.

_____. "Rethinking Emotions and the Moral Life in the Thought of Thomas Aquinas and Jonathan Edwards." PhD. diss., Duke University, 1991.

Lillback, Peter. *The Binding of God*: *Calvin's Role in the Development of Covenant Theology.* Texts & Studies in the Reformation & Post-Reformation Thought. Grand Rapids, MI: Baker, 2001.

Locke, John. *An Essay Concerning Human Understanding.* Edited by Peter Nidditch. Oxford: Oxford University Press, 1975.

_____. *The Reasonableness of Christianity.* Edited by I. T. Ramsay. Stanford, CA: Stanford University Press, 1958.

Lovejoy, Arthur O. *The Great Chain of being: A Study of the History of an Idea.* Cambridge: Harvard University Press, 1936.

Lyttle, David. "Sixth Sense of Jonathan Edwards." *Church Quarterly Review* 167 (Jan-Mar 1966): 50-59.

Malebranche, Nicholas. *The Search After Truth*. Cambridge Texts in the History of Philosophy. Thomas M. Lennon & Paul J. Olscamp, eds. Cambridge: Cambridge University Press, 1997.

Manuel, Frank. *The Eighteenth Century Confronts the Gods*. Cambridge, MA: Harvard University Press, 1959.

Marsden, George M. *Jonathan Edwards: A Life*. New Haven, CT: Yale University Press, 2003.

_____. *A Short Life of Jonathan Edwards*. Library of Religious Biography. Grand Rapids, MI: Eerdmans, 2008.

_____. "Perry Miller's Rehabilitation of the Puritans: A Critique." *Church History* 39 (1970): 91-105.

May, Henry. *The Enlightenment in America*. Oxford: Oxford University Press, 1976.

McClenahan, Michael. *Jonathan Edwards' Doctrine of Justification in the Period up to the First Great Awakening*. D. Phil. Diss. Oxford: Oxford University, 2006.

McClymond, Michael J. *Encounters with God: An Approach to the Theology of Jonathan Edwards*. New York: Oxford University Press, 1998.

_____. "God the Measure: Toward a Theocentric Understanding of Jonathan Edwards' Metaphysics." *SJT* 47 (1994): 43-59.

_____. "Spiritual Perception in Jonathan Edwards." *Journal of Religion* 77 1997: 195-216.

_____ and Gerald R. McDermott, *The Theology of Jonathan Edwards*. New York: Oxford University Press, 2012.

McCracken, Charles J. *Malebranche and British Philosophy*. Oxford: Clarendon Press, 1983.

McCracken, J. H. "The Sources of Edwards' Idealism." *Philosophical Review* 11 (1920): 537-55.

McDermott, Gerald R. *Can Evangelicals Learn from World Religions? Jesus, Revelation, and Religious Traditions*. Downer's Grove, IL: Inter Varsity Press, 2000.

_____. *God's Rivals: Why Has God Allowed Different Religions? Insights from the Bible and the Early Church*. Downers Grove, IL: Inter Varsity Press, 2007.

_____. "Jonathan Edwards and the American Indians: the Devil Sucks Their Blood," *NEQ* 72/4 (1999): 539-58.

_____. "Jonathan Edwards and the Salvation of Non-Christians." *PE* 10 (2001): 208-27.

_____. *Jonathan Edwards Confronts the Gods: Christian Theology, Enlightenment Religion, and Non-Christian Faiths*. New York: Oxford University Press, 2000.

_____. "Jonathan Edwards, Deism, and the Mystery of Revelation." *JPH* 77 (1999): 211-24.

_____. "Jonathan Edwards on Justification-More Protestant Or Catholic?," *PE* 17/1 (Winter 2008): 92-111.

_____. *One Holy and Happy Society: The Public Theology of Jonathan Edwards*. University Park, PA: Pennsylvania State University Press, 1992.

_____. "Response to Gilbert: 'The Nations Will Worship: Jonathan Edwards and the Salvation of the Heathen.'" *TJ* 23 (2002): 77-80.

_____. *Seeing God: Jonathan Edwards and Spiritual Discernment*. Vancouver, BC: Regent University Press, 2000.

_____, ed. *Understanding Jonathan Edwards: An Introduction to America's Theologian*. New York: Oxford University Press, 2009.

———. "What Jonathan Edwards Can Teach Us About Politics," *CT* 38/8 (18 July 1994): 32.
Miller, Perry. *Errand Into the Wilderness*. Cambridge, MA: Harvard University Press, 1956.
———. *Jonathan Edwards*. Westport, CT: Greenwood Press, 1949.
———. "Jonathan Edwards and the Sense of the Heart." *Harvard Theological Review* 41 (1948): 123-145.
———. *The New England Mind: From Colony to Province*. Cambridge, MA: Harvard University Press, 1981.
———. *The New England Mind: The Seventeenth Century*. Cambridge, MA: Harvard University Press, 1981.
——— and Alan Heimert, Editors. *The Great Awakening: Documents Illustrating the Crisis and Its Consequences*. Indianapolis, IN: Bobbs-Merrill Company, 1967.
——— and Thomas H. Johnson, Editors. *The Puritans: A Sourcebook of Their Writings*. Mineola, NY: Dover, 2001.
Minkema, Kenneth. "Jonathan Edwards in the Twentieth Century," *JETS* 47 (December 2003): 659-87.
Moody, Josh. *The God Centered Life: Insights from Jonathan Edwards for Today*. Leicester, UK: Inter Varsity Press, 2006.
———. *Jonathan Edwards and the Enlightenment*. Lanham, MD: University Press of America, 2005.
———, ed.. *Jonathan Edwards and Justification*. Wheaton, IL: Crossway, 2012.
Morais, Herbert M. *Deism in Eighteenth Century America*. New York, 1960.
Morimoto, Anri. *Jonathan Edwards and the Catholic Vision of Salvation*. University Park, PA: Pennsylvania State University Press, 1995.
———. "Salvation as Fulfillment of Being: The Soteriology of Jonathan Edwards and Its Implications for Missions." *The Princeton Seminary Bulletin* 20 (1999): 13-23.
Morris, William Sparkes. *The Young Jonathan Edwards: A Reconstruction*. Jonathan Edwards Classic Studies Series. Eugene, OR: Wipf & Stock, 2005.
Mossner, Ernest C. *Bishop Butler and the Age of Reason: A Study in the History of Religious Thought*. New York: Columbia University Press, 1936.
Muller, Richard A. *After Calvin: The Development of a Theological Tradition*. New York: Oxford University Press, 2003.
———. *Calvin and the Reformed Tradition: On the Work of Christ and the Order of Salvation*. Grand Rapids, MI: Baker Academic, 2012.
———. *Christ and the Decree: Christology and Predestination in Reformed Theology from Calvin to Perkins*. 3rd Ed. Grand Rapids, MI: Baker, 2009.
———. *Dictionary of Latin and Greek Theological Terms: Drawn Principally from Protestant Scholastic Theology*. Grand Rapids, MI: Baker, 1985.
———. *Post-Reformation Reformed Dogmatics: The Rise and Development of Reformed Orthodoxy, ca. 1520 to ca. 1725*. 4 vols. Grand Rapids, MI: Baker, 2003.
———. *The Unaccommodated Calvin: Studies in the Foundation of a Theological Tradition*. New York: Oxford University Press, 2000).
——— and James Bradley. *Church History: An Introduction to Research, Reference Works, and Methods*. Grand Rapids, MI: Eerdmans, 1995.
Murray, Iain. *Jonathan Edwards: A New Biography*. Carlisle, PA: Banner of Truth, 1987.
Murray, John. *The Imputation of Adam's Sin*. Phillipsburg, NJ: Presbyterian and Reformed Publishing, 1959.

Nash, Ronald H. *The Light of the Mind: St. Augustine's Theory of Knowledge*. Lexington, KY: University of Kentucky Press, 1969.

Newton, Isaac. *Philosophiae Naturalis Principia Mathematica*. Translated by Andrew Motte. New York: Prometheus Books, 1995.

———. *Optics or a Treatise of the Reflections, Refractions, Inflections, and Colours of Light*. New York: Dover Publications, 1954.

Nichols, Stephen J. *An Absolute Sort of Certainty: The Holy Spirit and the Apologetics of Jonathan Edwards*. Phillipsburg, NJ: Presbyterian & Reformed Publishers, 2003.

———. *Jonathan Edwards: A Guided Tour of His Life and Thought*. Phillipsburg, NJ: Presbyterian & Reformed Publishing, 2001.

———, ed. *Jonathan Edwards' Resolutions and Advice to Young Converts*. Phillipsburg, NJ: Presbyterian & Reformed Publishing, 2001.

———. *Heaven on Earth: Capturing Jonathan Edwards' Vision of Living in Between*. Wheaton, IL: Crossway, 2006.

Noll, Mark. *America's God: From Jonathan Edwards to Abraham Lincoln*. New York: Oxford University Press, 2002.

———. "The Contested Legacy of Jonathan Edwards in Antebellum Calvinism: Theological Conflict and the Evolution of Thought in America," *Canadian Review of American Studies* 19 (Summer 1988): 149-64.

Noth, Martin. *The Deuteronomistic History*. Sheffield, UK: Sheffield Academic Press, 1981.

Oberman, Heiko. *The Dawn of the Reformation: Essays in Late Medieval and Early Reformation Thought*. Grand Rapids, MI: Eerdmans, 1992.

Oliphint, K. Scott. *The Battle Belongs to the Lord*. Philipsburg, NJ: P&R Publishing, 2003.

———. "Jonathan Edwards On Apologetics: Reason and the Noetic Effects of Sin," in *The Legacy of Jonathan Edwards: American Religion and the Evangelical Tradition*. D. G. Hart, Sean Michael Lucas, and Stephen J. Nichols, eds. Grand Rapids: Baker, 2003, 131-146.

———. "Jonathan Edwards: Reformed Apologist." *Westminster Theological Journal* 57.1 (Spring 1995): 165-186.

———. *Reasons for Faith: Philisophy in the Service of Theology*. Phillipsburg, NJ: Presbyterian & Reformed Publishers, 2007.

———. "Review Essay: Epistemology and Christian Belief." *Westminster Theological Journal* 63 (Spring 2001): 151-83.

Opie, John, ed. *Jonathan Edwards and the Enlightenment*. Lexington, KY: D. C. Heath, 1969.

Orr, John. *English Deism: Its Roots and its Fruits*. Grand Rapids, MI: Eerdmans, 1934.

Otto, Randell E. "The Solidarity of Mankind in Jonathan Edwards' Doctrine of Original Sin." *Evangelical Quarterly* 62 (July 1990): 205-221.

Owen, John. *The Works of John Owen*. 24 vols. Edited by William H. Gould. Carlisle, PA: Banner of Truth, 1965-68.

Paley, William. *The Works of William Paley*. 5 vols. Boston: Joshua Belcher, 1810.

Park, Edwards Amasa. "Remarks of Jonathan Edwards on the Trinity," *Bibliotheca Sacra* 38 (January 1881): 147-87, (April 1881): 333-369.

Pasnau, Robert. *Thomas Aquinas on Human Nature*. Cambridge: Cambridge University Press, 2002.

Pauw, Amy Plantinga. *The Supreme Harmony of All: The Trinitarian Theology of Jonathan Edwards*. Grand Rapids, MI: Eerdmans, 2002.
Penner, Myron B. "Jonathan Edwards and Emotional Knowledge of God." *Direction* 1 (Spring 2001): 63-75.
Perkins, William. *The Art of Prophesying*. Carlisle, PA: Banner of Truth, 1996.
Pierce, Richard D. "A Suppressed Edwards Manuscript on the Trinity," *Crane Review* 1 (Winter 1959): 66-80.
Plantinga, Alvin. *God and Other Minds: A Study of the Rational Justification of Belief in God*. Ithaca, NY: Cornell University Press, 1990.
———. *Warrant: The Current Debate*. Oxford: Oxford University Press, 1993.
———. *Warrant and Proper Function*. Oxford: Oxford University Press, 1993.
———. *Warranted Christian Belief*. New York: Oxford University Press, 2000.
Powicke, Frederick J. *The Cambridge Platonists: A Study*. Hamden, CT: Archon Books, 1971.
Ramm, Bernard. *Varieties of Christian Apologetics*. Grand Rapids, MI: Baker, 1961.
Redwood, John. *Reason, Ridicule, and Religion: The Age of Enlightenment in England, 1660-1750*. London: Thames and Hudson, 1976.
Reventlow, Henning Graf. *The Authority of the Bible and the Rise of the Modern World*, J. Bowden, tr. Minneapolis, MN: Fortress, 1984.
Reymond, Robert L. "Dr. John H. Gerstner on Thomas Aquinas as a Protestant." *Westminster Theological Journal* 59 (Spring 1997): 113-21.
Reynolds, Charles H. "Proposal for Understanding the Place of Reason in Christian Ethics." *Journal of Religion* 50 (April 1970): 155-68.
Richardson, Herbert Warren. *The Glory of God in the Theology of Jonathan Edwards (A Study in the Doctrine of the Trinity)*. Ph.D. diss., Harvard University, 1962.
Ricketts, Allyn Lee. "The Primacy of Revelation in the Philosophical Theology of Jonathan Edwards." PhD. Diss. Westminster Theological Seminary, 1995.
Rupp, George. "The 'Idealism' of Jonathan Edwards." *Harvard Theological Review* 62 (April 1969): 209-26.
Sairsingh, Krister. *Jonathan Edwards and the Idea of Divine Glory: His Foundational Trinitarianism and Its Ecclesial Import*. Ph.D. diss., Harvard University, 1986.
Schafer, Thomas A. *The Concept of Being in the Thought of Jonathan Edwards*. PhD. diss., Duke University, 1951.
Scholder, Klaus. *The Birth of Modern Criticism: Origins and Problems of Biblical Criticism in the Seventeenth Century*. London: SCM, 1990.
Shea, William M. and Peter A. Huff, *Knowledge and Belief in America: Enlightenment Traditions and Modern Religious Thought*. Cambridge: Cambridge University Press, 1995.
Sher, Richard B. and Jeffrey R. Smitten, *Scotland and America in the Age of Enlightenment*. Princeton, NJ: Princeton University Press, 1990.
Skelton, Philip. *Ophiomaches; or, Deism Revealed*. London, 1747.
Smart, Robert Davis. *Jonathan Edwards' Apologetic for the Great Awakening*. Grand Rapids, MI: Reformation Heritage Books, 2011.
Smith, Claude A. "Jonathan Edwards and the 'Way of Ideas.'" *Harvard Theological Review* 59 (April 1966): 153-73.
Smith, Norman Kemp. *John Locke*. Manchester, UK: Manchester University Press, 1933.
Smyth, Egbert C. "Jonathan Edwards' 'Idealism.'" *American Journal of Theology* 1 (October 1897): 950-64.

Spinoza, Benedict de. *The Philosophy of Spinoza*. Edited by Joseph Ratner. New York: The World's Popular Classics, 1920.

Sproul, R. C., John H. Gerstner, and Arthur Lindsley. *Classical Apologetics: A Rational Defense of the Christian Faith and a Critique of Presuppositional Apologetics*. Grand Rapids, MI: Zondervan, 1984.

Stein, Stephen J., ed. *The Cambridge Companion to Jonathan Edwards*. Cambridge: Cambridge University Press, 2007.

Stewart, M. A. *Studies in the Philosophy of the Scottish Enlightenment*. Oxford: Oxford University Press, 1990.

Storms, C. Samuel. "Jonathan Edwards and the Freedom of the Will." *Trinity Journal* 3 (Fall 1982): 131-69.

———. *Tragedy in Eden: Original Sin in the Theology of Jonathan Edwards*. Lanham, MD: University Press of America, 1985.

Stout, Harry S. *The New England Soul*. New York: Oxford University Press, 1986.

Strange, Daniel. "The Secret Diaries of Jonathan Edwards Aged 54: A Reconstruction (and Deconstruction)." *Themelios* 27 (Autumn 2001): 32-43.

Stripes Watts, Emily. "Jonathan Edwards and Cambridge Platonists." PhD. diss., University of Illinois, 1963.

Strobel, Kyle C. *Jonathan Edwards's Theology: A Reinterpretation*. T&T Clark Studies in Theology Series. London: Bloomsbury, 2013.

Studebaker, Steven M. *Jonathan Edwards' Social Augustinian Trinitarianism: A Criticism of and an Alternative to Recent Interpretations*. PhD diss. Marquette University, 2003.

Sudduth, Michael. *The Reformed Objection to Natural Theology*. Ashgate Philosophy of Religion Series. Bristol, VT: Ashgate, 2010.

Suter, Rufus. "A Note on the Platonism of Jonathan Edwards." *Harvard Theological Review* 52 (1959): 283-4.

Sweeney, Douglas A. *Jonathan Edwards and the Ministry of the Word: A Model for Faith and Thought*. Downers Grove, IL: Inter Varsity Press, 2009.

Tattrie, George Arthur . *Jonathan Edwards' Understanding of the Natural World and Man's Relationship to It*. Ph.D. diss., McGill University, 1973.

Taylor, John. *The Plain Scripture-Doctrine of Original Sin, Proposed to Free and Candid Examination*. London: [No publisher listed], 1738.

Thomas Aquinas. *Summa contra Gentiles*. Translated by Anton C. Pegis. 5 vols. Notre Dame, IN: Notre Dame University Press, 1975.

———. *The Summa Theologica of St. Thomas Aquinas*. Translated by the Fathers of the English Dominican Province. 5 vols. Westminster, MD: Christian Classics, 1981.

Tertullian. *The Prescription Against Heretics* (*De praescriptione haereticorum*) in *The Ante-Nicene Fathers*. Translated by Peter Holmes. Edited byAlexander Roberts and James Donaldson. Grand Rapids, MI: Eerdmans, 1986.

Tindal, Matthew. *Christianity as Old as Creation*. London: 1730.

Tracey, Patricia. *Jonathan Edwards, Pastor*. Eugene, OR: Wipf & Stock, 2006.

Turretin, Francis. *Institutes of Elenctic Theology*. Edited by James T. Dennison and translated by George Geiger. 3 vols. Phillipsburg, NJ: Presbyterian & Reformed, 1993.

Van Mastricht, Peter. *Theoretica-practica theologia*. 2nd ed. Utrecht, 1724.

Van Til, Cornelius. *Defense of the Faith*. 4th ed. K. Scott Oliphint, ed. Phillipsburg, NJ: Presbyterian & Reformed Publishing, 2008.

_____. *Common Grace and the Gospel*. Philipsburg, NJ: P&R Publishing, 1972.
_____. *Christian Theistic Evidences*. Philipsburg, NJ: P&R Publishing, 1976.
_____. *Introduction to Systematic Theology*. William Edgar, ed. Phillipsburg, NJ: P&R Publishing, 1974.
_____. *Survey of Christian Epistemology*. Philipsburg, NJ: P&R Publishing, 1969.
Vincent, Tomas. "The Modernity of Jonathan Edwards." *New England Quarterly* 25 (1952): 60-84.
Vito, Miklos. "Spiritual Knowledge According to Jonathan Edwards." *Calvin Theological Journal* 31 (April 1996): 161-81.
Waddington, Jeffrey C. "Must We Believe? Jonathan Edwards and Conscious Faith in Christ," *Confessional Presbyterian Journal* 6 (Fall 2010): 11- 21.
Wainwright, William. "Jonathan Edwards and the Sense of the Heart." *Faith and Philosophy* 7 (January 1990): 49-62.
_____. "The Nature of Reason: Locke, Swinburne, and Edwards," *Reason and the Christian Religion*. Oxford: Clarendon Press, 1994: 91-118.
_____. *Reason and the Heart: A Prolegomenon to a Critique of Passional Reason*. Ithaca, NY: Cornell University Press, 1995.
Walker, Daniel P. *The Ancient Theology: Studies in Christian Platonism from 15th-18th Century*. Ithaca, NY: Cornell University Press, 1972.
Warfield, Benjamin B. "Edwards and the New England Theology," *Studies in Theology*. Grand Rapids, MI: Baker, 2000.
_____. "The Rights of Systematic Theology," in *The Selected Shorter Writings of Benjamin B. Warfield*. John Meeter, ed. Phillipsburg, NJ: Presbyterian & Reformed Publishing, 1973, 2: 219-279.
Weddle, David Leroy. *The New Man: A Study in the Significance of Conversion for the Theological Definition of Self in Jonathan Edwards and Charles G. Finney*. Ph.D. diss., Harvard University, 1973.
Westra, Helen Petter. "Jonathan Edwards and 'What Reason Teaches.'" *Journal of the Evangelical Theological Society* 34 (December 1991): 495-503.
Willey, Basil. *The Eighteenth Century Background: Studies on the Idea of Nature in the Thought of the Period*. New York: Columbia University Press, 1941.
_____. *The Seventeenth Century Background: Studies in the Thought of the Age in Relation to Poetry and Religion*. New York: Columbia University Press, 1967.
Withrow, Brandon. *"Full of Wondrous and Glorious Things": The Exegetical Mind of Jonathan Edwards in its Anglo-American Cultural Context*. Ph.D. Diss., Westminster Theological Seminary, 2007.
Wolters, Albert. *Creation Regained*. Grand Rapids, MI: Eerdmans, 1985.
Wolterstorff, Nicholas. *John Locke and the Ethics of Belief*. Cambridge Studies in Religion and Critical Thought. New York: Cambridge University Press, 1996.
Woodall, Joseph D. *Aesthetic Christian Apologetics*. Ph.D. diss. Fort Worth, TX: Southwestern Baptist Theological Seminary, 2005.
_____. "Jonathan Edwards, Beauty, and Apologetics," *Criswell Theological Review* 5/1 (Fall 2007): 81-95.
Young, B. W. *Religion and Enlightenment in Eighteenth-Century England: Theological Debate from Locke to Burke*. Oxford: Clarendon Press, 1998.
Zakai, Avihu. *Jonathan Edwards' Philosophy of History: The Reenchantment of the World in the Age of the Enlightenment*. Princeton, NJ: Princeton University Press, 2003.

www.ingramcontent.com/pod-product-compliance
Lightning Source LLC
Chambersburg PA
CBHW051634230426
43669CB00013B/2300